·THE·
LORD'S
SUPPER

· THE ·
LORD'S
SUPPER
BELIEVERS
CHURCH
PERSPECTIVES

EDITED BY
DALE R. STOFFER

HERALD PRESS
Scottdale, Pennsylvania
Waterloo, Ontario

Library of Congress Cataloging-in-Publication Data
The Lord's Supper: Believers Church perspectives/edited by Dale R. Stoffer.
    p. cm.
    Papers from the Eleventh Believers Church Conference held at
Ashland Theological Seminary, June 1994.
    Includes bibliographical references.
    ISBN 0-8361-3119-3 (alk. paper)
    1. Lord's Supper—Congresses. 2. Anabaptists—Doctrines—
Congresses. 3. Free churches—Doctrines—Congresses. I. Stoffer,
Dale R. (Dale Rupert), 1950- . II. Conference on the Concept of the
Believers Church (11th : 1994 : Ashland Theological Seminary)
BV825.2.L64 1997
264'.36—dc20   96-32559

The paper used in this publication is recycled and meets the minimum re-
quirements of American National Standard for Information Sciences—
Permanence of Paper for Printed Library Materials, ANSI Z39.48-1984.

Contents

Foreword by Franklin H. Littell 9
Editor's Preface 11
Contributors 15

Part One: Historical Perspectives on the Lord's Supper 19

1. The Lord's Supper in Church History:
   The Early Church Through the Medieval Period
   Everett Ferguson 21

2. Contrasting Views of the Lord's Supper
   in the Reformation of the Sixteenth Century
   William R. Estep Jr. 46

3. Believers Church Perspectives on the Lord's Supper
   Donald F. Durnbaugh 63

Part Two: Biblical Interpretation of the Lord's Supper 79

4. "Making a Meal of It": The Lord's Supper
   in Its First-Century Social Setting
   Ben Witherington III 81

Part Three: Theological Proposals for the Lord's Supper 115

5. Ecclesiology and the Lord's Supper:
   The Memorial Meal of a Peaceable Community
   Merle D. Strege 117

6. Eschatology and the Lord's Supper:
   Hope for the Triumph of God's Reign
   Robert G. Clouse 129

7. Making the Lord's Supper Meaningful
   Marlin Jeschke 140

Part Four: Denominational Perspectives on the Lord's Supper 155

8. Brethren Heritage of the Lord's Supper:
   Introduction
   Dale R. Stoffer 157
9. The Agape in the Brethren Tradition
   Jeff Bach 161
10. Footwashing Within the Context of the Lord's Supper
    John Christopher Thomas 169
11. Brethren Heritage of the Lord's Supper: Eucharist
    Dale R. Stoffer 185
12. The Lord's Supper as Viewed and Practiced
    by the Christian Churches, Churches of Christ,
    and the Disciples of Christ
    John Mills 193
13. A Quaker Interpretation of the Lord's Supper
    T. Canby Jones 200
14. Seventh-Day Adventists and the Lord's Supper
    Peter M. van Bemmelen 207
15. The Lord's Supper in the Free Methodist Tradition
    Howard A. Snyder 212
16. The Lord's Supper: The Perspective of the
    African Methodist Episcopal Church
    Thomas L. McCray 219
17. A Moravian Perspective on Holy Communion
    Kevin C. Frack 225
18. Sacrament, Ordinance, or Both?
    Baptist Understandings of the Lord's Supper
    William H. Brackney 231

Part Five: Special Presentations on the Lord's Supper 241

19. Toward an Anabaptist Theology of the Lord's Supper
    John D. Rempel 243
20. Social Implications of the Lord's Supper
    in the Early Church
    Reta Halteman Finger 250
21. Proposed Theses for a Believers Church Theology
    of the Lord's Supper
    Thomas Finger 256

Part Six: Reflections, Ecumenical Dialogue, and Findings 261

22. The Lord's Supper in the Mennonite Brethren Church
    David Ewert 263

23. Reflections on the Conference
    Timothy George 266

24. The Lord's Supper in Ecumenical Dialogue
    Jeffrey Gros 271

25. A Baptist Response
    William H. Brackney 278

26. Observations from the Orthodox Perspective
    Vladimir Berzonsky 281

27. Report of the Findings Committee 285

Appendix: Believers Church Conferences and Publications 289
Notes 293
The Editor 333

Foreword

This book, issuing from the Eleventh Believers Church Conference, carries an exciting message. It centers on the way in which the common table is a sign of the corporate nature of the Christian life—corporate both spiritually and practically. This witness is redemptive in an individualistic and broken world, as well as in the lives of those formed by the common life.

The authors come from the major Free Church traditions, as well as from the groups where the normative view of the early church model—with religious liberty in the world and Christ alone as Lord in the church—was first restored to authority. The core of the restitution of the true church was pioneered primarily by the Anabaptist-Mennonites in the sixteenth century, in the seventeenth century by the Quakers and Baptists in England, and in the eighteenth century by the Brethren in Germany.

In America religious liberty was recognized in colonial Pennsylvania and Rhode Island, and generally recognized in the states after the ratification of the federal constitution. So all religious associations are legally "Free Churches." In this setting, some churches that were part of the establishments in European Christendom have adopted a new understanding of church-state relations. In addition, other restitution or restoration movements have sprung up with a vision of the authority and power of the early-church model for Christian life.

The break from the compulsory model of "Christendom" is yet incomplete, however, as plainly indicated by the recent slide of some Baptists toward a hierarchical control and of some Methodists toward an indiscriminate pattern of church membership. Sadly, there are other signs that the manner of the "princes and powers of this world's darkness" has seductive force, even among those who are blessed to live in a time when "the eager witness of a willing heart" may flourish free of persecution.

The first discussions of the idea of a regular series of Free Church meetings took place at Earlham College, at a peace testimony session with host Wilmer J. Cooper. Mennonite and Brethren colleagues naturally joined the Quakers in the vision, and the first question was whether the parameters should include only "Peace Church" scholars. The decision was made to open the approach as widely as there were colleagues of common concern, since there were evidently pockets of peace-minded and "apostolic" teaching and practice in "mainline" churches. James Leo Garrett took the initiative to call the first Believers Church Conference, and the rest—as they say—"is history."

—*Franklin H. Littell*
  Ida E. King Distinguished Visiting Professor
  Richard Stockton College of New Jersey

Editor's Preface

Believers churches, those churches composed of people who have made a voluntary commitment of faith in Jesus Christ as Savior and Lord, have generally recognized two sacraments or ordinances: baptism and the Lord's Supper. Baptism has been the subject of much disputation, debate, and discussion over the years for these churches.

During the sixteenth and seventeenth centuries, disputations with pedobaptists inevitably caused baptism to be one of the central defining concepts for Anabaptists and Baptists alike. In the nineteenth century, especially in America, the topic of baptism became more of an in-house source of tension among believers churches. They sought through public debates to show how their form and understanding of baptism was the most biblical and true to that found in the primitive church. In the twentieth century, baptism has been a source of much discussion among all denominations. The ecumenical movement has forced mainline and evangelical churches alike to wrestle with the issue of recognizing baptism administered by other groups.

Compared to the deafening roar of discourse concerning baptism over the years in believers churches, the discussion of the Lord's Supper is a mere whisper. Several contributors to this volume note in their presentations the lack of literature on the Lord's Supper in their own traditions. The general silence on this topic in the Mennonite community is suggested in Howard John Loewen's "Editor's Preface" to John D. Rempel's comprehensive treatment of the Anabaptist view of the Lord's Supper: "The appearance of this volume represents a landmark, the first in-depth historical and theological inquiry into the Anabaptist understanding of the Lord's Supper. It is surprising that we had to wait this long for such a study to appear."[1]

This relative silence is partially due to the fact that most believers churches adopted a generally Reformed view of the Lord's Supper, thus diverting controversy and discussion away from this subject. For the most part, the lack of theological reflection on the Lord's Supper prevailed until recently. Ecumenical discussions, prompted especially by the *Baptism, Eucharist, and Ministry* statement of the World Council of Churches, brought the issue to the fore within the church at large.

But there may be another reason why discussion about the Lord's Supper is strangely lacking in believers church circles. What is true for Brethren groups may also be true for many other denominations within the believers church tradition. The Lord's Supper is not so much talked about as experienced. It is a living drama in which the believing community declares in existential fashion the core truths of what it means to be God's people.

The above observations reinforce why a symposium on the Lord's Supper in the believers church tradition, as found within this volume, is so significant. First, it can give voice to a significant tradition in the church that generally has been silent. Second, it can reacquaint believers churches with the richness and variety found within this tradition. All too often it is assumed that most believers churches have adopted a memorial view of the Lord's Supper, often referred to as the Zwinglian view. But not only did Zwingli have an understanding of the Lord's Supper that transcended the "Zwinglian view," so also have many believers churches. Third, this volume can aid the ecumenical dialogue on the Lord's Supper by making more accessible the perspective of a wide range of believers churches.

Fourth, churches whose identity is forged not so much by creeds, confessions, and traditions as by the shared experience of faith are in special need today to be reminded of the significance of the Lord's Supper. The church-centered culture of two generations ago in America has given way to a secular culture that has markedly restricted the forums for cultivating a common faith. The Lord's Supper represents a crucial link in maintaining our biblical heritage and faith. But even communion can lose its significance if the faith that it declares and embodies existentially is undercut by secularism. This volume can help to renew our commitment to the core truths embodied in the drama of the Lord's Supper.

The papers in this volume were originally prepared as addresses for the Eleventh Believers Church Conference, held at Ashland Theological Seminary, Ashland, Ohio, June 1-4, 1994. I wish to acknowledge the help of Richard Allison and Luke Keefer in serving with me on the planning committee for the conference. Lucy

DeLeonardis contributed to the preparation of the manuscript, as did Nancy Miller. My student assistant, Jeanne Bye, and her husband, Matthew, deserve special notice for their diligence in the tedious process of transcribing numerous audio tapes.

The logical structure of the book is as follows. Part one provides a historical overview concerning the thought and practice of the Lord's Supper, both in the larger church and the believers church. It includes essays by Everett Ferguson, William Estep, and Donald Durnbaugh. Part two, a paper by Ben Witherington, considers biblical interpretation of the Lord's Supper, noting especially the Supper's first-century social setting. The third part is comprised of papers by Merle Strege, Robert Clouse, and Marlin Jeschke and focuses on theological proposals for the Lord's Supper and its observance.

The fourth section is devoted to various denominational perspectives on the Lord's Supper. Jeff Bach, Chris Thomas, and Dale Stoffer address the three parts of the Brethren communion practice: the love feast, feetwashing, and the bread and cup. Presentations follow by John Mills (Disciples of Christ), T. Canby Jones (Quaker), Peter van Bemmelen (Seventh-Day Adventists), Howard Snyder (Free Methodist), Tom McCray (African Methodist Episcopal), Kevin Frack (Moravian), and William Brackney (Baptist).

Part five, from a more informal luncheon format, gives three supplementary presentations by John Rempel, Reta Finger, and Thomas Finger. The final part consists of reflections of a more ecumenical nature shared during a panel discussion on the last day of the conference. Participants were David Ewert, chair, Timothy George, Jeffrey Gros, William Brackney, and Vladimir Berzonsky. The report of the findings committee is included in this part as well. The findings committee was composed of David Ewert, chair, Christina Bucher, Timothy George, and Luke Keefer.

The appendix lists previous believers church conferences in this series and their associated publications. I express my thanks to Donald Durnbaugh, whose research made possible the compilation of this material. Finally, the forty pages of notes show that the contributors took their assignments seriously and provided good documentation.

Unfortunately, several elements that contributed substantially to the devotional atmosphere of the eleventh conference are not reflected in the papers reproduced in this book. Special thanks go to Myron Augsburger, former president of Eastern Mennonite College and of the Christian College Coalition and a Minister of the Word at

Washington (D.C.) Community Fellowship. His opening address for the conference, though not designed to be a formal paper, fulfilled its purpose of setting a devotional tone for the entire conference. He challenged the conference to view the Lord's Supper in terms of a covenant to which we pledge ourselves. This covenant has three important meanings.

First, the Lord's Supper is a covenant of commitment to the death. Jesus' atoning death for us lays a claim upon us. In solidarity with him, we are to die to our self-centeredness; only in this act can we become a participant in the unity of his body. Second, it is a covenant of celebration of redemption and reconciliation. In the Supper, Jesus is communicating his total giving of himself for our redemption and is calling us to give ourselves totally to him. In such self-surrender we find our identity in Christ. Third, it is a covenant of certification of Jesus' victory. The Supper is a declaration to the gathered church of his victory over evil. Thus, when we participate in the Supper, the symbols of bread and wine communicate to us what it means to live in solidarity with Jesus.

Thanks should also be extended to Jerry Flora, professor of New Testament theology and of spiritual formation at Ashland Theological Seminary. His daily devotions focused our attention on Jesus Christ as our "Maker, Defender, Redeemer, and Friend." Adding to the devotional richness of the conference was the music ministry of Ron Sprunger, professor of church music at Ashland Theological Seminary, and his wife, Linda. The hearty singing, which their accompaniment made possible, enabled those at the conference to experience the communion with Christ and his people about which we were talking. Finally, the highlight for many was the opportunity to share in a Brethren threefold communion service, led by Fred Finks, president of Ashland Theological Seminary. To unite with other believers in the love feast, feetwashing, and bread and cup experientially reinforced how powerful a symbol communion is.

—*Dale R. Stoffer*

Contributors

Jeff Bach is a professor of church history for Brethren studies at Bethany Theological Seminary, Richmond, Indiana, where he also serves as director of the Peace Studies Program.

Vladimir Berzonsky is an archpriest of the Orthodox Church in America. He pastors Holy Trinity Orthodox Church in Parma, Ohio, and is a lecturer at Baldwin-Wallace College. He also is a member of the governing board of the National Council of Churches of Christ.

William H. Brackney, an ordained Baptist minister, is currently principal and professor of historical theology at McMaster Divinity College in Hamilton, Ontario.

Christina Bucher, a member of the Church of the Brethren, teaches religious studies at Elizabethtown College in Pennsylvania. She edits the quarterly journal *Brethren Life and Thought*.

Robert G. Clouse, an ordained minister in the Grace Brethren Church, serves as a pastor in Clay City, Indiana, and as a professor of history at Indiana State University.

Donald F. Durnbaugh, former professor of church history at Bethany Theological Seminary, resides near Huntingdon, Pennsylvania, where he is an archivist at Juniata College. He is also a fellow of the Young Center for the Study of Anabaptist and Pietist Groups at Elizabethtown College.

William R. Estep Jr. is a minister in the Southern Baptist Church and former professor of church history at Southwestern Baptist Theological Seminary in Fort Worth, Texas. Though retired, he continues to teach classes and lecture in both Spanish and English.

David Ewert is a member of the Mennonite Brethren Church. He taught in several Mennonite institutions in North America and overseas. Now retired, he lives in Abbotsford, British Columbia.

Everett Ferguson is an elder in the Church of Christ and professor emeritus of church history at Abilene Christian University in Texas, with whom he is employed on a part-time basis.

Reta Halteman Finger, a member of the Mennonite Church and former editor of *Daughters of Sarah*, is a professor of New Testament at Messiah College in Grantham, Pennsylvania. Her dissertation at Garrett-Northwestern is on links between the Lord's Supper and sharing material goods in the New Testament.

Thomas Finger is a member of the Mennonite Church and a professor of systematic and spiritual theology at Eastern Mennonite Seminary in Harrisonburg, Virginia.

Kevin C. Frack is a minister in the Moravian Church. He pastored in Dublin, Ohio, for nine years and now serves a congregation in Winston-Salem, North Carolina.

Timothy George, a Southern Baptist minister, is dean of Beeson Divinity School of Samford University in Birmingham, Alabama.

Jeffrey Gros is a brother (F.S.C.) in the Roman Catholic Church and currently serving as an associate director of the Secretariat for Ecumenical and Interreligious Affairs for the U.S. Catholic Conference in Washington, D.C.

Marlin Jeschke is a member of the Mennonite Church and a former professor of philosophy and religion at Goshen College in Indiana. He is now retired and living in Berlin, Ohio.

T. Canby Jones is a member of the Friends and professor emeritus of religion and philosophy at Wilmington College in Ohio.

Luke L. Keefer Jr., a minister in the Brethren in Christ Church, is professor of church history and theology at Ashland Theological Seminary, Ohio.

Thomas L. McCray is a minister in the African Methodist Episcopal Church and currently pastors the Quinn Chapel A.M.E. Church in Cleveland, Ohio.

John Mills, a minister in the Christian Church, pastors in Brunswick, Ohio. He has also served congregations in Virginia, Oklahoma, Maryland, and Illinois.

John D. Rempel, minister in the Mennonite Church, pastors Manhattan (N.Y.) Mennonite Fellowship. He is an adjunct professor at Seminary of the East (Conservative Baptist) and serves as Mennonite Central Committee liaison officer at the United Nations.

Howard A. Snyder is a minister in the Free Methodist Church. He is the Heisel Professor of Evangelization and Church Renewal at United Theological Seminary in Dayton, Ohio.

Dale R. Stoffer is a minister in The Brethren Church (Ashland) and a professor of Historical Theology at Ashland Theological Seminary, Ohio.

Merle D. Strege, ordained minister in the Church of God (Anderson, Ind.), is a professor of historical theology at Anderson University.

John Christopher Thomas is a minister in the Church of God (Cleveland, Tenn.) and a professor of New Testament at the Church of God School of Theology. He also is an associate pastor of the Woodward Avenue Church of God in Athens, Tennessee.

Peter M. van Bemmelen is an ordained minister in the Seventh-Day Adventist Church and a professor of Systematic Theology at the Seventh-Day Adventist Theological Seminary, Andrews University, Berrien Springs, Michigan.

Ben Witherington III, an ordained minister in the United Methodist Church, has moved from Ashland Theological Seminary to Asbury Theological Seminary, as a professor of New Testament.

❧ PART 1 ❧

HISTORICAL PERSPECTIVES ON THE LORD'S SUPPER

‍ 1 ‌

The Lord's Supper in Church History: The Early Church Through the Medieval Period

Everett Ferguson

Introduction

Many aspects of the Lord's Supper could be considered both liturgical and doctrinal. To limit the subject, I have chosen to consider the real presence, a topic where many of the confessional differences in the history of Christianity center. As a second limitation, I will largely confine myself to Western history, with apologies to my Orthodox and other Eastern Christian friends. As a further limitation, instead of attempting a complete survey,[1] I will make some soundings at strategic places in the history of eucharistic theology: the second century, with attention to Justin Martyr and others on the topic; the fourth century, with special reference to Ambrose and Augustine; the ninth century, with its treatises by Radbertus and Ratramnus; the eleventh century, with the controversy involving Lanfranc and Berengar; and concluding in the thirteenth century, with special attention to the contributions of Thomas Aquinas.

I need to state my understanding of the apostolic and New Testament point of departure for thought about the Lord's Supper. If one has a different interpretation of the New Testament texts, then the course of development will look different. I think my understanding is consistent with the future unfolding of thought on the Lord's Supper, but I trust the sample excavations of certain chronological sites will be objective enough to hold up regardless of the starting point and interpretive framework.

I understand Jesus' words at the Last Supper in terms of the Old Testament description of the Passover, in keeping with the Passover atmosphere if not Passover context of the meal. The meal "is the passover of the Lord," according to the first reference to it in Exodus

12:11. The Passover meal commemorated the death of the firstborn of the Egyptians and the deliverance of the Israelites (Exod. 12:14).[2] More than that, it was a reliving in the present of those events, a bringing of them into the present so that those participating could think of themselves as experiencing the exodus.[3] As the Mishnah put it, "In every generation a man must so regard himself as if he came forth himself out of Egypt" (Pesahim 10.5). I consider Jesus' words, "This is my body" (Mark 14:22), in the same way. The bread brings the body into the present. The presence is real, but not literal. The meaning of the event is made present once more. Similarly, the "remembrance" (*anamnēsis*) of 1 Corinthians 11:24-25, according to the Jewish background, was neither simply mental recollection nor the actual repetition of something but the celebration of a past event in order to live in its experience and to participate in its redemptive qualities. The historical deliverance is unrepeatable, but its effects are reaffirmed.

In biblical thought something, including food for nourishment, is sanctified to a given purpose "by God's word and by prayer" (1 Tim. 4:5).[4] Similarly, the effects of commemoration are accomplished by reason of God's appointment of what is to be done (declared by the Word of God) and the human intention to do what is appointed (expressed by prayer). In the context of the Lord's Supper, this means that the bread and wine now have a different function from what they do as table food. Their purpose now is the memorial of Jesus' giving of himself for human forgiveness.

In this Jewish context of thought and practice, the first Christians broke bread and blessed the cup. In so doing, they relived their time when Jesus was personally present. They made Jesus' body and blood offered on the cross and its effects real in their assemblies. Other aspects were also present—fellowship, eschatological joy, a thank-offering to God, and so on. But for now we focus on the question of Jesus' "presence."

Second Century

What happened to this Jewish understanding of memorial and sanctification by God's Word and by prayer in a Greco-Roman intellectual and social environment? How was this to be expressed in a different thought world? Greeks and Romans obviously had the concept of memorial and knew a distinction between the holy and the unholy, but other philosophical understandings were also at work.

This situation required Christians to make many adjustments and reinterpretations in their effort to communicate with their society. The interpretation of the Lord's Supper was included in those matters influenced by new ways of looking at things.[5] A major aspect was a shift from Jewish thought in terms of function and relationships, to Greek philosophical thought about ontology (or being, where Plato had directed his attention) and substance (where Aristotle had made important analyses).[6]

Justin Martyr, who was born at the Roman colony near Samaria and died as a martyr at Rome ca. 165, knew well the Jewish context of Christianity but had his intellectual formation in Hellenistic philosophy.[7] He made the earliest surviving effort at communicating the words of the Last Supper in this philosophical environment.[8] In his Dialogue with Trypho, Justin recorded his debates with Jews who were quite hellenized. This work addressed Jewish concerns, even if Justin may have had his eye on Gentiles who wanted to know the differences between Jews and Christians.[9]

To Jews, Justin speaks of the eucharist (the common term in use from the second century until the Reformation) as a memorial. He describes the bread as a "memorial (*anamnēsis*) of the incarnation" and the cup as a "memorial of his blood" (*Dial.* 70.4). In these things there is "remembered his passion" (*Dial.* 117.3). The word "memorial" suggests the intention or purpose behind the act. As we have said, a memorial for the Jews involved more than what the word itself said: it was to bring God's activity of the past into the present and to make it effective. How was this idea to be expressed to educated pagans?

Here we turn to Justin's *First Apology,* addressed to pagans. Justin includes two accounts of the eucharist. The first is in chapter 65 as part of a description of Christian initiation that included instruction and baptism and was followed by first communion. The second is in chapter 67 as part of the description of the continuing Christian life that included the regular Sunday assembly. This shows that the baptismal eucharist was not different from the weekly eucharist. Both observances had a congregational context in which the president and the people together were involved. Between the two accounts, there is an explanation of the meaning of the rite (chap. 66).[10]

Justin's "explanation" has been more confusing than helpful to modern readers. The difficulty that has plagued interpreters comes from his struggle to express a fullness of meaning that terminology carrying a Jewish content did not adequately convey to educated pagans. Justin says,

> We do not receive [the eucharist] as common bread and drink. In the same manner as Jesus Christ our Savior became flesh through the word of God and had flesh and blood for our salvation, so also the food for which thanks was given through the prayer of the word that is from him [or, through his word of prayer], from which our blood and flesh are nourished by metabolism, we have been taught to be the flesh and blood of that Jesus who became flesh. (*Apol.* 1.66.2)

The following points are important: (1) The bread and beverage were now no longer "ordinary" food and drink, for they now served another purpose. (2) This change was effected by the word of the Lord (he cites in the next section, 66.3, the institution narrative as the justification for the Christian practice) and by prayer, as in 1 Timothy 4:5. (3) The description of the prayer is so unclear as to be particularly puzzling,[11] but the nature of this prayer or formula of words is of more liturgical than doctrinal interest; for my purposes it is sufficient to note that Justin still reflects the Jewish and New Testament thought about what effects sanctification for a particular use. (4) The bread and wine are still real food, for they bring nourishment to our physical bodies by the regular process of digestion. (5) Nevertheless, the comparison with the incarnation opened up the line of thought along which doctrinal interpretation was to proceed.

Did Justin by his explanatory words intend to help his pagan readers understand the significance the bread and wine had for Christians and to emphasize the true humanity of Christ, or is he an early witness to a belief in the substantial conversion of the elements? By his comparison to the incarnation, is Justin describing the meaning that the consecrated ("eucharistized") elements had for Christians, that is, a change in their relationship or function so that the bread and drink now mean the real flesh and blood of Jesus that suffered for us? Or is he describing some real ontological change of the bread and drink into the flesh and blood of Jesus? Or is he suggesting in some sense an addition of the flesh and blood of Jesus to the material elements?[12] I do not know how literally to take Justin, but I am suspicious of efforts to read too much of later developments into his words. Nonetheless, his parallelism between the word of God giving flesh and blood to Jesus and the bread and wine becoming flesh and blood does show how the transition to a realistic interpretation could have occurred.

Irenaeus, bishop of Lyons in the late second century,[13] may serve as a supplement to Justin's words or possibly an interpretation of them. Irenaeus mainly makes incidental rather than deliberately descriptive remarks about the eucharist.[14] Most of his statements are in an anti-Gnostic context, stressing the real humanity of Christ.[15] He set up a three-track parallel between the Lord having flesh and blood, the material elements of bread and wine receiving the word of God,[16] and our human bodies having the hope of resurrection for a twofold purpose: to affirm the goodness of creation and the redemption of the body against the Gnostic denial of these doctrines, and to argue that the use of bread and wine is an indication that the Savior had a real human body.

> How can they [Gnostics] say that the flesh which is nourished from the body of the Lord and from his flesh comes to corruption and does not partake of life? Let them either change their views or avoid offering the bread and wine. But our view is in harmony with the eucharist, and the eucharist confirms our view. We offer to God his own things, proclaiming rightly the communion and unity of flesh and spirit. For as bread from the earth when it receives the invocation of God is no longer common bread but the eucharist, consisting of two things—one earthly and one heavenly—so also our bodies when they partake of the eucharist are no longer corruptible but have the hope of the resurrection to eternity. (*Adv. haer.* 4.18.5)

Irenaeus offers several parallels to Justin's language: "no longer common bread," yet this cup and bread furnish true physical nourishment,[17] and the elements are sanctified by a prayer of thanksgiving (*Adv. haer.* 4.18.6). These similarities indicate that Irenaeus is acquainted with and developing Justin's thought. His statements, furthermore, make clear which option in the interpretation of Justin's ambiguous language he would take: the prayer to God adds a new dimension to the material elements; now they have a heavenly as well as an earthly reality. The partaking of this heavenly reality through the earthly brings eternal life. Nowhere does Irenaeus make a literal identification of the elements with the body and blood; his point is that Christ by acknowledging material elements in relation to his body and blood was affirming that they too were material realities. I would contend that for Irenaeus, there is not a conversion or change in the elements,[18] but a new reality is added to them by reason of their consecration through calling upon God.

There were two other ways in which early Christian authors expressed the relationship between the bread and wine of the eucharist and the body and blood of Christ: in Greek by the word *symbolon*, as represented by Clement of Alexandria, and in Latin by the word *figura*, as represented by Tertullian.

Clement of Alexandria[19] makes such allusive reference to the eucharist in talking about other matters that his thought is difficult to interpret.[20] I want here only to note his use of the words "symbol" and "allegory" to describe the bread and wine of communion. "The holy Scripture named wine a mystical symbol of the holy blood" (*Paed.* 2.2.32). He interprets the eating the flesh and drinking the blood of Jesus in John 6:53-56 as spoken "through symbols" and "allegories" about the partaking of faith and the promises, of the Holy Spirit, and of the divine Word (*Paed.* 1.6.38, 43, 47).[21] Later he makes more explicit reference to the eucharist:

> The blood of the Lord is twofold. There is his fleshly blood by which we are ransomed from corruption; and there is the spiritual blood by which we are anointed. And this is to drink the blood of Jesus, to partake of the Lord's immortality. The Spirit is the strength of the Word, as blood is of the flesh. By analogy, as the wine is mixed with water, so the Spirit is with man; the mixed wine and water nourishes to faith, and the Spirit leads to immortality. And the mixing of both the drink and the Word together is called eucharist, a praiseworthy and beautiful grace. Those partaking of it in faith are sanctified in body and soul. (*Paed.* 2.2.19-20)

Thus does Clement in his own highly symbolic style describe Irenaeus's earthly and heavenly realities.[22] By drinking of the eucharistic wine, a person partakes of the Lord's Spirit and so of his immortality.

Tertullian of Carthage, the formative influence on ecclesiastical Latin,[23] speaks more expressly than Clement about the Lord's Supper but again only in discussing other subjects.[24] His viewpoint seems to be the same as his predecessors we have considered. He alludes to the physical properties of the wine that Jesus consecrated as a memorial of his blood (*An.* 17.13), yet he expresses the concern felt when the wine or bread of the eucharist falls to the ground (*Cor.* 3). Realist language is joined to a spiritual benefit: "The flesh feeds on the body and blood of Christ," but the soul is nourished (*Res.* 8.3; *Pud.* 9.16).

In opposing Marcion, Tertullian had anti-Docetic concerns similar to those of Irenaeus, as shown in his use of the term *figura*.

> Taking bread and distributing it to his disciples, Jesus made it his own body by saying, "This is my body," that is a "figure of my body." On the other hand, there would not have been a figure unless there was a true body. (*Adv. Marc.* 4.40.3-6; cf. 5.8)

Figura has a prophetic or typical meaning for Tertullian. The bread of the eucharist has the same significance as the words of the prophets: both proclaim or point to the body of the cross (*Adv. Marc.* 3.19.3-4). A "figure" is not the same as something else; the symbolic or figurative meaning is confirmed by Tertullian's parallel use of *image, allegory,* and *enigma.* Nevertheless, there is a correspondence between a figure and what it reflects. "The bread . . . represents [Jesus'] own proper body" (*Adv. Marc.* 1.14.3). As the passage quoted from book 4 argues, "A phantom is incapable of a figure"; or to paraphrase, "Without a substance, there is no shadow."

Protestants have tended to make *symbol* mean "bare symbol" and *figure* mean "mere figure." Catholics and some others have stressed the connection in ancient thought (especially in Platonism) between symbol and reality; the symbol partakes of or participates in the nature of what is symbolized. Or from the perspective of Plato's theory of ideas, the reality manifests itself in material imitations. The usages of Clement and Tertullian lie somewhere between these interpretations. The philosophical language offered an approximation to the Jewish idea, so it presented a means of communication while at the same time carrying the potential of misunderstanding. The symbol or figure carries with it the reality of which it is a symbol; in this instance the symbol makes the body present and effective.

Certainly if one read the statements of Justin, Irenaeus, Clement, and Tertullian as a Platonist, attention was called to the heavenly reality behind the earthly manifestations. But the way was also opened for a more realistic understanding of the presence of the body and blood. That feature would have been preserved by the Jewish and early Christian emphasis on historical events. Some precision for their understanding is given if the Alexandrians and North Africans were trying to express in philosophical or legal-rhetorical language some grasp of the biblical-Jewish language of religious reality. The biblical-Jewish realism concerning the present benefits of historical events was combined with philosophical-Greek realism about ideas and their material manifestations. I think this best accounts for the dual language of symbolism and realism found in Christian thought about the Lord's Supper, often in the same writers.[25]

Fourth Century

Third-century thinkers sometimes expressed themselves in the language of figure or symbol that we have described; sometimes they employed the language of simple realism. At what point these statements are to be taken at face value is not clear. In the fourth century, however, we know that thought moved to a new level of explicitness, because of the use of the language of a conversion of the elements to express the real presence. The future of eucharistic theology belonged to this language of conversion.

The explicit language of conversion occurs first in Greek authors of the fourth century. Cyril, bishop of Jerusalem (ca. 349-378),[26] explained to the newly baptized the ceremonies they had experienced. He first speaks in general terms without detail:

> The bread and wine of the eucharist before the holy invocation of the worshipful Trinity was simple bread and wine, but when the invocation is done, the bread becomes the body of Christ and wine the blood of Christ. (*Catech. mys.* 1.7)

This statement does not reveal how realistic a content Cyril intends. But he later affirms that the elements in some sense really are the body and blood (*Catech. mys.* 4.1), the evidence of the senses to the contrary (*Catech. mys.* 4.6), and compares the wine becoming blood to the water becoming wine in Jesus' miracle at Cana (John 2:1-11; *Catech. mys.* 4.2). In further elaboration, he distinguishes between the elements and the gift but declares a real partaking of Christ:

> In the type (*tupos*) of the bread there is given to you the body, and in the type of the wine there is given to you the blood, in order that you may become by partaking of the body and blood of Christ the same body and blood with him. For even so we become bearers of Christ since his body and blood are distributed in our members. (*Catech. mys.* 4.3)

Then he explains that in response to the invocation of God, the Holy Spirit effects a real change:

> We beseech the loving God to send forth the Holy Spirit upon
> what is offered in order that he may make the bread the body of
> Christ and the wine the blood of Christ. For whatever the Holy
> Spirit touches he sanctifies and changes (*metaballō*). (*Catech.
> mys.* 5.7)[27]

The nature of the change is still not spelled out; Cyril only says that
there is a reality present now that was not present before—the body
and blood of Christ. It could be a functional change, but I suspect he
means something more. At least, later thinkers, as we shall see, took
the language of change more literally.

The language of change became more explicit with reference to
the elements in Gregory, bishop of Nyssa (d. ca. 395).[28] Gregory might
seem to be moving in the biblical frame of thought when he describes
the working of the Spirit with material elements and describes how
benediction consecrates something to the service of God. He illustrates the working of the Spirit through common water in baptism by
the way an ordinary table of stone becomes an altar, common bread
and wine become the body of Christ, oil becomes sacramental, and a
man by ordination is set apart from the mass of men (*Bapt. Chr.*, in
Migne, *Patrologia Graeca*, 46.581B-C).

Yet he means something more than biblical consecration, for he
speaks of a transformation and gives examples of real change occurring, both in the Bible and in nature. Elsewhere he applies this idea of
change in the elements expressly to the Lord's Supper. After noting
that when Christ ate bread it was transformed (*metapoieō*) into his
body and quoting 1 Timothy 4:5, Gregory affirms the effects on believers:

> He disseminates himself through that flesh whose substance
> comes from bread and wine in everyone who believes in the
> economy of grace, blending himself with the bodies of believers,
> as if by this union with what is immortal, man too may become a
> partaker in incorruption. He gives these things by the power of
> the benediction through which he transelements (*metastoi-
> cheioō*) the natural quality of these visible things to that immortal
> thing. (*Or. catech.* 37)

Gregory was a pioneer here in expressing a thought that was to have
an abundant future.[29]

Justin Martyr did not say that the bread and wine were "converted into" but that they "are" the body and blood. Irenaeus then spoke of a heavenly reality added to the material elements. Cyril and Gregory next spoke of a change in the elements, illustrating it but not explaining philosophically how it came about.[30]

This idea of a change in the elements was introduced from the East into the West by Ambrose, bishop of Milan (374-397).[31] He is the major representative of the realist strand of thought in the West, as Augustine, bishop of Hippo (395-430)[32] is of the symbolist strand of thought. Yet both have statements that sound like the other.[33] This fact indicates that thinkers at that time did not fit into the neat categories refined by later thought.

Ambrose affirms that John 6 means that we receive the Lord's "true flesh . . . and true blood"; lest this literalism be offensive, he also explains, "You receive the sacrament in a similitude, but truly obtain the grace and virtue [or power] of the nature." His addition, "You who receive his flesh partake of his divine essence in that food" (*De sacram.* 6.1.3, 4),[34] shows that the eucharistic food has a spiritual character. The sign and the reality are treated as identical so that the physical and the spiritual eating are united.[35]

The bread and wine become a sacrament by consecration, and that is effected by the working of the words of Christ. Ambrose declares that the priest uses the words of Christ himself at the Last Supper, which he quotes. Then he explains:

> Before consecration, it is bread, but when the words of Christ have been added, it is the body of Christ. . . . And before the words of Christ, the cup is full of wine and water. When the words of Christ have operated, then is made the blood which redeems the people. (*De sacram.* 4.5.23)[36]

Ambrose follows Cyril and Gregory in speaking of a change in the nature of the elements. But once more, there is an element of ambiguity for the modern reader. The flesh and blood of John 6:54 are the "merits and power of the Lord's death." "Now we, as often as we receive the sacramental elements, which by the mysterious efficacy of holy prayer are transfigured into the flesh and blood, 'do show the Lord's death' " (*De fide* 4.10.125). The significance of *figure* for Ambrose would seem to be still that of Tertullian, for he can speak of the manna in the wilderness and other experiences of Israel as a figure of the body of the Lord, and "the reality is better than the figure" (*Mys.* 8.49).[37]

At other times, Ambrose can speak of a metabolism that concerns the elements themselves, not simply their effects or power.[38] By a blessing "even nature itself is changed," as may be seen in Old Testament miracles of transformation. The words of the Savior are even more powerful, so as even "to make out of nothing what was not" as well as to change natures. A new reality is added to the elements. The body of Christ was not present before the consecration, but after the consecration it is, and that body is identical with the body born of Mary. But Ambrose then calls attention once more to the spiritual aspect. "Therefore it is not bodily food, but spiritual." This declaration follows from the teaching that "the body of Christ is the body of a divine Spirit, because Christ is a Spirit." The purpose of the bread and wine is to nourish and strengthen the church: "With these sacraments, therefore, Christ feeds his church."[39]

Ambrose can be read as trying to elaborate the language of Irenaeus about two realities, earthly and heavenly, or as anticipating later language about a physical change in the elements. There are both components to his thought. He probably saw them as no different, for it is likely that by the language of physical change, he was making more vivid the presence of the spiritual blessings.

Later readers of Ambrose noted as distinctive in him the idea of a change in the elements effected by the repetition of the words of Christ at the Last Supper. They found in Augustine, on the other hand, an emphasis on the symbolic and spiritual aspects of the Lord's Supper. Nevertheless, there is once more a combination of language about a real presence and about a symbolism, so that both Roman Catholic and Protestant interpreters have claimed Augustine as supporting their views. Augustine, true to his Platonic philosophical heritage, put more emphasis on the spiritual reality than on the material sign, but true to his North African theological heritage, he took the material elements seriously.

Sometimes Augustine speaks in the ordinary realist language without explanation: "That bread you see on the altar, sanctified by the word of God, is the body of Christ. That cup, or rather what the cup contains, sanctified by the word of God, is the blood of Christ" (*Serm.* 227).[40] He anticipates the language of later Scholastic theologians, but I assume without their meaning: "The appearance is the same, but not the substance" (*Sermo Morin* 7). Augustine also connects the practice of adoring the Lord's Supper by bowing before it to the reality of Christ's flesh in it. He explains that Christ took flesh and "gave that very flesh to us to eat for our salvation; and no one eats that flesh unless he has first worshipped."[41] He continues, however, as an interpretation of John 6:54 and 63, by having Jesus say the following:

> Understand spiritually what I have said; you are not to eat this body that you see; nor to drink that blood that they who will crucify me will pour forth. I have commended to you a certain mystery; spiritually understood, it will give life. Although it must be visibly celebrated, yet it must be spiritually understood.

This latter statement agrees with Augustine's commentary on John 6, where he declares, "Believe, and you have eaten" (*In euang. Ioh.* 25.2). Or again, "This then is the eating of that meat and the drinking of that drink: to dwell in Christ and to have Christ dwelling in him" (*In euang. Ioh.* 26.18).[42] These interpretations accord with and result from Augustine's understanding of a sacrament: "One thing is a sacrament [the sign]; another the virtue [power] of the sacrament" (*In euang. Ioh.* 26.11).[43] This definition he applies to John 6:50, "so that one may eat of it and not die":

> That which pertains to the virtue of the sacrament, not that which pertains to the visible sacrament: he that eats inwardly not outwardly; he that eats in the heart, not he that presses with his teeth. (*In euang. Ioh.* 26.12)

In another context, Augustine uses the word *sacrament* expressly of the Lord's Supper in comparison to baptism: "As, then, in a certain manner the sacrament of the body of Christ is the body of Christ, and the sacrament of the blood of Christ is the blood of Christ, so the sacrament of faith [baptism] is faith" (*Ep.* 98.9).[44] In addition to the words *sign* and *sacrament,* Augustine could also use the word *figure* with reference to the elements. He says that at the Last Supper, Jesus gave a *figuram* (*In Ps.* 3.1).

Augustine sometimes interpreted the symbolism of the bread and wine with reference to the unity of the church. Participation in the elements was a sign of incorporation into the mystical body of Christ, the church.[45] This understanding, also based on biblical language, was an extension of the symbolism of the body of Christ and was not itself a contradiction of a real presence.

I conclude that Dugmore's description of Augustine's doctrine is accurate: For Augustine, the sign is distinct from the reality, but the reality is conveyed by and through the sign. Augustine believed in a symbolism of the visible sign and the realism of the supernatural invisible gift.[46] There is one passage that comes the closest to bringing these two ideas together and seems to sum up his thought: "The body and blood of Christ will be life to each one, when that which is received visibly in the sacrament is in very truth spiritually eaten, spiritually drunk" (*Serm.* 131.1). The influence of Augustine maintained a dynamic alternative to the popular realism in medieval thought.

Ambrose and Augustine were major influences on the eucharistic theology in the West. That they themselves did not see symbolism and realism as opposed suggests to me that the realism was not what it became later. Indeed, each was interpreted in terms of the other. So, at times the emphasis was on Ambrose's metabolic realism; sometimes more emphasis was laid on Augustine's symbolic realism.

Ninth Century

The succeeding centuries saw a growth of popular literalism about the real presence of the body and blood in the Lord's Supper. Authors sometimes made distinctions between the sign and the reality; often they did not. The next major period of writing on the subject of the Lord's Supper came in the ninth century in Carolingian Gaul. Many writers contributed to the discussion of the subject, including Rhabanus Maurus, Gottschalk, and John Scotus Erigena. The major alternatives of interpretation were voiced by Paschasius Radbertus and Ratramnus.[47] Quotations from Ambrose and Augustine recur in the writings of both men. The two "R's" assumed that the two "A's" agreed. However, Radbertus used Ambrose to interpret Augustine, and Ratramnus used Augustine to interpret Ambrose.

Radbertus was a monk at Corbie near Amiens (and its abbot from 844 to 853). His treatise, *On the Body and Blood of the Lord*, opened the discussion and indeed was the first treatise we have devoted to the eucharist.[48] It was written about 831 and then revised and sent to the Frankish King Charles II the Bald in 844. There followed a flurry of writing on the subject in the revived intellectual life of the Carolingian renaissance. Radbertus united the Augustinian with the Ambrosian-Greek view, borrowing the language of earlier writers but understanding the presence of Christ in the elements literally. Radbertus had two overruling points to make: (1) There is a real presence of the body and blood of Christ in the elements. (2) Body and blood in the eucharist are identical with the body and blood of the man who walked the earth and died on the cross.

For Radbertus, the appearance to the senses of the consecrated bread and wine is a symbol of Christ's body, but the essence of the consecrated elements is the true historical body itself.

> Because it is not right to devour Christ with the teeth, he willed in the mystery that this bread and wine be created truly his flesh and blood through consecration by the power of the Holy Spirit; . . . as from the Virgin through the Spirit true flesh is created without union of sex, so through the same, out of the substance of bread and wine, the same body and blood of Christ may be mystically consecrated. (*Corp.* 4.1)

Thus there is both a reality and a figure, because the appearances of bread and wine remained.

> He is speaking [John 6:53] about no other flesh than the true flesh and the true blood, that is, in a mystical sense. And because the sacrament is mystical, we cannot deny the figure, but if it is a figure, one must ask how it can be truth. . . . That sacrament of faith is rightly called truth; truth, therefore, when the body and blood of Christ is created by the power of the Spirit in his word out of the substance of bread and wine; but a figure when, through the agency of the priest at the altar, outwardly performing another thing, in memory of his sacred Passion, the Lamb is daily sacrificed as he was once for all. (*Corp.* 4.1)

Radbertus used *figura* in the sense of "outward appearance" and *veritas* for "what faith teaches."

> It is rightly called both the truth and a figure, so that it is a figure or character of truth because it is outwardly sensed. Truth however, is anything rightly understood or believed inwardly concerning this mystery. (*Corp.* 4.2)

For Radbertus, it was important that Christ did not say, "This is a figure of my body," but, "This is my body." He made two fundamental affirmations: (1) At every eucharist there is a new creation of the body of Christ. (2) There is a complete identification of the sacramental body with the historical body. Through the agency of the priest in repeating Christ's words, the consecration by the Holy Spirit (*Corp.* 4.3) creates the sacrament of his flesh:

No wonder that the Spirit which without seed created the man
Christ in the womb of the Virgin, from the substance of bread
and wine daily creates the flesh and blood of Christ by invisible
power through the sanctification of his sacrament, though outwardly understood by neither sight nor taste. (*Corp.* 3.4)

Furthermore, there is more than an analogy between the creation of the body of Christ in the womb and the creation of the body
on the altar. It is the same body that is created. Such is affirmed near
the beginning of the treatise:

These [bread and wine] must be believed to be fully, after the
consecration, nothing but Christ's flesh and blood. . . . And, to
put it in more miraculous terms, nothing different, of course,
from what was born of Mary, suffered on the cross, and rose again
from the tomb. (*Corp.* 1.2)

The reader may have noticed how prominent the Holy Spirit is in
Radbertus's exposition, a feature usually associated with Greek
thought on the eucharist. It is important, also, to note the centrality of
faith for Radbertus. The sacrament presupposes faith and is meant to
arouse faith; hence, the physical appearance remains so that the body
is hidden.

He has left us this sacrament, a visible figure and character of
flesh and blood, so that through them our soul and our flesh are
richly nourished for grasping things invisible and spiritual by
faith. (*Corp.* 4.2)

The believer alone receives the *virtus sacramenti*, the power of the
sacrament. The unbeliever eats for condemnation, but the believer
receives the body and blood for salvation.

They all eat, without distinction, what they often receive as sacraments of the altar. They receive them, of course, but one man
spiritually eats the flesh of Christ and drinks his blood; another
man, however, does not, although he may seem to receive the
wafer from the hand of the priest. (*Corp.* 6.2)

Radbertus stressed in his exposition the salvific purpose. "Therefore, the true flesh and blood of Christ, which anyone worthily eats

and drinks, have eternal life abiding in them" (*Corp.* 1.5). "We do not spiritually take the flesh and blood for the sake of this life so that we may not die temporally, but for the sake of life eternal" (*Corp.* 5.2). This theme from John 6 may have contributed as much to the popularity among theologians of realist language about the body and blood as the literal reading of John 6 itself did.

We conclude this survey of Radbertus with a passage setting forth his synthesis of what a sacrament is.

> They are called sacraments either because they are secret in that in the visible act divinity inwardly accomplished something secretly through the corporeal appearance, or from the sanctifying consecration, because the Holy Spirit, remaining in the body of Christ, latently accomplishes for the salvation of the faithful all these mystical sacraments under the cover of things visible. (*Corp.* 3.1)

Many who disagreed with Radbertus might have subscribed to this statement. The difference was that Radbertus had a realistic understanding of the presence of Christ in the eucharist.

Ratramnus, another monk at Corbie, represents a different way of looking at what happens and what is involved in the sacrament of the altar.[49] Charles the Bald requested his views on the eucharist. Ratramnus responded with a treatise bearing the same title as Radbertus's, *On the Body and Blood of the Lord*, probably written shortly after 844.[50]

The king raised questions concerning the two points that were fundamental to Radbertus's exposition: (1) What is the nature of the presence of Christ in the elements?[51] What is the relation of the eucharistic body to the historical body?[52] Ratramnus concludes,

> It has been most clearly shown that the bread which is called Christ's body, and the cup which is called Christ's blood, is a figure, because it is a mystery, and that there is no small difference between the body which exists through the mystery and that which suffered, was buried, and rose again. (*Corp.* 97)[53]

Ratramnus interpreted Ambrose as teaching not an actual but a sacramental presence of Christ. As human beings are body and soul, so the consecrated elements have an outward and inward aspect that nourish respectively the body and soul of the recipient.

They are called Christ's blood and body, because they are received, not as what they outwardly seem, but as what inwardly,
through the agency of the divine Spirit, they have been made. . . .
Just as the substance of this visible bread and wine nourishes and
stimulates the outer man, so the Word of God, who is living
Bread, refreshes faithful souls that share in it. (*Corp.* 43)

The emphasis on the dual realities is a position that may be described as dynamic symbolism. There is, as for Augustine, a symbolism
of the elements and a realism of the spiritual benefits. "In one respect
they are what they outwardly signify, and in another they are what
they effect inwardly and invisibly" (*Corp.* 47). The change is not in
appearance or substance but in effective power.

Christ's body and blood which are received in the mouth of the
faithful in the church are figures according to their visible appearance; but according to their invisible substance, that is the
power of the divine Word, they truly exist as Christ's body and
blood. Therefore, with respect to visible creation, they feed the
body; with reference to the power of a stronger substance, they
feed and sanctify the souls of the faithful. (*Corp.* 49)

A superficial reading might not see a great difference in
Ratramnus from some of Radbertus's statements, especially in the use
of *figura*. However, Ratramnus normally made a different distinction
between *figura* and *veritas* from the one Radbertus made. *Veritas*, or
"truth," for Ratramnus is "representation of clear fact," or what is perceived by the senses; *figura* or *figure* usually refers to the "intent [or
reality] under some sort of veil" that may be seen by the eye of faith.[54]

Drawing on Augustine's distinction between "sacraments" and
"the things of which they are sacraments," Ratramnus offers an illustration. The giving of the name of the Lord's body and blood to the
"sacraments of these two things" may be compared to the name Pas-
cha for the annual celebration of the Lord's death and resurrection.
Those things happened only once, yet the same name is used for the
annual remembrance. In the same way, when the sacraments of the
Lord's passion are celebrated, the name body and blood is employed.
There is a resemblance, but not an identity.[55]

Within this framework of thought, the similarities with Radbertus
are to be seen in their true light. The objective efficacy of the sacraments was due to the spiritual presence of the body and blood.[56] And

this, no less than for Radbertus,[57] requires the exercise of faith: "They [the sacramental body and blood] are commonly called sacraments because under cover of corporeal objects the divine power secretly dispenses the salvation of those who receive it by faith" (*Corp.* 48).

The treatises by Radbertus and Ratramnus sharpened the issue by more fully presenting two different ways of looking at the sacrament: a change in the elements versus a change in their effects. Radbertus, however, offered no explanation of how the sacramental change in the elements could be understood (other than to state it was a mystery). Nevertheless, the future belonged to him. His viewpoint was dominant by the end of the tenth century.

Eleventh Century

There was doctrinal disagreement over the Lord's Supper in the ninth century but not much evidence of real controversy. The eleventh century was different, for it saw genuine controversy—theological, conciliar, and political. The occasion was a letter in 1049 from Berengar, archdeacon and treasurer of the cathedral at Angers and later scholasticus (or master of the schools) at Tours, to Lanfranc, prior at Bec and later archbishop of Canterbury.[58] The ensuing controversy was the first in which dialectical reasoning shaped by Aristotelian logic assumed a formative place. The outcome was the beginning of a philosophical explanation for the real physical presence that had been lacking from the presentations by Ambrose and Radbertus.[59] This explanation came to be formulated in terms of the Aristotelian distinction between substance (the essential underlying reality of what something truly is) and accidents (the thing's nonessential external appearances). This development was a response to dialectical arguments against the possibility of a real physical presence of Christ in the elements.

Roman Catholics charge Berengar with being an innovator because he placed dialectical reasoning at the foundation of his theology instead of starting with traditional theology. Protestants defend him by seeing him as part of a tradition that reached back through Ratramnus to Augustine. The main surviving source for Berengar's eucharistic teaching is *De sacra coena* (On the holy Supper), written 1068-70.

As first of all a grammarian, Berengar drew on grammar and logic to argue against the popular realism with regard to the Lord's Supper. We will give some samples of his reasoning that give the flavor of his use of both verbal and physical arguments.[60] (1) Grammarians of the time said that a pronoun signified things in their substance only; nouns referred to substance and accidents. Hence, when Jesus said, "*This* is my body," he was referring to bread in its substance.

(2) No proposition can stand if the subject is denied, destroyed, or contradicted by the predicate. "This bread is the body of Christ" would be self-contradictory if it implied the substance of the subject of the sentence ceased to exist; the bread and wine must still exist or the proposition is false.[61]

(3) "Qualities" or "accidents" of something cannot exist apart from their substance, and any change in substance would involve a change in its accidental qualities (the first use of this terminology so characteristic of later Scholasticism).

(4) A change into a real bodily presence is contrary to the senses.

(5) The resurrection body, since it is impassible and incorruptible, is incapable of being handled, broken into little pieces, and chewed.

(6) The doctrine of a real presence of the body and blood involved two bodies of Christ (one in heaven and one on earth).[62]

(7) A change into the body and blood is contrary to nature, for it requires either the breaking up or annihilation of what was originally there (denied by the senses) or the creation of a substance that had not existed before (contradicted by the teaching itself). The whole doctrine, therefore, was impossible and blasphemous.

Although Berengar often does not allow any form of real presence in his attacks on the current teaching, he does sometimes express himself in more positive ways. The only conversion that he allows, however, is of the spiritual significance of the elements, that is their value or efficacy. Moreover, he consistently maintained the distinction between realities that are spiritual and material, divine and earthly. A balanced statement of his positive teaching is found in the following quotation:

> The eucharistic sacrifice has two constituents, the sacrament, which is visible, and that to which the sacrament refers (the *res sacramenti*), which is invisible. The latter is the body of Christ. If it were before our eyes, it would be invisible, but being exalted into heaven and sitting at the right hand of the Father "until the time of the restoration of all things," . . . it cannot be summoned down from heaven, as the person of Christ consists of God and man.[63]

Although repeatedly condemned by councils, made to read a grossly materialistic oath in 1059, and finally made to submit to the doctrine of his opponents before Pope Gregory VII in 1079, Berengar was never excommunicated or officially declared a heretic. The defeat of Berengar limited the range of options in eucharistic thought but did not establish a single acceptable approach to the sacrament of the altar in Catholic thought.[64]

Apart from forcing his opponents to clarify their own views, Berengar made two contributions to the development of Catholic thought. His definition of a sacrament as a "visible form of invisible grace" became standard; and his use of Aristotelian categories of substance and accidents helped establish these concepts.[65]

Lanfranc was one of Berengar's principal opponents.[66] He championed with modifications the realistic interpretation of Radbertus. He recognized, however, that simply repeating the traditional realism was not sufficient to answer the objections, so he attempted to meet Berengar on his own grounds and provide a dialectical justification for the doctrine of Radbertus. In his work, *On the Body and Blood of the Lord*, he put forward in effect the theory of transubstantiation, that the substance of bread and wine changes while the accidents remain, but without using that terminology. He spoke instead of "to be changed in the essence."

> The material objects on the Lord's Table which God sanctifies through the priest are by the agency of God's power indefinably, wondrously, in a way beyond our understanding, converted to the body of Christ in their being (*converti in essentiam dominici corporis*). Their outward appearance and certain other qualities remain unchanged, so that those who receive them are not shocked by the naked flesh and blood, and so that believers may receive the greater rewards of faith. . . .
>
> What we receive is the very body which was born of the virgin, and yet it is not. It *is*, in respects of its being and the characteristics and power of its true nature; it *is not*, if you look at the outward appearance of the bread and wine.[67]

This explanation of a change of the essence pointed toward the technical language of transubstantiation.

Berengar and Lanfranc themselves both preferred not to use the word substance (*substantia*), but the discussion they initiated was the first major controversy in the medieval Latin West to be dominated by this Aristotelian idea.[68] When Platonism was the ruling philosophy, theologians spoke of symbol and reality in explaining the real presence in the eucharist. With the (re)introduction of Aristotelian philosophy, substance and accidents became the way to account for the real presence. The concept of a change in substance made possible the affirmation of a real presence without there being a presence discernible by the senses.

The next century credited Lanfranc with the major part in the overthrow of Berengar's teaching. Yet Humbert, Cardinal-Bishop and papal adviser, appears to have had more to do in an official way with Berengar's condemnation. And Guitmund, a monk at Bec, had a more important role in the literary controversy.

Humbert, it seems, was responsible for drafting the oath of 1059 that many even of Berengar's opponents later found embarrassing. It stated the doctrine of the real presence in a way that was quite literal and even crude, some might say:

> The bread and wine which are laid on the altar are after consecration not only a sacrament but also the true body and blood of our Lord Jesus Christ, and they are physically taken up and broken in the hands of the priest and crushed by the teeth of the faithful, not only sacramentally but in truth.[69]

Berengar later repudiated his repeating this oath.

Guitmund's treatise *On the Reality of the Body and Blood of Christ in the Eucharist* shows him a more subtle thinker than Humbert. As a dialectical realist, he defined the change of the elements in clearer terms than his predecessors. He emphasized faith, but he also raised the doctrine of a metabolism of the elements to a more philosophical plane. He argued that Berengar's position robs human beings of salvation, for they must receive the substance of Christ in order to receive his immortal life. There is the total and complete presence of the body of Christ in the tiniest fragment of the consecrated bread. The eucharist represents a unique kind of change, known only by faith, the change of that which exists into something already in existence.[70] Guitmund did not introduce the wording *substantialiter mutari* ("to be changed in the substance") but he popularized it. This modification of Lanfranc's formula became the accepted way of describing the sacramental change in the eucharist.

The oath required of Berengar in 1079 contained a variation on the wording of Guitmund:

> The bread and wine which are placed on the altar . . . are
> changed substantially (*substantialiter converti*) into the true and
> proper vivifying body and blood of Jesus Christ our Lord, and af-
> ter the consecration there are the true body of Christ which was
> born of the virgin . . . and the true blood of Christ which flowed
> from his side, not however through sign and in the power of the
> sacrament, but in their real nature and true substance.[71]

The first uses of *transubstantiation* (*transsubstantiatio*) to express the change in the elements of bread and wine, but not their accidents, oc-curred about 1140 in a work of Rolando Bandinelli, the future Pope Alexander III, and about the same time in a work attributed to Ste-phen of Autun.[72]

Thirteenth Century

Theologians of the twelfth century elaborated the doctrine of transubstantiation and related it to the rest of Catholic theology. In the thirteenth century, transubstantiation received official approval at the Fourth Lateran Council (1215) under Pope Innocent III, and full theological justification and philosophical explanation in the *Summa theologiae* of Thomas Aquinas.[73] Thus the doctrine of transub-stantiation in the technical sense is a latecomer to Catholic theology. It functioned as an explanation of how the change in the elements oc-curred without affecting the sense perception of that change. The doctrine of the real presence is much older, going back at least to the fourth century, depending on how it is defined. Transubstantiation was a theory of how the real presence of body and blood was accom-plished when the bread and wine continued to have the appearance of bread and wine. The doctrine, as we shall see more fully in Thomas Aquinas, made use of the Aristotelian distinction between substance and accidents. The substance, what something is in itself, becomes the body and blood of Christ, but the accidental qualities of what one sees, smells, tastes, and feels remain bread and wine.

The word *transubstantiation* occurs in the creed approved at the Fourth Lateran Council (the twelfth ecumenical council of the West-ern Church) in opposition to the Cathars, or Albigensians, who repre-sented a revival or continuation of the ancient dualist heresy held by the Gnostics, the Manichaeans, and the Bogomils—a heresy that con-sidered matter to be evil. Canon 1 of the council includes in its exposi-tion of the faith the following statement:

There is one Universal Church of the faithful, outside of which there is absolutely no salvation. In which there is the same priest and sacrifice, Jesus Christ, whose body and blood are truly contained in the sacrament of the altar under the forms of bread and wine; the bread being changed by divine power into the body, and the wine into the blood (*transsubstantiatis pane in corpus et vino in sanguinem potestate divina*), so that to realize the mystery of unity we may receive of Him what He has received of us.[74]

Theologians of the early thirteenth century did not understand this conciliar confession as containing a definitive statement on the mode of the real presence. They read it as a strong rejection of the anti-materialist heresy of the Cathars but not as deciding the manner of the eucharistic presence of the body of Christ.[75]

By the mid-thirteenth century, theologians began to give to the word *transubstantiation* a very exact meaning. Thomas Aquinas, Dominican friar and one of the great theological thinkers of all time, became the most influential defender and exponent of transubstantiation.[76] For him, transubstantiation provided the only way in which the real presence could be explained in such a way as to preserve the physical presence without gross materialism and to preserve the sign quality of the sacrament without a purely symbolic interpretation. This was one example of his theological program of fusing Aristotelian philosophy with Catholic theology: to the eucharistic elements, he applied Aristotle's distinction between *substance* (what a thing is in itself as grasped by the mind) and *accidents* (the appearance of a thing as grasped by the senses). Actually, as his critics later pointed out, Aquinas departed from Aristotle in this instance by allowing the accidents to be separated from their substance.

Aquinas devoted questions 73 to 83 of part 3 of his *Summa theologiae* to the eucharist, and of these question 75 considers "The Change of Bread and Wine into the Body and Blood of Christ," in 8 articles. (1) "Is the body of Christ really and truly in this sacrament, or only in a figurative way or a sign?" He answers, "We could never know by our senses that the real body of Christ and his blood are in this sacrament, but only by our faith which is based on the authority of God."[77] (2) "Does the substance of the bread and wine remain in this sacrament after the consecration?" The position of those who say it does, he replies, "cannot be sustained." (3) The substance of bread and wine, however, is not annihilated or reduced to a more elementary kind of matter. (4) The bread can be turned into the body of Christ;

"this conversion, however, is not like any natural change, but it is entirely beyond the powers of nature and is brought about purely by God's power." Such a change is unique and so has "a name proper to itself," "*transubstantiation*."

(5) Logically the accidents of bread and wine ought not to be present, but by God's power they remain when their substance is changed. (6) The substantial form (according to Aristotle's distinction of matter and form) of the bread does not remain after consecration. (7) The change is wrought instantaneously. (8) "The body of Christ comes from the bread." "The conversion of the bread into Christ's body has certain resemblances both to creation and to natural change, but in some respects it differs from each of them." Aquinas, furthermore, affirmed that the whole Christ was present in each of the species (bread and wine) and in every part of each species (*Summa*, 3:Q. 76, art. 1-3), a doctrine that gave theological justification to communion in one kind.[78]

The importance of transubstantiation for Aquinas is that it guarantees the presence of Jesus Christ in the sacramental species on the altar. Transubstantiation is independent of place and all local movement, does not modify the quantity of the body of Christ, and is invisible. The great miracle of transubstantiation involves other miracles as well: the complete disappearance of the substance of bread and wine, the permanence of the accidents after the disappearance of their substance, the existence of a human body (in this case that of Christ) without any of its natural accidents, and (most extraordinary of all) the apparent "multilocation" of Christ (actually Christ is present in the elements because the accidents are present in him).[79] Throughout his treatment of the change of the elements, to overcome objections Aquinas constantly invoked the infinite power of God. God is able to effect what is contrary to sense and logic.

Aquinas's interpretation was disputed by theologians of the Franciscan order such as Alexander Hales and Bonaventura. One point of difference had to do with the connection between the body of Christ and the accidents of the elements. For Aquinas, the substance of the body of Christ after consecration remained attached to the accidents, whatever happened to the bread and wine; thus if a mouse ate them, the body of Christ was there, although Christ would be unaffected and the mouse would derive no benefit. For the Franciscans, on the other hand, the body of Christ was detachable from the consecrated elements so that only those capable of understanding (not a mouse) and believers (not Jews or pagans) could receive sacramentally.[80]

In the later thirteenth century, the Franciscan Duns Scotus (ca. 1265-1308) considered *consubstantiation* more plausible on philosophical grounds than transubstantiation. (Consubstantiation is the view that the substance of the body and blood of Christ is present along with the substance of the bread and wine in the eucharist.) Duns nevertheless adhered to transubstantiation on the authority of the church, and he appears to have begun the interpretation of the Fourth Lateran Council as a dogmatic affirmation of transubstantiation over against other alternatives.[81] These other alternative approaches continued to be taken by various theologians through the later Middle Ages. Transubstantiation remained one explanation among others but increasingly prevailed until the Council of Trent (1551) condemned those who rejected it.

Summary

We have traced a long history of interpretation of the Lord's Supper, reflecting in turn the influence of Hebrew commemoration, Platonic ontology, and Aristotelian analysis of substance and accidents. This history has traveled from a Hebrew realism of meaning to a Greek realism of presence, or in other words, adding to a change in significance a change in the elements themselves. Within the context of Greek thought, the philosophical background moved from Plato's idealism of spiritual forms to Aristotle's explanation of material reality. These changes of intellectual climate culminated in the teaching of transubstantiation as an explanation of how the change in the reality of the sacrament of the Lord's Supper occurred.

Discussion continued among Roman Catholic theologians of the late Middle Ages concerning the correct and best way to define and explain the real presence in the Lord's Supper. Yet the stage was now set for the various options to be taken in the age of the Reformation.

The modern preference by some Roman Catholic thinkers for the term "transignification" promises a way to overcome the debates of the Reformation era. The term itself may fairly be interpreted in such a way as to agree with the early understanding of the Lord's Supper which was proposed at the beginning of this essay.

❧ 2 ❧

Contrasting Views of the Lord's Supper in the Reformation of the Sixteenth Century

William R. Estep Jr.

On Christmas Day of 1521, Andreas Bodenstein von Karlstadt led in the first public Protestant observance of the Lord's Supper in the Castle Church in Wittenberg. Even though he read the traditional canon of the mass in Latin, there were some significant differences. First, Karlstadt preached a sermon extolling the virtues of faith. Then he proceeded to celebrate mass without the usual vestments, omitting all references to sacrifice, and the host was not elevated. After consecration, both elements were distributed; for the first time in their lives, the two thousand or so present heard, as Karlstadt shifted into German, "This is the cup of my blood of the new and eternal testament, spirit and secret of the faith, shed for you to the remission of sins."[1]

This event, eagerly anticipated by the citizens of Wittenberg, received the approval of neither the cautious Elector nor the exiled Reformer. Upon his return to Wittenberg in March, Luther turned on Karlstadt with a vengeance and restored the traditional Latin mass, with the exception of any reference to it as a sacrifice. It would be two more years before Luther would permit communion in both bread and cup. It remained for Thomas Müntzer to translate the mass into German, adding Psalms and hymns in German in the process. Later in the same year, 1523, Luther began his own liturgical reforms.[2]

Although Luther felt that Karlstadt's celebration of the Lord's Supper in both kinds was an unwarranted, precipitous act, until 1523 the two Reformers were in essential agreement regarding the theology of the mass. They both held to the presence of Christ in some sense and the necessity of faith on the part of the recipient in realizing that presence. But early in that year, Luther published *Vom Anbeten des Sakraments*, in which he embraced the concept of the "real presence." Before the end of 1523, Karlstadt had brought out his *Vom Priestertum und Opfer Christi*, in which he revealed his complete rejection of the "real" presence. Instead, Karlstadt held that Christ pointed to himself as he said, "This is my body," when he instituted the Lord's Supper.[3] In back of this acrimonious disagreement between colleagues was the centuries-old clash of diverse positions on the mass. The Reformation accelerated the controversy, while adding new dimensions to it.

Medieval Antecedents

For five centuries, at least, the nature of the presence of Christ in the eucharist had been the subject of controversy within the Roman Church. In 844, Paschasius Radbertus was apparently the first to publish a treatise in which he argued that the bread and wine were changed at the time of consecration into the very body and blood of Christ. This was disputed by Ratramnus, Lanfranc, and others, who cited Augustine as the authority for teaching the spiritual and not the physical presence of Christ in the Lord's Supper.[4] After years of debate, Radbertus's position finally gained the support of Aquinas, who provided an elaborate theological undergirding of the sacraments with a synthesis of Aristotelian philosophy and Catholic dogma. *Transubstantiation*, a term that had come into use to indicate the miraculous change in the bread and wine, became official dogma at the Fourth Lateran Council in 1215. This position was affirmed by the Council of Trent.

With the decree of the Fourth Lateran Council, the building blocks of a sacral society were in place. The two acts which bound this society together were infant baptism and the mass. Although all the sacraments were significant as means of grace, it was the eucharist that symbolized the indispensable role of the priest in the sacramental system. Salvation then became dependent upon the one dispensing the sacraments, the most important of which involved the miracle of transubstantiation. Thus, sacramentalism and sacerdotalism became characteristic of the medieval church, against which numerous individuals and dissenting groups began to raise their voices, particularly as the Scriptures became more widely dispersed among the literate classes. Some of these early protesters were priests, such as Berengar of Tours and Tanchelm of Flanders. However, those who articulated alternative interpretations of the Lord's Supper most effectively arose after transubstantiation became official dogma of the church. The first of these was John Wycliffe.

John Wycliffe

In 1379, for the first time, Wycliffe, often referred to as "the Morning Star of the Reformation," made public in two works, *De apostasia* and *De eucharistia*, his own views on the mass. Wycliffe believed that his understanding of the Lord's Supper was true to Augustine's teaching and that of the Bible. Therefore, he rejected transubstantiation but not the presence of Christ which can be perceived by faith alone. The bread and the wine for Wycliffe remained simply bread and wine after consecration as sacramental signs. He deemed it idolatry to identify the bread with the physical body of Christ. His position on the Lord's Supper became known as the "remanence" theory.[5]

John Huss

John Huss, who was closely identified with Wycliffe theologically, was also accused at Constance (1415) of holding the same heretical opinion as that of Wycliffe on the Lord's Supper. He denied the accusation, although he admitted that after consecration the bread and the wine remained bread and wine. He claimed to the hour of his death that he held to the miracle of transubstantiation. Matthew Spinka, his major biographer, writes that Huss "held tenets which he understood to be the orthodox dogmas of the sacraments, which he regarded, just as inconsistently as did Augustine, to be necessary to the process of sanctification."[6] Apparently, according to his close friend Jakoubek of Stribo, Huss also held that both elements should be given to lay participants in the mass.[7]

Wessel Gansfort

In spite of the fact that, at Leipzig, Luther had spoken approvingly of the teachings of John Huss and/or Wycliffe as found in Huss's *De ecclesia*, it was the lesser-known Wessel Gansfort of the Netherlands whose writings had the greatest impact upon the Protestant reformulation of the Lord's Supper in the Reformation era. In a letter to Hinne Rode (Rhodius), Luther wrote: "If I had read his works earlier, my enemies might think that Luther had absorbed everything from Wessel, his spirit is so in accord with mine."[8] However, Gansfort exerted far more influence upon the thinking of both Karlstadt and Zwingli, mediated through Cornelius Hoen, than upon Luther. It is indeed enigmatic that Gansfort, who died in the good graces of the Catholic Church, became, in a sense, the intellectual father of the theology of the Lord's Supper that is still characteristic of the majority of evangelicals today.

During his lifetime, Gansfort (1419-1489), escaped the inquisition, due to the intervention of powerful friends, including the bishop of Utrecht. Although his teachings were not above suspicion, he never attacked the dogma of transubstantiation; he simply bypassed it with a fresh interpretation of the Lord's Supper. The heart of its observance for Gansfort was "in remembrance of his broken body and shed blood." "For it is this remembrance of him," he writes, "that constitutes the true eucharist. . . ."[9] Everything that the Lord's Supper was intended to mean and to do for the recipient is encompassed "in the remembrance of Him."

A few excerpts from Gansfort's treatise *De sacramento eucharistiae* will illustrate how thoroughgoing was Gansfort's memorial interpretation of the eucharist.

> "Take, eat; for this is my body which is broken for you; this do ye, as often as ye do it, in remembrance of me." Here Christ made a great assertion and strengthened it with two commands. He commanded us to take and eat, and to do it in remembrance of him. It is as though he said: "Remember what I endured in my body, not only as an example of patience for your imitation but more than that—as the price I paid to redeem you from misery. For indeed my body was given to endure pains that you might not bear what you must have borne, had I not endured it for you. Thus my body broken for you will be your bread and food, feeding, nourishing, refreshing, preserving, strengthening, quickening, exhilarating, gladdening, stimulating you. Therefore you have eaten of it, as often as your remembrance of me has been thus efficacious, healthful, and beneficial."[10]

Gansfort emphasizes the necessity of the spiritual appropriation of the Lord's Supper, for man is a spiritual being. "Just as therefore the inner man is a spirit and his life also is spiritual, so this bread must be spiritual and must be eaten spiritually. For except we eat the bread, we have not life in ourselves."[11] Perhaps Gansfort's memorial view of the Lord's Supper would have simply gathered dust in a professor's library and remained unknown to later generations but for Cornelius Hoen.

Cornelius Hoen

Cornelius Hoen (Honius), a lawyer at the Hague, was asked by Martin Dorp of Louvain to examine a library he had been given by an uncle. In this library, Hoen discovered Gansfort's work on the eucharist and was thoroughly captivated by it. From his reading, he drew the conclusion that there was no basis in Scripture for the dogma of transubstantiation. Instead, he interpreted Christ's words of institution, as set forth in the canon of the mass, "*Hoc est corpus meum* (this is my body)," to mean that the bread signifies the body of Christ. Further, he insisted that one can no more say that the bread is literally the body of Christ than one can say that Christ is substantially the door or the vine. Following Gansfort's understanding of the significance of John 6:63, Hoen declared that whoever believes in Christ partakes of the true bread, Christ himself.[12] Hoen also rejected the mass as a repetitive sacrifice.

Hoen determined to share his insights and those of Wessel with Luther, but, due to his age, he commissioned Hinne Rode (Rhodius) to make a 1521 journey to Wittenberg on his behalf. In addition to Hoen's own manuscript on the subject, Rode carried with him the works of Gansfort to share with Luther and also with Oecolampadius and Zwingli. By 1523, it was evident that the seed thus planted had begun to bear fruit in Germany and Switzerland.

Two Reformers: Luther and Zwingli

Marburg, 1529, will always mark the failure of the two leading Reformers and their colleagues to find common ground for an acceptable Protestant position on the eucharist. The outbursts of both men in the heat of debate provide a historical engraving of dramatic proportions as inescapable as it is painful. But it was not always so. Both Reformers before Marburg, for a time, had traveled parallel paths but by 1525 had reached divergent positions. Marburg demonstrated how irreconcilable the differences were or appeared to be.

Both Zwingli and Luther had been Roman Catholic priests who had celebrated the eucharist with the traditional liturgy and the theological understanding prescribed by the canon of the mass. The host and the cup were elevated and the miracle of transubstantiation was invoked with the words of consecration, *"Hoc est corpus meum"* and *"Hic est sanguis meus* (this is my blood)." Thus they both had accepted the distinction between accident and substance, the concept of the repetitive sacrifice of Christ upon the altar, the "real" presence, and the *ex opere operato* (effective through the mere action) nature of the mass. The first indication that Luther, at least in his mind, had begun to seriously question the church's teaching came with his 1520 treatise on the sacraments, *On the Babylonian Captivity of the Church.*

Martin Luther

Luther gave credit to Peter D'Ailly, the cardinal of Cambrai, for prompting him to examine more closely the teachings of the church on the mass. D'Ailly was probably led to examine the dogma of transubstantiation at Constance by the testimony of the condemned Huss. Subsequently, Luther attributed the decree of the Fourth Lateran Council to a pagan philosopher, Aristotle. He claimed that for 1200 years the "holy fathers" knew nothing of "this transubstantiation (a monstrous word and a monstrous idea), until the pseudo philosophy of Aristotle began to make its inroads into the church in these last three hundred years."[13]

In place of the traditional understanding, Luther's bold reconstruction considered the eucharist a testament or promise of "life and salvation" "actually granted those who believe the promise." He proceeds to link the promise of the forgiveness of sins which comes through Christ's sacrifice on the cross to the memorial of his death, which the Lord's Supper commemorates with the faith of the recipient.

> From this you will see that nothing else is needed for a worthy holding of mass than a faith that relies confidently on this promise, believes Christ to be true in these words of his, and does not doubt that these infinite blessings have been bestowed upon it. Hard on this faith there follows, of itself, a most sweet stirring of the heart, whereby the spirit of man is enlarged and enriched (that is love given by the Holy Spirit through faith in Christ), so that he is drawn to Christ, that gracious and bounteous testator, and made a thoroughly new and different man.[14]

At this stage in his theological development, Luther sounds much like Wessel Gansfort. However, he identifies the *"est* (is)*"* in the institution of the Lord's Supper with the flesh and blood of Christ. Therefore, he never quite forsook the concept of the "real presence" although, in 1520, he subordinated it to the "promise of the forgiveness of sins and salvation," to which it testifies when received by faith. But the Luther of Marburg is "the Catholic Luther." Even though he had discarded the concept of sacrifice in the mass, he had now a heightened emphasis upon the bodily presence of Christ in the eucharist. Faith is subordinated to the miracle, not of transubstantiation but of consubstantiation.

How does the historian account for the change in Luther's position evident by 1525? In all probability, a number of factors influenced him to retreat from the bold stance of 1520. Doubtless his altercation with Karlstadt, who had done nothing more than initiate the changes in the celebration of the mass which Luther had taught, reflected Luther's opinion of Karlstadt, which was formed during his ten months in the Wartburg from reports of Spalatin and Melanchthon. During this period Luther's own development as a Reformer may have been arrested. Again, Karlstadt's crossing of swords with Luther in 1524 on the "real presence," in which Karlstadt reflected Hoen's influence upon his thinking, apparently drove Luther into a corner that he refused to forsake. Besides, the "old Luther," as some viewed him, or the "responsible Reformer," according to others, was beginning to emerge. When he faced Zwingli, he probably saw Karlstadt or, even worse, a sharper "Swiss Karlstadt."

Marburg, 1529

The Colloquy of Marburg, planned by Philip of Hesse to provide a show of unity in the face of Roman Catholic resurgence, became instead a symbol of division. As with numerous ecumenical ventures since, the sticking point was the Lord's Supper. The leading Reformers, Luther and Zwingli and their respective colleagues, upon the Landgrave's insistence, drew up a list of fifteen articles upon which they were in agreement. The last, on the Lord's Supper, was ambiguous enough to lend itself to a variety of interpretations. But the list did provide Philip with a paper agreement. Although Philip knew that Luther and Zwingli were strong-willed and tough-minded men, he never understood how deep was the cleavage in their positions on the eucharist until Marburg, if even then.

The predominant element in the colloquy at Marburg was conflict. Controversy revolved around the nature of the presence of Christ in the eucharist. Luther came to Marburg determined not to depart from his literal interpretation of the words in the Latin Vulgate, "*Hoc est corpus meum*"—nor did he. Zwingli, who knew Luther's position well and had in print refuted it point by point, was just as insistent upon his own interpretation, which relied heavily on his understanding of John 6:63.[15] Behind the interpretations were a different understanding of the human and divine natures in Christ and different meanings ascribed to the term, "the testament in my blood." Luther's final argument for the real presence was based upon a concept of the ubiquity of Christ's physical body. Zwingli rejected that concept upon the basis of his own exegesis of the relevant passages in the Greek New Testament, which he tried to explain. To this, Luther replied, "Don't speak Greek to me. Speak in Latin or German."

Behind the outbursts of both Reformers was a deep commitment to Scripture and particularly to their own interpretations of the disputed passages. Yet there were also many nontheological factors at work which preconditioned each Reformer not to accept the position of the other. A part of the problem lay in Luther's apparent retrenchment from the theology of the Lord's Supper which by 1520 he had embraced, at least in theory. Zwingli had once held essentially a Lutheran position, as reflected in his *De Canone Missae epichiresis*, in which he had rejected the concept of the mass as a fresh sacrifice of Christ on the altar but had continued to insist on the adoration of the host together with the proper vestments. He later apologized for holding to his earlier position in *De Canone Missae libelli apologia*.

Ulrich Zwingli

Ever so gradually, Zwingli changed in his understanding from an uncritical acceptance of the Roman Catholic canon on the mass as late as 1522, to what has been called, with some justification, a "symbolic view." (A simple reductionism implied by the term "symbolic" fails to appreciate the fully developed theology of the mass set forth by Zwingli in 1529.) The change for Zwingli apparently began from his examination of Luther's *The Babylonian Captivity of the Church*. By the First Zurich Disputation in January 1523, he had not only rejected the mass as a sacrifice but also adopted the memorial view of Gansfort and probably also the signifying concept of Hoen. Article 18 of the Sixty-Seven Articles drawn up for the occasion stated:

That Christ having sacrificed himself once, is in all eternity a
true and sufficient sacrifice for the sins of all believers; therefore
the mass is not a sacrifice but a thanksgiving memorial (*ein
Widergedechtnuss* = *Wiedergedächtnis*) and an assurance of the
forgiveness that Christ has made known to us.[16]

By 1529, Zwingli's eucharistic theology was fully developed. He
had denied the mass as a sacrifice and the "real presence" (the carnal
eating of the flesh of Christ); and he had enriched his own understanding by insisting that the *Abendmahl* was a memorial of the one
sacrifice of Christ in which the taking of the bread and the wine were
acts of thanksgiving. He affirmed the spiritual presence of Christ for
those who received the elements in faith. In partaking of the Lord's
Supper, the believers testify that they have forgiveness through
Christ's sacrifice on the cross.

Zwingli did not like the word *sacramentum* but used it, with res-
ervations, and only as an equivalent of the German word, *Pflichtzei-
chen*, meaning pledge or covenant sign.[17] Initially, apparently under
Hubmaier's influence (1523), Zwingli adopted the concept that in
partaking of the mass, a pledge is given to God by the believer and to
one's brothers in Christ. Therefore, the Lord's Supper was viewed as a
communion not only with Christ but also as an act of fellowship within
the community of faith. Thus, in his eucharistic theology, Zwingli
sought to avoid the perceived errors of Luther and the Roman Catholics and attempted to restore the Lord's Supper to its simple New Testament meaning and practice.

By Easter Sunday of 1525, Zwingli was at last ready to discard the
Roman Catholic mass, which he had been celebrating in Latin for
some twenty years, for a simple communion service with bread and
wine. For this initial observance, he discarded the monstrance and
the silver chalice, replacing them with wooden plates and wooden
cups, into which wine was poured from pewter pitchers.

Although Zwingli's sacramental theology was in the final analysis
uniquely his, it was not without considerable input from other
sources, including the Anabaptists. In fact, as Peter Stephens points
out, there was a significant change in Zwingli's understanding of the
covenant signs in 1525, due to his conflict with the Anabaptists. "Until
this (1525) the sacraments have been seen as the covenant or pledge
made between the Christian and his fellow Christians. This development takes place in terms of the eucharist but is of particular importance in Zwingli's controversy with the Anabaptists."[18] From this point

on, Zwingli abandoned his earlier concept of communion (*koinōnia*) for a new understanding of the signs of God's covenant with his people. This enabled him to find a parallel between circumcision as a sign of the covenant with Israel, and infant baptism as a sign of the new covenant. This change also reflected a shift in his theology from people's free response to the gospel in faith, to an Augustinian emphasis upon God's sovereignty and predestination.[19]

The Anabaptists

In 1955, Heinold Fast presented a paper to the Mennonitischer Geschichtsverein at Göttingen, Germany, on "The Dependence of the First Anabaptists on Luther, Erasmus, and Zwingli," later published in *The Mennonite Quarterly Review*. First he summarizes major theological points which the Anabaptists held in common with Luther, Erasmus, and Zwingli, and their possible indebtedness to all three. Then he raises the question of the apparent influence of Karlstadt and Müntzer upon the Swiss Brethren. Of these, Fast insists that the major influence upon the emerging Anabaptist movement was that of Ulrich Zwingli, even in the matter of baptism. In fact, Fast holds that the early Anabaptists were dependent upon Zwingli for their theology and their understanding of both baptism and the Lord's Supper.[20] While Fast is undoubtedly correct up to a point, his position needs some qualification. As every historian of the period knows, Zwingli rejected believers baptism and turned against those who followed his earlier lead in the matter. Although the situation is not quite the same with the Lord's Supper, the Anabaptists represent a distinct development beyond Zwingli in this regard as well.

While Fast admits that Grebel and his colleagues had developed a more advanced theology of baptism than Zwingli, he does not hold that the same was true of the Lord's Supper. To the contrary, he writes: "A comparison with Zwingli's corresponding views shows (and this has frequently been ascertained in summarized form) that in Grebel's exposition on communion, every point has been taken over from Zwingli."[21] Fast goes on to state that it is "Zwingli's concept of communion as creating fellowship and obligating to fellowship (which was made known in May 1524) that constitutes the chief theme also for Grebel."[22] Then he gives in parallel columns phrases from Zwingli's works and Grebel's letter to Thomas Müntzer in twenty-five points. However, Fast ignores the possible influence of Balthasar Hubmaier, who spoke at length at the Second Zurich Disputation in the discussion on the mass, and the fact that the concept of the Lord's Supper as a pledge of fellowship did not appear in Zwingli's writings until more than a year and a half after the break between Zwingli and the Grebel-led group.

The Second Zurich Disputation

On October 26, hundreds of men, priests, and laymen gathered in the *Rathaus* (town hall) to attend the second disputation held in Zurich in 1523. The agenda called for three days to discuss before the two councils of Zurich the topics of images, the mass, and purgatory. The discussion on images was dispensed with in relatively short order, with hardly a dissenting voice. Most were apparently agreed that images were an "abomination" before the Lord and should be abolished in an orderly fashion after the people were properly instructed. Balthasar Hubmaier, one of the ten theologians present with a doctor's degree, spoke eloquently to the accompaniment of "amens." The second day was given to a discussion of the mass, which some of Zwingli's more zealous followers were anxious to abolish.

About two weeks before, Zwingli had published his second book on the canon of the mass (October 9), which constituted both a defense and an apology. He confessed he had been wrong regarding the traditional use of vestments but right about liturgical prayers and chants. He was still the cautious Reformer striving to hold his more aggressive disciples in check while appeasing those who still clung to the traditional Roman Catholic mass. As the second day of the disputation came to a close, it was clear that Grebel was not satisfied. He had anticipated much more and said as much.

The next day (the 28th) the meeting was called to order by Joachim von Watt (Vadian), Grebel's brother-in-law. Grebel began where he had left off the night before, declaring that there were still many abuses in the mass which should be pointed out and abolished by "Milords" (the city councils). Then, he almost immediately deferred to "those more eloquent than he." Whereupon, as if by prearrangement, Balthasar Hubmaier arose to speak. By this time, Hubmaier had clearly established himself as a knowledgeable reformer who sought to test everything by the Bible. His comments represented a position in advance of that of Zwingli and Grebel. The day before, instead of appealing to conciliar authority for the abolition of images, as others had done, including Grebel, Hubmaier declared that the decision should be left to the local church.

At the beginning of his remarks on the mass, Hubmaier diplomatically declared his agreement with the position of Zwingli and Leo Jud. But from his subsequent statements, it was clear that his thinking on the mass was beyond anything Zwingli had written or was reported to have said on the subject. Of course, as Rempel has pointed out, it did not represent the final formulation of Hubmaier's theology of the Lord's Supper.[23] Even though Hubmaier's was a preliminary word, it appears to have been a seminal one, not only for the Grebel-led group but for Zwingli as well.

With his introductory remarks, he declared that the mass was not a sacrifice but a "testament" or a "memorial" and a proclamation of "the covenant of Christ." He went on to refer to the mass as a sign and *sigill* (seal) of the once-for-all sacrifice of Christ, by which we are assured of the forgiveness of our sins. Then, before delineating his position in five points, he cited six passages of Scripture upon which his remarks were based. Noticeably lacking in these was John 6:63, which was so prominent in Gansfort's work on the mass. It is also clear that his supreme authority in matters of faith was Jesus Christ. Christ speaks, "*Hoc facite* (do this)." He does not say, "*Hoc offerte* (sacrifice this)."[24] After these preliminary statements, Hubmaier proceeded to set forth his view regarding the reform of the mass. While he still used the term *missae*, this would soon give way to *Nachtmahl* or *Abendmahl*.

It is evident that Hubmaier had given considerable thought to what he planned to say, a summary of which follows. First, the mass is not a sacrifice. Instead, it is a testament of personal faith. It follows that one cannot celebrate mass for another. Second, the mass is a sign or seal of the body and blood of Christ. Therefore, only the words of Scripture should be used when it is celebrated. Third, the gospel must be preached every time mass is celebrated. If it is not, there is no mass. Fourth, mass should be celebrated in the language of the people wherever it is held, not in Latin, which people do not understand. Fifth, mass is to be taken together in fellowship with the entire congregation with both bread and wine. Therefore, there is no biblical basis for private masses.

It is the last point that both the Swiss Brethren and Hubmaier were to develop into a distinctive Anabaptist understanding of communion. Implicit in this statement is the concept of *koinōnia* within the congregation of believers who take the Lord's Supper together. Later, believers baptism became closely linked with the *Abendmahl* or *Nachtmahl* in Anabaptist theory and practice.

Grebel and the Swiss Brethren

In his letter to Thomas Müntzer on behalf of himself and six others, Grebel admonishes Müntzer to observe the Lord's Supper according to scriptural guidelines and discard his own innovations. He refers to the Lord's Supper as a "Supper of unity." In referring to the bread, he writes:

> Although it is simply bread: where faith and brotherly love prevail, it shall be partaken of with joy. When observed in that way in the congregation, it shall signify to us that we are truly one loaf and one body, and that we are and intend to be true brothers one with another. 18. But if one should be found who is not minded to live the brotherly life, he eats to his condemnation, for he does not discern the difference from another meal. He brings shame on the inward bond, which is love, and on the bread, which is the outward bond. . . . The Supper, however, is to be an exhibition of unity. It is not a mass or a sacrament. Therefore, no one shall receive it alone, neither on a deathbed nor otherwise.[25]

Evidently the first Lord's Supper among the Swiss Brethren was not observed until after the first baptism on January 21, 1525. The next day, baptisms followed near Zollikon, and that evening or on January 23, Conrad Grebel led in the observance of the Lord's Supper in the home of Jacob Hottinger at Zollikon. These attempts at restoring a simple New Testament pattern took place while Zwingli was still following the traditional Roman Catholic rites in both infant baptism and mass, except for any reference to the mass as a sacrifice.

The first baptisms were followed by a rash of baptisms in Zollikon until interrupted by the arrests of some thirty new converts. The prisoners were placed in the Augustinian monastery and interrogated. Judging by answers the untutored farmers gave the authorities, it is evident that a deep desire to live the Christian life had led to repentance and baptism, followed by the Lord's Supper as a sign of their unity in Christ and love for the brethren and even for those beyond their own community of faith—their neighbors. Jörg Schad, after telling of his baptism at the hands of Felix Manz, said that "they sat at a table and broke bread, pledging to have God in their hearts always and, while thinking of Him, show brotherly love to every man."[26] Conrad Hottinger's testimony is similar. He related that after baptism, "they sat together at a table and like the disciples of Christ at the Last Supper (*Nachtmal*), broke bread and gave to each as a sign that they should show brotherly love to one another and live in peace."[27]

Fritz Blanke held that in the observance of the Lord's Supper, one catches a glimpse of "the real heart of the young church." He continues: "In them they feel themselves to be a holy community tied together by the same bond and united in love of God and their fellow believers."[28] For these first Swiss Anabaptists, the Lord's Supper was a communion of those bound together by a common commitment to Christ signified in baptism and a commitment to one another to walk together in love. This ethical dimension to live according to the precepts of Christ in relation to others also included those outside the community of faith.

Balthasar Hubmaier

Hubmaier, who was burned at the stake in Vienna on March 10, 1528, developed the initial insights of the Swiss Brethren into a rather complete theology of the Lord's Supper, tying it even more closely to believers baptism. Hubmaier's theology and practice of the Lord's Supper receives the fullest treatment in two works written for use by the Anabaptist congregation in Nikolsburg, Moravia. The first, published in 1527, antedates Luther's catechisms by two years. Given the title, *Eine christliche Lehrtafel*, it was written in the form of a dialogue between Leonhart Leichtenstein and his nephew Hans.

In this work, Hubmaier has Leonhart ask: "What is the Lord's Supper?" Hans answers:

It is a public sign and testimony of the love in which one brother pledges himself to another before the congregation, that just as they now break and eat the bread with each other and share and drink the cup, likewise they wish now to sacrifice and give their body and shed their blood for one another in the strength of our Lord Jesus Christ, whose suffering they are now commemorating by the breaking of the bread and sharing the wine and proclaiming his death until he comes.[29]

In the next exchange, Hubmaier stresses the memorial aspect of the Lord's Supper; then he links baptism to the Supper.

The Lord's Supper is a sign of the pledge to brotherly love just as water baptism is a symbol of the commitment of faith. The water relates to God, the Supper to our neighbor; therein lie all the Law and the Prophets. No other ceremonies were instituted by Christ and left behind on earth and whoever teaches correctly these two signs teaches faith and love.[30]

In *Eine Form des Nachtmahls Christi*, Hubmaier gives a much fuller development of his eucharistic theology. It is presented within the context of a liturgy that he had composed for the observance of the Lord's Supper for the church at Nikolsburg. The liturgy has ten parts, with several recurring themes: (1) The gospel must always be proclaimed and the appropriate passages of Scripture used. (2) The spiritual nature of the observance is stressed: " 'I have fellowship with Christ and all his members, 1 Cor. 10:16, therefore I break bread with all believers in Christ according to the institution of Christ.' Without this inner communion in the spirit and in truth, the outward breaking of bread is nothing but an Iscariotic and damnable hypocrisy." Hubmaier says further: "This [Lord's Supper] is the true communion of saints, 1 Cor. 10:16. It is not a communion (*gmainschafft*) for the reason that bread is broken, but the bread is broken because the fellowship has already been established inward in the spirit, since Christ has come in the flesh, John 4:27."

(3) For Hubmaier, there was a close relationship between baptism as an initiatory sign and the Lord's Supper as the sign of fellowship. "For just as water baptism is a public testimony of the Christian faith," Hubmaier declares, "so is the Supper a public testimony of Christian love. Now he who does not want to be baptized or to observe the Supper, he does not desire to believe in Christ nor to practice Christian love and does not desire to be a Christian." (4) The ethical demands of the Christian life are touched upon in the self-examination one experiences prior to taking communion. Out of gratitude for what God has done for us through his Son, comes the desire to respond in love to the needs of others. Deeds for Hubmaier were more important than words. After referring once again to Christ's great love for us, he admonishes the "righteous Christian," "So we must not only speak the word of brotherly love, hear it, confess ourselves to be sinners, and abstain from sin; we must fulfill it in deeds, as Scripture everywhere teaches us."

Hubmaier insists on two prerequisites for a proper observance of the Lord's Supper: first, the priest must clearly explain that the bread is bread, not flesh, and the wine is wine alone, not blood; second, the communicant must repeat "The Pledge of Love (*Die Liebepflicht*)," which incorporated all the themes he had repeatedly stated in addition to an admonition to live a life above reproach. He concludes the entire liturgy by reminding the reader of the scriptural order: "For as faith precedes love, so water baptism must precede the Lord's Supper."[31]

Regardless of perceived inadequacies in Hubmaier's sacramental theology, it represents an admirable attempt at constructing an alternate communion liturgy for his own church at the time. As such, it reflects the most thorough theological undergirding for the Lord's Supper developed among evangelicals. Although he probably drew upon the same sources that informed both Zwingli and Grebel, Hubmaier seems to have been further along in this development than Zwingli in 1523. His relationship with the Grebel-led Swiss Brethren appears to have been reciprocal. However, Hubmaier's final formulation was apparently more dependent upon his own study of the biblical record than upon any other source.

Conclusion

While it is regrettable that some of the most bitter conflicts arose over the "sacraments" (a term that Zwingli reluctantly used and Hubmaier used one time as a synonym for pledge or oath), it was probably inevitable. Given the time frame of less than ten years in which Conrad Grebel, Michael Sattler, George Blaurock, and Balthasar Hubmaier began and ended their ministries, it is indeed remarkable that they were able to develop such an enduring theology of the Lord's Supper for those of the believers church tradition.

The theology and observance of the Lord's Supper underwent a number of changes during the Reformation. While all factions within the Protestant movement rejected the concept of the mass as a sacrifice, only gradually was the adoration of the host eliminated. In a further development, the Lord's Supper became a thanksgiving memorial in remembering the one all-sufficient sacrifice of Christ, of which the bread and the wine were symbols.

In addition to its relationship to Christ, the Lord's Supper also became an act of fellowship testifying to the unity of those brothers and sisters in the community of faith by virtue of their faith commitment to Christ as witnessed in believers baptism. Thus, it became a communion. Underlying the symbolism involved in every aspect of its observance was the *kerygmatic* (proclamatory) nature of the Lord's Supper and believers baptism. In the liturgical writings of Hubmaier, baptism and the Lord's Supper became inseparably linked to the two keys given to the church by Christ.

This understanding of the Lord's Supper as a communion eventually became pervasive in Protestantism. Thus the Supper signified the unique unity which the believer experiences in Christ and with fellow believers. Anabaptists first enunciated the concept of the Lord's Supper as an expression of the love that fellow believers experience in the community of faith. For most Protestants, even for those who retained infant baptism, this became an essential element in observing the Supper. Even now the term "Communion" or "Holy Communion" in many churches has become a synonym for the Lord's Supper. The recovery of the ethical dimension of the Lord's Supper as embodied in the concept of the Lord's Supper as communion may have been the most significant contribution of the Anabaptists to the theology and practice of the Lord's Supper.

⚘ 3 ⚘

Believers Church Perspectives on the Lord's Supper

Donald F. Durnbaugh

Two writers introducing the recent comprehensive study on the Lord's Supper in Anabaptist perspective by John D. Rempel express surprise that such an important topic has been so little studied. Hans-Jürgen Goertz begins his foreword:

> Much has been written about the Anabaptist concept of the church. Strangely, however, little has been said about the most important symbol of their fellowship: the Lord's Supper, which they celebrated in a unique manner. . . . The Lord's Supper was deeply rooted in Anabaptist piety. Congregation, Christian discipleship, and martyrdom were central. It was not an ancillary ritual but the essential manifestation of their corporate worship.

The editor of the book, Howard John Loewen, agreed: "This volume represents a landmark, the first in-depth historical and theological inquiry into the Anabaptist understanding of the Lord's Supper. It is surprising that we had to wait this long for such a study to appear."[1]

By extension, we can express similar bemusement that it has taken this long in the series of believers church conferences since 1967 for such a central theme to engage our direct attention. And even here, the initiative is based on the prior ecumenical discussion in Faith and Order circles that produced the "Baptism, Eucharist, Ministry" document of 1982. The planners of the present consultation at Ashland Theological Seminary deserve appreciation for their rectification of this lapse.[2]

Many here will likely agree that understanding the Lord's Supper is vital for an appreciation of the genius of the believers church. As one example, it is a commonplace among members of Brethren denominations that inquirers into their faith-tradition are told that they can best comprehend this ethos by attending and participating, so far as their conscience and church discipline permit, in the distinctive Brethren love feast. In 1967 a delegation of Russian Orthodox clergy and laity were visiting Church of the Brethren congregations in the United States. When they came to Bethany Theological Seminary, Oak Brook, Illinois, their visit coincided with the semiannual love feast of the nearby congregation at York Center. The richly vested visitors were invited to participate in the observance to the extent they could with integrity. They engaged in the service of examination, feetwashing, and fellowship meal, refraining only from the bread and the cup. Metropolitan Nikodim, leader of the delegation, had hosted Brethren in the Soviet Union and participated in a previous visit to the USA. After this love feast at the seminary, he exclaimed, "Now, I finally understand the Brethren!"[3]

Complexity of the Topic

Perhaps one reason for the delay in addressing the topic of the Lord's Supper is the evident difficulty of mastering it. Upon closer examination, understanding the true meaning of the Lord's Supper proves to be problematic; this is the case if one looks at any of the church bodies identified as belonging within the believers church tradition, to say nothing of the attempt to delineate an interpretation of the Lord's Supper that could encompass the totality of such church groups. Recent discussion makes clear that it will not do simply to identify the position as one of remembrance or memorial, often identified as Zwinglian. John D. Rempel's study of Anabaptist-Mennonite views of the Lord's Supper, to take one example, documents a richer and more varied understanding from early Anabaptist writers, including Balthasar Hubmaier, Pilgram Marpeck, and Dirk Philips. In a concluding chapter, he also finds diversity in current Mennonite eucharistic thought and practice, reflecting theological orientations from evangelicalism to liberalism.[4]

John D. Rempel provides a succinct summary of his lengthy monograph in his article in *The Mennonite Encyclopedia*, volume 5, by describing three characteristics of the Anabaptist understanding of the Lord's Supper:

(a) The "body of Christ" signifies not only the historical person of Jesus and not only the bread and wine, but also the church. The church is the body of Christ because it is made up only of those who have personally covenanted with Christ as fellow believers in baptism. In the breaking of bread, this reality is recreated; in it Jesus' incarnation is prolonged through time. (b) The Lord's Supper is, inseparably, an act of remembrance of and thanksgiving for Jesus' suffering sacrifice for the world. It is a visible word by which the church "proclaims the Lord's death until he comes" (1 Cor. 11:26). (c) It is a communion of the body and blood of Christ. The elements do not change, but in a gathering of believers who break bread in faith and love, there is an assured participation in Christ's saving presence.[5]

Inasmuch as Anabaptism is in many ways foundational for many bodies within the believers church, this may serve as a reasonably comprehensive summary of varied denominational belief. That it does not fit all those associated with the believers church is made clear, to take but one example, by scholars describing major Baptist bodies. While bemoaning the lack of serious Baptist attention to the issue, the active ecumenist and church historian Ernest A. Payne (1902-1980) concluded that the influence of both a "Zwinglian" memorial view and a Calvinistic spiritual presence view of the Lord's Supper have been equally strong.[6]

Another variant is added by members of the Religious Society of Friends, who understand all of life as sacramental. Therefore, they have rejected stated and specific observance of the Lord's Supper. As the Friends World Conference of 1937 explained,

> Neither silence, nor words, nor music, nor baptism with water are in themselves religious ends. We are called upon to partake of the sacrament of communion at every meal; when alone; and when in Friends' Meetings, where our form of worship gives a unique opportunity for corporate union in the Spirit of God.

Echoing this orientation, Stephen Grellet (1773-1855), a French-American Friend active in the early nineteenth century, stated,

> I think I can reverently say that I very much doubt whether since the Lord by His grace brought me into the faith of His dear son, I have ever broken bread or drunk wine, even in the ordinary

course of life, without devout remembrance of, and some devout feeling regarding the broken body and the blood-shedding of my dear Lord and Saviour.[7]

Quaker Robert Barclay (1648-1690) argued in his *Catechism* of 1673 that the followers of Christ were indeed asked to commemorate his life and sacrifice by breaking bread and drinking wine. It was to continue until the Lord comes. But Jesus *did* come to his followers, according to John 14:18-23: "Those who love me will keep my word, and my Father will love them, and we will come to them, and make our home with them" (NRSV). There is, therefore, no need to continue the observance.[8] Barclay also devoted a long chapter in his famous *Apology* (1676-1678) to the sacrament of communion, contending that the Lord's Supper, like other early church practices, was no longer commanded, since God was to be worshiped in spirit and in truth. As such practices, ordinarily called sacraments, are "but shadows of better things, they are no longer to be practiced by those who have obtained the substance."

Barclay, however, concluded (with generous intent, considering that polemical age):

Finally, if there are any in this day who practice this ceremony with a true tenderness of spirit, and with real conscience toward God, and in the manner of the primitive Christians, as recognized in scripture, that is another matter. I do not doubt but that they may be indulged in it. The Lord may take these facts into consideration and appear to them for a time when they use these things. Many of us have known him to do this for us in our own times of ignorance.[9]

According to D. Elton Trueblood, Barclay's chief concern was to emphasize the reality of sacraments such as baptism and communion in the daily life of the committed Christian, liberating their essence from any external act. "[If] a person has the reality, nothing else is required, and if he does not have the reality, nothing else will suffice."[10]

Besides the wide sweep of theological understandings on the meaning of the Lord's Supper as reflected by the variety of terms used to describe it—sacrament, ordinance, communion, eucharist, love feast, ritual, symbol, and the like—there is great difference in manner and time of observance. The Polish Brethren (Anabaptists sometimes known as the Minor Party) wrote to other Anabaptists in

Strasbourg in 1591 that they observed the Lord's Supper if possible every day, following apostolic practice (Acts 2:42-46). When Conrad Grebel (1498-1526) wrote in 1524 to Thomas Müntzer (1488/89-1525), he urged the holding of the Lord's Supper "much and often," asserting that the emerging Swiss Brethren fixed no definite time for its observance, but implying that it occurred often.[11]

One of the issues in the Amish-Mennonite split of 1693 was that the latter faction held the Lord's Supper only once a year, whereas Jacob Ammann (c.1656-c.1730) stridently maintained that it must be held twice; it is current Amish practice to hold the Lord's Supper twice a year in each district, a pattern followed in many Mennonite bodies. The Christian Church (Disciples of Christ) and related bodies are accustomed to hold communion each Sunday. The traditional love feast of the Brethren was an annual event, but most congregations now hold them in the spring and fall with some adding two additional Sunday morning bread-and-cup communions. Yet other patterns of observance could be named.[12]

Since the outline of the conference suggests that the theological meaning of the Lord's Supper, with particular attention to Christ's presence, will be specifically addressed by others, this paper will address that essential only in passing. Instead, it will focus on the relationship between the individual believer and the community as members participate in (or are excluded from) the Lord's Supper. This focus entails discussion of such issues as self-examination, group assessment, church discipline, closed communion, and mutual aid. Illustrations will be drawn from a number of different bodies often identified as believers churches, with particular emphasis upon Anabaptism.

The Discipled Body

The role of the Lord's Supper finds early expression in the constituent confession of Swiss Brethren Anabaptism, the Brotherly Union or Schleitheim Confession of 1527; it deals with the Lord's Supper in the third of its seven articles:

> Concerning the breaking of bread, we have become one and agree thus: all those who desire to break the one bread in remembrance of the broken body of Christ and all those who wish to drink of one drink in remembrance of the shed blood of Christ, they must beforehand be united in the one body of Christ, that is the congregation of God, whose head is Christ, and that by bap-

tism. For as Paul indicates, we cannot be partakers at the same time of the table of the Lord and the table of devils. . . . That is: all those who have fellowship with the dead works of darkness have no part in the light.[13]

Here is a clear declaration that the Lord's Supper is intended to express the unity of those sisters and brothers who have taken a covenant with God and each other through adult baptism to follow Jesus Christ as Lord in all things. Stated negatively, those who have not undertaken this covenant will not be admitted to the solemn meal. This underlies the practice spoken of in later years as closed or close communion.

This was a strong rejection of the medieval church emphasis upon the sacraments controlled by the hierarchy, the threat of the withdrawal of which was often used to elicit obedience from disobedient laity. The Anabaptists posited in some ways a more daring interpretation—the congregation, the gathered community, was seen as the body of Christ. As such, it must be kept clear of evident sin. This immediately brings into play the role of church discipline. As Grebel put it to Thomas Müntzer, the Lord's Supper "should not be used without the rule of Christ in Matt. 18:15-18, . . . for without that rule every man will run after the externals. The inner matter, love is passed by, if brethren and false brethren approach or eat it [together]."[14]

Thus understood, the Lord's Supper is seen as a celebration of church unity based upon free acceptance of God's grace made possible by the sacrifice of Christ. "The body of Christ, understood by Anabaptists in a very literal sense as the visible community of believers, was the presence of God in the world. The new peaceful, reconciling community was reality" (Klaassen). Sharing the Lord's Supper testifies to the marks of unity, joy, and obedience, as those taking on themselves Christ's discipleship gather in remembrance of him for encouragement and strengthening in their resolve.[15]

The flat rejection of a medieval sacramental understanding is found in the above-cited letter of Conrad Grebel to Thomas Müntzer, written before the first baptisms of early 1525:

The supper of fellowship Christ did institute and plant. . . . Ordinary bread ought to be used, without idols and additions. For [the latter] creates an external reverence and veneration of the bread, and a turning away from the inward. An ordinary drinking vessel too ought to be used. This would do away with the adoration and bring true understanding and appreciation of the Supper, since the bread is nought but bread. In faith, it is the body of Christ and the incorporation with Christ and the brethren. But one must eat and drink in the Spirit and love, as John shows in ch[apter] 6 and the other passages. . . . Although it is simply bread, yet if faith and brotherly love precede it, it is to be received with joy, since, when it is used in the church, it is to show us that we are truly one bread and one body, and that we are and wish to be true brethren with one another.[16]

The concept of one bread and one body here articulated was amplified in a striking image often repeated in Anabaptist circles, first found in the Didache or the Teaching of the Twelve Apostles (c. 120). The version used by Andreas Ehrenpreis (1589-1662) in 1652 read:

As the grain-kernels are altogether merged and each must give its content or strength into the one flour and bread, likewise also the wine, where the grapes are crushed under the press, and each grape gives all its juice and all its strength into one wine. Whichever kernel and whichever grape, however, is not crushed and retains its strength for itself alone, such an one is unworthy and is cast out. This is what Christ wanted to bring home to his companions and guests at the Last Supper as an example of how they should be together in such a fellowship.

Peter Rideman (Riedemann, 1505-1556), also a prominent Hutterite leader, had earlier limned the same image in powerful phrases in his first *Rechenschaft* (c. 1530):

Just as many kernels [from several fields] which are ground by the millstone and become one mass of flour and put together become one bread, so that in the bread one can no longer recognize of what flour one or another [loaf] is made, so also among people, when we are ground by the noble millstone of the divine force and believe his Word and place ourselves under the cross of Christ, so then are we brought together by the bond of love in one body, of which Christ is the head, as Paul says (1 Cor. 2:16).

It is not surprising to find this in the circles of Hutterian Brethren, with their emphasis upon complete sharing of communal property, or that the Amish to this day repeat it. What is perhaps more interesting is that both Luther and Calvin used this imagery upon occasion in reference to the Lord's Supper.[17]

Comparable statements can be found in the literature of the Society of Brothers (often called the Bruderhof), the twentieth-century counterpart of the Hutterites. Not only is adherence to community standards of behavior made mandatory; great effort is also exerted to ensure that the correct spirit is found in each member. Much of the turmoil that has periodically wracked this communal movement derives from the attempt to attain complete community.[18]

Harold S. Bender (1897-1962) found as one of the three essential marks of the Anabaptist vision the ideal of the brotherhood of love, of the covenanted community. Scholars of Mennonite bodies describe frequent schisms in their history as the ironic result of efforts of conscientious elders and bishops to maintain absolute unity, with much tension coming from varied responses to technological innovations in the surrounding society.[19]

When Menno Simons (c. 1496-1561) wrote on the signs of the church, he included the Lord's Supper. (Interestingly, he did not hesitate to call it a sacrament.) The true church is known by the "right and scriptural use of the sacraments," namely that of baptism and the Lord's holy Supper. Those who participate will be the "penitent, who are flesh of Christ's flesh, and expect grace, reconciliation, and the remission of their sins in the merits of the death and blood of the Lord." To underline concerns for ethics and community, Menno added that these penitent are "those who walk with their brethren in love, peace, and unity, who are led by the spirit of the Lord into all truth and righteousness, and who prove by their fruits that they are the church and people of God."[20]

These illustrations make clear the emphasis upon unity in the discipled community. But this is not the whole story. Accompanying the central emphasis upon community in Anabaptism and later manifestations of the believers church is the balancing emphasis upon the individual. Community itself is founded upon prior acts of volition by its members. Stated somewhat differently, membership in the body derives from a voluntary act of the witting person, freely choosing a life of discipleship. Although a truism, the fact needs constant reiteration that the concept of the believers church is based upon the knowing decision of the uncoerced person. One reason infant baptism was discarded was that it was held to be coercion of conscience, just as irregular as the forced baptisms of entire peoples in the histories of medi-

eval Teutonic folk groups. The classic expression is that of Claus Fel-
binger (d. 1560): "God wants no compulsory service. On the contrary,
he loves a free willing heart that serves him with a joyful soul and does
what is right joyfully."[21]

In John D. Rempel's study of the Christology of the Anabaptists
as reflected in their understanding of the Lord's Supper, he highlights
the subjectivism of the Radical Reformation, going beyond that of the
Magisterial Reformation. He accepts the interpretation of the Roman
Catholic scholar Joseph Lortz, who contrasted the "attitudes of objec-
tivism, traditionalism, and clericalism" of late medieval Catholicism
with the "subjectivism, spiritualism, and laicism" of the Reformation.
Because many Anabaptists understood their position as carrying the
reform of classical Protestantism to its consistent conclusion, they
were fairly identified with individualism.[22]

Not the least of Luther's and Calvin's objections to Anabaptism
were their correct perceptions that Anabaptists emphasized the importance of free will and thus remained closer to the spirit of Christian humanism and reformed Catholicism than did their own theological positions. George H. Williams and others have commented on
this—in Williams' words: "Like the Catholics, most of the radicals defended the freedom of the will in the realm of faith and stressed sanctification as the goal of the Christian life and the foretaste of salvation." This being the case, as one corollary, Anabaptists and later
movements have pursued what Williams has provocatively called a
"sectarian ecumenicity," asserting that "the radicals professed membership in a universal Church not linked to race or nation, a people
with corporate loyalties and internal disciplines transcending any
earthly state and never to be subsumed under one, a people characterized by the pursuit of holiness, separated from the world." This ex-
pansive orientation, again, is founded upon acts of individual choice,
not bound by passivity and predestination.[23]

The practice of believers baptism in itself is dramatic evidence of
this stance. Dirk Philips (1504-1568) argued that infants had as much
right to commune at the Lord's Supper as at the other sacrament of
baptism, namely none. The churches were inconsistent in forbidding
infants to commune but demanding that they be baptized.[24]

Current practice among the Amish prior to their communion services as well as traditional patterns for other bodies reflects the constant appeal to individual volition. Two weeks prior to the semiannual communions of the Amish comes the *Attnungsgemee* (preparatory service), in which members examine themselves to see if they are

in accord with the *Ordnung* (church rules and practice). This day-long service (children are not present, contrary to usual practice) is described by John A. Hostetler: "Each member is asked whether he is in agreement with the *Ordnung*, whether he is at peace with the brotherhood, and whether anything 'stands in the way' of his entering into the communion service. Faults must be confessed and adjustments made between members who have differences to settle."[25]

The Brethren pursued the same unity among the congregation by the traditional "deacons' visit." In these, church leaders made the rounds of the membership, asking if members were at peace with one another, if they still stood with their statements made when baptized, and whether there were issues for the congregation that must be brought to open discussion. Much as with the Amish, it was expected that any grievances among members be settled before the love feast could be observed. It was not unknown for the love feast to be postponed if a satisfactory unity were not achieved. As will be discussed later, in a variation of the above practice, individual members could be set back from the love feast if resolution of their individual shortcomings was not effected in time. The strong preference, however, was to achieve or restore unity so that all could commune.[26]

Although members of the Society of Friends did not have similar ordinances, a similar practice was followed annually. At first directed to the separate meetings and then to the stated ministry, over the years the "advices and queries" have developed into guidance and challenge for all Friends. Members are asked to ponder a lengthy list of queries, covering most aspects of life. It amounts to a searching review of the relationship of Friends with God and with their fellows.

The first such queries to be answered systematically in North America were laid out in the *Book of Advices* of 1755. Some sense of their tenor and specificity may be derived from the three initial queries, which read:

> 1st—Are all Meetings for Religious Worship, and Discipline duly attended, the Hour observed, and are Friends preserved from Sleeping, or any other indecent Behavior therein, particularly from chewing Tobacco, or taking Snuff?
> 2nd—Is Love and Unity maintained amongst you, as becomes Brethren, are Talebearing, Backbiting, and evil Reports discouraged, and where any differences arise, are Endeavors used Speedily to End them?
> 3rd—Are Friends careful to bring up those under their Direc-

tion, in plainness of Speech, Behavior and Apparel, in frequent reading the Holy Scriptures, to restrain them from reading pernicious Books, & the Corrupt Conversation of the World?[27]

Current expectations are phrased: "Although the corporate use of the advices and queries is governed by more flexible regulations than in the past, it is believed that they will continue to be a challenge and inspiration to Friends in their personal lives and in their life as a Christian community." Insight into the spirit of such advices is provided by an oft-cited postscript issued by a meeting of elders at Balby in 1656:

Dearly beloved Friends, these things we do not lay upon you as a rule or form to walk by, but that all, with the message of light which is pure and holy, may be guided; and so in the light walking and abiding, these may be fulfilled in the Spirit, not from the letter, for the letter killeth, but the Spirit giveth life.[28]

The Disciplined Body

As has already become evident, the Lord's Supper, discipleship, and church discipline were all integrally connected. If unity were not present, then communion could not follow. Examination preceded celebration. These practices also reflected the understanding of the meaning of the Lord's Supper. "This is my body" broken for Jesus' followers was understood to apply directly to the church membership. Balthasar Hubmaier (c. 1480-1528) wrote in answer to those spiritualizers of his day who objected to any tangible practices such as water baptism and the Lord's Supper:

These are only outward symbols. They are nothing other than water, bread, and wine. . . . These people have in all their lives never learned even to understand why these symbols were ordained by Christ, what their purpose is, or to what end they are to be practiced. The end is the gathering of a church, the covenanting publicly to live according to Christ's word in faith and brotherly love, and the submitting themselves to a brotherly discipline and the Christian ban because of their sins. . . . This is the important thing . . . and not the water, bread, or wine. Our water baptism and breaking of bread have become but empty illusions, indeed, nothing better than the futile infant baptism and spoon-feeding of children in communion has been where brotherly discipline and the Christian ban are not also present.[29]

Because the Lord's Supper had this meaning for members of the believers churches, they found it only appropriate to reserve the breaking of bread and drinking of wine to those who had seriously committed themselves through baptism to follow Christ. This is the reasoning, as mentioned previously, behind the widespread early practice of the closed or close communion.[30]

For the same reason, given this high Christology, a central focus of church discipline involved exclusion from the Lord's Supper if reconciliation and restoration could not be accomplished. The Short Treatise of Philadelphia Baptists of 1743, for example, provided that if and when a congregation "is informed that a member hath acted amiss, either in matters of faith or practice," and investigation of the same was in process by the elders, the member should be immediately suspended "from communion at the Lord's table." Similar references are customary in other believers church bodies.[31]

An amusing anecdote is told about Brethren antiquarian Abraham Harley Cassel (1820-1908) and such exercise of church discipline instigated by his attendance at the International Centennial Exposition of Philadelphia in 1876. At that time, Brethren were forbidden to attend worldly amusements and exhibitions. When Cassel was brought before the church council on this matter, he apologized to the membership for causing offense and promised that he would never attend another centennial. He was fifty-six years old at the time.

The individualistic aspect of the disciplined body relates again to the foundational character of voluntary membership. As first clearly explained by Balthasar Hubmaier, church discipline can take place with integrity only when it is grounded on the prior willingness of the member both to proffer and accept admonition and correction. Discipline, correctly understood, amounts to other members helping the individual to be or become what that person truly wants to be. Although earlier patterns of structured visitation or queries have been dropped in many congregations, there still emerge testimonies of the effectiveness of examination prior to the Lord's Supper in producing reconciliation. A student at Bethany Theological Seminary reported as follows:

My most profound experience at Bethany occurred at the love feast in the spring of 1974. It had been a difficult year. There had been a lot of friction among the people and groups on campus. I was a member of the planning committee for the love feast, and there was much discussion as to whether we should even have it or not. We were well aware of the admonition of taking communion in an unworthy manner. Communion was supposed to be for brothers and sisters who were in unity with one another, and we felt far from that. After much debate, we decided to go ahead with the love feast, not so much as an expression of the reality among us but of obedience: "Do this in remembrance of me."

The night of the love feast, we gathered in the chapel for a time of reflection. We read 1 Corinthians 11:27-29, which led to many honest confessions such as, "It's been a bad year, and I didn't want to come. I don't know why I'm here."

After the conclusion of the sharing, we went downstairs. The chairs had been placed in an oval with three chairs, wash basins and towels placed inside. We were instructed that as we felt led, we should seek out someone and wash their feet. We sat for what felt like a very long time. Slowly, individuals began to seek out one another. Being in an oval, we could all observe what was happening. We began to see individuals whom we knew had broken relationships seeking out one another and washing their feet. We witnessed those who had struggled with each other for most of the year, embracing with tears in their eyes. Others would join them, making confession and seeking forgiveness. . . . That evening I witnessed the broken body of Christ become so identified with the brokenness among us that God was able to resurrect new life through the healing and reconciling of relationships.[32]

Of interest is a parallel story coming from the Quaker heritage. In what became the Marlborough Friends Meeting of Chester, Pennsylvania, two members who owned neighboring farms had a long-standing boundary dispute. All attempts at adjudication had failed to restore good feeling. Finally, a party to the dispute, Richard Barnard (1726-1813), whose position had been held by all to be correct, had a leading that he should go and wash the feet of his troublesome neighbor.

Very early one morning, he went to the neighbor's home with water, bowl, and towel. He announced to the startled neighbor, who was still in bed, that he intended to wash the latter's feet in order to restore harmony between them. The neighbor resisted, but, according to the account, when he

was rising, to dress himself, Richard took hold of his foot, and
began the operation of washing it. He at first resisted; but soon
became calm, and suffered Richard to wash both his feet, and
wipe them with his towel. . . . An evident change now took place
in his neighbor's disposition; and Richard left him to his own
reflections.

According to the account, the unusual action in fact established the
desired harmony; when Friends decided to erect a meetinghouse in
the vicinity, both neighbors donated land and funds, allowing the
meetinghouse to be erected squarely on the boundary line.[33]

The Available Body

In a continuum found strange only to those to whom the concept
of the believers church seems odd or offensive, aid to the brother and
sister was understood to flow inexorably from the shared Lord's Supper and its attendant church discipline. True love and aid for the possibly erring co-member was seen in the correction and patient dialogue necessary until the harmful conduct or attitude was corrected
and unity regained. This concern for spiritual well-being merged
readily into concern for bodily well-being.[34]

In a liturgy called the "pledge of love" developed by Balthasar
Hubmaier in Moravia, willingness to aid the near and far neighbor is
made a condition of breaking bread. After first pledging to love, hon-
or, and adore God, the communicant is asked: "If you will love your
neighbor and serve him with deeds of brotherly love . . ., lay down
and shed for him your life and blood, . . . according to the will of God,
. . . then let each say individually, I will." Made at a time of ongoing
prosecution and execution of scores of believers, this pledge had bitter reality. It was not idle phrasing.

The next pledge asked:

If you will practice fraternal admonition toward your brethren
and sisters . . ., make peace and unity among them, and reconcile
yourselves with all those whom you have offended, willingly
cease all action and behavior which causes harm, disadvantage,
or offense to your neighbor, . . . then let each say individually, I
will.[35]

This attitude of service finds dramatic expression in the practice of feetwashing, bowing or kneeling in humility to wash and dry feet, brother to brother, sister to sister, as described earlier. The symbolism of John 13 is preserved to this day in the Catholic and Orthodox traditions on Maundy Thursday of Holy Week when the pope or patriarch washes the feet of twelve laymen. Yet they do not expect each member to engage in the service, as do many in the believers churches. In Robert Barclay's discussion of the sacraments in his *Apology*, he used the neglect of this practice by the established churches to good polemical advantage. He pointed out the inconsistency of insisting on baptism and communion and omitting feetwashing, which actually had as much or even more scriptural authority.[36]

Ecumenical participants have on occasion found deep meaning in the practice of feetwashing, asking Brethren or others to guide them in the practice during interconfessional gatherings. M. R. Zigler (1891-1985), the peace advocate of the Church of the Brethren in Geneva, related that the communication department of the World Council of Churches sought to explain the remarkable extent of Brethren aid to refugees and survivors following World War II. Staffers found it, he recounted, in the practice of feetwashing. It was an easy transition to move from the washing of feet in local congregations to symbolically washing the feet of the world in programs of relief and rehabilitation. Not the least of the merits in those in the believers church tradition is the recognizable willingness to share income, time, and material goods with those in need.[37]

As with other aspects of the Lord's Supper, mutual aid maintains a balance between individualism and communalism. Just as an individual is expected to come to the aid of neighbors near and far, so each can expect that in case of one's own need, others will be attentive and supportive. For long periods in the histories of these bodies, various forms of insurance were suspect or forbidden, in part because it was held to be evidence of lack in faith in a loving God. In addition, organized commercial schemes were considered unnecessary because the ready response of informal mutual aid made such structures superfluous. When members no longer lived in self-contained rural communities, insurance became necessary and accepted.[38]

The long-standing and still active practice of barn-raising for neighbors struck by catastrophe has become symbolic of this stance of mutual support. Various forms of disaster aid have found expression in believers church bodies. This is widely recognized in the larger society as emblematic of a stance of availability to those in critical need.[39]

Conclusion

We have looked at some issues relating to the understanding and practice of the Lord's Supper by members of the believers churches, with special attention to the foundational years of the sixteenth century. We have seen strong emphasis upon community, unity, and mutual aid, balanced by concern for individual volition, integrity, and conscience. We conclude with a comment on the spirit in which such issues may be considered.

In the late eighteenth century, Alexander Mack Jr. (1712-1803) wrote about a controversy among the eastern Pennsylvania Brethren on the correct timing of the feetwashing service. Because of the scriptural account of Jesus rising from supper to perform this (John 13:2-4), some believed that feetwashing should be observed following the meal and before the breaking of bread. Mack responded that in his experience, Brethren had washed feet *after* the meal and the breaking of bread, *after* the meal and *before* the breaking of bread, and currently *before* the meal and breaking of bread. For his part, he averred that

> if a brother or any other person can in love and moderation instruct us according to the word of the Lord more fully and otherwise than is here pointed out, we should be ready to accept of it not only in this point of feetwashing but also in other matters, and not at all rest on long usage, but let the word of the Lord be our only rule and guide.

Mack pointed out that Christ did not reveal that his disciples would be known by the manner of washing of feet or breaking of bread, but rather through this word: "By this everyone will know that you are my disciples, if you have love for one another" (John 13:35). He concluded with an admonition that has been meaningful for many through the years: "Therefore, dear brethren, let us watch and be careful. *Above all let us preserve love, for then we will preserve light.* Then our great God, who is love purely and impartially, can and will add by degrees what may be wanting in this or that knowledge of truth" [emphasis added]. Whether the question involves the Lord's Supper or anything else, this admonition by Alexander Mack Jr. can be commended to us all.[40]

PART 2

BIBLICAL INTERPRETATION OF THE LORD'S SUPPER

৺ 4 ৡ

"Making a Meal of It": The Lord's Supper in Its First-Century Social Setting

Ben Witherington III

"In the Beginning Was the Ritual"

Christianity, on several accounts, must have seemed an odd social phenomenon to both early Jews and Gentiles. On one hand, for most early Jews, what religion was really all about was *Torah, temple,* and *territory.*[1] Christianity did not perpetuate the focus on temple, nor did it pass on the territorial mandate, so far as one can tell. Furthermore, its christological handling of Torah set early Christian exegesis apart from the interpretive moves made by most early Jews.

On the other hand, to pagans, Christianity must have seemed much more like a philosophy or a social club than a religion. If it was a religion where were the Christian priests, the sacrifices, and the temples? While the Greco-Roman world knew much about the religion of hearth and home, the idea of a religion centered solely *in* the home as the setting for worship would have seemed peculiar indeed. The book of Acts tells us that early Christianity was seen as a *superstitio* by the pagans or a "sect" by the Jews (cf. Acts 16:21; 17:7, 18; 24:5, 14), charges we find also in the Greco-Roman literature (Pliny, *Ep.* 10.96; Tacitus, *An.* 15.44.2-4; Suetonius, *Nero* 16). In addition to these charges, Christianity was also criticized for being a form of atheism, since Christians refused to worship not only the emperor but also the traditional gods.[2] Yet there *were* some indicators that outsiders, whether Jew or pagan, would have recognized that Christians were practicing a religion of a sort, for early Christianity had its religious rites and ceremonies.

Social historians have taught us much of late about new ways to look at early Christianity. For example, they have taught us to distinguish between a ritual and a ceremony.[3] The former is practiced only

81

once on a particular person or group of persons, and frequently deserves the label "a rite of passage." Good examples of these would be an ordination ritual, a bar mitzvah, a circumcision rite, a ritual where citizenship or freedom from slavery is granted, or an act of baptism. In each case, the rite marks the crossing of a boundary that can be crossed only once. Rites of passage make clear the difference between the in-group and outsiders, between the clean and the unclean, between members and nonmembers, between youth and adults, between freedom and slavery, between one religious group and another.[4] In antiquity, the mistaking of a ritual for a ceremony would likely have been seen as sacrilege, the profaning of something holy that was meant to set one apart permanently. One can cross a permanent boundary for the first time only *once*.

By contrast, ceremonies are repeated and repeatable and have a rather different social function than rituals. While the ritual of baptism can symbolize the initial passage into the people of God or the body of Christ, the Lord's Supper does not serve this function. It is a ceremony of communion or reunion, not a rite of initial union. Rituals are about status change, status reversal, status transformation, while ceremonies are about status *confirmation*, including the confirmation of roles within the in-group. To put it another way, baptism is a group-creating exercise; the Lord's Supper is a group-sustaining or group-renewing exercise. We will have something to say about a social view of footwashing; in anticipation, footwashing seems to have been viewed as a repeatable ceremony rather than a rite, and thus for insiders rather than candidates for admission to the community.

It is not accidental that rites and ceremonies tend to be administered differently. The former tend to involve a passive recipient. No one baptizes oneself as a Christian, ordains oneself, circumcises oneself, or naturalizes oneself. Rather a gatekeeper, someone who monitors the boundary of the community or nation or society, must perform the function for the recipient. By contrast, a ceremony involves one or more active participants and is something shared regularly by the in-group. The elements or actions must be freely taken up or consumed in a ceremony. While there normally were prerequisites for participants in both rituals and ceremonies in antiquity, as today, these prerequisites vary precisely because the social function and effect of each event is intended to be different. While the Lord's Supper can be said to be a ceremony of *koinōnia*, of active participation or sharing something in common with others, this is not the case with baptism. It is done for and on another by a baptizer.

Social historians have reminded us of another crucial point: rituals and ceremonies depict and encode at least some of the major values of the community that practices these exercises.[5] We can learn much about what was at the heart of early Christianity by asking: What is depicted and what is said about the rite of baptism and the ceremony of the Lord's Supper? What values are inculcated by these exercises?

For example, it is surely no accident that *both* baptism and the Lord's Supper are associated with aspects of Christ's death and resurrection. These two occurrences were the group-founding events, those events without which there would be no community. These events must not merely be remembered; they must be enshrined in the hearts of believers. Indeed, in some sense believers must participate in these events.

Furthermore, these founding events must be proclaimed when the community gathers. Rituals and ceremonies are a form of symbolic proclamation of a community's basic beliefs and values. From even a superficial analysis, baptism depicts the need to be *united* to the Christ events, to the Christ, and to his community if one is to be cleansed and saved; and the Lord's Supper, as a ceremony of confirmation, is about the need for ongoing *union* and *communion* with the Christ events, with Christ, and with his community.

Even more to the point, the Lord's Supper shows that the early Christian community valued: (1) *koinōnia*, (2) equality in Christ; (3) reconciliation and unity as opposed to factionalism; (4) servanthood as a paradoxical model of leadership; (5) group awareness ("discerning the body," 1 Cor. 11:29, NRSV); and all of this was inculcated in the light of the expectation of (6) the return of Christ. These suggestions can be confirmed by a close analysis of the key texts we will examine shortly from 1 Corinthians and the Gospel of John.

There is, however, much more that can and should be said about the social function and dimensions of each of these pictographic exercises. Our task here is to focus on the Lord's Supper. I have concluded that perhaps the greatest service I could render to a group of Anabaptists is to review in some depth what can be said about the social setting, function, and values of the early practice of the Lord's Supper. I serve as one who stands outside the circle of that Anabaptist faith tradition but who has looked in on it for over a decade with both respect and admiration. No Protestant group that I know of has been more concerned with the proper social dimensions of the Lord's Supper than Anabaptists. They are the ones who have asked the sticky questions about the relationship of the Lord's Supper to things like foot-washing and Christian meals.

Since non-Anabaptist fools rush in where angels fear to tread, I propose to look in depth at two sets of texts dear to the hearts of Ana-baptists; they tell us the most about the social context and practice of the Lord's Supper in the early church: first, 1 Corinthians 10-11; and second, John 13-17. I realize that these texts have been the subject of endless debate in Anabaptist circles, so I am under no delusions about being able to say anything radically new. Nor do I intend to merely re-hearse the various exegetical options that other New Testament (NT) scholars before me, such as J. Jeremias or I. H. Marshall, have laid out in full.[6] I do, however, intend to present what is a somewhat new ave-nue of approach to these texts in hopes that this study may provide the basis for further discussions in Anabaptist circles.

Meals Sacred and Profane in Corinth
1 Corinthians 10–11

Meals, perhaps more than any other social event in antiquity, en-coded the values of the larger society, or in some cases the values of a subculture. While we might call them rules of etiquette, the rules and taboos which dictated who would be invited to a Greco-Roman meal, how a meal would be eaten, who would be served where and when, who would sit where, and the like—these mirrored the essential val-ues of the society with regard to social structure and the roles and sta-tus of individuals. As Mary Douglas has put it, if "food is treated as a code, the message it encodes will be found in the pattern of social re-lations being expressed. The message is about different degrees of hi-erarchy, inclusion and exclusion, boundaries and transactions across boundaries. . . . Food categories encode social events."[7]

Ancient Greco-Roman society had a high degree of social stratifi-cation, consciously reinforced by its dining customs. The more-impor-tant guests were placed nearest the host when reclining for a meal, and also got better food at the dinner. Where one reclined, what one ate, beside whom one was placed for conversation—all reflected how the host evaluated one's status and degree of honor in society. The satirist Martial reveals the stratifying character of ancient meals:

> Since I am asked to dinner, . . . why is not the same dinner served
> to me as to you? You take oysters fattened in the Lucrine lake, I
> suck a mussel through a hole in the shell; you get mushrooms, I

take hog funguses; you tackle turbot, but I brill. Golden with fat, a
turtledove gorges you with its bloated rump; there is set before
me a magpie that has died in its cage. Why do I dine without you
although, Ponticus, I am dining with you? . . . Let us eat the same
fare. (*Epigram* 3.60)[8]

This text explains a great deal of what we find especially in 1 Corinthians 10–11, but also in John 13–17.

Our first window on the social practice of the Lord's Supper
among early Christians comes to us from Paul's first letter to the Corinthians, written in the mid-fifties A.D.[9] In order to understand what
Paul tells us in 1 Corinthians 10–11, we must first review what we
know about the social practice of meals in the Greco-Roman world in
the first century. Our concern is not with meals eaten in public places
but with dining in homes, the locale of early Christian worship.

I am assuming that no one needs reminding that due to the
spread of Hellenism all over the ancient Mediterranean crescent before NT times, Greco-Roman dining customs were extremely widespread, even among very orthodox Jews dining in the Holy Land. This
would be all the more the case in a context like Roman Corinth,
where a significant number of Gentiles would be involved. We will
say more about the Jewish adaptation of Greco-Roman meal patterns
when we discuss John 13.[10]

Well before the time of the Roman Empire, the distinction had
become somewhat blurred between the "feast" (*deipna*) and the symposium (from *sumposion*, a group sharing a meal) as a ceremony that
constituted a closed club. The latter had started in classical Greece as
a drinking party where a close-knit group enjoyed company, conversation, and wine mixed with water. A second important change from
classical times is in the feast that followed the communal sacrifice,
with its extensive meat courses. In earlier times, it had been held in
private homes, but before the time of Augustus, it was moved to the
temple precincts. The result was that the *deipna* in a private home became increasingly more like a symposium, mainly featuring drinking.[11]
It was not uncommon for *deipna* and *symposion* to form two stages of
the same evening's entertainment—a feast followed by a drinking
party.[12] This is of some importance for understanding 1 Corinthians
11:17-22. It would explain how and why some Corinthian Christians
gorged themselves and got drunk at the Christian meal.

Even a cursory perusal of Plutarch's *Lives* will show drinking parties with disorderly conduct, flaunting of excess and extravagance,

treachery and plotting, sexual daliance, and immorality. The drinking parties were generally all-male affairs, as the classical club meetings had earlier been. But entertainment might include dancing and flute-playing girls, and *hetairai*—as well as prostitutes at less-refined meals, such as those held by some freedmen.

At the symposium, besides drinking, the chief entertainment was, at least officially, conversation about all sorts of things, including politics, philosophy, religion, and economics. Sophists and rhetors were regularly the guests of honor at such feasts, because with a simple *encomium* or some other form of epideictic rhetoric, they could entertain the guests and get the conversation going (cf. Athenaeus, *Deipnosophists*; Philostratus, *Vit. Soph.* 20). Tacitus (*Agric.* 21) tells us that the chief enticements to romanization among non-Romans were the cultivation of rhetorical oratory and elegant banquets, along with the use of the promenade and the toga.

Plutarch (*Lyc.* 13.607; cf. *Mor.* 227C) relates what the meals of the wealthy were like in Roman Corinth, telling the tale of a Spartan named Leotychidas who, when dining at Corinth, gazed up at the expensive coffered ceiling and asked his host if trees grew square in Corinth; he was used to simple feasts held outside in a grove. Plutarch also polemicizes against the vulgarity of silver-footed couches, purple coverlets, gold cups, and the like being found in a simple home or the home of a nouveau riche freedman. He does so because, like other writers of the period, he took behavior at the *convivia* as an indicator of the level of civilized behavior in general. What happened at such occasions was seen as an example of the society's character in microcosm.[13] This may explain why Paul spends the space he does in 1 Corinthians regulating eating practices in Corinth.

The term *convivia* usually refers to smaller private dinner parties as opposed to formal banquets, such as an official city banquet, called *epulae*. At *convivia*, guests normally were served by male slaves, called *ministri*. They also served as gatekeepers, to prevent anyone from crashing the party, and as bouncers, when a guest became too unruly.

While there was some concern for equality at a banquet, it was common for the choicest foods and wines to be reserved for the master and the higher-status guests, just as it was the usual practice to observe a pecking order of who got to recline on which couch. The closer to the host and the head of the table, the more important you were thought to be.[14] A. Booth rightly reports that the Roman *convivium* was legendary for fostering a degree of decadence "associated not only with the pleasures of the palate but also of the pillow."[15]

With regard to who could and did attend such *convivia*, Booth is correct in saying that it was basically a *male* venture; Roman males, when they arrived at their late teens, first gained entrance to them, having donned the toga *virilis*.[16] Wives and daughters, while they might attend the beginning of a feast in their home, would retire when it was time for the heavy drinking to begin. The public banquets were also largely male feasts.[17]

In an important essay, K. E. Corley summarizes the evidence:

> It is clear that women who were associated with banquet settings were seen in the popular imagination as prostitutes. Certain Greco-Roman women did in fact attend dinners with their husbands, but the practice may not have been all that common, even in the associations, and its pervasiveness outside the upper classes is difficult to determine. Areas still influenced by Greek ideals and practices would also still adhere to a certain extent to the exclusion of women from some meals, and certainly from those meals characterized as *sumposia*. Women who did attend such parties would have engendered a great deal of social criticism, particularly after the time of Augustus, when the interest in the maintenance of the nuclear family as a means to insure the political stability of the Empire caused a shift in the social consciousness which reemphasized ideal women's roles. Absence from public banquets became part of that complex of ideas which eventually determined a woman's social classification, and eventually limited her ability to participate in the public sphere in the centuries to follow.[18]

Study has been made of the *triclinium* in places like the Asklepion in Corinth, and of dining couches and space in private homes. These show that Romans liked the *triclinium* pattern of three couches aligned in a C shape, each couch comfortably holding up to three diners. In a large dining room in a home, one might have space for twelve to fourteen guests, while in the dining facilities at a temple about twenty-two was the maximum.[19] Vitruvius describes a Corinthian-style dining room as having rows of columns along three sides, separating the dining area from a surrounding gallery, where slaves would linger to wait on the guests (6.3.8). Garden *triclinia* could be hired, both at *taberna* and at temples for outdoor dinner parties, but *taberna* catered to private affairs, while temples catered to *public* dinner parties. Dining was a highly ritualized affair during the empire, and dinner parties were highly androcentric in character. All the above must be borne in mind as we turn to examining 1 Corinthians 10–11 in some detail.

The primary key for understanding the material we find in 1 Corinthians 10–11 is grasping Paul's rhetoric about meals. His basic concern is to make two things clear: (1) Christians should not attend meals or banquets in pagan temples at all. (2) Christians should not hold the common meal ("*agapais*, love-feasts" of Jude 12) according to the customs of Greco-Roman dining, especially because the Lord's Supper was part of this larger common meal. In Corinth we find converts only partially socialized as Christians; they were holding the Christian meal as if it were a normal Greco-Roman meal. This affects both how Paul says what he does and why he says it.

In 1 Corinthians 10 we have an example of typology, and Paul uses the word *tupos* (type, example) to describe what he is doing. The idea behind typology is that since God's character never changes, God acts in similar ways in different ages of history. Perhaps more importantly, God provides persons and events that foreshadow other later persons and events in salvation history. Combined with this is the concept that all previous ages of salvation history prepare the way for and point toward the final eschatological age, which Paul believes has already begun.

For Paul, all those things that happened to the Old Testament (OT) people happened as examples, and ultimately for the benefit of the last age of believers. The OT is seen as the *ekklēsia*'s (church's) book, meant to teach Christians by analogy and example how one ought to live and ought not to live, with Israel providing both negative and positive examples. Paul sees an analogy between the wicked behavior of the Israelites and at least some of the Corinthian Christians. Since God still judges such behavior, Paul warns them that their outcome could be the same as those Israelites. Paul thus reckons with the possibility that some Corinthians might even willfully wrench themselves free from the grasp of God and so be judged by God.

These examples drawn from the Pentateuch are especially apt to promote concord among a group of factious Corinthians willing to sacrifice the unity of the body of Christ for the sake of eating meat, whether in a temple or at home, according to their own preferred social customs. Paul suggests that it mattered little if the Israelites had, so to speak, been baptized into Moses in the Red Sea, and partaken of the OT "sacrament" of manna. They still were judged by God as rebellious people unworthy of making it to the Promised Land. Underlying the relevant OT texts and the discussion in 1 Corinthians 8–10 is the charge of idolatry and thus the apostasy of God's people.[20]

Paul begins by stressing that the Israelites received the benefits of the Exodus-Sinai experiences and the manna and water in the wilderness. It is crucial to point out that *all* had these spiritual experiences. Paul is not really arguing that the Red Sea crossing was a sacrament, since actually the Israelites went across on dry ground and did not get wet. Nor is he suggesting that the manna was in some sense a sacramental food that was just like the Lord's Supper. His point is that the Israelites had the same sort of benefits that Christians do, even benefits from Christ himself. Yet this did not secure them against perishing in the desert and losing out on God's final and greatest blessing.[21] Christ was the one who provided the miraculous water back then, just as he provides benefits to the Christian now, as the Lord's Supper makes clear.

Paul in 1 Corinthians 10:3 calls the manna "spiritual" food, by which he presumably means food miraculously provided by the Spirit of God, not heavenly tasting or textured food. Nor indeed was the water spiritual in character. Instead, it was spiritually provided, just as the rock was spiritually enabled to give water. Yet despite all these spiritual benefits to all Israelites, even some of which came from Christ, God judged most of those Israelites. They died, and their bodies were strewn around in the wilderness.[22]

Here as before, Paul is largely arguing against those who wrote him, who were urging the right to eat in pagan temples. They in particular are being warned of possible disastrous spiritual consequences. Possibly the Corinthians had a magical view of the Christian sacraments. They may have thought that since they had partaken of the Christian initiation rite (baptism) and the Christian communion ceremony (Lord's Supper), they were immune to spiritual danger at pagan feasts. They seem to have held to some form of an "eternal security by means of sacraments" view. Paul is trying to disabuse them of this false sense of security.

Such an attitude is understandable, in view of the mystery rites in Greece and elsewhere in the Greco-Roman world which were apparently thought to put one on a different spiritual plane.[23] The Corinthians viewed the Christian rites as being like such pagan rites in their efficacy and benefits.[24] Thus, they may have assumed that they were immune to harm now or later, whatever they did; "Everything is permitted!" (cf. 1 Cor. 10:23; 6:12). This may also explain why Paul responds as he does about temptations and their danger.

Paul then corrects them by drawing an analogy between the so-called Jewish sacraments and the Christian ones, *rather than* the analogy the Corinthians "in the know" had apparently assumed with pagan rites. Paul says that the OT story has become an example so that the Corinthians might not likewise suffer destruction. He accuses them of being coveters of evil things, grasping for whatever they might gain at a feast in a pagan temple.

One key to catching Paul's point here is his use of the term *pneumatikon*. In what sense was the rock and the food and drink "spiritual" for the Israelites (1 Cor. 10:3-4)? Paul likely has chosen the term to stress the source of this sustenance (from God, who is spirit). The parallel to 1 Corinthians 2:13ff. is noteworthy. Spiritual people should be wise enough to discern the deeper spiritual significance or meaning of such phenomena. The bread and drink given to the Israelites are called spiritual because they come from God; thus they need interpretation, aided by the power of discernment given by the Holy Spirit. The food was not figurative or allegorical but real. It is a matter of seeing its real significance.[25] Paul's addition to the wilderness traditions is the idea that such gifts actually came from Christ, for he was present and helping God's people back then. This is a strategic rhetorical move. Otherwise, some might have objected that the Israelites had sacraments inferior to those available for the Corinthians.[26]

Paul exhorts the Corinthians not to be idolators and then quotes directly from Exodus 32:6, the story of the golden calf. Probably Paul uses this text for its special relevance, in particular its allusion to sexual play or amusement after the idol feast.[27] This is why in 1 Corinthians 10:8 the warning against sexual sin immediately follows. Paul believes that more is going on in the pagan temple than just an idol feast. While it may be true that there is no clear evidence of sacred prostitution in Roman Corinth, there certainly were numerous stories of sexual immorality happening in pagan temples.[28] This common association in the larger culture would explain why sexual immorality and idol food are also *always* linked in the NT (cf. Acts 15:29; Rev. 2:14, 20). It is worth adding that the rabbis certainly interpreted "play" in Exodus 32:6 to refer to sexual play (cf. B.T. Sot. 6.6).[29]

It is also wrong to underestimate the religious character of meals held in temple precincts. Plutarch says, "It is not the abundance of wine or the roasting of meat that makes the joy of festivals, but the good hope and belief that the god is present in his kindness and graciously accepts what is offered" (*Mor.* 1102A). Nor was this only true at public festivals for, as R. MacMullen stresses, one must place religion at the heart of social life as surely as it must be placed at the heart of cultural activities of every sort. For most people, to have a good time with their friends involved some contact with a god who served as guest of honor, as master of ceremonies, or as host in the porticoes or flowering, shaded grounds of his own dwelling. For most people, meat was a thing never eaten and wine to surfeit never drunk save as some religious setting permitted. There existed—it is no exaggeration to say it of all but the fairly rich—no formal social life . . . that was entirely secular. Small wonder, then, that Jews and Christians [held] themselves aloof from anything the gods touched.[30]

This suggests that, in their letter to Paul, the more well-to-do Gentile male converts in Corinth were arguing for the right to go to idol feasts.[31] Paul says that the Corinthians by participating in these idol parties are trying to provoke Christ just as the Israelites did.[32] First Corinthians 10:12 is a clear warning that the Corinthians had better watch themselves or they might fall as the Israelites did.

The Corinthians then are to endure and prevail over the temptation to go to idol feasts. God will provide them with an out so they can escape their present malaise. Paul believes that God never allows a Christian to be tempted to such a degree that by God's grace one can't resist or find a way of escape. This does not mean one *will* necessarily resist. At 1 Corinthians 10:14, Paul gives the directive toward which the entire section of 1 Corinthians 8-10 has been arguing: flee from idolatry.

A further argument for avoiding idolatry is presented in 1 Corinthians 10:16ff., not a discourse on the Lord's Supper. Paul only mentions those elements that are relevant to the present discussion and will help in getting them to avoid idolatry. In 10:16 (NRSV) he refers to the "cup of blessing," a technical term for the wine cup drunk at the end of a Jewish meal and over which the thanksgiving or grace is said: "Blessed art thou, O Lord, who gives us the fruit of the vine." In the Passover meal, this was the third cup of the four to be drunk. This was probably the cup which Jesus in the Last Supper identified as the cup of the new covenant in his blood. The point is that this new covenant was enacted by Christ's death.

The Greek term *koinōnia* (1 Cor. 10:16, NRSV: "sharing," NIV: "participation") has as its fundamental meaning to have or to share something in common with someone.[33] This term may refer to sharing between God and the worshiper, or between the worshipers, or perhaps both. I maintain that some of both is entailed. Barrett's translation "common participation" is a good one.[34] It is something worshipers do together and share as an act of the body of Christ, the church. What believers are sharing or participating in is not just each other, nor is it just a matter of an individual's private communion with God.

What then does it mean to share or participate in the blood of Christ, especially since for Jews drinking blood was considered something horrible? Apparently, Paul believes that more than mere symbols are involved. There seems to be some real spiritual communion with Christ, or one might say, an appropriation of the benefits of his death—forgiveness, cleansing, and the like.

G. D. Fee makes the intriguing suggestion that the sharing in the cup is vertical (with Christ), but the sharing in the loaf represents and facilitates believers in sharing with one another as the body of Christ.[35] This requires that the reference to the body of Christ in 1 Corinthians 10:16b refer to the body of believers, *not* either the physical or transcendent body of the individual Christ in heaven, or some spiritual participation in that ascended one's body. Paul would not have been so upset with the Corinthians participating in idol feasts unless he believed it really entailed some type of spiritual communion with demons. He thought one was giving, at least tacitly, one's allegiance and self over to that demon by participating in the feast.

First Corinthians 10:17 (NIV) says that "because there is one loaf, we, who are many, are one body." Paul is talking about that which binds believers together into one body, not merely the common sharing in bread but the more profound spiritual uniting that it signifies. They all share from the common loaf. Another clue to the meaning of *koinōnia* here must be the use of the verb to "partake," share (*metechō*). The stress on *all* sharing is because of the coming 10:18 analogy with OT Israel.

First Corinthians 10:18 says that the eating of the sacrifice entailed a common participation in the altar. Philo, *De spec. leg.* 1.221, may be relevant: "He to whom sacrifice has been offered makes the group of worshipers partners in the altar and of one table" (using *koinōnia*). Thus Paul likely sees the Lord's Supper as a sacrificial meal. But what does it mean to be a common participant in the altar? Is it merely to share in the meat and the benefits of the sacrifice, or does it also mean participation in the god as well? Deuteronomy 14:22-27 seems to be in view here, and so it is unlikely that Paul envisions the participants actually consuming the deity. In Judaism, the sacrificial food was never thought to convey God in that sense.[36] Sharing in the altar would mean sharing in the material and spiritual benefits of the sacrifice. Likewise, in the Lord's Supper, believers share in the material and spiritual benefits of Christ's sacrifice. Paul does not mean sharing in Christ's metaphysical being directly, much less in his physical or glorified flesh.

Though idols and idol food are not anything in themselves (1 Cor. 10:19), Paul nonetheless believes that the demons who use them are something. In his mind, one cannot offer allegiance to demons and share in the dubious benefits demons have to offer while also sharing in God's meal and benefits. Paul says bluntly that he does not wish them to become sharers in or common participants with demons by partaking of idol food in the temple (10:20). There is a fundamental incompatibility between eating and drinking at the table of the demons, sharing activities and benefits with them, and doing so with the Lord. These are mutually exclusive fellowships. Paul concludes this subsection at 10:22 by asking: Are you trying to make the Lord angry, or do you think yourself stronger than even he, by binding yourself to two supernatural sources at once and receiving "benefits" from both?

First Corinthians 10:30 (paraphrased) brings up a further crucial point in the form of a hypothetical rhetorical question from the Corinthians to Paul: "If I partake of food after giving thanks to God, why should someone denounce me for partaking with gratitude?" Paul's answer is because it is not just a matter of one's relationship with God, not purely a vertical matter. There are also the horizontal relationships and the effects which eating will have on others. Verse 31 then states the basic Pauline principle: "Whether you eat or drink, or whatever you do, do everything for the glory of God," and thus also for the building up of Christ's body.

Paul's missionary or evangelistic approach then is re-enunciated in 1 Corinthians 10:32: in matters adiaphora (of neutral value), one should strive to give no offense to Jews, Greeks, and to the church of God.[37] This includes everyone outside or in the congregation. The rule is, "Consider others first." Verse 33 explains further that Paul strives to fit in with everyone in all such matters, not for his own benefit so things will go smoothly for himself, but in order to save many for Christ. Paul isn't saying he is trying to be a people-pleaser in a way that would amount to compromising the gospel. But in indifferent matters such as food, he is more than happy to be socially accommodating.[38] Finally, this section closes with the exhortation, "Imitate me as I imitate Christ" (1 Cor. 11:1, adapted). All along, Paul has been holding himself up as an example, but only because he follows the model of Christ. This may suggest that he is alluding to Jesus' practice of eating with anyone, even notorious sinners, and to his ruling about no food being unclean. It may also refer to Christ's servanthood example of giving up all for the sake of others, even to the point of death on the cross.

To sum up, in 1 Corinthians 8–10, Paul is exhorting primarily certain "in the know" Gentile Christians who have been arguing for their freedom, including the right to attend feasts in pagan temple precincts. To set an example for them to imitate, so that the factions between this group and the weak will be healed, Paul identifies with the weak in three ways: (1) by manual labor, (2) by defending the weak to "those in the know," and (3) by using slave language and casting himself as a servant. Paul deliberately defies the social expectations and concerns, especially of the upwardly mobile, or those who had already arrived. Here he sets up an alternate vision of what a Christian meal, including the Lord's Supper, should entail.

The material about the Lord's Supper in 1 Corinthians 11:17ff. continues the discussion begun in 11:2 about abuses in worship, a discussion which will not end until at least 1 Corinthians 14. Since Paul is correcting abuses here, he does not provide a full positive exposition of his views on the Lord's Supper. Nonetheless, we learn a great deal here about how the Lord's Supper was being practiced in Corinth and about Paul's views on such matters. In 1 Corinthians 11:17-34, we hear about divisions created in an act of Christian worship, involving an agape (love-feast) meal, the setting for sharing in the Lord's Supper. These divisions seem to have been created by some more well-to-do members of the congregation treating the agape meal like a private dinner party, perhaps a banquet followed by a drinking party (*convivia*). The result of this activity was that the social stratification of the congregation was not only emphasized but further exacerbated. Thus, a serious division between the haves and have-nots was threatening the fragile unity of the Corinthian Christian community.[39]

Paul is concerned with at least two social facets of the problem: (1) the disorderliness of the proceedings, and (2) the inequality of the proceedings.[40] Neither of these problems was at all unusual at Greco-Roman banquets followed by drinking parties. Even the larger dining rooms in homes were equipped to hold only nine to twenty people, and there were certainly more Corinthian Christians than this. It was the normal practice to rank one's guests in terms of social status, with the higher-status guests eating with the host in the dining room and others eating elsewhere and getting poorer food.

The only exception to this rule was in the Saturnalia, a meal where the normal social values were turned upside down for a day and slaves or the poor were treated well. Lucian recounts such an occasion, contrasting it with the normal practice of a Greco-Roman banquet (*Sat.* 21-22):

> Tell them to invite the poor to dinner, take in four or five at a time, not as they do nowadays, though, but in a more democratic fashion, all having equal share, not one man stuffing himself with dainties with the servant standing waiting for him to eat himself to exhaustion, . . . only letting us glimpse the platter or the remnants of the cake. And tell him not to give a whole half of the pig when it's brought in, and the head as well, to his master, bringing the others bones covered over. And tell the wine servers not to wait for each of us to ask seven times for a drink but on one request to pour it out and hand it to us at once, filling a great cup as they do for their master. And let the wine be one and the same for all the guests—where is it laid down that he should get drunk on wine with a fine bouquet while I must burst my belly on new stuff?[41]

Paul *expects* the meal Christians share to be of a more democratic nature, and thus more like a Saturnalia. For the Christian community, he is trying to construct a practice at variance with the customs of ordinary meals. He is upset that some Corinthians are treating the agape as an ordinary banquet.[42] Paul's strategy, as S. C. Barton argues, is to make a distinction between private meals in one's own home, and a meal shared in and by the *ekklēsia*, whoever's home may have been the venue.[43] This is not a matter of sacred space but rather of sacred time and occasion.[44] Paul does not talk about sacred buildings, but he does talk about holy persons and holy occasions when they gather for worship and fellowship. These occasions are to be regulated by sacred traditions, in this case the narrative about the Last Supper. The Lord's Supper was meant as a sacrament of communion in both a horizontal and vertical character, *not* a rite of incorporation.[45]

It is, however, both possible and likely that some would have viewed Christian meetings as a type of association or *collegia* meeting, especially since early Christianity had no temples,.no priests, and no sacrifices. Early Christian meetings may also have been viewed in this way because association meetings could involve a variety of people from up and down the social strata. It could include a wealthy patron either male or female, a group of artisans both free and freed, and even some slaves, who perhaps had taken up a trade or started a business, using their *peculium* (private property).

There was a trade association of leatherworkers.[46] Paul practiced his trade in Corinth and stayed with Priscilla and Aquila, who also practiced this trade (Acts 18). Thus it may have been assumed that Paul was involved in setting up or participating in some trade association which, to avoid suspicion or being banned by the authorities, had a variety of religious functions and activities. One of the main functions of these associations was to provide for those who were not among the wealthy or aristocrats but had social aspirations. They were given a venue in which they could feel appreciated and gain honor and acclaim from their peers.

We have clear evidence of what club or association rules for their banquet meetings could look like in this era. D. E. Smith summarizes the more common rules:

> (1) Injunctions against quarreling and fighting, (2) injunctions against taking the assigned place of another, (3) injunctions against speaking out of turn or without permission, (4) injunctions against fomenting factions, (5) injunctions against accusing a fellow member before a public court, (6) specifications for trials within the club for intraclub disputes, (7) specifications for worship activities.[47]

Paul addresses nearly *all* of these concerns in this letter, which strongly suggests that the Corinthians and perhaps Paul as well saw the Christian community as functioning rather like the more egalitarian associations of the day.

Smith goes on to argue that 1 Corinthians 11 should be connected with 1 Corinthians 12–14, and that what Paul is discussing is a worship event. This event involves a meal, a *sumposia*, followed by religious acts as described in chapters 12–14; it is patterned after the normal order of events in a Greco-Roman meal, including club meals.[48] A formal transition was made between the meal and the drinking party by a wine ceremony, where wine was poured out to the god. Smith suggests that to make the formal transition, the Christians replaced the wine-pouring ceremony with the postmeal wine cup of blessing of the Lord's Supper.

After the transition (cf. Plato, *Sympos.* 176A), there would be a hymn or chant sung to the god, perhaps a calling upon a god as savior (cf. Athenaeus, *Deipnos.* 15.675b-c). The drinking party could then continue with entertainment or, for the more sober-minded, conversation, considered an essential feature of the *sumposia.* Plutarch, writing shortly after Paul's time, says the proper conversations at such an occasion could be about history, current events, lessons on philosophy, lessons on piety, or exhortations to charitable or brave deeds (cf. *Quaest. conviv.* 697E). The conversation often was prompted by a guest teacher or Sophist.[49]

In many ways, meals were an occasion for gaining or showing social status, being a microcosm of the aspirations and aims of the culture as a whole. Paul's attempt to deconstruct the social stratifying that was happening at the Lord's meal goes directly against the tendency of such meals.[50] The *ekklēsia* of course was not exactly identical with an association. As Meeks says,

> the Christian groups were exclusive and totalistic in a way that no club nor even the pagan cultic association was. . . . To be "baptized into Christ Jesus" nevertheless signaled for Pauline converts an extraordinarily thoroughgoing resocialization, in which the sect was intended to become virtually the primary group for its members, supplanting all other loyalties. The only convincing parallel in antiquity was conversion to Judaism. . . . Students of private associations generally agree that their primary goals were fellowship and conviviality. . . . The goals of Christians were less segmented; they had to do with "salvation" in a comprehensive sense. . . . The Christian groups were much more inclusive in terms of social stratification and other social categories than were the voluntary associations.[51]

The point is not that the *ekklēsia* was identical with such an association. Instead, their similarities were great enough to make it believable that various Corinthians view the Christian assembly as some sort of association, perhaps even a cultic one, and have *behaved* accordingly at fellowship meals.[52] In addition, as Paul advises the Corinthians, he seems to be cognizant of the kinds of rules set up in such associations. For Paul, the function of reciting the sacred tradition about the Lord Jesus and the Last Supper is to encourage social leveling, overcome factionalism created by stratification and its expression at meals, and create unity and harmony in the congregation.

Paul has yet another problem in Corinth for which he can give his audience no praise (1 Cor. 11:17). There are divisions (*schismata*) among the Corinthians when they gather for worship (11:18). G. Theissen is likely right that the division here discussed is between the relatively well-to-do and the poor, the haves and the have-nots.[53] Some are going hungry at the meal, while others are gorging themselves and getting drunk. Here is more evidence that the main troublemakers for Paul in Corinth were the more well-to-do Gentiles who continued to follow the social conventions of the larger pagan culture, in this case in their dining and drinking.

There are several ways to envision this. The text could imply that the wealthy are going on ahead without the poor, who would arrive late after work and thus go without a fair share. This depends on translating *ekdexesthe* in 11:33 as "wait for" one another, which is perfectly possible.[54] More likely is the suggestion that the wealthy are eating in the *klinē* (dining room with couches) while the poor are eating in the atrium; and that there are two sorts of food being served, as customary at ancient pagan banquets. The verb here often has the sense of "welcome" or "entertain" when it is used in the context of an act of hospitality (cf. 3 Macc. 5:26; Josephus, *Ant.* 7.351). The result, whether the problem is timing or location, is a split in the congregation between haves and have-nots.

Paul says he half believes there are these sorts of divisions, not because he has any doubts about it, but because he feels this is a monstrous violation of Christian unity, however common the behavior may have been in pagan contexts. In 1 Corinthians 11:19, Paul seems to be alluding to a tradition, perhaps a Jesus tradition, that there must be various divisions about such matters so the real Christians can be discerned in the end. J. Jeremias points to both Matthew 10:34-37 (or 24:9-13) and the extracanonical saying of Jesus found in Justin, the Didascalia, and elsewhere: "There shall be divisions (*schismata*) and dissensions (*haireseis*)."[55]

The focus here is on the sociological divisions and the assumption that, as was the practice at a pagan feast, it was all right to separate or distinguish between wealthier and poorer Christians. Paul is taking the side of the poor or weak, and arguing against the strong or rich, whom he is addressing. They would be the ones hosting these Christians meals and thus would be responsible for the protocol that was followed.

First Corinthians 11:20 mentions coming together in one place. Apparently the Corinthians did not always do this. Paul implies that the reason for a big meeting of all together was for the Lord's meal. The Lord Supper's was being taken in conjunction with a normal meal, perhaps after the meal, in the midst of it, or even surrounding it. Possibly the breaking of the bread preceded the regular meal and the drinking of the wine cup followed the meal. Since some are drunk at the Lord's meal, the Lord's Supper was likely coming *after* the common meal, and perhaps also after the drinking party as well.

Paul does not mean in 1 Corinthians 11:21 that literally "everyone" has his own meal, since some of the have-nots are going without. He likely does mean that those whom he is particularly addressing, the hosts and the wealthy in Corinth, have their own dinners. Much depends on how we take the verb *prolambanei* in 11:21. Does it mean "to go beforehand" or "anticipate," in which case the haves were eating before others? Or does it mean simply "to take" coupled with "to eat"? The lexical evidence slightly favors the former. But even if so, then the point may not be about late-arriving poor people, but rather that while all are present, the wealthy are being served first and get the better portions, while the poor in the atrium get what is left over.[56]

The end result is that one gets gorged and drunk, and another goes hungry. This hardly amounts to a shared and common meal. As the letter develops, Paul's concern for unity and equality in the Corinthian congregation becomes clearer and clearer, climaxing in 1 Corinthians 12–14. The difficulties he deals with in the congregation in Corinth are primarily problems that violate that unity. The goal of Paul's rhetoric here is to remove obstacles to that unity.

First Corinthians 11:22a shows plainly that the problem is with the well-to-do, who have houses enough in which to have their own feasts. Paul doesn't try to rule out such sumptuous banquets; his point is that pagan rules of normal protocol do not apply when one meets at the Lord's table. The better-off Christians are showing no respect for the have-nots, humiliating them, and thus giving no respect to the *ekklēsia* of God, which is supposed to be a united body.

Part of Paul's way of correcting the abuses is to remind the Corinthians of the traditions he and they share about the Lord's Supper. In 1 Corinthians 11:23, he uses the technical language of Judaism for the passing on of sacred traditions. Likely there was a systematic transmission of at least some of the Jesus material. This is only what we would expect since the earliest Christians were all Jews. When Paul says he received these traditions from the Lord, he presumably means that they ultimately come from the Lord,[57] not that these words were directly revealed to him. The latter view is surely ruled out by the closeness of the Lord's Supper tradition found here and in Luke.[58]

In the main, there were two forms of this Lord's Supper tradition:

the form we find in Mark and Matthew, and the form we find in Luke and Paul. Luke prefers Paul's form, or they share a common form.[59] Paul's version is the earliest record we have of this tradition, but Paul has only selectively quoted it to make his point about the abuse in Corinth.

First Corinthians 11:23 makes clear that the Lord's Supper was seen as a tradition involving a historical memory; thus the Lord's Supper is set off from all pagan memorial meals. It was not uncommon for those who could afford it, to leave in their last will and testament a stipend and stipulation that there be a memorial feast in honor of the deceased. Diogenes Laertius records (10.16-22) that Epicurus left provision for an annual celebration "in memory of us." The Corinthians may have seen the Lord's Supper as a funerary meal. The main difference between such meals and the Lord's Supper is that, in the latter, one is not just celebrating the memory of a deceased person; one is also proclaiming his death until he comes.

The Lord's Supper also stands out from Passover in that the Supper celebrates a person and his final deeds on earth, but the Passover simply celebrates the divine actions—the Exodus-Sinai events. There were thus salient differences among the three kinds of meals. The reference to Jesus' betrayal or being handed over (*paredideto* can mean either in 1 Cor. 11:23) marks off the Lord's Supper from all pagan celebrations that focused on a myth. As Fee says, this betrayal word is poignant: we are reminded that it is one of Jesus' own disciples who handed him over, and this in the context of a meal meant at least in part to stress loyalty to Christ, and the forgiveness received from him.[60]

Reading 1 Corinthians 11:23ff. in their own historical context reveals the following points:

1. There is no association here of the breaking of the bread with the breaking of Jesus' body (despite the later textual variants). Nothing is said here about reenacting the passion.[61]

2. Notice the double reference to "unto my memory/memorial" or "in remembrance of me" after both the bread word and the cup word. This may be due to Paul's own stress here. Only Luke and Paul have the memory clause.[62]

3. Only Paul says that they are to celebrate the Lord's Supper as often as they drink of the wine cup. Not all meals involved wine; for many, this was only for special occasions.

4. In the original Last Supper meal, Jesus' language had to be figurative since he was physically present and had not yet died. Jesus

was likely modifying the Passover traditions, which also had elements of symbolic significance, such as the bread of haste and the bitter herbs. This must also count against any overly literal interpretation.

5. The phrase "*to huper humōn* (which is for you)" is found only in the Pauline-Lukan version of the Supper words (1 Cor. 11:24; Luke 22:19-20). They probably allude to Isaiah 53:12, indicating that Christ gave his body on the believers' behalf and/or in the believers' place. The breaking of the bread is associated with and reminds of that act of self-giving of his body.

6. What Jesus did at the Last Supper should not be seen as the institution of a funerary rite. This is not Jesus' last will and testament, for the word *new* here is fatal to that view. The "*diathēkē* (covenant)" here should be seen as a reference to the founding of a new covenant relationship, probably by Christ's death. Thus the remembering is not merely a matter of an occasional memorial service for Jesus, perhaps once a year. Indeed, the mention of having this meal whenever all the Corinthians came together suggests a frequent occasion. Something more positive is also involved. It is the proclamation of the dying but risen Lord and what he has done for believers through his death and resurrection.

7. Jesus is said to have broken the bread only after giving thanks. This does not prove that Jesus was celebrating a Passover meal since the giving of thanks over the bread was a part of every Jewish meal: "Blessed art thou, O Lord our God, King eternal, who brings forth bread from the earth." Nevertheless, other factors suggest that he was observing a Passover meal.[63]

8. The reference to the wine cup surely means that the drinking of wine was a part of the early celebration of the Lord's Supper. Why else would Paul accuse some of getting drunk?

9. Paul does not specifically link the cup to the blood, but he says it is the cup of "the new covenant." The new covenant is "in my blood," instituted by Christ's death. It is beyond Paul's (or Jesus') meaning that the disciples could have been asked to drink blood—something a Jew would react against with horror. Paul says nothing about the wine representing Christ's blood.[64]

10. Paul stresses that the celebration of the meal entails both eating and drinking but also includes the words said for proclaiming Christ's death, until he returns. Thus the meal has both a past, present, and future reference.[65] The "*marana tha*" cry, which likely means "Our Lord, come," was an integral part of the Lord's Supper for early Jewish Christians.[66] The Lord's Supper then is part of the Christian

witness to the crucified, risen, and returning Lord. The mention of the Lord's coming prepares the way for the discussion about judgment that follows in 1 Corinthians 11:27ff. It is part of Paul's plan to encourage the Corinthians to add a not-yet to their eschatological already.

The reference in 1 Corinthians 11:27 is to Christ's actual body, which was crucified, as the reference to blood makes clear. *Anaziōs* has been translated "unworthily" and sometimes incorrectly thought to modify not the *way* of partaking but the character of the persons who partake. Paul refers to those who are partaking in an unworthy manner, not those who *are* unworthy.[67] He is concerned about the abuse of the actions involved in participating. Those who partake in an unworthy fashion, abusing the meal, are liable or guilty in some sense of the body and blood of the Lord. They are partaking without discerning or distinguishing the body, the church (cf. below).

Perhaps Paul means they are guilty of standing on the side of those who abused and even killed Christ—an atrocious sacrilege. The concept of sacrilege was widespread in antiquity with regard to religious meals and customs. For example, Dionysius of Halicarnassus says that "those who tried to abolish a custom were regarded as having done a thing deserving both the indignation of human beings and the vengeance of the gods . . . [resulting in] a justifiable retribution by which the perpetrators were reduced from the greatest height of glory they once enjoyed to the lowest depths" (*Rom. ant.* 8.80.2). Paul is saying something similar about those who have become sick and died. These Corinthians had partaken of the Lord's Supper in an unworthy manner and had been judged by God for doing so. Paul uses this as a solemn warning to the other Corinthians against continuing to abuse the Christian meal.

Juridical language dominates and sets the tone for this entire section: *enoxos*, guilty/liable (1 Cor. 11:27); *dokimazetō*, examine (11:28); *krima*, judgment; *diakrinōn*, distinguishing/recognizing (11:29); *ekrinometha*, be judged (11:31); *katakrinōmen*, condemned (11:32).[68] The examination referred to in 11:28 means that one must consider how properly to partake of the meal, not whether one is worthy, as decided through introspection. With regard to discerning or recognizing the body, note that Paul says only "the body" (11:29, NRSV), with no reference to the Lord or to blood. While this might refer to forgetting Christ's death when one eats, more likely it refers to believers as the body of Christ.[69] The Corinthians are eating without taking cognizance of their brothers and sisters. They are to partake with them as one body in Christ, rather than following selfish pagan protocol.

The Corinthians are bringing judgment on themselves, both temporal in the form of weaknesses and illnesses, and possibly even eternal condemnation. Paul even says that because of this failure, some have died (1 Cor. 11:30). Paul must have believed he had some prophetic insight into the situation which we do not have. It is not the food that has made them ill, but the judgment that has come upon them for partaking of the meal in an unworthy manner. This disaster can be avoided, says Paul, if they will simply examine themselves and their behavior before they partake (11:31). Perhaps Paul sees the judgment of illness as a temporal judgment, meant to prevent a worse disaster of being condemned with the world of nonbelievers at the last judgment. Paul may view this temporal judgment as not final, but remedial or disciplinary in character.[70]

First Corinthians 11:33 then provides a final word of remedial advice. *"Ekdexesthe"* may mean wait for one another, a common meaning of the word; more likely it means to welcome one another, meaning all should partake together as one, without distinctions in rank or food. The point of the Lord's meal is something other than satisfying hunger, or at least this is not the main point; and so the meal must not be treated as just another banquet.

First Corinthians 11:34b lets us know that Paul had more to say on these matters; it demonstrates the occasional or *ad hoc* character of the letter. Paul's letters are not preconceived divine treatises, but occasional rhetorical arguments given in the heat of battle.

What have we learned from 1 Corinthians 10–11 about the early practice of the Lord's Supper? First, the Lord's Supper was partaken of in homes as a part of a larger fellowship meal.

Second, Paul is exercised to try to distinguish what is proper at the Christian meal from the usual stratifying customs of Greco-Roman meals. The Christian meal was to depict the radical reversal that the kerygma proclaimed: the first would be last, and the last first, and whoever would lead must take the role of a servant. This social leveling was meant to make clear that there was true equality in the body of Christ. All were of equal status in the eyes of the Lord, and they should also be viewed that way by Christians, leading to equal treatment for all.

Third, the Lord's Supper was clearly not simply a reenactment of the Passover meal, and not least because of its prospective element, looking forward to the Lord's return. For that matter, neither was the

Last Supper simply an ordinary Passover meal, for Christ modified both the interpretation of the elements, and selected elements to bear the freight of symbolic interpretation. There seems to have been no attempt on the part of early Christians to simply use the Lord's Supper as an occasion to reenact or dramatize either Passover or the Last Supper. Instead, it was incorporated into the different and larger context of the agape or fellowship meal. Christ clearly enough was seen as the Christian's Passover in his death and its benefits, but this did not lead to seeing the Lord's Supper as simply a Passover meal.

Fourth, nothing in this Pauline discussion suggests that the Lord's Supper was seen as foreshadowing the Messianic banquet. Yet that would have been appropriate, especially in view of the Jesus tradition about not partaking again until the kingdom came (Mark 14:25).

Fifth, it was perhaps the very setting of where this meal took place, the home, that led to some of the abuses evident in 1 Corinthians 10–11. In such a setting, it was natural to assume one was dealing with a usual Greco-Roman meal.

Last, it is clear enough from the sacrilege issue and from 1 Corinthians 10 that Paul does not assume that the Lord's Supper is simply a symbolic matter. On the contrary, he assumes that some spiritual transaction takes place in the Christian celebration, which can be contrasted with the wrong sort of spiritual communion with demons that happened in pagan temple meals. In short, Paul was no Zwinglian, but then it turns out that even Zwingli would have flinched at the purely symbolic interpretation of the Lord's Supper.

A Farewell Dinner and Symposium
John 13-17

Scholars have long had difficulty in assessing various features of the material in John 13–17, precisely because these chapters seem so different from the Synoptic accounts of the Last Supper. For instance, there is no clear indication that Jesus is celebrating a Passover meal at all in these chapters. Instead, we are told that this event transpired not only before Passover day but "before the festival of the Passover" (13:1). The speculation of the disciples about Judas leaving to buy things for the Festival (13:29) also suggests a meal prior to the Passover.[71] The time reference in 13:1 may be compared to the one in John 12:1, "six days before the Passover." This could mean that the meal is depicted as occurring even before Jesus was anointed by

Mary. But in all probability, we are meant to think of it as occurring *sometime* during the week before the actual celebration of Passover, *not necessarily on the eve of Passover.*

The vast majority of scholars of all theological stripes, including more conservative ones,[72] have recognized that we do not have just one theological discourse in John 13:31—17:26 but several, combined here likely to indicate the sort of in-house teaching Jesus offered to the disciples at the close of his ministry when he was preparing them for his departure. Some of this teaching seems to have been offered on one occasion, some on another. Certainly 14:31 indicates that the discourse is over, and the natural sequel to 14:31 is 18:1. Perhaps this teaching was offered on successive nights of the Passover feast leading up to Good Friday, and the Fourth Evangelist has put the material into his own idiom and combined it to convey the gist of these occasions. Clearly enough from 13:21-30, the section includes some Last Supper traditions as well as other material. More importantly, why has the Evangelist presented the material as he has done? And what is the significance of it? Is it really true that John 13:1-30 is only loosely connected to what follows it?

Here is my basic framework for interpreting John 13–17:

1. The Fourth Evangelist is portraying the disciples sharing a farewell dinner with Jesus.

2. This dinner is *not* portrayed as a Passover meal; this is shown not only by the time reference in 13:1, but also by the lack of any discussion of or reinterpretation of the Passover elements in any of these chapters. This may be because, as Craddock stresses about the Johannine portrayal, "Jesus does not *eat* the Passover, he *is* the Passover,"[73] and he will be portrayed as dying as the Passover Lamb at the appropriate time in John 19:31-37.[74]

3. Instead of a Passover meal, what we have in these chapters is a portrayal of a Greco-Roman banquet complete with closing *sumposia* and the religious rites associated with such meals. Jesus acts as the sage and offers the teaching. This is not unlike what we find in 1 Corinthians 11–14, where Paul describes a worship event which involves a meal, a *sumposia*, and closing religious acts. In order to see this, a few remarks are in order about the *Jewish* celebration of Greco-Roman meals.[75]

As we have seen, the normal Greco-Roman banquet in the first century A.D. involved a meal and a *sumposia* (a teaching, dialogue or entertainment period following the meal but during the drinking party). The *sumposia* in particular tended to be an all-male affair. Women who had been present at the meal would politely excuse themselves before the *sumposia*. In a Jewish setting, this was all the more likely to be the case. A formal transition was usually made between the meal and the drinking party or *sumposia* by a wine ceremony, where wine was poured out to the god. After the transition (cf. Plato, *Sympos.* 176A), a hymn or chant would be sung to the god, perhaps calling upon a god as savior (cf. Athenaeus, *Deipnos.* 15.675b-c).

The drinking party could then continue with entertainment or, for the more sober-minded, conversation, considered an essential feature of the *sumposia*. Plutarch, writing shortly after Paul's time, says the proper conversations at such an occasion could be about history, current events, lessons on philosophy, lessons on piety, or exhortations to charitable or brave deeds (cf. *Quaest. conviv.* 697E). Often the conversation was prompted by a guest teacher or Sophist.[76]

In 1 Corinthians 11-14, we have seen Paul's attempt to deconstruct the social stratification that was happening at the Lord's meal in Corinth, an action which went directly against the tendency of such meals. Jesus is in part depicted as doing the same thing in John 13. For Paul, the function of reciting the sacred tradition about the Last Supper in 1 Corinthians 11 is to encourage social leveling, overcome factionalism created by stratification and its expression at meals, and create unity and harmony in the congregation. The same may be part of the intent of the footwashing episode in John 13, coupled with the prayer in John 17 for the unity of Jesus' followers.

We know for a fact that early Jews, including even the more religiously conservative among them, by Jesus' day had adopted and adapted the customs of Greco-Roman dining to suit their own ends and religious practices. A good example of this can be seen in Luke 7:36-50, where Jesus is portrayed as "reclining at table" (the Greco-Roman practice) with Simon the Pharisee. It is clear from the discussion in 7:44ff. that Jesus expects footwashing to be a regular service of hospitality the host would provide for the guest, at the beginning stages of the meal. He missed that service when Simon did not supply it.[77] Putting the above things together, we can now give an in-depth and coherent analysis of the structure of John 13-17 as follows:

1. The meal depicted in John 13 is definitely a Greco-Roman style meal, as is shown by the remark in John 13:23, 25 that the Beloved Disciple was *"reclining next to [Jesus]."*[78]

2. The act of footwashing by Jesus depicts him as the host of this banquet, who quite extraordinarily is assuming doing what the host's slave or other family members would normally perform for the guest

in Israel. The act is portrayed as a typical Johannine sign act, but the point is reinforced because it was a regular part of hospitality at the Jewish celebration of a Greco-Roman style banquet. Here this opening act, coupled with the closing prayer, in part serves the purpose of creating unity among the inner circle of disciples, especially in view of the coming betrayal, denial, and general desertion of Jesus. It works against social stratification within the inner circle.[79]

3. The mention of the common purse in John 13:28-30 is reminiscent of Greco-Roman meals held by *collegia* or trade associations. There would be a treasurer's report, and charitable acts or future spending would be discussed.[80]

4. After the meal, Jesus provides discourses with some dialogue, as was common for a sage or Sophist to do at a Greco-Roman banquet. A good deal of this material is like other farewell discourses or "testaments" of those about to die found in the Bible and elsewhere in early Jewish literature. Yet this should not obscure the fact that this material is said to be conveyed in the *meal* setting. In other words, John 13:31—16:33 is the appropriate sequel to the meal mentioned in 13:1-30.

5. Jesus' "high priestly" prayer of John 17 was an appropriate closing act at such a meal, though sometimes this act would happen at the transition between the meal and the *sumposia* (cf. above).[81] Notice the similar closing prayer and the exhortation to the sage's disciples in Sirach 51. The character of this prayer may suggest that the situation of the Johannine community is or has recently been the one described in the Johannine epistles, where some factionalism has happened. Like Judas in John 13, some have gone out and betrayed the Christ (cf. 2 John 7-11).

6. Jesus is portrayed as not just any kind of great teacher in the discourses but as a Jewish sage (John 16:25-27) who speaks parabolically and explains his figures of speech to his disciples in this setting. More importantly, he is portrayed as Wisdom in these discourses. Jesus is like Wisdom in Proverbs 9, who built her house and then called her disciples to a feast, including the simple and immature: "Come eat of *my* bread, and drink of *my* wine, . . . live and walk in the way of insight" (9:5-6). Once more before his rejection and departure, Jesus calls his disciples to hear and heed the voice of Wisdom (cf. 1 Enoch 42), even though as the "simple" they do not spiritually perceive what is going on between Jesus and his betrayer in John 13:28-29.[82]

7. The *reason* for the portrayal of Jesus' last meal with his disci-

ples as a Greco-Roman banquet, instead of bringing out its associations with the Jewish Passover meal, is because this material is now a part of a missionary document. While Jesus is portrayed as a Jewish sage and as Wisdom in John 13–17, this portrayal is presented in a fashion that highlights the more universal aspects of his character, ministry, and mission—traits that would appeal to Gentiles, as well as some Diaspora Jews among the potential converts. In other words, Jesus is portrayed as offering teaching and sharing fellowship in a setting that anyone in the Greco-Roman world could identify with—at a Greco-Roman banquet.

These chapters conclude with words and allusions to the ongoing missionary work of Jesus' disciples (cf. 15:16; 17:21, 23). In short, these chapters are not written so much *about* the Johannine community and its communal history and development; instead, they are written to encourage the Johannine community to continue their missionary work, proclaiming Jesus as universal Savior and Wisdom. They are to evangelize even though they face persecution when they enter synagogues and other places to witness (cf. 15:18ff.; 16:1; 17:4), and even though there are divisions within the Christian community.[83]

At the outset, we note the parallels between the story in John 12:1-8, and the one in 13:1-30. In the former, Jesus is anointed on the *feet*, and that action is interpreted as a symbol of his coming burial. In John 13, Jesus himself washes the feet of his disciples, and this is seen as foreshadowing two things: (1) the coming death of Jesus, by which all those who believe in him will be made clean; and in particular, (2) the cleansing of Peter, which foreshadows his future need for cleansing after he betrays his Master. Peter then is depicted as fallible but redeemable; Judas is portrayed as one who by contrast becomes possessed by Satan and chooses darkness over light. When he goes forth to do his dastardly deed, it is suddenly said to be "night" (13:30). John 13:1-30 then has links both with what has come before and with what is yet to come in the narrative of this Gospel. Nevertheless, it is a mistake to assume that all that is said about the anointing in John 12 also applies to the footwashing in John 13. These are two distinguishable actions with different social functions and overtones.

The Evangelist is *not* interested in speaking about the disciples taking part in the specifically Jewish celebration of Passover with Jesus. He may even be suggesting that this non-Passover meal took place earlier in the week than Thursday. Instead, he is interested in portraying this meal as a Greco-Roman banquet which leads to discourses after the meal proper. If this interpretation is right, then all speculation attempting to relate the account in the Fourth Gospel to the accounts of Passover and the Last Supper in the Synoptics are pointless and will prove fruitless.[84]

The account of the footwashing begins in John 13:1 not only with a time reference, "before the festival of the Passover," but with an indication that Jesus knew his time was up, his hour to culminate his ministry had come. It is important to the Evangelist to portray Jesus being in control every step of the way, even to the point of ordering Judas to get on with his treachery (13:27b), a feature not found in the Synoptic accounts of the Last Supper. John 13:1 is a long, unwieldly sentence in the Greek. It climaxes with the assertion that Jesus loved his disciples *eis telos*, likely meaning "unto the end" (of his life). The evidence of Jesus' love for his disciples to the very end is going to be shown in the material that follows. This appears not only in the footwashing and in the Farewell Discourses, but also in Jesus' testamentary dispensations for his mother and the Beloved Disciple even while he hangs on the cross (John 19:25-27).

By contrast with Jesus' love is the evil the devil has put into the heart of Judas that will lead him to betray Jesus (John 13:2). The shocking character of this meal lies not just in the announcement that one of the inner circle would betray Jesus; the decision to betray would also take place at a fellowship meal and furthermore would involve the one sitting near to Jesus, a place of honor. Irony is piled on irony when we are told that the very one to whom Jesus gives a "choice morsel" at that moment decides to betray Jesus. Thus Judas's act violates a basic rule of ancient hospitality that one does not break fellowship with one's host while one is sharing in a meal with him, regardless of the animus one may bear for that host (cf. Ps. 23:5). Jesus gives Judas a sign of friendship; Judas chooses that moment to get on with betraying him (13:26-27).[85]

John 13:3 tells us that Jesus chose to perform a dramatic act during the meal, knowing that he had come from and would soon go back to God, and knowing furthermore that the Father had delivered into his hands his own fate.[86] We are told that Jesus not only chooses to perform a task reserved for those at the lower end of the social spectrum in the household; he even strips himself down to the Spartan attire of a slave, disrobing and tying a towel around himself.[87] It is sometimes overlooked that Jesus washes not merely Peter's feet but that of at least some of the other disciples as well, apparently including Judas. Jesus washed their feet with water from a basin and then wiped them with a towel.

John 13:6 and 8 says that Simon Peter questions and then rejects such shocking behavior on the part of his Master. This is a role reversal for which he is not prepared; it might be appropriate for a pupil to do this for his teacher, but not the other way around. John 13:7 is quite important because it indicates that Peter will only *later* understand the real significance of this act, which points us forward to Peter's denials of Christ in John 18, and perhaps also the story of his restoration, now found in John 21. Jesus responds that unless he washes Peter, "you will have no share in me." The language, that of having a kind of inheritance, is further developed in 14:3 and 17:24. Jesus himself is seen as the disciple's promised land, the prized possession.[88]

Peter responds in John 13:9 with his typical impulsiveness and exuberance: "Well then, Lord, wash my hands and head as well."

John 13:10 has sometimes been thought to refer to both baptism and the later Christian rite of footwashing, but as D. A. Carson says, the focus here is christological, *not* sacramental.[89] It is Jesus, not some rite, that cleanses in particular by his death, as is symbolized in this act of footwashing. The disciples are said to be clean, "though not all of you." The Evangelist once again clarifies matters for the listener in 13:11, revealing that Jesus knows who will betray him. Such an explanation would hardly be necessary for a Christian in the Johannine community, but it makes sense if this narrative was written to be used with outsiders for missionary purposes. Having performed this symbolic act, Jesus dons his robe again and returns to the table (13:12). How are we to evaluate this act? Does it have any bearing on later Christian practices?

In the first place, it must be seen as doubtful that the act has any bearing on the practices of Christian baptism or the Lord's Supper. If it were meant to symbolize baptism, we would hardly expect the feet to be the prime object of attention. More to the point, we would definitely not expect Jesus to reject the option of pouring water on the head and hands of Peter, as if Jesus were an advocate of an anti-immersion form of baptismal practice! The footwashing rite points forward to the actual cleansing work of Christ on the cross, not to later sacraments such as baptism which look back retrospectively on Christ's cleansing death. Even Schnackenburg, who once held a baptismal view of the significance of the footwashing story, came in due course to reject such a view as implausible.[90] He says the "washing of the disciples' feet is interpreted in the christological and soteriological sense as a symbolic action in which Jesus makes his offering of himself in death graphic and effective, not in a sacramental manner, but by virtue of his love, which his disciples experience to the extreme limit (see 13:1)."[91]

With regard to the connection of this rite to the Lord's Supper, if our conclusions offered at the outset of the discussion of this chapter are correct, then *even if* this act took place at the Last Supper, the Evangelist makes *nothing* of any connection of it to the Lord's Supper ritual. Washing someone's feet can hardly be a symbol parallel to the bread and wine and words of institution of the Lord's Supper; the latter refers to partaking of Christ, while footwashing symbolizes the cleansing necessary *before* one can have a part in Christ.[92] This is clear from Jesus' rejoinder to Peter in 13:8. In short, if this act is to be made into a Christian ceremony, then it would seem appropriate that it serve the same function as it did in early Judaism and early Christianity—as a preparatory ceremony symbolizing the necessary cleansing of the individual needed *before they can partake of the meal.*

Jesus then proceeds to interpret the act he has just done. He is indeed the Teacher and Lord of his disciples, and this act should have taught them something about their need and his provision of cleansing. He suggests that they ought to wash one another's feet, doing as he has done. Does Jesus mean, "Follow the ceremony I have just instituted," or does he mean, "Practice the forgiveness of and cleansing from sins that I have just symbolically depicted," or both? In view of this Gospel's lack of interest in sacraments in general, I suspect that the point here is not to institute a new ceremony, but to insist on the practice of what the ceremony symbolizes. Here, as elsewhere in this Gospel, one is encouraged to read the story at a level beyond the material one, and look for the spiritual significance behind or within it. Jesus asks, "Do you know what *I* have just done to you?" not "Do you understand now how to perform this rite?"

Jesus sees his followers as his agents and messengers sent out into the world to do what he has just symbolically done—offer cleansing from sin through Christ. They are blessed if they do the same sort of loving and forgiving acts as Jesus performed. They, like Jesus, are called to be servants performing self-sacrificial deeds. In short, while the ceremony is not *mandated* here, nevertheless there is nothing to rule it out as a viable expression of the symbolic message about cleansing and forgiveness.[93]

John 13:23 provides us with the first clear reference in the Gospel to "the one whom Jesus loved." It is said that he reclined on the bosom of Jesus. This is likely an allusion to John 1:18, where Jesus as God's Word and Wisdom is said to be in the bosom of the Father.

"The Evangelist introduces the Beloved Disciple as standing in analogous relation to Jesus as Jesus to the Father with respect to the revelation he was sent to make known; behind this Gospel is the testimony of the one who was 'close to the heart' of Jesus."[94] This sentence then is making a claim about the authenticity of the witness of the Beloved Disciple—he understood the mind and meaning of the Word and Wisdom of God.

To sum up, this story does not focus on Jesus' last meal with the disciples being a Passover meal. Indeed, the evidence can be read to suggest that what is being portrayed is footwashing with some other meal being shared during Passover week. This might explain why none of the Synoptics seem to know anything about the footwashing episode in connection with the Last Supper.

Second, this meal, perhaps for missionary purposes, is portrayed as a Greco-Roman meal with the diners reclining at table. This makes natural the connection between the meal and the teaching that follows. Jesus is portrayed as the ultimate after-dinner speaker at an ancient banquet, offering his teaching to the disciples.

Third, one may debate whether the footwashing episode is meant to be seen as setting a precedent for a future Christian ceremony. Yet I think what may not be debated is that this act is seen as an *entrance ceremony* for the meal, something that prepares the partaker to partake in a worthy manner, having been cleansed of one's sins. As such it foreshadows the death of Christ and its cleansing effect. Notice how this rite, like both baptism and the Lord's Supper, alludes to Christ's death and its sequel, the foundational events of the community. This leads to some final overall conclusions and suggestions.

Conclusions and Conjectures

The footwashing episode in John 13 serves the same function here as Paul's exhortations in 1 Corinthians 10–11: it counters social stratification. If even the most honorable participant takes on the role of the slave, then it is no longer possible to conduct Christian meals according to the larger conventions of society. Servant leadership sets a precedent for servant discipleship as well. In short, the social implications of John 13 must not be overlooked. They clearly went against the trends and customs of the larger society. Christianity was indeed a counterculture movement within the Roman Empire. The church was not interested in simply baptizing the values of the larger society, especially when they conflicted with the most foundational values of the community—union and unity in Christ and his body, the church, as expressed in the communal meal.

The sobering outcome of all the above is that to take the Lord's Supper outside of its meal context, and perhaps also to take it out of the context of the Christian home, are hermeneutical moves the NT neither suggests nor endorses. Perhaps this is why the significance of the Lord's Supper has too often been trivialized or marginalized or over-ritualized. To denude the ceremony of its social context leads to the distortion of its essential meaning and function.

What would happen if we really heeded Paul's hint that the Lord's Supper was partaken of every time the entire *ekklēsia* came together (1 Cor. 11:18)? The Lord's Supper suggests that the family of faith, *not the nuclear family*, is the primary family for Christians. What would happen if we really took this concept seriously?

Doubtless, there are many other implications both social and spiritual one could draw from this material. I leave you with this simple suggestion: we must learn once again what it means to make a meal of the Lord's Supper in such a way that it creates *koinōnia* among Christians. It must not be merely an occasional ceremony tacked on to an already overly long worship service. If we manage to do this, then perhaps we may recapture once again what it means to be the family of faith, the true body of Christ.

~§ **PART 3** §~

THEOLOGICAL
PROPOSALS
FOR THE
LORD'S SUPPER

❧ 5 ❧

Ecclesiology and the Lord's Supper: The Memorial Meal of a Peaceable Community

Merle D. Strege

In his masterful treatment of the frontier theme in the American mythos, *Gunfighter Nation*,[1] Richard Slotkin traces that theme as it has been cast in the various media of popular culture. In the course of his study, he analyzes Hollywood films and especially the genre of the Western as primary vehicles of the myth of regeneration through violence. In commenting on one film, director John Ford's *Rio Grande*, Slotkin contends that the frontier motif has been employed to separate a range of social and ideological categories: wilderness versus civilization, Eastern metropolitan corruption versus a crude but virtuous West, and so on. He argues that the frontier also has been interpreted in such a way as to divide contending moralities. "The borderline may also be construed as the moral opposition between the violent culture of men and the Christian culture associated with women."[2]

In American popular culture, especially films such as *Rio Grande*,[3] narrative plots are typically resolved through a definitive moment of violence. A plot's tension is often heightened through conflict between a female whose antipathy toward the violence of the male-dominated cavalry rests in a set of implicitly Christian virtues, and a male hero who embodies the pragmatic code of the West. That code regards violence as necessary to the accomplishment of higher ends: "A man's gotta do what a man's gotta do." Dramatic tension is resolved when, almost inevitably, the female representative of Christian morality is converted and accepts the male morality with its code of regeneration through violence. With equal inevitability, John Wayne seems to have played a starring role in films where the plot develops in this fashion.

What have American cultural myths to do with the topic of "Ecclesiology and the Lord's Supper"? Slotkin's penetrating insights prompt questions which do, I think, bear on our topic: Why is this opposition—between a nonviolent Christian morality and our culture's myth of regenerative violence—so obvious to Slotkin and yet so obscure to most Americans and to many in the American churches? Might the Lord's Supper be understood as the central liturgical discourse within the larger web of the narratives and discourses of Christianity, by which the church can be distinguished from its host culture? Are there ethical implications for the church which rise from members' participation in the Lord's Supper as the central liturgical discourse?

Some ecclesial traditions read the conflict between the opposing moral traditions of redemptive violence and Christian nonviolence in a way which concedes and justifies the necessity of violent force. Does this concession shape the social reality of the church in these ecclesial traditions such that the celebration of the Lord's Supper is undermined as the memorial of one whose love called forth the laying down of his life? Can we then think about the Lord's Supper apart from issues of ecclesiology and ethics without serious harm to that celebration, and harm to our character as followers of the crucified and risen Lord? Such questions form the background for the following reflections.

Consequences for Worship When the Church Moves Too Close to the State

Old Testament theologian Walter Brueggemann provides us with a convenient biblical reference to consider the relationship between the church's social location and the shape of its liturgy. His essays collected under the title *Old Testament Theology*[4] develop the theme of Israel's capacity to hear and give voice to those who are in pain and otherwise oppressed. His study of the Psalter[5] explores the manner in which the monarchy recognizes and suppresses the subversion inherent in the liturgical forms of such cries. The possibility that these cries might find advocacy in the temple liturgy is diminished by the royal patronage of the temple; Israel's religious leaders teach the people to sing to the Lord a song which secures kings against the possibility of revolution even as it praises Yahweh. The temple bureaucracy will not bite the royal hand that feeds them. Thus the liturgy, which *should* form Israel as a people who recognize themselves as the people of Yahweh and an oddity in the world of *realpolitik*, is corrupted and put in the service of the Israelite monarchy's application of that politics.

Brueggemann identifies four ways in which royal power vitiates the liturgy's capacity for shaping Israel as a hopeful people who will cry to Yahweh in confidence that their cry will be heard and answered. He develops these from an unusual and rather daring reading of Psalm 150:

> Praise the Lord!
> Praise God in his sanctuary;
>   praise him in his mighty firmament!
> Praise him for his mighty deeds;
>   praise him according to his surpassing greatness!
> Praise him with the trumpet sound;
>   praise him with lute and harp!
> Praise him with tambourine and dance;
>   praise him with strings and pipe!
> Praise him with clanging cymbals;
>   praise him with loud clashing cymbals!
> Let everything that breathes praise the Lord!
> Praise the Lord!

First, says Brueggemann, the God whom this psalm praises

> does nothing and has done nothing and will do nothing. . . . It takes no great imagination to think that the psalm reflects a community of self-sufficient people who are engaged in absolutizing the present because it is so good, and the god needed for that absolutizing is one with an eternal present, no past and no future.[6]

The liturgy underwritten by the monarchy "articulates a God who does nothing concrete or specific."[7]

Second, once the liturgy establishes praise to a God who sits in the heavens apart from Israel's life, then it follows that the only legitimate social order will be that secured by the monarchy, Yahweh's "representative." Such social order will be above criticism or possibility of change—even if unjust.

Third, the psalm's praise of a God who will do nothing and who has no history, coupled with the ideology of a social order which can be neither criticized nor changed, will eventually cost Israel the narratives from which its social reality first rose. "The royal liturgy . . . evokes persons who become loyal conformists without capacity to judge, discern, critique, or risk."[8]

Brueggemann's fourth point is the cumulative effect of the first three. Together they produce

> a situation in which pathological social relations are generated through the liturgy. The liturgy trains and disciplines one not to notice or to speak about any noticed dysfunction. In such a doxological system as the royal liturgy, the justice questions disappear from one's moral religious horizon.[9]

Brueggemann's work suggests a process whereby the state coopts religious institutions. However subtly, in this process the state nevertheless revises the church's liturgy to the end that worship will serve the purposes of the state. There are contemporary examples of this tendency: the German church's experience at the hands of the Nazis, and American society's coopting of Christian terminology and symbols in moments of national crisis and the celebration of state holidays.

That nation-states will co-opt the church's liturgy raises an important ecclesiological consideration. John Howard Yoder has best articulated this matter in his observation about the Constantinian church and the new ecclesiology it brought forth. As Yoder says, "After Constantine, the church was everybody."[10] As the dimensions of the church began to approximate those of the society, a new ecclesiology was necessary. The old notion of the church as a gathered and visible community was replaced by a conception of the church as simultaneously visible and invisible.

This replacement profoundly altered the ethical teaching of the church. No longer could the Sermon on the Mount be interpreted as moral guidance for a community of disciples. The new ecclesiology required that the Sermon no longer be taken literally for all so-called Christians. Jesus' instruction to his disciples that they not return violence for violence might be intelligible to a church of disciples; it made no sense to a church of Roman society as a whole.[11] How could a government or society exist if all its members agreed to turn the other cheek?

The new ecclesiology altered the form of the church's polity even as it revised interpretations of its moral tradition. Since the identities of true Christians could not be determined in the post-Constantinian church, "believer" came to mean "all the baptized." Yoder asserts that such a diverse mass could no longer be trusted to provide definitions of the faith. "As a result, therefore, the eyes of those looking for the church had to turn to the clergy, especially to the episcopacy, and henceforth 'the church' meant the hierarchy more than the people."[12] Correlative to the widening distinction between clergy and laity was the former's reservation to itself of certain liturgical responsibilities, among them the authority to officiate at the eucharist. We must consider the possibility that the growing conception of the church as clergy shaped the interpretation and practice of the Lord's Supper.

The second-century apologist Justin the Martyr described the celebration of the Lord's Supper as a simple ceremony with considerable freedom of participation. Prayers were said along with readings from Scripture, and the blessing and distribution of bread and wine.[13] Summarizing Justin's description, historian Gary Macy writes, "The earliest celebrations of the liturgy were truly community celebrations, and it seems that there was no clear distinction between those who led the liturgy and those who did not. More accurately, no one led the liturgy; everybody seems to have worshiped together."[14]

By the early fourth century, this simple ecclesial egalitarianism had been replaced by episcopal pomp and ceremony. Macy's description deserves a full citation:

> Privileges associated with the highest ranking officials of the empire would be accorded to the leader of the church. The bishop would be met at the church by a chorus, a rite reserved only for the emperor. He was waited on by deacons with covered hands, again a mark of imperial dignity. People would genuflect in front of the bishop and kiss his feet. By the seventh century, a procession would precede the patriarch, at least in Rome, and the clergy would sit around the bishop's throne just as the emperor's advisers sat at his side. The bishop would be dressed as an imperial dignitary with not only special clothes but also special shoes and headgear. All of these clothes were marks of imperial dignity, and clearly secular and political in origin.[15]

Under such circumstances, we should not be surprised that the communion celebration became more stylized, formal, and the special prerogative of the clergy and hierarchy. Indeed, with regard to the Lord's Supper, one way to interpret these developments is to think of them as a shift in the church's consciousness from communion as the memorial meal of the Lord's Supper to communion as the hierarchical celebration and distribution of the eucharist to the laity.

A strong correlation exists between the development of the new Constantinian ecclesiology and the emergence of conceptions of the elements of communion as the medicine of salvation. In such conceptions, the believer approaches the altar as an individual to consume the body and blood of the Lord. If we ask to whose benefit this reception occurs, the answer seems clear enough: the primary beneficiaries will be individual believers. Only in a secondary sense will the corporate body of the church be shaped by the Lord's Supper celebrated in such terms. This inference seems warranted by Cyril of Jerusalem's fourth-century description of a believer's proper reception of the eucharist:

> Coming up to receive, then, do not have your wrists extended or your fingers spread, but making your left hand a throne for your right, for it is about to receive a King, and cupping your palm, receive the Body of Christ, and answer, "Amen." Carefully hallow your eyes by the touch of the sacred body, and then partake, taking care to lose no part of it. . . . After partaking of the body of Christ, approach also the cup of His blood. Do not stretch out your hands, but bowing low in a posture of worship and reverence as you say, "Amen," sanctify yourself by partaking of the blood of Christ. While it is still moist upon your lips, touch it with your fingers, and so sanctify your eyes, your forehead, and other senses. Then wait for the prayer, and give thanks to God, who has counted you worthy of such high mysteries.[16]

The Constantinian hierarchical ecclesiology correlates with a eucharistic practice and theology which underwrote a curiously individualistic acceptance of the communion elements by the laity. Such hierarchical conceptions of power and clerical authority left laypeople virtually as passive recipients of all the sacraments, the Lord's Supper included. While the hierarchy might have had some sense of a corporate church, the laity did not. Eucharistic theology and practice emphasized the believer's reception of the sacrament as a divinely gracious antidote to the moral and spiritual illness of sin; such theology and practice could do little but further erode any corporate sense of the church which might have existed among the laity.

We have arrived at a point where we might make some provisional assertions. We have good historical warrants for questioning the consequences for the Lord's Supper of those ecclesiological arrangements which create close working relationships between the church and the secular political order. Further, in the example of Constantinian ecclesiology, we have reason to conclude that the way liturgy devolved has not strengthened the church's ethical life. The broadening of the church to include all those baptized without commitment seriously weakens the potential link between worship and ethics. In the Constantinian ecclesiology, the Lord's Supper remains a meal of import to the eternal salvation of each believer as an individual worshiper. But the Supper's capacity to shape the character of disciples is vitiated by this state-church ecclesiology, which thinks of the church as Christendom rather than as the community of disciples.

Does a Relationship Exist Between Worship and Ethics?

Some of us, perhaps many of us, who came to our first intellectual and political awareness during the 1960s applied that decade's universal standard of value to the church and found it wanting. The church was "irrelevant," we thought. Our judgment often was based on what many now think a false separation of worship and ethics. We judged the church irrelevant because it spent too much of its time in worship and not enough effort in the realization of justice. In our hasty judgment, we did not see any connection between worship and ethics.[17]

The sixties' preponderance of interest in utilitarian and deontological theories of moral reasoning facilitated the separation of worship and ethics. After all, worship is in some part an affective and aesthetic experience. Either of the two aforementioned theories are not well prepared to appreciate the role of worship in ethics, particularly when ethics is construed as the practice of moral reasoning. However, we are not left without alternative approaches to ethics. The reemergence of the ethics of virtue or character gives us an alternative which establishes strong connections between the liturgical and moral life of believers.[18]

In the concluding section of his important article, "The Elements of Character,"[19] Richard Bondi puts forward several implications of this approach to ethics for the liturgical life of the church. He thinks that there is no more fundamental way to talk about character than as the "self in relation." Selves cannot be formed other than through their relationships with the creation, with human society, and in Christian ethics, with God. Here we recognize the lines of a discussion shaped by the work of Alasdair MacIntyre, Stanley Hauerwas, Gilbert Meilaender, and others.

On this view, a crucial element in the formation of character will be the self's relationship to a primary community. The narratives and symbols of this community are primary sources, forming the person's conception of the good life. For Christians, the stories of God, Israel, Jesus, and the church are this source. The liturgical symbols drawn from them "may often be more clearly at work in the formation of character than the larger stories from which they come."[20]

Within the life of the church, Bondi thinks, the character of Christians must be formed by preaching and teaching, but these activities must also be accompanied by "evocation, by the urging and enabling of our affective participation in the story. It is finally the heart that must be reached, and it is the emotions as well as our intentions that must be formed. This is particularly true in the formation of Christian character, where it is said we will be known not by our doctrines but by our love."[21] Bondi thus establishes a strong connection between worship and ethics. We might extend that discussion to inquire specifically about the relationship between the Lord's Supper and Christian ethics.

In his exegesis and interpretation of 1 Corinthians 11:17-34, Peter Lampe contends that Paul drew an explicit connection between the church's celebration of the Lord's Supper and ethics.[22] Indeed, Lampe observes that Paul often discusses the sacraments when faced with the necessity of correcting misconduct. The apostle "deals with baptism and the eucharist predominantly in ethical contexts."[23]

In the specific case of 1 Corinthians 11:17-34, Lampe establishes three possible Pauline connections between the "sacramental proclamation of Christ's death" and ethics: (1) Christ died for the weak; therefore the strong Christians at Corinth should neither demean nor offend their weaker brothers and sisters. (2) The eucharist represents Christ's self-denial on the cross for the benefit of others. In view of Christ's example, the wealthy Corinthians should not ignore the hunger of the poor. (3) "In the eucharist a close relationship is established between us and Christ's suffering on the cross. In the sacrament we die *with* Christ. . . . Such cross-existence includes self-denial and active love for others. . . ."[24]

Thus Lampe concludes:

What, then, does it mean to "proclaim" Christ's death in the eucharist? In the eucharist, the death of Jesus Christ is not made present and "proclaimed" (11:26) only by the *sacramental acts* of breaking bread and drinking wine from one cup. In the eucharist, Christ's death is proclaimed and made present by means of our giving ourselves up to others. Our love for others represents Christ's death to other human beings. Only by actively loving and caring for others does the participant in the eucharist "proclaim" Christ's death as something that happened for others.[25]

The celebration of the Lord's Supper is thus a "sanctifying ordinance," in William Willimon's terms. It is a symbol of God's grace active in the lives of the church. "Our characters are formed, sanctified, by such instruments of continued divine activity in our lives."[26]

Thus far I have argued that one important way to think about the relationship between ecclesiology and the Lord's Supper lies in the connection between the celebration of the Supper and ethics. I have employed the negative example of the Constantinian ecclesiology to demonstrate how at least one ecclesiology, and a dominant one at that, with its correlative interpretation of communion, weakens the force of the New Testament's ethical teaching. On the basis of some elements of character ethics and an exegesis of the eucharistic passage in 1 Corinthians, I have claimed a strong link between the celebration of the Lord's Supper and Christian ethics. This link presupposes the existence of a particular kind of community and its way of interpreting the Lord's Supper. We can finally turn to a description of the church as a community of remembrance, and to the communion service as a liturgy of memory.

The Politics of Remembering and the Lord's Supper as *Anamnēsis*

James McClendon has described a vision of the Christian community which he believes peculiar to the believers church tradition. "The vision can be expressed as a hermeneutical motto, which is a shared awareness of *the present Christian community as the primitive community and the eschatological community. In other words, the church now is the primitive church and the church on the day of judgment is the church now.*"[27] Some meetinghouses of congregations in my own tradition, the Church of God (Anderson), have cornerstones which carry the inscription "Founded A.D. 30." Those congregations sing gospel songs of the Church of God Movement which also anticipate the dawn of the eschatological age, the "evening light," as we once sang. Such congregations understood themselves to be the visible restoration of New Testament Christianity. As such, they clearly embody McClendon's hermeneutic, and they illustrate the importance of memory in the life of the believers church tradition.

McClendon's description of the believers church vision includes the implicit claim of such churches that "this is that." This present congregation of Jesus' followers gathers as the present-day embodiment of that congregation or those congregations which incarnated Jesus' teaching in the first century. The New Testament thus provides the norm for contemporary disciples who ask the question, "What kind of people is God calling us to be?" Answers to that question can be discerned only through re-presenting the New Testament community; that is a function of memory.

We remember the New Testament church as we take it as normative for our existence. But we also remember the saintly examples of our forefathers and foremothers whose sacrifices and suffering model the life of discipleship. This surely has been among the chief functions of books like van Braght's *Martyrs Mirror* and Foxe's *Book of Martyrs*. In my own tradition, the Wednesday night prayer meeting once served a similar function. Especially in that meeting, believers were invited to give a testimony to God's activity in their lives since "the saints" last gathered. In other words, they were invited to remember and share that memory for the edification of the entire community. They were also confident that their testimonies of God's goodness were of a nature consistent with those which might have been uttered in Philippi or Rome in the first century.

The church that lives through memory lives as a community with an order markedly different from the liberal politics of our culture. No contemporary theologian has explored this difference with greater insight or pointedness than Stanley Hauerwas. In so doing he has drawn upon resources of the believers church tradition in a manner which may clarify for us some of the claims of our own tradition. Churches that order themselves by a politics of memory should understand that a congregation is more than an aggregation of individuals who are free to determine their own characters and, perhaps worse, the congregation's corporate life.[28] If the past is the norm and memory is the means of re-presenting that norm, then clearly the church must practice a way of being together that is communitarian rather than liberal.[29]

Given the believers church vision as described by McClendon and its foundation in memory, we should not be at all surprised that its several ecclesial expressions have tended to interpret the Lord's Supper as a memorial meal. As Israel understood the Passover, so we in the believers churches have primarily understood Lord's Supper as a memorial. As such, the determinative questions about this meal have not been inquiries about the manner of Christ's presence or of divine operations under the species of bread and wine. Instead, we come to the Lord's Table to ask the same question posed by the child who asks at the Passover table, "Why have we come here?" We have come because of that singular event which demands our remembrance as an act of reverence. This remembrance constitutes the moral shape of us, the present-day people of God, even as Israel's moral life was shaped by its Passover memory of the Exodus. *Anamnēsis* ("remembrance," 1 Cor. 11:24-25) is the process of identification with this past event such that it becomes *our* event and determinative of *our* character.

Israelites of all centuries have been taught to say, "A wandering Aramaean was my ancestor . . ." (Deut. 26:5) and "We were Pharaoh's slaves in Egypt . . ." (6:21). Perhaps that education explains the Hebrew capacity for identification with the past and why such identification is more difficult for us.[30] However, such difficulty does not excuse us from identifying with and imitating the crucified and risen Lord. The celebration of the Lord's Supper, in which we remember the Lord's exemplary sacrificial death, provides us with the most powerful and evocative means for gaining this identification. Our corporate act of remembrance forms our character after the image of Christ. In eating bread and drinking the cup, we remember and identify with the crucified Lord so that our lives might proclaim his sacrificial death until he returns.

American culture threatens the politics and morality of the church as envisioned by the believers churches. A society dominated by the values of individualism, a culture of therapy, progress, and entertainment will scarcely appreciate, let alone understand, a politics and morality built on the necessity of memory and identification with the past. Moreover, the constituents of our churches, who live the vast majority of their lives as members of that culture, will be hard-pressed to see why their church should be different from others who have made peace with it. Indeed, some of those constituents already ask why worship cannot be more "contemporary" (which, being interpreted, means "less boring and more entertaining") and why we, unlike the Burger King ads, cannot have the church our way.

At stake in this threat is the believers church vision of the church as a disciplined community of moral expectation living under the cross of Christ.[31] I have tried to suggest that the celebration of the Lord's Supper is related to our ecclesiology through the concept of the moral expectations of this disciplined community. At the table of the Lord, our worship centers in remembering the sacrificial death, the preeminent example of both the church's life together and its mode of being in the world.

If we will be faithful to the believers church vision of the church, then we will celebrate the Lord's Supper as a memorial feast. In this act of remembrance, we will identify with the crucified Lord whose sacrifice redeemed us as it exemplified the life of agape. Our corporate act of remembrance also employs powerful symbols which evoke the slow and often subtle transformation of our character as we put off the old nature and put on Christ. Only a church which understands the gospel in a way that sets the church over against the world can take the ecclesiological shape of a visible community which can make such expectations and so live.

To the extent that we practice the politics of remembering, especially in the central liturgical act of the Lord's Supper, we will become a people less likely to wait for John Wayne and the cavalry to ride to our rescue by employing the violent weapons of this world. Instead, like Elisha of old, we will become people of such character that we will be enabled to see the armies of the Lord ranging on the hills surrounding those who would destroy us, armies of a Lord who will instruct us not to kill our enemies but invite them to a banquet before sending them home in peace.[32]

❧ 6 ❧

Eschatology and the Lord's Supper: Hope for the Triumph of God's Reign

Robert G. Clouse

It seemed possible in the decade of the 1960s to change American society for the better. Although we came from conservative socially noninvolved groups, the direction of change as well as the protests against many of the established institutions led us to join the new movements. So we argued and worked against the radical right, for the dismantling of the military-industrial complex, for civil rights for all peoples, for peace in the Middle East through the recognition of Palestinian rights, for empowerment of the poor and an end to the war in Southeast Asia.[1] As the decade of the 1970s dawned, new concerns were added to this list, especially feminism and environmentalism.[2]

A few of these noble goals have been partially attained, and yet most of them are farther from fulfillment than ever. Even the movements to achieve these ends have fragmented into so many antagonistic divisions that it is quite discouraging. The radical right seems stronger then ever, having taken advantage of the failure of some social programs and the antiabortion movement to gain new adherents. The struggle against racism falters when quotas are used to thwart democracy; the antiwhite rhetoric of Black Muslims strains the faith of those who believe in a just society. Our environment is threatened by the desire for jobs and a frightening growth in population. The ravages of ethnic and mini-nationalist slaughter in Bosnia, Somalia, the Commonwealth of Independent States, and Rwanda remind one that war is taking on new and more deadly forms despite the demise of the anticommunist crusade. Even the marvelous advances of medical science are dimmed by the difficulty of creating an adequate health-care delivery system and the horror of the AIDS epidemic.

What went wrong with the hopes of thirty years ago? Perhaps they were too sanguine. Yet it was always necessary to have hope to try to accomplish these worthwhile goals. The challenges that society and individuals face can be met only by an adequate eschatology. Ironically, while working and arguing for the goals of this "great society," the writer also engaged in research in the apocalyptic and millennial tradition.[3] However, most of the time the concerns for social justice and eschatology were not related together. The details about the return of Christ can be studied as merely a distant and almost irrelevant, final chapter in God's redemptive program.

The important question remains about the final judgment, the restoration of Israel, the millennium, the new heavens and the new earth. How do these doctrines tie in with other Christian beliefs such as the creation, the fall of humankind, the incarnation of Christ, the work of the Holy Spirit, and the mission of the church? There is a meaning and a purpose to these great events toward which God is moving history that makes them important at the present time. Yet I was so preoccupied with the sequence of events, the geography and the schedule of the end-times, that I missed the most important question. When one considers the implication of Christ's coming, eschatology is absolutely necessary for a Christian view of life.

As the former president of Fuller Seminary stated, eschatology

> is the North Star from which theological study gains its bearing, the giant floodlight by which God brightens the whole landscape of human life and history, the clearest picture we possess of what God really wants, what our place is in his plan, and what power he has to make all creation serve his glory. . . . The landscapes of the Bible's future are not polluted with the sights of injustice, the sounds of war, or the pangs of deprivation. Peace, righteousness, and plenty dwell there as celebrated achievements of the King of kings. It is the ethical perfection of that kingdom which both prods and guides us to get on with the task of loving our neighbors, living as peacemakers, and offering the cups of cold water in the Savior's name. Christian ethics flow from our view of the future: we not only pray for God's will to be done on earth as it is in heaven, but we work to be part of the answer to that prayer.[4]

Perhaps the greatest encouragement for Christians to work for a better society is through the eschatological emphasis of the Lord's

Supper. This statement could be emphasized even farther by suggesting that the threefold observance of this Christian ordinance is an especially helpful way to accomplish this purpose. The bread and the cup signify the death of Christ and our justification through him. The feetwashing service emphasizes our present fellowship with the risen Lord through sanctification. The meal directs us toward the future, when we reach our goal, glorification, the celebration of the marriage supper of the Lamb.[5] However, the Grace Brethren as they observe this service usually emphasize doctrinal considerations, often forgetting that it is necessary to go beyond such explanations and stress the moral and social implications of the ordinances.

The Lord's Supper focuses on the Christian hope not just in a doctrinal but also in an ethical way. The coming of Jesus brought hope to the world. He fulfilled Israel's desire for the coming Messiah (Luke 1:31-33, 54, 68-69; 2:29-32; John 1:41). Many Israelites did not accept Jesus, however, and cooperated in his death. Despite this seeming defeat, he rose from the dead and sent the Holy Spirit to work in the world. His coming in the Spirit was the promise of his return in glory (Rev. 3:11; 22:7, 12, 20).

The early Christians believed that Jesus was coming soon, and they cried out with the apostle, "Our Lord, Come" (1 Cor. 16:22). Contemporary believers must continue to hope that Christ will come soon because a deferred hope is forlorn and disappointed. Those who base their belief on the New Testament do not look forward to a dark and uncertain future. We are secure in Jesus Christ, and therefore it causes our faith to be active in love. We cannot believe and love without hoping, because faith, hope, and love are three forms of human response to "him who is, and who was, and who is to come" (Rev. 1:4, 8; 4:8; 11:17; 16:5). The Lord's Supper is a feast of love and joy eaten in faith that the reign of God has come and is coming. Jesus held the Last Supper as the final meal with his disciples before he would eat and drink with them in the kingdom of God (Mark 14:25 and par.). He wished the supper to be observed as the meal "between the ages," celebrating the new age of "already" which is overcoming the old age of "not yet" (cf. 1 Cor. 10:11). Thus it is an eschatological supper, "until he comes" (1 Cor. 11:26).

The reign of God, which has come and been revealed in the ministry of Christ, has ushered in the new creation, and the present is really the "last days" or "the end of the times" (1 Pet. 1:20; 1 John 2:18; 1 Tim. 3:1; 2 Pet. 3:3; James 5:3; Heb. 1:2; and Acts 2:17). Wars, famines, disease, earthquakes, and social injustice—these are but the last gasps of a world that is passing away. The Lord's Supper should cause joy in the celebration of the church; it is a promise and foretaste of the final appearing of the Lord. Then the saints of God will see what now they only believe.

One of the more thoughtful presentations of the eschatological significance of the Lord's Supper is by Geoffrey Wainwright, who states that it brings the second coming into the present:

> Christ's coming at the eucharist is a projection in the temporal sense that it is a "throwing forward" of Christ's final advent into the present. What is part of the final purpose of the eternal God but is still future in the dealings between God and man is, by the divine initiative, thrown forward into man's present experience. . . . [Thus] man may order himself according to what he thereby sees the kingdom of God to imply in the way of fellowship between God and man and the extirpation of all that would oppose the divine sovereignty.[6]

The present realization of Christ's coming involves the attempt to anticipate as far as possible the conditions of the kingdom of God. This should encourage the church in the work of sharing the gospel. The command, "Go therefore and make disciples of all nations, baptizing them . . . and teaching them," closes with the assurance, "And remember, I am with you always, to the end of the age" (Matt. 28:19-20).

We must honestly admit that many who are involved in the believers church tradition do not take opportunities to share their faith with unbelievers. Often there is agreement with statements such as, "I think the work that people do ought to speak for itself, and if people are truly involved and committed to what they believe, little verbal explanation is required." Many secular humanists do excellent work for others, and yet they are not able to share the good news of Jesus Christ. Christians are able to help people spiritually and should not confuse tactful witnessing for Christ with an offensive in-your-face religion. These words of witness must be supported by acts of decency, kindness, and justice.

In Matthew 25 are three parables which deal with the wedding feast and the important question about how those who await its coming spend their time. The last of these, that of the sheep and the goats, asks whether they fed the hungry and clothed the naked. Paul is also concerned about the way the Corinthian Christians ate the Lord's

Supper, while they allowed others to go hungry (1 Cor. 11:20). It is quite obvious from passages such as these that believers are to alleviate the suffering of the poor and oppressed.[7]

Those who proclaim the theology of liberation have much to teach the church on this subject. One need not agree with all of their conclusions to approve of the comment of Desmond Tutu: "If you are neutral in a situation of injustice, you have chosen the side of the oppressor. If an elephant has his foot on the tail of the mouse, and you say you are neutral, the mouse will not appreciate your neutrality."[8] There is an extreme divergence between the rich and poor of today's world, a contrast often described in terms of the North-South divide. Experts in demographics estimate that by the year 2000, the world's population will be 6.3 billion, and by 2025 it may reach 8.5 billion. Moreover, 95 percent of the global population growth over this period will be in the developing countries of Latin America, Africa, and Asia. By 2025, Mexico will have replaced Japan as one of the ten most-populous countries on the earth, and Nigeria's population will exceed that of the United States.

Despite progress made in economic growth, public health, and literacy in the third world, at least 800 million live in "absolute poverty." This is defined as a condition of life where malnutrition, illiteracy, disease, squalid housing, high infant mortality, and low life expectancy are beyond any reasonable definition of human decency. The stark reality is that the North (including Eastern Europe) has a quarter of the world's population and 80 percent of its income, while in the South (including China) three-quarters of the world's people live on one-fifth of its income. Also, approximately 90 percent of the global manufacturing industry is in the North. While the quality of life in the North rises steadily, in the South every two seconds a child dies of hunger and disease.

Still, the contrast between wealth and poverty does not correspond exactly with the North-South division. Many of the OPEC countries are rich, while poverty is found in North America and Europe. In the United States 14 percent of the people and 20 percent of the children are beneath the poverty line. In Britain over 10 percent live below the legal definition of poverty, and another 10 to 15 percent are close to this point. A great disparity between wealth and poverty is found not only between nations but also within them.

On the other hand, one-fifth of the world's population lives in relative affluence and consumes approximately four-fifths of the world's income. Moreover, according to a World Bank report in the year 1988, the "total disbursements" from the wealthy nations to the third world amounted to $92 billion, a figure less than 10 percent of the worldwide expenditures on armaments; but this was more than offset by the "total debt service" of $142 billion. The result was a negative transfer of some $50 billion from the third world to the developed countries. This disparity between wealth and poverty is a social injustice so grievous that Christians dare not ignore it.

God has provided enough resources in the earth to meet the needs of all. It is not the fault of the poor themselves, since for the most part they were born into poverty. Christians today are tempted to use the complexities of economics as an excuse to do nothing. However, God's people need to dedicate themselves not only to verbal evangelism but also to relieving human needs as part of sharing the good news (Luke 4:18-21), both at home and to the ends of the earth.

This explains why Christians in the two-thirds world place issues of poverty and economic development at the top of their theological agendas. Some Christians in the North have difficulty in understanding why "liberation" is so central to the thinking of their counterparts in Latin America, Africa, and Asia, but they have never faced the stark, dehumanizing reality of grinding poverty.

Christians in the more-developed lands must share their material means with others. This can be done by supporting public and private efforts to aid the poor, by scaling down our standard of living, and by working for the empowerment of those who do not have the ability to represent themselves.[9]

The eschatological vision of the Lord's Supper also projects into our time a desire for peace. The image of the future found in the closing chapters of Revelation is that of a peaceful existence with city gates that never shut; the kings of the earth are bringing their glory to God, and the nations are being healed. Are we working for peace? It is needed more than ever.

The relaxation of cold war tensions following the demise of the Soviet Union led many into complacency about the continuing threat of war. The menace of international communism faded and with it the fear of a nuclear holocaust. Its place was taken by a fragmenting nationalism. A variety of mini-nationalisms pointed to the great paradox of the times: bitter divisions in an otherwise increasingly unifying world. Since the end of World War II, over one hundred new states have declared their independence and started on the road to nationhood. Usually unstable and economically weak, these states face severe problems. The appearance of so many new, small countries has even stimulated nationalism among minority groups in the larger and older nations. Most of these states have been accepted as members of the United Nations, thus setting a precedent for other dissident groups that they too should be heard, even those living in situations that have not traditionally been seen as "colonial."

The existence of so many new nation-states is a serious matter, because they are in such a precarious condition. Given their small land areas and limited resources, the hopes to which independence gave rise cannot be fulfilled by peaceful development. Consequently, they may resort to arms to gain what they want. These wars may be fought with conventional weapons, but there is always the temptation to turn to atomic, biological, and chemical (ABC) warfare. The use of chemical weapons by the Iraqis in the 1980s illustrates this point.

What makes this so frightening is the proliferation of atomic weapons. In the 1980s only five countries had them—the United States, the Soviet Union, Britain, France, and China. By the early 1990s, it was known that seventeen more countries had the capability to produce them. Many believe that in the first decade of the twenty-first century, the "nuclear club" will have many more members. With that many countries possessing nuclear arms, the possibility that they would be used in a war is extremely high. This gives great urgency to Christian efforts on behalf of peace. As Jesus said, "Blessed are the peacemakers, for they will be called children of God" (Matt. 5:9).

An objective observer from another planet would conclude that earth is indeed a strange place. There is such a surplus of weapons, and yet a scarcity of food for the hungry and shelter for the homeless. Thus, the task confronting believers is an urgent one. They must teach people to build a peace in the world based upon a true knowledge of God and just relationships among nations.[10]

The quest for peace consequently involves more than the struggle against violence. Individuals as far apart as Pope Paul VI and Reinhold Niebuhr have observed, "If you want peace, work for justice."[11] This brings one to the universal scope of the eschatological hope. The Revelator claimed that all nations would flow into the final kingdom. The prophecies of the Old and New Testaments indicate an acceptance of people from all groups who turn to God (Isa. 66:18; Joel 3:2; Rev. 5:9; 21:24). When we compare this outlook with the present age, we are challenged to join the struggle against racism and ethnic hatred.

A widely accepted definition among the international Christian community holds that racism is ethnocentric pride in one's own racial group and preference for the distinctive characteristics of that group; belief that these characteristics are fundamentally biological in nature, strong negative feelings toward other groups who do not share these characteristics, coupled with the thrust to discriminate against and exclude the outgroup from full participation in the life of their community.[12]

Ethnicity has to do with cultural or group identity. Members of an ethnic group share a common language and social and cultural institutions; they perceive that these set them apart from other people.

Racism and ethnicity are global matters, not something just limited to the West. Before European expansion (ca. 1500), the various races of the human family lived in relative isolation. This was gradually modified by mass migrations, both free and forced, and presently there are varying degrees of racial mixture in the world. The change in the racial map of the world did not necessarily make conflict inevitable. What actually promoted it was the nature of European expansion. Possessing technological and military superiority, the Europeans conquered vast colonial possessions in Africa, Asia, and the Americas. In the process, Westerners developed a myth of racial superiority to justify their conduct. In the contemporary world, racial and ethnic tensions have been steadily increasing.

Christians are especially equipped to deal with this situation, as the apostle Paul showed in his remarkable address to the Athenians (Acts 17:22-31). Athens was perhaps the most racially, ethnically, and culturally diverse city in the Roman Empire. Paul addressed the questions of their differences in the sight of God. His sermon emphasized four points. First, he affirmed the unity of humanity because God is the Creator, Sustainer, and Father of all humankind. Consequently, racism is not only foolish but evil, since it violates the creative purposes of God.

Second, Paul acknowledged the diversity of ethnic cultures. Despite the fact that God made all nations from one man, "he allotted the times of their existence and the boundaries of the places where they would live." Scripture acknowledges that cultures enrich the total picture of human life, so Christians may affirm both the unity of humankind and the diversity of ethnic existence.

Third, although the apostle accepted the richness of the various cultures, he did not carry this over into the realm of religion. He did not accept the idolatry on which they were based because God does not tolerate rivals to his Son, Jesus Christ, the only Savior and Judge of humankind.

Finally, the apostle declared the importance of the church, which would be a new and reconciled community to which all may belong (Acts 17:34).

John R. W. Stott eloquently sums up the thrust of Paul's address to the Athenians:

> Because of the unity of humankind, we demand equal rights and equal respect for racial minorities. Because of the diversity of ethnic groups, we renounce cultural imperialism and seek to preserve all those riches of inter-racial culture which are compatible with Christ's lordship. Because of the finality of Christ, we affirm that religious freedom includes the right to propagate the gospel. Because of the glory of the church, we must seek to rid ourselves of any lingering racism and strive to make it a model of harmony between races, in which the multiracial dream comes true.[13]

The ideal of equality must extend, as Paul states, to gender as well as race and class. Women are to be accepted as equals; this is affirmed in such passages as Galatians 3:28. A just society is inconceivable without the recognition of the gifts and abilities of women; this must start with the church. One thoughtful writer eloquently states,

> People (in the nineteenth century) asked why such and such differences were relevant to the distribution of social benefits and deprivations. "Why is my being born of a commoner and your being born of a noble relevant to whether we will become educated?" At each point a question of justice was raised, for people are being treated unjustly where benefits and deprivations are distributed on the basis of differences that are not relevant. The question that women in the church are raising is a question of justice. There are, indeed, a good many more dimensions involved than this one of justice, but justice is basic. Women are not asking for handouts of charity from us men. They are asking that in the church—in the church, of all places—they receive their due. They are asking why gender is relevant for assigning tasks and roles and offices and responsibilities and opportunities in the church. The gifts of the Spirit are relevant. But why gender?[14]

The eschatological view of the Lord's Supper projects a final characteristic of the kingdom into our age: the need to protect the environment. According to the final chapter of the Bible, the water is clear as crystal, and the trees bear abundant fruit in every month. In short, the curse is removed from creation, and Edenic conditions return (Rev. 22:1-5; cf. Rom. 8:22). This encourages us to tackle perhaps the most serious challenge facing humankind, that of preserving the earth. The extent of environmental destruction is alarming, represented by such recent disasters as the 1984 leak of poisonous gas from a chemical plant at Bhopal in India, the 1986 Chernobyl nuclear power plant accident in the Ukraine, and the 1989 Exxon Valdez oil spill in Alaska. Such alarming events as the destruction of the tropical rain forests, the southward advance of the Sahara desert, the acid-rain crisis, and the elimination of innumerable species of animals and plants—these and other crises have made many individuals aware of the need for environmental responsibility.

Unfortunately, secular ecologists accuse Christians of being a principal source of the problem because of the statement in Genesis 1:26, 28 that humankind should "subdue" the earth and all the life that is in it. Some even say believers bear a huge burden of guilt for the exploitation of the environment, and they call for a pantheistic religion, joining humans and nature together.

Christians must respond to these charges by showing that Genesis chapters one and two balance each other. God delegates dominion to humans, but they are responsible to God and are to cooperate with the forces of nature. This requires conservation of the earth's resources by wisely using and recycling manufactured products. More Christians must promote awareness of environmental responsibility.

Respect for the natural world; love for all people regardless of race, gender, or class; justice for the poor; and the establishment of peace—these are some of the goals that the Christian vision of the kingdom puts before society. What chance is there that the present age will ever reflect these values? One must frankly admit that currently there is no complete realization of these goals. However, one can separate complete from partial accomplishments.

On the cornerstone of the headquarters of the United Nations are these words: "They shall beat their swords into plowshares, and their spears into pruning hooks; nation shall not lift up sword against nation, neither shall they learn war any more" (Isa. 2:4). This passage states what will happen when Christ returns to transform the world. While the United Nations can reduce conflict, there will be no final peace until his coming. In a similar manner, there will be no final solutions to the other problems until then. Yet there can be partial answers.

> Even though we know that we are "strangers and pilgrims on the earth," we should do all we can to improve the conditions of men's lives. Why? Because love and justice and all the values which will be basic in heaven are God's will for men now. The Church is to be a sign of God's kingdom, pioneering things which are God's will for men. That is what the Church at its best has always been. Who pioneered mass education? Who pioneered hospitals? Who pioneered the abolition of slavery? In each case Christians played a leading role in causing progressive change. . . . If there has been progress in the past, there can be progress in the future.[15]

We can pursue these goals with a certainty born of the conviction that the Christian hope

> leads somewhere—to the triumph of God. As people who have heard God's loving invitation to share in his victory, we long for the day when the shout will be heard: "Praise God! For the Lord, our Almighty God, is King! Let us rejoice and be glad; let us praise his greatness! For the time has come for the wedding of the Lamb, and his bride has prepared herself for it." (Rev. 19:6-7)[16]

✒ 7 ✑

Making the Lord's Supper Meaningful

Marlin Jeschke

Whoever goes away from the Lord's Supper without the love of [brothers and sisters] being awakened [within] has received nothing; [that one] was present in vain, for it is by love to the [brothers and sisters] that we have fellowship with Christ.
—*Emil Brunner* (Our Faith, *138*)

Introduction

With the stated title, I do not intend to say that the celebration of the Lord's Supper is not meaningful in our churches at present, or that I will supply the magic formula to make it meaningful. The title I first tried, "Making the Lord's Supper Meaningful Again," seemed to suggest that it once carried meaning but had lost at least some of its meaningfulness. Yet the celebration of communion in our churches could and should be more meaningful than it currently is, and I believe that what follows will show that this is the case.

Other essays above have chronicled and documented that the Lord's Supper has indeed lost meaning in the wider Christian church. The main question before us is this: Have we believers churches recovered the meaning that the Lord's Supper should have? Is the understanding *and practice* of the Lord's Supper in our churches what it should be, measured by the criteria we accept? We stress our biblicism and our restorationist vision, with a conviction that the Magisterial Reformation did not necessarily complete the task of reformation. These criteria lead us seriously to consider restoring the agape meal (love-feast) form of the Lord's Supper of the New Testament church.

My own reading has identified at least two important developments that contributed to the loss of the agape meal in the patristic church in the middle of the second century.[1] The first was the intrusion of behavior patterns from the Greco-Roman *eranos* custom.[2] This custom, remarkably similar to modern church potlucks, dated back to Homer's time. The host for the occasion provided such items as wreaths, perfumes, and sweets. The guests contributed the food: fish, various kinds of meat, and baked goods. Ideally, everyone present would pool their contributions so that they would be equally satisfied.

Second, the rise of the cathedrals with the Constantinianization of the church[3] led to the discontinuation of the full supper, because they did not have the "fellowship rooms" that our modern churches do. This rendered the supper *as a supper* awkward and led eventually to the "cafeteria" form of celebration in medieval and modern Christendom.[4] Thus the loss of form and change of meaning went together.

One way of trying to make the Lord's Supper more meaningful today (misguided in my opinion) is to take our cue from the high churches. Not a few people in our churches seem enchanted by the vocabulary and style of these traditions. To solemnly intone words such as *anamnēsis* and *epiclēsis* and eucharist and real presence and transignification and to "break bread together on our knees" (wafers preferably[5])—all this seems to some members to promise more sanctity and grace, heightened reverence, profounder piety, and richer blessing.[6] We are tempted to have an ecclesiastical inferiority complex as we look at high-church traditions.

Yet there are rich meanings in historic church practice, views we hold in common with the larger church. These can and should be preserved, even if in some cases we need to reinterpret them to remain true to the biblical tradition. So in what follows, I first critique the larger tradition and then suggest what our meaning and practice should be.

Some writers do us the service of gathering up the constellation of meanings they think the Lord's Supper is supposed to have.[7] But there are some dimensions of the biblical meaning of the supper that traditional theology and forms of celebration have overshadowed or even lost. These ought to be recovered. If it is difficult to recover them under present forms of celebration, then we must be willing to reform so we can recover these biblical and essential meanings.

Few writers discuss the form of the supper or attempt to relate meaning to form. They do not say the supper should be at the chancel rail or in the pew. They seem to assume that form is irrelevant—

that from the New Testament church until today's World Council of Church's "Baptism, Eucharist, and Ministry" statement by Faith and Order, the meaning is the same regardless of form.[8] Is that credible? I think any reflective anthropologist would say that form *does* influence meaning; and meaning can and does influence form.

The two dominant forms in Christianity today are (1) the procession to the chancel rail or communion rail—Orthodox, Catholic, Anglican, Lutheran, Methodist; and (2) communion while seated in the pews, being waited upon by servers. Both of these, however, are departures from a third form, (3) that of the Last Supper and of the New Testament church—participation by believers in an actual meal around a table.

About Terminology

If the meaning—*and form*—of the Lord's Supper are important, so also is terminology. Alister McGrath, for example, claims that Lord's Supper, communion, eucharist, and mass all intend the same thing, but that for simplicity he will use the most acceptable common denominator, eucharist. However, I think we know these terms *do not* all mean the same thing and that it *does* matter.[9] My preliminary claim —and I do not feel any need to argue it at length—is that the term *Lord's Supper* is the most basic but also the most full-orbed term and that it carries the richest meanings. The term eucharist identifies only one aspect of what the Lord's Supper means, only one act in the liturgy. Why use the more limited term?[10]

Some theologians object to calling the Lord's Supper a sacrament. But I find one basic meaning in that term quite acceptable and even useful for our purposes.[11] A *sacrament* is "a sign and the thing signified." The sign of a restaurant can point you to good food but itself gives you no nutrition. However, a kiss between spouses signifies love and is already an experience of what it signifies. So the Lord's Supper is a sign of numerous things, and it is intended to convey, in the act of celebration, what it signifies.

I make no brief for the use of the term sacrament rather than of the term ordinance in our regular church life. Our believers churches do well to stay with the term ordinance. I am merely noting that we don't need to feel deficiencies in comparison with other churches that prefer the term sacrament, because these other traditions can be shown *on the basis of the term sacrament* to have deficiencies in manifesting in their church life much of what the Lord's Supper signifies.

We are believers churches talking to each other. So the question may again be pressed: Are *our* Lord's Suppers an experience of what they signify? It may not be difficult to find agreement among us on what applies to Orthodox, Catholic, Episcopal, and Lutheran churches. But do we have theological and practical deficiencies in our own church communion doctrine and practice? Here the Church of the Brethren restoration of the New Testament agape feast form of the supper may point the way more truly toward a sacramental Lord's Supper than those traditions that would like to claim the word as their trademark. Maybe the term sacrament can prod us toward more meaningful forms of celebration.

The rest of this essay will take up (1) meanings of the Lord's Supper on which we have substantial agreement with historic Christianity, (2) meanings on which we are obliged to offer substantial critiques and reinterpretations, and (3) meanings on which we need to critique ourselves. As believers churches we have—or should have—something to offer the Christian church at large concerning this rite of the church.

Preserving Historic Meanings

Thanksgiving

I cannot imagine anyone from the believers church tradition objecting to the claim that the Lord's Supper is an act of thanksgiving even though it obviously says and does more than give thanks. No worthy celebration would not include thanksgiving in some sense according to the liturgical pattern of 1 Corinthians 11. We offer thanks not just for food but for all that Christ wrought. Yet as stated, I see no reason to replace the earlier, broader, richer, and clearer term Lord's Supper with the term eucharist (gratitude) that derives from only one aspect of the liturgy.

Memorial

Believers churches have not usually been faulted for neglecting this aspect of the meaning of the Lord's Supper. If anything, they are charged with having *only* this meaning. We are allegedly Zwinglians; the supper tends to be for us a mere memorial.[12] The subject merits clarification.

New Testament scholars remind us that the word remembrance, *anamnēsis*, means not only remembering a past event but bringing its significance into the present. " 'To make remembrance' of Christ is more than the performance of an act of worship; it is to accept living under the sign of the cross. . . ."[13] Good family reunions don't merely reminisce about a forebear. They keep alive that forebear's values and family traditions. This kind of remembering is not just warehousing; it is keeping something from the past alive and transmitting it.

In that light, it is undeniable that Lord's Supper celebrations of all denominations are keeping alive some tradition. The pertinent question: What configuration of meanings resides in the supper that Christ and the New Testament church bequeathed to us, meanings that we strive to keep alive and transmit? For the moment we can safely say that those churches are doing the best job of memorializing Christ's death who most adequately reflect the life of the kingdom that Christ inaugurated.

Proclamation

The Lord's Supper is also a proclamation. This recalls the word of Paul in 1 Corinthians 11:26, "For as often as you eat this bread and drink the cup, you proclaim the Lord's death until he comes."

The Protestant Reformation with its restoration of preaching has made good a serious deficiency in the pre-Reformation church.[14] Word and sign are both needed: word to explicate the sign, and sign to enact and incarnate the word.

That observation logically prompts the question: How adequately do word and sign complement each other? It is never out of season to call for good preaching. Is there, however, a commensurate celebration, an enactment in the supper which then conveys all the rich meaning that the preaching has claimed the supper contains? Do our words and deeds at the supper conjointly proclaim our unity, our love, joy, and peace? Our *koinōnia*? Or is there an inconsistency whose more serious name is hypocrisy? There is a risk that the sign does not make good on what the preaching claims.[15]

Critiquing Historic Meanings

Sacrificial Offering

Seeing offering as one of the meanings of the Lord's Supper goes back to the earliest church: believers brought food for the agape meal or Lord's Supper.[16] Few writers today defend the old Catholic doctrine of the Lord's Supper as the repetition of the sacrifice of Christ.[17] Most even reject the view that the supper is a reminder to God of the once-for-all sacrifice of his Son, as though God needed reminding.

This leaves us with the view that the supper is intended to remind *us* of Christ's sacrifice, and that as our high priest (according to the book of Hebrews), he is presently making intercession on our behalf before the Father on the basis of his once-for-all sacrifice. On this last point the believers church tradition has always, happily, concurred. But there is a motif in our heritage that can enhance this view. I refer to our emphasis on discipleship, our awareness that being a Christian means taking up our cross and following Christ, our commitment to suffering servanthood.[18] Here we owe it to ourselves to seriously consider the restoration of the rite of washing feet, to recover this dimension of the meaning of the supper.

The question is not whether Christ's sacrifice is complete but whether ours is complete,[19] whether we have recognized the implication of Christ's sacrifice for our call to sacrifice. This means sacrificing money in church offerings, time in the service of the church, or literally sacrificing our lives in keeping faith with our Christian calling. In any case, the Lord's Supper, rightly understood, calls us to a life of sacrifice.[20]

Real Presence

The heavy emphasis upon the term *real presence* in contemporary discussions of the Lord's Supper betrays the long shadow of the doctrine of transubstantiation. In current high-church thought, bread and cup may not literally be made body and blood of Christ in the act of consecration. In its place, theologians have sought some assurance or guarantee of the efficacy of grace in terms of "real presence." It is alleged that the consecration charges the elements with a power that merits the term "real presence of Christ."[21]

Unfortunately, the focus upon real presence removes attention from where the New Testament places it—on the church.[22] The *church* is the body of Christ. In effect, then, the answer to the question of the presence of Christ is whether the church is really the church. If it is, Christ is present. If therefore we want real presence, the only way to realize it is to be a real church. Without real church life, without congregational samples of the coming kingdom that Jesus brought, other attempts at guaranteeing Christ's presence are in vain.[23]

It is clear that "no denomination celebrating the eucharist has a doctrine of the absence."[24] However, one writer draws attention to the sense in which we must recognize a "real absence."[25] What else would it mean to confess the hope of Christ's "coming again"? The church should not deny its present position between the first and second advents of Christ. There is a need for us to accept our present eschatological place. And in our present place, we accept the presence of Christ in the form he himself has ordained until his return.

There really shouldn't be any question about whether Christ is present if the church has invited his presence. If the church prays, "Be present at our table, Lord," whether in those specific words or not, does our Lord not hear that prayer?[26]

There is absolutely *no* correlation between affirming faith in the real presence of Christ in the bread and cup and the real presence of Christ to his believers in the Lord's Supper. If anything, dogmatic assertions of real presence are in danger of detracting from examination of confirming signs of whether Christ really *is* present—in signs of love of the brothers and sisters, turning from sin, commitment to lives of self-sacrifice, and the like.

Transignification

A new word has appeared in contemporary theological discussion of the Lord's Supper which also still carries the long shadow of the doctrine of transubstantiation. Though surrendering much, it is calculated to salvage some of the overtones of the classic doctrine. As I understand it, *transignification* is supposed to mean that through the act of consecration, the bread and cup *cross over* (transit) into a new meaning; they come to signify something *other* than food for the body.[27]

It is preferable to say that the bread and cup have a dual signification rather than undergoing a transignification. The food remains food for the body and never ceases to signify that. But it also signifies spiritual fellowship of God's people, conscious of themselves as living under the lordship of Christ, being his followers, called out of the world, being renewed for their mission in the world. There is therefore a dimension or quality to this eating that sets it apart from just any secular meal, such as Friday night at Bob Evans. Hence, it is appropriate that invitations to the Lord's table discriminate and identify the guests as the baptized "who are living in fellowship with God and their neighbor." It is not inappropriate for this table to have boundaries.[28]

There may be an apprehension that these two don't fit easily together. We suppose that if we recognize the spiritual significance of the Lord's table, we must suppress the ordinary signification of food and eating; that we must make it as unlike normal eating as possible;

that if we do have normal patterns of eating, we will fail to recognize its spiritual significance. This makes it look as though it must be one or the other but can't be both.

On this question, we do well to compare the treatment of the two natures of Christ in the Chalcedonian Creed. Christians have been notorious for having difficulty respecting the two natures and not confusing them. As an early heresy such as Eutychianism shows, Christians tend to sacrifice one nature or the other, usually surrendering the humanity of Christ. So it is here. If the Lord's Supper is a full meal, it can't be spiritual, too many Christians think. If it is spiritual, we can't have a normal meal.

However, in the attempt to heighten the sanctity of the Lord's Supper by abbreviating the meal, by suppressing its ordinary social significance, we actually surrender some of its spiritual significations. We give up such things as (1) the sense of joyful feasting in appreciation of the present form of the kingdom and in anticipation of its future realization, and (2) the awareness of congregational solidarity, community, *koinōnia*, mutual support.

Forgiveness of Sins

The Lord's Supper has long been held to be a means of grace, specifically to mediate forgiveness of sins. Yet paradoxically almost all traditions stress the need for confession of sin by communicants *before* they come to the Lord's table.[29]

It is not acceptable to think of forgiveness in the supper—or anywhere else, for that matter (including the weekly service in Protestantism)—as a ritual, routine, perennial lament of failure and perpetual absolution.[30] The real meaning of forgiveness is empowerment to overcome sin. So if the Lord's Supper is a means of grace, it is more than absolution; it is acceptance of the power of the Spirit to transform us. (Of course, the Lord's Supper is also not the opposite—a weekly accrual or accumulation of merits.)

Some believers churches have neglected, however, to see how the Lord's Supper is a means of effecting forgiveness and aiding sanctification. I refer to the preparatory service, which demands that members of the church have their sins forgiven—practically to be free of known sin—to be qualified to approach the Lord's table. The intent is to heed Paul's injunction to believers to examine themselves so as not to come to the Lord's table unworthily and thereby eat and drink damnation upon themselves (1 Cor. 11:27-32). (The church in which I grew up did not have a preparatory service; that service suggests to me that members of the church are presumed guilty until they declare themselves innocent.)

There is a sense in which the order of preparatory service followed by the Lord's Supper has it backward. Instead of believers pulling themselves together to be worthy to appear at the Lord's table, may it not be that the Lord's table graces them to live worthy of their calling? Does it not engender love and openness, helping to create a community living in sacrifice, hope, holiness, service, love, and peace? A Christian's appearance at the Lord's table ought not to be considered a sign of a special sanctity at that particular hour or during that particular week. Instead, it is a sign of regular, ongoing, normal Christian life.

I have no interest in disputing Paul about Christians examining themselves in the context of the Lord's table. But isn't it equally important for us to be open to examining each other? We should not assume that sin is adequately dealt with in a private, subjective fashion. If there are strained relationships or offenses between me and another member of the congregation, those are not resolved in the seclusion of my heart but only by actually getting in touch with my fellow believer to restore the relationship. Isn't this what the Lord's table is, the context in which healing can occur?

The church must be careful about using the Lord's Supper as an instrument of church discipline, as the preparatory service implies. The preparatory service is connected with the threat of withholding communion. There should be church discipline, but not at the expense of coloring the supper with punitive connotations. The Lord's Supper should not lose its value as an instrument to grace believers with the power of love and the joy of the kingdom.

Recovering Historic Meanings, Reforming Patterns

The Messianic Feast

"This is the most neglected aspect of the church's celebration of communion."[31] All too few Lord's Supper observances look like anticipations of the messianic feast, and this assessment applies to believers churches as much as to other churches.[32] Numerous writers remind us that the Lord's Supper is not just a remembrance of the *Last* Supper, even if the Last Supper instituted it. There was a resurrection, after which Christ met with disciples at Emmaus and by the Sea of Galilee. As Peter says, "God raised [Jesus] on the third day and allowed him to appear, not to all the people but to us who where chosen by God as witnesses, who ate and drank with him after he rose from the dead" (Acts 10:40-41).[33]

The present meaningfulness of the Lord's Supper may seem diminished because it seems stranded between the historic Christ event of the past and the yet unrealized future life of the kingdom. The apostle says we "do this in remembrance" of Christ "until he comes." But how can we make something come alive in the present that seems part of a receding past or a still-unreached future?

Our present life in the church is a foretaste of the life of the kingdom. We already experience some of its joys, triumphs, and blessings. Communion celebrations are thus not merely marking time between those momentous events of the time of Jesus and his second advent. Shouldn't our communions show it then?[34] Let us not be "dispensationalist" in our Lord's Supper observance, as though the kingdom is postponed, still totally future. If many of the present celebrations of the Lord's Supper that we see are supposed to be samples of the kingdom, let us not be surprised if some people hesitate over whether they want it.

Do our somber and introspective "celebrations" reflect what we *really* believe and where we *really* live? Do they show that our lives have caught all too little of the life of the coming kingdom? If one of the essential meanings of the Lord's Supper is anticipation of the messianic feast, we need to revamp our style to let our celebrations reflect it.

Communion, Koinōnia

Most theologians on the subject say the fellowship of believers in the community of faith is one of the essential meanings of the Lord's Supper. If this is true, we have come to the point where our believers churches potentially possess their greatest strength and could make their most important contribution.[35] Whatever else it may be said to mean, at its heart the Lord's Supper speaks the universal language of table fellowship. When we invite someone for supper in our homes, we are telling them—and anyone else who cares to notice—that we are friends. The act of eating together intends to reinforce and deepen and perpetuate that friendship. If we are not friends, the invitation to supper likely is intended to initiate a friendship, perhaps to overcome an estrangement.

To sit down to the Lord's Supper is to confess to one another—and to the world—that we are brothers and sisters in *Christ*. The act of eating together deepens and strengthens that covenant bond.[36] If there are strains upon our fellowship, the supper provides the means to overcome estrangements, to restore fellowship.

Let us recall what it means to say that the Lord's Supper is a sacrament in the sense of "a sign and the thing signified." In the act of signifying that we live in fellowship, we should already be unabashedly enjoying the fellowship we are signifying. On this definition, we can ask whether communion-rail forms of celebration do not fail to fulfill this sign. We can also ask whether patterns of celebration in most of our churches—sitting in benches and incommunicado—fail to fulfill this sign.[37]

We have so abbreviated the Lord's Supper and removed it from any natural location (such as the space rightly called the "fellowship hall") to the improbable space of a church sanctuary. As a consequence, we have tended to lose sight of its most basic meaning of table fellowship.[38] Under any other circumstances, we would chide someone who carried a cup of coffee and sweet rolls into the church sanctuary: "Don't bring food in here." But then we turn right around and bring "food" in there for the "Lord's Supper." The incongruity does not, however, usually get noticed, because we don't think of the Lord's Supper as *food,* and we think even less of that ritual as *fellowship* over food.[39]

If we did with the sermon what we have done with the Lord's Supper, what would that look like? Imagine the minister offering a three-sentence outline of the sermon, or only a thirty-second introduction. Now, some people might welcome such an abbreviation of the sermon (!), but think what an impoverishment that would mean for the teaching ministry of the church.

That is how our communion has been impoverished by our abbreviation of the meal itself and by our perpetuation of the Constantinian pattern of observing this rite in the awkward setting of the sanctuary. In addition, we have the audacity to say we have communion while we sit in silence with our backs to each other.[40]

Thus the supper is abbreviated from a full agape meal to token eating,[41] what one might call the "crumb and drop" form of communion. About this change, one may ask what Martin Marty does about the declining quantity of water at baptism.

> The baptismal river became a pool, the pool a . . . cistern, the cistern a . . . barrel, the barrel a font, the font a . . . finger bowl. If the trend continues, . . . shall we soon be experiencing the waters, the Flood, the Red Sea, the Jordan, the water of life in the minuscule antisepsis of an aerator, an atomizer, or a humidifier?[42]

Individualism and lack of community are recognized as among the biggest problems in contemporary society. Why do we reinforce them in a Lord's Supper pattern that is a private and subjective experience, in which people can come and go without saying a word to each other?[43] We already live in an eat-and-run culture. Some families no longer sit down at meals to cultivate family identity, caring, and loyalty. A sit-down Lord's Supper has the chance of making an impact upon such a culture.[44]

As believers churches, we are biblicist, and some of us are restorationist. Hence, we speak of the Lord's Supper or Lord's table and communion (1 Cor. 11). We have communion *tables*, not altars. But do we sit down to a table? Do we actually partake of a supper? Do we commune in the most basic meaning of that term—"to make known, impart; exchange thoughts and feelings" (*American Heritage Dictionary*).

High-church theologians love to talk about "real presence" in the eucharist. Shouldn't we start talking about a "real supper," a "real table," "real eating" ("real food for real people")? Then maybe we could experience "real communion," in which members of our congregations have an opportunity to make known to each other their joys and pains. They could offer counsel and support, and build up the body of Christ.

D. B. Gibson, a Church of the Brethren writer of a past generation, argues in a logic that should register with all biblicists and even more with immersionists: If *baptizō* means to immerse, it is even more indisputable that *deipnon* means a full meal, and in particular a supper.[45]

One of the noteworthy developments in recent American Christianity is the appearance of the church fellowship hall. Believers churches will need to admit that they have not taken the lead in this development. The now almost ubiquitous fellowship hall of the standard Protestant church in the U.S. and Canada indicates rather clearly the felt need of Christians for some expressions of fellowship and communion beyond the time spent in the sanctuary. This fellowship commonly includes food. Witness the modern and well-equipped kitchens beside most church fellowship rooms today.

I would like to test the straightforward suggestion that we seriously consider returning to the agape meal, that is, the full meal form of communion. Not a few voices are calling for this today.[46] I know that this suggestion will run into serious opposition in many quarters. This is so not only because of inertia and stubbornness in congregations.

This is also so because of a general impression among us, as in other Protestant churches, that somehow *our* particular tradition finished the work of the Reformation; *we* removed *all* unbiblical accretions of church history and restored our church to pristine Christianity. We stoutly resist the suggestion that there may be some points on which the Reformation never did get completed.

My claim is that a candid review of the story of the Lord's Supper shows that, for whatever reason, *on this matter the believers church movement, with the exception of our Brethren friends, did not return the church to New Testament patterns.* We need to continue the Reformation. Our restorationist convictions should make us, especially us believers church people, open to the idea of respecting the model of the New Testament, when that model is explained and called for.[47]

To return to an agape form of the Lord's Supper does not surrender the meanings invested in this rite in historic Christianity. But *not* to return to the agape meal continues to obscure the aspect of fellowship.

While some believers may resist my suggestion for reform—and we should be aware of its risks—I nevertheless urge it. I am convinced that it reflects a legitimate impulse, a conviction that *ecclēsia* means not a building but people. Church people need to find the time and setting to celebrate the life of the kingdom, to be informed about each other, to offer support, to bear one another's burdens, and even to cultivate the necessary acquaintance to make authentic congregational life happen.

There should be enough freedom in our believers church denominations for congregations who wish to return to an agape form of communion to do so without precipitating splits. If majorities in congregations are unwilling to move in this direction, there should be freedom for subgroups to do so, provided things are done decently and in order.

If someone pleads that congregational size is a problem, let us notice that size is not usually an insuperable obstacle to carry-in dinners of various kinds. Indeed, many megachurches have quite efficient and modern dining facilities. If size is really a problem, then it is a problem for authentic congregational life in other respects as well. Also, if large size is a hindrance to authentic communion, then are megachurches a nonnegotiable form of church life which we will not surrender as a price for true communion?

Some may be concerned about the church's fellowship hall activities degenerating into mere socializing. But bringing the Lord's Supper into the fellowship room of the church is one of the best ways to sanctify that space and to remind ourselves that it is as *Christ's body* that we function in that space. Thus, as noted, something of the spirit and meaning of the Lord's Supper should carry over into *every* meal that Christians eat together. Let them always be conscious of living everywhere under the lordship of Christ.

If some object that this will demean the sanctity of the Lord's Supper or decrease reverence, then Jesus and the apostles are the first ones to be instructed about that danger.[48] If others object that this will open the door again to the abuses Paul dealt with in 1 Corinthians 11, then let us ask our Brethren friends if that has been their experience. Whenever abuse appears at the table, it should be corrected— not "solved" by being relegated to the tavern or Holiday Inn or the nightclub. We have dichotomized life and worship: out of concern for "reverence" and solemnity at the Lord's table, we have sacrificed fellowship, only to seek such fellowship elsewhere, sometimes in places where we sacrifice sanctity. If our church people claim they are not guilty of gluttony or alcohol abuse at those places, then that shows that fear of abuse at the Lord's table is a bogus issue.[49]

This conference has met at an auspicious place to consider this topic. The Brethren tradition is one of the few that has had the insight and courage to seek to restore the apostolic, New Testament church form of celebration of the Lord's Supper.[50] If we venture to follow their lead in this, we do it not out of some merely formal reason to imitate apostolic Christianity, as though imitation were a virtue in itself. Instead, let us see that sanctified *koinōnia* around the table is inherently the Christian way, the way consonant with the believers church vision. If we are truly believers churches, we will want to eat together. If we eat together, we will be helped to deepen and perpetuate a believers church quality of congregational life in which we incarnate the love, righteousness, joy, peace, hope, freedom, and power which God intends for us.

DENOMINATIONAL PERSPECTIVES ON THE LORD'S SUPPER

৶ 8 ৾

Brethren Heritage
of the Lord's Supper:
Introduction

Dale R. Stoffer

A tradition that adds a unique facet to the varied communion practices among believers churches is the Brethren or German Baptist Brethren tradition. The five main Brethren groups, the Church of the Brethren, the Old German Baptist Brethren, the Brethren Church, the Dunkard Brethren, and the Fellowship of Grace Brethren Churches, all have a common origin in early-eighteenth-century Germany. The Brethren derived most of their thought and practice from the Pietist and Anabaptist movements.

All five Brethren groups continue to practice a form of communion that can be traced back to the earliest documents of the movement, the writings of the foremost leader among the Brethren, Alexander Mack Sr. The form, sometimes called threefold communion, combines feetwashing, the love feast, and the bread and cup. In the papers that follow, each of these parts of the Brethren communion service is examined separately to explore their biblical, theological, and historical significance. In this introductory presentation, I briefly explain why the early Brethren joined these three practices into one service and clarify the interpersonal dynamic that all three practices share.

Certain terminology has been used by the Brethren to refer to the communion service in its totality and in its separate parts. Initially, if Alexander Mack's writings can serve as a gauge, Brethren of the eighteenth century referred to the total service as the *Lord's Supper*, borrowing the term that was generally used by other groups of the time to refer to the eucharist. The term could also be used more narrowly to refer to the meal; the word *communion* was reserved for the bread and cup.[1] Certainly by the mid eighteenth century, however, the term *love feast* also began to be used interchangeably with Lord's Supper for the entire service. Again, both terms could also be used to refer strictly to the meal.[2]

During the nineteenth century, reflecting the competitive and contentious mood among American denominations, the Brethren became dogmatic that the term *Lord's Supper* referred to the meal alone and that the word *communion* should refer only to the bread and wine.[3] During that century, the term *love feast* came into vogue for the total service of feetwashing, Lord's Supper, and bread and cup, even though love feast, using Dunker or Brethren logic, should also have been reserved for the meal alone.

The twentieth century brought some Brethren groups into a more cooperative relationship with the larger American church. This development led more progressive Brethren groups to refer to the total service with terms common in the broader church: Lord's Supper and communion. When these Brethren want to emphasize their distinctive approach to this ordinance, they sometimes call it threefold communion. However, among conservative Brethren groups, love feast is still the preferred designation for the total service. Progressive Brethren will at times also use the technical terms *agape* and *eucharist* to refer to the love feast and bread and cup respectively.[4]

The Brethren were by no means the only group in the early eighteenth century which practiced feetwashing or even which observed a love feast. Certain Mennonite groups already had a long history of practicing feetwashing, though not necessarily in connection with communion; and the Moravians and Methodists observed the love feast, though the Moravians practiced it separate from communion. What made the Brethren unique was their observance of both feetwashing and love feast in conjunction with the eucharist. What led the Brethren to such a practice?

The answer to this question is found, in large measure, in their approach to Scripture. The Brethren, following the Mennonites, were committed to complete obedience to all Christ's commands and examples. In this, the early Brethren were quite scrupulous. They went beyond the Mennonites in insisting, for example, not only on adult baptism, but adult baptism by immersion; likewise, they went beyond Mennonites in maintaining that feetwashing and the love feast were ordinances that should be observed with communion.

Why? The Brethren found that, according to all the synoptic Gospels, the bread and cup were shared in the context of a meal; and in John's Gospel, Jesus washed the disciples' feet in conjunction with the same meal. In addition, Jesus explicitly stated regarding feetwashing in John 13:15 that he had given "an example that you should do as I have done for you." That alone would have sealed the issue for the biblicist Brethren.

However, there are several other intriguing pieces of this puzzle that should be set in place. One of the hermeneutical principles that guided the Brethren was a harmonizing approach to Scripture which sought to give due consideration to all the biblical data.[5] Alexander Mack Jr., after describing how the early Brethren harmonized the Synoptic and Johannine accounts of the Last Supper, states this hermeneutical principle: "All of which [process] evolves into a glorious harmony for a believing soul and gives testimony at the same time of how the Holy Spirit has avoided in [the writings of] the holy evangelists all unnecessary repetition of words."[6]

The Brethren, reflecting both Anabaptist and Pietist influence, also gave great weight to the example of the early church up through the third century and to those "witnesses of the truth" who had been faithful to the apostolic faith following the fall associated with the Constantinian church.[7] The Brethren found from Radical Pietist historical sources that the early church had practiced the love feast with communion. They read in both Mennonite and Radical Pietist sources that such "witnesses of the truth" as the Anabaptists had practiced feetwashing and even, according to one account, the love feast with communion. This information only reinforced what they found in the scriptural record.

The weight of these biblical and historical sources of authority led the Brethren to the conviction that they should observe feetwashing, love feast, and communion in conjunction if they were to be fully obedient to Christ's teaching and example.

These three parts of the service have a distinctive interpersonal dynamic. Within the Anabaptist, Pietist, and Brethren traditions, there is a strong conviction that the love relationship between God and the believer must evidence itself in love for one's brother, sister, and neighbor. This vertical (divine-human) and horizontal (believer-to-believer) dynamic is visibly reinforced by each of the three acts.

Feetwashing emphasizes the vertical message of the necessity of spiritual cleansing and the horizontal message of humble service to the community of faith. The love feast emphasizes the vertical message of Jesus' love for his disciples and the horizontal message of our love for one another. The eucharist emphasizes vertically Jesus' sacrificial death for us and horizontally our unity within the body of Christ. Thus, within the Brethren tradition, these three acts form one powerful reminder and proclamation of the central core of truths that have guided the Brethren faith from the beginning.

ஃ 9 ஃ

The Agape in the Brethren Tradition

Jeff Bach

The Schwarzenau Brethren arose in Germany in 1708 from the mingling of separatist radical Pietism and contact with Mennonites and Anabaptist writings. The Pietist influences which shaped them included Reformed and Lutheran Pietism and radical Pietism inspired by the thought of Jacob Böhme, transmitted through Hochmann von Hochenau.[1] Here I briefly deal with one practice of the Brethren, the love meal or agape, part of their observance of the Lord's Supper. I explain the grounding of this practice in the Brethren reading of Scripture, their restitutionist preference for primitive Christianity, and some of the changes and significance of the love meal during their history.

Biblical Background

The early Brethren realized that 1 Corinthians 11:17-34 describes a meal eaten together when bread is broken and a cup shared in remembrance of the Lord Jesus Christ. They believed that the New Testament could continue to shape the present community of believers. So the Brethren added a love meal to their Lord's Supper, as had the Christians of the New Testament community. Alexander Mack, the first Brethren leader, wrote in 1715,

> In the first place, it says in the Scriptures, a "supper" (1 Corinthians 11:20). The believers learned it that way, having learned it from Paul. . . . Paul, in turn, had himself received from the Lord Jesus that which he gave to the Corinthians (verse 23). They thus held an evening meal or supper.[2]

Although Jude 12 refers to "love feasts" (*agapais*, the only New Testament use of the term), the early Brethren did not cite it in their writings which survive.[3]

In the twentieth century, Hans Lietzmann shaped international scholarly opinions on the New Testament meal traditions. He identified two separate strands of tradition that he believed had been distinct from the beginning. One tradition was that of the communal fellowship meal, *koinōnia*, portrayed in the Gospels as the feeding miracles and in the meals of 1 Corinthians 11, Acts 2, Jude, and 2 Peter. The other strand represented the eucharist of the bread and cup, commemorating Jesus' death, a remembrance, *anamnēsis*, in the bread-and-cup passages of the Gospel accounts of the Last Supper, and in 1 Corinthians 11.[4]

Recently, some biblical interpreters have challenged Lietzmann's claim. Thus Michael Townsend has argued that the New Testament offers no evidence that two traditions were separate from the beginning. In his view, the communal meal was the setting in which the bread and cup were shared.[5] Interestingly, Graydon F. Snyder, writing on Corinthians from a "faith community perspective," continued Lietzmann's older interpretation,[6] which has since been questioned by some scholars of Magisterial Reformation traditions.

The attention of the early Brethren to the details of the New Testament community's meal traditions guided their reshaping of the Lord's Supper to include a love meal with the bread and cup.

Christian Antiquity

The first Brethren consisted of dissenters who had separated from the Lutheran or Reformed territorial churches of their native lands, the Palatinate, Switzerland, Hesse, and others. In addition to criticizing contemporary churches for no longer observing practices instituted by Christ according to the New Testament, the Brethren (and other separatist Pietists) maintained that the contemporary churches had fallen away from apostolic Christianity and had failed to preserve it against the ravages of time and enemies.

Gottfried Arnold (1666-1714) inverted the traditional telling of institutional Christian history with his *Unparteyische Kirchen- und Ketzer-Historie* (A Nonpartisan History of Churches and Heretics, 1699-1700). He did not adopt the customary picture of the church continually preserving correct doctrine and practice against the threat of heretics. Instead, Arnold portrayed a church corrupted by power since Constantine, destroying the marginalized faithful who attempted to call it to faithfulness. Arnold had laid the groundwork with an earlier book on primitive Christianity, *Die erste Liebe* (The First Love, 1696). This book was a response and correction to William Cave's *Primitive Christianity* (1673), translated into German as *Erstes Christentum* (1694).[7] While Cave championed the era of Augustine as the culmination of early Christianity, Arnold located the pristine era of the church's "first love" for its Lord in pre-Constantinian (and pre-Augustinian) Christianity.[8]

Arnold described the *Liebesmahl* (love feast) or agape among the practices of early Christianity. He quoted authors such as Tertullian and Hippolytus, explaining that the meal was an expression of loving fellowship and ministry to the hungry poor. Arnold concluded that the first Christians had observed the eucharist in the context of a communal meal.

From their first considerations of formation, the Brethren intended to include a love meal in the Lord's Supper. Hochmann von Hochenau, the radical separatist, responded to their query for advice in July 1708, that he was not opposed to holding "the Lord's love feast," as long as it was "based on the love of Jesus and the appropriate community of members." But he could not support the love feast as "an outward, legalistic work."[9]

Explaining how the Lord's Supper (*Abendmahl*, supper, evening meal) had been distorted, Alexander Mack criticized contemporary liturgical practice.

> When an evening or a noon meal is to be held, there must be something to eat! But here the people go to their so-called "supper" and return from it hungry and thirsty. Some do not even receive a bit of bread and others not a drop of wine.[10]

For the eighteenth-century Brethren, the love meal as liturgical practice expressed critique against what they perceived as the fallenness of the established churches. The Brethren love meal aimed at demonstrating a loving fellowship sharing material and spiritual support along with mutual discipline. The love meal contrasted especially with the Reformed eucharist, at which the unknown elect shared in the Lord's Supper with people known by their neighbors to violate teachings of the Heidelberg Catechism.

For the Brethren in Europe and to a certain extent in America, the love meal served a helpful social function. Most of them were impoverished by their flight from religious persecution. The love meals helped to share resources to feed the group. In America, after Brethren settled and became more prosperous, the love meals provided hospitality when they would gather from distances for the love feast.

The love meal also had eschatological significance. Indeed, Brethren restitutionism must be seen in light of their eschatological expectations. Arnold's *Kirchen- und Ketzer-Historie* appeared when he and many other Pietists expected the end of the age and the beginning of Christ's reign.[11] Thus the only fitting, faithful response, in the separatists' view, was to flee Babel (the established traditions), to flee the individualism of the separatists, and to join a group being restored to the purity and vigor of the first church of Jerusalem.[12] The Brethren believed they were constituting such a group.

Frequently the love meal was interpreted in light of the wedding feast of the Lamb in Revelation 19. On the title page of *Rights and Ordinances* (1715), Alexander Mack designated himself as "one also called to the Great Supper."[13] Believers must persevere during suffering "in true obedience of faith even to the cross so that they may partake of the great Supper with [the Lamb] at the end of the world."[14] In the eighteenth century, Brethren considered the agape to symbolize the coming kingdom of the conquering Lamb as much as loving fellowship in the community.

The eschatological interpretation of the agape continued into the following century. In the mid-nineteenth century, Peter Nead wrote that the meal is observed "to remind the believer of the marriage supper of the Lamb."[15] Nead and John Kline identified the love meal as the "Lord's Supper," not the bread and cup.[16]

After the first emigration to Pennsylvania in 1719, the Brethren were slow to reorganize. When they did on Christmas Day of 1723, the love feast concluded the baptisms of new members. M. G. Brumbaugh wrote an inspirational account of the first love feast in America, basically importing his perception of early twentieth-century practice back into the eighteenth century.[17] From the nineteenth to the early twentieth century, there was little change in the Brethren love meal.

Love Feast at Ephrata

The love feast formed a central part of the piety at Ephrata (Pa.), a development from the second Brethren congregation in America. Georg Conrad Beissel (1691-1768) was a Pietist separatist who sojourned among the Inspirationists in Wetteravia (1715-1720). After emigrating to Pennsylvania (1720), he was eventually baptized by Peter Becker (1724) into the Conestoga congregation of Brethren.

By 1728, Beissel was insisting on worship on the Sabbath and advocating celibacy. The congregation he led at Conestoga divided, and a communal society had its beginnings on the farm of Rudolf Nägele. The community consisted of former Mennonites and Brethren who followed Beissel. Before the group moved to the banks of the Cocalico, Johann Adam Gruber, the Inspirationist, wrote from Germantown in 1730 that "the men and the women daily observe spiritual exercises and the breaking of bread."[18]

After the group moved to what became the Ephrata Cloister, love feasts continued frequently. Love feasts could be hosted by an individual or family, or held for the entire community, including the married householders. In addition, the celibate orders held love feasts within their convent houses. The celibates interrupted their rigorous discipline of one vegetarian meal a day for the love feast, which added needed nutrition to their diets. Thus, in one sense, Ephrata celibates had a love-feast piety, reminiscent of the medieval tradition of mystics who fasted for long periods, taking for nutrition only the host at communion.

The eschatological meaning of the love meal as a foretaste of the wedding feast of the Lamb (Rev. 19) was especially pronounced at Ephrata. This was possible because they linked the Lamb's banquet (Rev. 19) to his appearance in Revelation 14, where his virgin followers on Mount Zion sing a song that only they can learn. Indeed, Ephrata's unique system of music theory and prolific composition of texts (and illustrations thereof) came as the fruition of their faith that, as virgin followers of the Lamb, they had received this "secret of our spiritual singing work."[19]

In the early years at Conestoga, love feasts occasioned special manifestations of spiritual power, "usually lasting till midnight, sometimes even till the dawn."[20] Typically, Beissel presided as celebrant at the love feasts and distributed the elements of the eucharist into the hands of each communicant.[21] At times, he "held love feasts with the female portion, no brethren participating, at which the sisters were his *diaconnae* (deacons) and officiated in all things."[22] Because Beissel reserved the role of officiant to himself, it is doubtful that sisters ever distributed the eucharistic elements. Their ministry of assisting at love feasts, however, would have been a unique role for women compared to European churches, and probably even in Pennsylvania.

Also at Ephrata, love feasts were held in memory of members

who had died. The Ephratans thus combined the ancient traditions of communal love meals and meals for the dead.

Further Historical Significance of the Love Meal

During the course of the nineteenth century, the Brethren struggled with pressures to sacralize the menu of the meal. Annual Meetings minutes record several queries whether only lamb should be served (1827, 1849, 1850, 1853-55, 1858, 1863) since some Brethren believed that the Last Supper was a Passover meal. A division occurred when the Christian Brethren of Ohio (Landisites, after the leader, Michael Landis) left the main body in 1835, in part over Landis's insistence that only lamb be served at the fellowship meal. Brethren leaders refused to identify the love meal as a Passover meal and have stressed love and unity rather than prescribing a menu.

Early in the nineteenth century, Brethren allowed open communion (Annual Meeting minutes, 1832, 1841), but communion was closed in 1849. Minutes from Annual Meetings in the early nineteenth century mention leftovers from the love meal being taken to the poor (1835, 1849, also 1915). It is unclear how long this practice persisted. If it occurs in the twentieth century, it is only in isolated instances. One other controversy was whether or not food should be on the table before feetwashing took place (Annual Meeting minutes, 1822, 1833, 1844, 1849, 1850, 1853-55, 1858, 1863).

In the twentieth century, the love meal has changed little except in local variations of what is served. The meal has been interpreted mostly as an expression of fellowship. Vernard Eller added a renewed emphasis on the covenantal character of the community in which the living Christ is embodied at the Lord's Supper.[23] Twentieth-century Brethren make little or no appeal to the example of early Christianity or to an eschatological interpretation of the agape.[24] In the last quarter of the twentieth century, the love meal, indeed the whole love feast, has sometimes been interpreted as a part of Brethren heritage, but not the longer Christian tradition.

The full love feast was the only format for the Lord's Supper for the Church of the Brethren until 1958. At that time, Annual Conference authorized open communion and the observance of bread-and-cup communion during Sunday morning worship in addition to the full love feast.

Most Church of the Brethren congregations still have a love feast at least once a year, many twice. However, during the twentieth century, attendance at love feasts has generally declined, and the morning bread-and-cup communions have found an increasingly secure place. The more progressive Brethren groups (Brethren Church, Grace Brethren) have continued to practice the love feast, though some individual congregations have begun to observe the bread and cup separate from the love feast. The more conservative Brethren groups (Dunkard Brethren, Old German Baptist Brethren) practice love feast as the only form for celebrating the Lord's Supper.[25]

For believers churches, the love meal might once again find broader practice. The witnesses of the New Testament and of earliest Christianity indicate that the bread and cup were shared in the context of a communal meal. Although a biblicist or primitivist argument may no longer appear sustainable, the believers church tradition has challenged the progressivist idealism of magisterial Christianity that developments along the course of time are to be expected and accepted. While so-called New Testament churches are often accused of being ahistorical, of attempting an end run around history, assuming they can recreate a long-gone past, there is an ahistorical element to arguments which dismiss New Testament and early Christian practices. Such debaters assume that the past story of the faith need not have formative influence on the present. They are frequently unable to account for changes in tradition except by assigning a "that was then, this is now" irrelevance to the past.

Eating together remains an important social act in the late twentieth century, as it was in the first. If Christianity makes a body of people sharing filial love out of strangers (as 1 Corinthians argues), then face-to-face table fellowship is an important way to express that character of covenanted communal love. In North America, families spend less time eating together. For such, the love meal can offer a critique of the fragmented alienation of culture and an experience of good news: Christians are becoming a spiritual family that takes time to eat together.

Some might resist combining such meals with the eucharist, pointing to fellowship meals at other times in congregations to fill this need. However, Christian fellowship is grounded in the love Jesus Christ expressed most supremely in surrendering life on the cross. Thus the context of the bread and cup in memory of Christ's death and resurrection may be precisely the time to eat together in fellowship.

Two further suggestions might make the agape more a practice for the present. First, members of the congregation might bring the food for the agape, as is done among Nigerian Brethren. This could increase shared ownership in the meal. Second, congregations might once again use the surplus to feed the poor. At best, members would take the food personally to those in need. At the crassest level of efficiency, leftovers could be donated to soup kitchens or homeless shelters.

Perhaps the current decline in mainline Protestantism may present a unique moment to give a more lively role for the agape in the believers churches.

ᷤ 10 ᷧ

Footwashing Within the Context
of the Lord's Supper

John Christopher Thomas

It is an extraordinary honor for me to be invited to expound on footwashing, not only because others may be better prepared for such an assignment, but also because I am to represent a church tradition not my own. For such a distinctive privilege, I express my thanks.

It is dangerous to invite someone to offer a short presentation on a subject to which one's Ph.D. thesis was devoted. Faced with this dilemma, I have pondered what might be the best way to proceed. Since the bulk of my more academic work on this topic is readily available in print,[1] I do not feel pressed to cram all of that material into this section devoted to the Brethren heritage of the Lord's Supper. But I still am under the pressure of trying to convey an understanding of the justification of a practice not part of the tradition of many readers. Given the assigned purpose and space, I have decided to concentrate on three questions: (1) What is the theological justification for the practice of footwashing? (2) What does footwashing mean? (3) What is the relationship of footwashing to the Lord's Supper?

Theological Justification
for the Practice of Footwashing

The primary theological justification for the practice of footwashing is grounded in the explicit nature of the commands Jesus gives to his disciples to wash one another's feet in John 13:14-17.

> If, therefore, I your Lord and Teacher have washed your feet,
> you also ought to (must) wash one another's feet. For I have given

you an example in order that you should do just as I have done. Truly, truly I say to you, no servant is greater than his Lord, neither is a sent one (apostle) greater than the one who sends. If you know these things, blessed are you if you do them.

(Scripture in this essay is translated by the author)

Not all readers of John 13:14-17 interpret these verses as calling for a literal fulfillment of the commands. But those communities of faith which observe this rite are convinced of the mandatory nature of Jesus' words. Although in some communities this interpretation has resulted simply from a surface reading of the text, there is additional evidence which indicates that John 13:14-17 was intended to result in the actual practice of footwashing as a religious rite.

A hermeneutical gap exists between twentieth-century readers and their ancient counterparts. Yet it is possible to narrow that gap somewhat by examining attitudes toward footwashing and its practice in Greco-Roman and Jewish antiquity. When this evidence is examined, it becomes clear that footwashing was a remarkably widespread practice in the ancient world and functioned in a variety of ways: as a sign of hospitality, for the purpose of comfort and hygiene, as a sign of servitude, and as a religious or cultic cleansing. In other words, footwashing was a part of everyday life. As such, in antiquity footwashing came to be regarded as a sign of preparation. It was so commonplace that to approach a task without adequate preparation could be described in a traditional saying as acting "with unwashed feet."

Descriptions of footwashing most frequently occurred in banquet settings or before a meal of some type. A host would provide water, in some cases spiced wine or ointments (if the home were an affluent one and the guest was deserving of special honor), for the guests to remove from their feet the dirt which had accumulated on their journey. Such a practice was commonplace and appears to be presumed. Most texts place the washing at the time the guests arrive.

When the commands of John 13:14-17 are read against the cultural context of Western antiquity, it seems probable that the first readers (members of the Johannine community) would have taken verses 14-17 as calling for compliance on their part. Given the extensive practice of footwashing in antiquity, it is reasonable to assume that the readers of the Fourth Gospel would have been familiar with footwashing of one kind or another through actual participation. These first readers were in a different position than modern Western readers, who, due to their unfamiliarity with the practice of footwashing, seem unable to take seriously that a literal fulfillment of the command is in view. The first readers' familiarity with the practice in general makes it likely that, after reading John 13:14-17, they would be inclined to carry out its literal fulfillment.

In addition to the evidence from Western antiquity, the most natural reading of the text of John 13:14-17 is one that calls for a literal fulfillment of the commands. In 13:14, "therefore (*oun*)" serves to make clear the connection between Jesus' own actions in 13:4-12 and the following commands. In the light of his actions, the disciples are instructed to wash one another's feet. The emphasis of his instruction is borne out by the appearance of "also (*kai*)" and the emphatic use of the personal pronoun, "you (*humeis*)." The verb in this verse, often translated as "ought (*opheilō*)," further highlights the nature of the act. Rather than a suggestion, this verb carries with it the idea of necessity and/or obligation.

The force of this *ought* can be seen from elsewhere in the Johannine literature. According to John 19:7, in an attempt to convince Pilate that Jesus should be crucified, the Jews say, "We have (the) Law, and according to the Law he must (*opheilei*) die." In the epistles, the same verb is used to describe the mandatory nature of moral conduct. Thus 1 John 2:6, "The one who claims to remain in him *ought* himself to walk just as that one walked." Likewise, it is used to command Christian service to other brothers and sisters. Thus 1 John 3:16, "In this we have known love, because that one laid down his life for us; we also *ought* to lay down our lives for the brothers." First John 4:11, "Beloved, if God so loved us, we also *ought* to love one another." Third John 8, "Therefore, we *ought* to receive such ones as these, in order that we might be fellow-workers in the truth."

The only other time Jesus uses the term *ought* (*opheilō*) in the Gospels is also in a context of mandatory service, that of a slave to a master (Luke 17:10). Normally, in the other New Testament uses of this verb, the nuance is that of

> an obligation towards men which is deduced and which follows from the experienced or preceding act of God the Saviour. In many instances the sentence construction indicates the connection between human obligation and the experienced act of salvation.[2]

Here, the disciples' directive to service is based upon the salvific action of the Lord and Master, for "now that Jesus, their Lord and

Teacher, has washed his disciples' feet—an unthinkable act!—there is every reason why they also should wash one another's feet, and no conceivable reason for refusing to do so."[3] The disciples have received cleansing at the hands of Jesus. Now, they are instructed to preserve this practice. The stress of this verse lies upon washing one another's feet. Because of the connection of these verses with John 13:6-10, there is the implicit and contextual directive that the disciples receive this service-sign (from one another) as well as render it.

The force of Jesus' command for the disciples to practice footwashing among themselves in John 13:14 is strengthened by referring to the footwashing as an example (*hupodeigma*) in verse 15. While a general call to humble service cannot be ruled out altogether, there are three reasons to think that the readers would see in *hupodeigma* a reinforcement of the direct command to wash one another's feet.

The first consideration is the context of the verse. In John 13:14, it has been clearly stated that the disciples are to wash one another's feet. Following so closely upon this explicit command, it is likely that *hupodeigma* would be taken in a specific fashion. Second, this is the first (and only) *hupodeigma* given by Jesus, which the readers encounter in the Fourth Gospel.[4] Third, the combination of "just as . . . also" (*kathōs . . . kai*) emphasizes the intimate connection between Jesus' action (washing the disciples' feet) and the action of his disciples (washing one another's feet).[5] They are to act precisely as he acted. The instructions to wash one another's feet are rooted and grounded in the actions of Jesus in 13:4-10. Therefore, the footwashing is far more than an example. "It is a definite prototype."[6] In all probability, the readers, as well as the disciples in the narrative, would take *hupodeigma* with reference to footwashing in particular, not humble service generally.

In John 13:16, there is another appeal to the person and status of Jesus as the basis of the command to wash one another's feet. This time it comes in the form of a saying that also appears in a synoptic context (Matt. 10:24). The authority of the statement is understood by the double amen (*amēn*) which precedes the rest of the saying. The *amēn amēn* formula denotes a particularly solemn saying which issues forth from Jesus' own authority. As Schlier concludes:

> The point of the *Amen* before Jesus' own sayings is: to show that as such they are reliable and true, and that they are so as and because Jesus Himself in His Amen acknowledges them to be His own sayings and thus makes them valid.[7]

Having already identified himself as Teacher and Lord (John 13:12-13), Jesus here expands upon the implication of his lordship. Since as Lord he has washed the feet of his disciples, they have no choice but to take similar action, on account of their own position as slaves in relation to Jesus. Their own status and consequent actions cannot hope to be on a higher level than that of their superior. That the Gospel is describing identical action between Jesus and the disciples is borne out by the use of this saying in John 15:20, where the world's hatred for Jesus and the disciples is said to be the same. Another maxim-like saying underscores the point. "No one who is sent is greater than the one who sends him." Again, the clear emphasis is upon the authority of Jesus' actions in relation to the similar activity of the disciples. This interpretation of the master-slave language, which agrees perfectly with the context, is much to be preferred over reading *service* back into 13:15 and thereby making it simply an ethical example. In any event, the full authority of Jesus is given to the injunction to wash one another's feet.

In John 13:17 a final exhortation is given to ensure that the disciples might not fail to carry out the footwashing among themselves. This time the command takes the form of a blessing. It is not enough for the disciples to know what to do; they must actually do it in order to be considered blessed. The grammar of this verse bears out that the disciples possess some knowledge of the footwashing, now that Jesus has given this explanation, but must follow through with action. This contrast is accomplished by the use of a first-class conditional clause, which indicates a future possibility.

The use of the term blessed (*makarioi*) in this context clearly underscores the importance of acting out Jesus' commands to wash one another's feet. Such emphasis is similar to that of John 13:8, where Peter is warned that his solidarity (*meros*) with Jesus is dependent upon reception of the footwashing. Therefore, not only have the disciples received footwashing from Jesus as a sign of continued fellowship with him; they now are also instructed to continue this practice. In light of its earlier meaning, it is likely that the footwashing to be practiced by the disciples would convey a similar significance—continued fellowship with Jesus. Obedience to Jesus' commands to wash one another's feet results in a declaration of *makarioi*.

In sum, the narrative contains not one, but three directives for the disciples to practice footwashing. It seems improbable that either the disciples (in the narrative) or the readers implied by the text would understand such emphatic language as not having primary reference to the actual practice of footwashing. Consider this as a question: If the Johannine Jesus had intended to institute footwashing as a continuing religious rite, how else could he have said it to get his point across? When compared with the words of institution associated with water baptism and the Lord's Supper in the New Testament, the commands to wash feet appear to be the most emphatic of the three.

But support for taking John 13:14-17 as calling for a literal fulfillment is not limited to the evidence from Western antiquity and our own reading of the text of the Fourth Gospel. This interpretation may be tested by how actual readers in the early church understood these commands. A number of early Christian texts give evidence of the regularity with which a reading of John 13:14-17 resulted in the practice of footwashing. In these cases, the relationship of the practice to John 13 is explicit. Such evidence comes from Tertullian (*De corona* 8), the Canons of Athanasius (66), John Chrysostom (*Homilies on John* 71), Ambrose (*Of the Holy Spirit* 1.15), Augustine (*John: Tractate* 58.4), the *Apostolic Constitutions* (3.19), John Cassian (*Institute of Coenobia* 4.19), Pachomius (*Rules* 51-52), and Caesarius of Arles (*Sermon* 202 and 86).

In addition to these texts, others indicate that Christian footwashing was observed in a variety of contexts in the early church. Such evidence comes from 1 Timothy 5:10, Tertullian (*To His Wife* 2.4), Origen (*Genesis Homily* 4.2), Cyprian (*Epistles* 5; *Treatises* 11.3; "Testimonies" 39), the Synod of Elvira (Canon 48), Ambrose (*Sacraments* 3.4, 7), Augustine (*Letter* 55.33), Sozomen (*Ecclesiastical History* 1.11.10), John Chrysostom (*Genesis Homily* 46), Caesarius of Arles (*Sermon* 1, 10, 16, 19, 25, 67, 104, 146), and Benedict of Nursia (*Regula monachorum* 35).

When the Fourth Gospel is taken as the starting point, there is every reason to believe that footwashing was practiced as a religious rite in the Johannine community. A careful reading of the text reveals that the implied readers would have understood John 13:14-17 as calling for a literal fulfillment. In addition, the cultural environment of Western antiquity demonstrates that readers of the Fourth Gospel would have been predisposed to practice footwashing as a result of reading John 13:1-20. The evidence from early Christianity shows that a number of people read the text in just such a fashion. The geographical distribution of the evidence is impressive, in that it comes from North Africa (Tertullian), Egypt-Palestine (Origen), Asia Minor (1 Timothy, John Chrysostom), Italy (Ambrose, Augustine), and Gaul (Caesarius). The diverse contexts in which the commands were fulfilled are also noteworthy; they range from congregation to monastery to the home. Enough examples have been given to show that the implications of the reading of the John 13:1-20 were somewhat consistent and that the practice of footwashing was widespread.

The evidence for the practice of footwashing based on John 13 is of sufficient strength to conclude that in all likelihood, the Johannine community engaged in religious footwashing as the direct result of John 13:1-20 (or the tradition that lies behind it). Indeed, those within footwashing communities would want to argue that instead of interpreters needing to demonstrate the probability of the practice in the Johannine community, the burden of proof is on those who would deny such a probability.

The Meaning of Footwashing

Since there is sufficient reason to believe that Jesus, as depicted in John 13, desired that footwashing be practiced, what was the intended meaning of this act? Several aspects of the text point in the direction of an answer.

Footwashing and the Passion of Jesus

A variety of indicators in the text demonstrate that a close tie exists between the passion of Jesus and the footwashing. First, the reader is prepared for this connection in John 12:1-8, where Mary's anointing of Jesus' feet is said to be a preparation for his burial. Second, the location of the footwashing within the farewell materials (John 13-17) indicates that the footwashing, along with the rest of the materials, was intended to prepare the disciples for Jesus' departure. Third, the tie to the passion is made explicit in 13:1, which serves as the introduction to the entire Book of Glory (John 13-21), where the reader learns that Jesus' hour has come. Fourth, the statement that Jesus loved his own *"eis telos* (to the end)" at least suggests to the reader that Jesus' "end" is near. Fifth, the appearance of Judas in 13:2 ominously foreshadows the betrayal of Jesus. As Raymond Brown notes,

> The betrayal is mentioned in [verse] 2 precisely so that the reader will connect the footwashing and the death of Jesus. Jesus undertook this action symbolic of his death only after the forces had been set in motion that would lead to crucifixion.[8]

Mention of the betrayer will also be made in John 13:11. Sixth, in 13:3 the return of Jesus to the Father is mentioned again. Seventh, more than one commentator has seen a reference to the death of Jesus when in 13:4 he is described as laying aside (*tithēsin*) his clothing, since this term (*tithēmi*) has reference to Jesus' death in over half its Johannine occurrences. Additionally, the mention of Jesus disrobing foreshadows in the footwashing the humiliation connected with laying down his life. The stark reality of nakedness presents a clear reference to the crucifixion. As P. G. Ahr concludes,

> The reference to the crucifixion is ever more clearly present in the statement about Jesus' nakedness: anyone familiar with the story of Jesus' death can grasp the reference to the removal of clothes, and, indeed, it is the very unexpectedness of this statement which points the reader to this reference.[9]

"All of this serves to relate the footwashing to the death of the Lord."[10]

The Unusual Nature of this Footwashing

The reader learns in John 13 that this is no ordinary footwashing. The first indication that there is more to this footwashing than meets the eye is the fact that it is chronologically out of place. When footwashing occurs in the context of a meal, it precedes the meal, most often occurring at the door of the host. However, the footwashing which Jesus provides for the disciples is interrupting the meal rather than preceding it.[11] The Evangelist underscores the importance of the footwashing by its unusual placement.

Another indication that this footwashing is unusual is the highly deliberative way in which Jesus' actions are described. Instead of simply saying that Jesus washed the feet of the disciples, John methodically underscores the significance of Jesus' actions by specifically mentioning each element of the procedure.

In John 13:7, Jesus himself indicates that this footwashing is no ordinary one when he informs Peter that he will not understand the significance of this action until "after these things (*meta tauta*)." Just as the disciples are unable to comprehend other events in the Fourth Gospel fully until after the resurrection (John 2:22; 12:16), so Peter (and the other disciples with him) are unable to understand the full significance of the footwashing until after the resurrection.

Responding to Peter's emphatic refusal of the footwashing, Jesus informs Peter that this act is not optional and that its significance is far-reaching: "If I do not wash you, you have no *meros* (part) with me" (John 13:8). One of the first things the reader would see in *meros* with Jesus would, no doubt, be a share in eternal life. The prologue promised such to those who believe (1:12), and it has also been stated that Jesus bestows eternal life upon those who are placed in his hands (cf. 3:35-36; 6:40; 10:28-29). The immediate referent is found in 13:3, where the reader is reminded of Jesus' knowledge that all things were placed in his hands by the Father.

This interpretation is supported by the many New Testament texts where *meros* appears in contexts which deal with issues of eternal life and/or punishment (cf. Matt. 24:51; Rev. 20:6; 21:8; 22:19). Therefore it seems safe to assume that one idea which having *meros* with Jesus conveys in John 13:8 is eternal life. Yet, this understanding does not exhaust the significance of *meros*. The closest structural parallels to this verse suggest that to share a person's *meros* is to share that one's identity or destiny: Matthew 24:51, Ignatius' *Epistle to Polycarp* 6:1, and the *Martyrdom of Polycarp* 14:2. Matthew 24:51 describes the unfaithful servant as being assigned "a place with the hypocrites (*kai to meros autou meta tōn hupokritōn*), where there will be weeping and gnashing of teeth" (par. Luke 12:46). In affirming the legitimacy of ecclesiastical offices, Ignatius (*Letter to Polycarp* 6) claims,

> Give heed to the bishop, that God may also give heed to you. I am devoted to those who are subject to the bishop, presbyters, and deacons; and may it be mine to have my lot with them in God (*kai met' autōn moi to meros genoito schein en theō*). Labour with one another, struggle together, run together, suffer together, rest together, rise up together as God's stewards and assessors and servants.[12]

As part of his last prayer, Polycarp (*Martyrdom of Polycarp* 14.2) gives thanks:

> I bless thee, that Thou has granted me this day and hour, that I may share, among the number of the martyrs (*tou labein me meros en arithmō tōn marturōn*) in the cup of thy Christ, for the Resurrection to everlasting life, both of soul and body in the immortality of the Holy Spirit.[13]

If anyone has cast their lot with Jesus in the Fourth Gospel, it is the disciples. To have a share in his destiny includes not only eternal life, but also being sent as Jesus himself was sent (4:31-38; 20:21-23), resurrection at the last day (6:40), and the hatred of the world (15:18-16:4). Simply put, it appears that *meros* here denotes continued fellowship with Jesus,[14] and a place in his community which ultimately results in uninterrupted residence in the Father's house (14:1-14). Such a view of *meros* dovetails neatly with 15:1-17, where remaining in Jesus is the key to life. Without such remaining, one's fate is like unproductive branches which are cut off and cast out to be burned.

Consequently, the footwashing is a sign which points beyond itself to some deeper meaning. Two things point to the crucifixion-exaltation as essential to that deeper meaning. First, the qualities represented by *meros* (eternal life, identity with Jesus, sharing his destiny, mission, resurrection, and martyrdom) are ultimately secured through Jesus' death. Second, Jesus' act of humiliation in washing the disciples' feet foreshadows his ultimate act of humiliation on the cross. These hints in the narrative make it easier to understand the importance of footwashing. By refusing the footwashing, Peter is ultimately refusing the effects of the cross. The emphatic language of John 13:8 removes all doubt concerning footwashing's importance. Without it, Peter will have no *meros* (part, share) with Jesus.

Footwashing as a Sign of Cleansing

Clearly, the meaning of the footwashing is given in John 13:10, where, in response to Peter's request for washings in addition to his feet, Jesus says, "The one who has bathed has no need to wash except the feet but is wholly clean; and you are clean, but not all of you." To understand the function of footwashing, one must accurately identify (1) the meaning of the two verbs used to describe a washing, (2) the bath to which Jesus makes reference, and (3) the kind of cleansing which footwashing provides.

On the first question, John appears to intend a distinction between the two verbs "to bathe" and "to wash." The former (*louō*) always has reference to a bath when it is found in the same context with the latter (*niptō*), and is never used in extant Greek literature to refer to a footwashing. Therefore, Jesus views the footwashing as a supplement to or an extension of an earlier bath.

Jesus' explanation, which uses these two verbs, draws upon the ancient custom of the day. A traveler or guest would bathe at home before leaving on a trip. During the course of the journey, dirt and dust would become attached to the feet. Upon arrival, the host would offer water to remove that which accumulated on the way. There would be no reason to bathe again, only to wash those parts of the body which had become soiled. Jean Owanga-Welo affirms[15] the proverbial and parabolic character of John 13:10a by pointing to a parallel found in Seneca (*Epistulae morales* 86.12):

> It is stated by those who reported to us the old-time ways of
> Rome that the Romans washed only their arms and legs daily—
> because those were the members which gathered dirt in their
> daily toil—and bathed all over once a week.[16]

Together with the evidence mentioned earlier, this text demonstrates the common character of the practice. The analogy is used by Jesus to convey the deeper meaning attached to the action.

On the second question: To what is Jesus alluding when he speaks of a complete bath that makes someone clean? For the disciples in the narrative, there is one option that seems most likely: baptism. Not only do the first disciples come from the Baptist's circle (which would imply an acquaintance with and appreciation for baptism), but Jesus (3:22) and/or his disciples (4:2) are said to have baptized others and to have been more successful than John. Regardless of the way in which the tension between 3:22 and 4:2 is handled, the implication is the same. Baptisms are either performed by Jesus or under his auspices. Whether John's baptism, of divine origin (1:33), is being exalted by the subsequent actions of Jesus and the disciples, or his baptism is subsumed by the later practice, the implication for 13:10 is the same. It is highly probable that the disciples, who baptize others, have experienced baptism themselves, either at the hand of John or Jesus.

The readers, while familiar with baptism and its role, might be able to discern another meaning for *leloumenos* (John 13:10). On the basis of the post-resurrection perspective of several statements in the narrative, the reader may suspect that the bath which cleanses has reference to the death of Jesus. Other passages in the Johannine literature testify to the connection between Jesus' death and cleansing. Notice the special qualities of Jesus' blood in Johannine thought (John 6:53-56; 1 John 1:7-9; Rev. 1:5; 5:9; 19:13), as well as the remarkable usages of water in the Fourth Gospel; every time water appears, something significant takes place. Hence, it is difficult to avoid interpreting the water and blood which come from Jesus' side in 19:34 as having reference to the life-giving and cleansing qualities of his death. First John 1:7-9 gives clear evidence of the connection between cleansing from sin and the blood of Jesus:

> But if we walk in the light as he is in the light, we have fellowship with one another and the blood of Jesus his Son cleanses (*katharizei*) us from all sin. If we say that we have no sin, we deceive ourselves and the truth is not in us. If we confess our sins, he is faithful and righteous to forgive us (our) sins and cleanse (*katharisē*) us from all unrighteousness.

There can be little doubt that such statements are based upon reflection about the crucifixion of Jesus. In Revelation 7:14, one of the elders responds to John concerning the identity of certain ones who are dressed in white clothes: "These are the ones who are coming out of the great tribulation, and have washed their clothes and made them white in the blood of the Lamb." Again, the cleansing efficacy of the blood should be noted. The readers, then, might already see the significance of *leloumenos* (John 13:10) in terms of Jesus' death, especially in light of *meta tauta* (13:7, "after these things"). But it is unlikely that the cleansing through baptism and through the blood would have been seen as mutually exclusive.[17]

It would appear then that *leloumenos* (John 13:10) most likely has reference to baptism (and Jesus' death). Several additional pieces of evidence tend to corroborate this decision. One of the reasons for this identification is the effects of the bathing. Jesus says, "The one who has bathed (*leloumenos*) . . . is wholly clean." In early Christian literature, no rite signifies complete cleansing from sin as does baptism. Certainly, the crucifixion is that event which accomplishes the cleansing, but it is baptism which signifies the cleansing. The occurrence of *leloumenos* fits well with such a theme.

In addition, Jesus implies that there is no reason to repeat the complete bath one has received. Likewise, baptism is a rite which is once-and-for-all. Further support for this nuance is the tense of *leloumenos*. The perfect tense designates a past action with abiding results, and it is difficult to assign the choice of tense to coincidence. Finally, there is some philological support for taking *louō* as a reference to baptism. In several New Testament passages, *louō* and its cognates are likely references to baptism (Heb. 10:22; Eph. 5:26) or are closely related to it (Acts 22:16; 1 Cor. 6:11; Titus 3:5).[18] Therefore, it seems likely that the readers would make the connection between *leloumenos* and baptism, as most scholars believe.

On the third question: By following the ancient banquet practice to its completion, the deeper meaning of the footwashing comes into view. The one who travels any distance at all on the dusty paths in the ancient orient accumulates dust which must be removed. In the analogy Jesus uses, if *louō* represents baptism, then it makes best sense to take the function of the footwashing as an additional act of cleansing. Dodd concludes:

> In [John] 13:10 *louesthai*, to take a bath, is contrasted with *niptein*, to wash a part of the body. Baptism is a bath (*loutron*, Eph. 5:26; Tit. 3:5). The Christian reader is assured that having undergone the *loutron* he is *katharos* [clean], yet may need some kind of recurrent washing.[19]

More than one interpreter has seen in the footwashing an allusion to forgiveness of post-baptismal sin.[20] This association is due in part to the occurrence of *katharos* (clean) in John 13:10. A cognate of this term appears in later Johannine literature (1 John 1:7, 9) with explicit reference to forgiveness of sin through the blood of Jesus. In addition, a multitude of ancient texts use *katharos* (and its cognates) in contexts which describe the forgiveness of sins. The LXX (Greek Old Testament: Lev. 16:30; Ps. 18:14 [19:13]; 50:4 [51:2]) and certain para-biblical literature (Sirach 23:10; 38:10; Josephus, *Ant.* 12.286; *Testament of Reuben* 4:8) use *katharos* in such a fashion.

Although *katharos* may designate other kinds of cleansing (cf. John 2:6), its frequent associations with forgiveness of sin make it likely that the readers of the Fourth Gospel would have understood *katharos* to have reference to forgiveness of sin. Thus, while sin is not explicitly mentioned in John 13:10, its presence is implied. Such an interpretation fits well with Jesus' emphatic language in 13:8. On this view, Peter is told that he would have no *meros* with Jesus because of (post-baptismal) sin which had not been removed by cleansing. This meaning would become clear to Peter *meta tauta* (13:7, "after these things").

Another point concerns the Book of Glory (John 13–21). This understanding of footwashing fits well within the context of belief, of which John 13 is a part. The disciples are not being initiated into belief in this passage, but are continuing in their belief. Their earlier baptism, which the community probably understood as being at the hands of John (1:19-39) or possibly Jesus (3:22; cf. 4:1-2), would designate initial belief and fellowship with Jesus, while footwashing would signify the continuance of that belief and fellowship.[21] As a sign of preparation for Jesus' departure, footwashing signifies the disciples' spiritual cleansing for a continuing relationship with Jesus and taking on his mission in the world.

Yet another point concerns evidence from the LXX which demonstrates that footwashing could be used in a sacred or cultic way (Exod. 30:17-21; 40:30-32; 1 Kings 7:38; 2 Chron. 4:6). For Jesus to treat footwashing as a religious rite would not be wholly without precedent.

Finally, the efficacious nature of the washing is emphasized by the way the footwashing "foreshadows the self-giving involved in Jesus' death on the cross."[22] In light of preceding considerations, an identification of footwashing with the cleansing from the sin contracted through daily life in this world is an appropriate one. Just as a banquet guest would bathe at home and only wash the feet at the visited house to remove the dust and debris accumulated on the road, so Peter (the believer) who experiences baptism (which signifies complete cleansing from sin) does not need to be rebaptized. Instead, one is to undergo footwashing, which signifies the removal of sin that might accumulate as a result of life in this sinful world. In a sense, footwashing is an extension of baptism, for it signifies the washing away of post-baptismal sins in Peter's (the believer's) life.[23]

The Relationship of Footwashing to the Lord's Supper

While the Fourth Gospel does not make the connection of the footwashing to the Lord's Supper altogether clear, three things may be deduced about the community's practice. First, because of its placement in the Fourth Gospel, the footwashing was probably observed in conjunction with the eucharist. If so, it is possible that the footwashing took place in the context of a meal (perhaps the agape) together with the eucharist. It cannot be determined whether every eucharistic celebration would involve the footwashing.

Second, if the footwashing was observed in connection with the eucharist, then in all probability it *preceded* the Lord's Supper. John 13:1-30 is certainly open to such an interpretation. Of particular relevance are 13:12, which describes Jesus as rejoining the meal, and 13:27, which records that the meal had been completed.

In 1 Corinthians 11:28, Paul admonishes the Corinthian believers to examine themselves before approaching the Lord's table. According to the Didache (14), in some early Christian circles a period of confession of sin preceded the eucharist:

> 1. On the Lord's Day of the Lord come together, break bread and hold Eucharist, after confessing your transgressions that your offering may be pure; 2. but let none who has a quarrel with his fellow join in your meeting until they be reconciled, that your sacrifice be not defiled. 3. For this is that which was spoken by the Lord, "In every place and time offer me a pure sacrifice, for I am a great King," saith the Lord, "and my name is wonderful among the heathen."[24]

If the Johannine community's eucharistic celebration allowed for a period of self-examination or was anything like that described in the Didache, the footwashing would most easily fit at this point. It would serve as the sign that confessed sin was forgiven. The believer would then be able to sit at the Lord's table with a clear conscience.

Third, more than likely the footwashing itself was carried out by all members of the community. Such participation would accord well with the commands of John 13:14-17 and also with the emphasis upon mutual intercession in 1 John. Since the confession of sin may have been a public one to the community, the brotherly intercession could well have been quite specific in its petitions.

It is not too difficult to envisage a footwashing of this sort in the context of the house church of the late first century. The environment of the home, as well as the small number of people involved, would be conducive to such mutual confession and intercession.

Conclusion

In the first-century church (as well as that of the Protestant Reformers), baptism and eucharist were regarded as established by Jesus himself, directly related to his atoning death, and continuing in the worshiping community. In view of these attitudes, several reasons may be offered in support of the classification of footwashing as a sacrament for the Johannine community and, consequently, for the contemporary church.

When John's account of the footwashing is examined, each of the above characteristics are present: (1) There is no question that as portrayed in the Fourth Gospel, the footwashing is instituted by Jesus.

(2) It is clear from a number of literary allusions in John's Gospel that the footwashing is viewed as rooted and grounded in Jesus' atoning death. (3) On the basis of John 13:14-17, it is evident that footwashing is to be continued in the Johannine community. (4) John 13:14-17, taken as words of institution, are as explicit in terms of perpetuation of the practice as the eucharistic words of institution. If the Johannine community is familiar with the Synoptic traditions, the comparison between the two sets of words of institution could hardly be missed. (5) Finally, by taking the traditional place of the eucharist in the passion narrative, the footwashing appears in a sacramental context. There are even some writers in the early church who use sacramental language in describing the footwashing.[25]

In conclusion, while there appear to me to be a number of appropriate contexts for the religious practice of footwashing, I am personally convinced that, with regard to its relationship to the Lord's Supper, the Brethren tradition has gotten it just about right. Since the footwashing serves primarily as a sign of the continual forgiveness of sins available for the believer, its observance just before the Lord's Supper is most appropriate.[26]

⮨ 11 ⮩

Brethren Heritage
of the Lord's Supper:
Eucharist

Dale R. Stoffer

At first glance you may think that we have already covered the areas of Brethren uniqueness with the consideration of the love feast and feetwashing. Judged by the practice of the eucharist service, this is probably true. The traditional Brethren practice was to pass unleavened bread, from which participants were to break a piece; several common cups of wine were then passed to the participants. Variations today would involve unleavened wafers that are broken between two people or the use of a common leavened loaf. Today, progressive Brethren drink grape juice from individual cups; conservative Brethren use wine in a common cup. All of these practices can be found in other denominations today.

Even theologically, the Brethren seem to have little that is distinctive. Together with the Anabaptists, they share what is known as the Zwinglian view of the eucharist, a remembrance of Jesus' sacrificial death for us which serves as the foundation for the Christian life and church. (Yet the Brethren and Anabaptists, like Zwingli, hold a view that is not merely a memorial of Jesus' death.)

But there are other themes in the Brethren view of the eucharist that give a unique twist to its celebration. One of these themes is the rehearsal of the flow of salvation history as proclaimed by the bread and cup. There is a past, present, and future reality that is represented by the elements. Alexander Mack Sr. summarizes these three tenses of communion in his summary of the meaning of the rite:

> In the first place, it is called a supper which the Son of God established as a memorial for His beloved disciples. He commanded

that they should thereby proclaim His death on the cross, break the bread of communion, drink the cup of communion, and covenant with one another in love as members of Christ to be ever faithful to their Lord and Master. Further, that they should remain steadfast with Him in true obedience of faith even to the cross, so that they may partake of the Great Supper with Him at the end of the world.[1]

For Mack, the rite points to the past in its memorializing and proclaiming Christ's death on the cross. He places special emphasis on the present significance of participating in the rite. He stresses four points, all of which have strong Anabaptist overtones. Participating in communion represents (1) a covenanting with the gathered body to love one another, (2) a covenanting with Christ to be faithful to him, (3) a call to remain steadfast in the obedience of faith, and (4) a call to endure suffering, even the cross. The future perspective appears in the anticipation of the fulfillment of communion when believers will be present with Christ at the Great Supper in the consummation.

These themes have remained strong in much of the Brethren tradition. Writing in 1908, C. F. Yoder, a scholar and missionary in the Brethren Church, enumerated seven points in discussing the meaning of the eucharist. Note again the development of salvation history in his points. Eucharist represents (1) a memorial of atonement, (2) a symbol of divine life, (3) a type of the union of Christ and the church, (4) a testimony of faith, (5) a confession of sin, (6) a covenant with our Lord to live the life he gives, and (7) an earnest or foretaste of heaven.[2] Though similar to Mack, Yoder does give a different slant to the significance of the eucharist for the present. There is a clear shift away from the strong corporate accountability of Mack's statements toward a more individual, experiential emphasis in Yoder's listing.

This shift in teaching can be accounted for by a movement, in progressive Brethren circles, away from a strong Anabaptist concept of the church as a mutually accountable community of believers. The movement was toward a revivalistic model that upheld an experiential, individualized relationship with Christ. Even though communion continues to be seen as a reenactment of salvation history, there has been a shift in emphasis from the corporate to the individual by early in the twentieth century. Intriguingly, this same shift is found in the meaning associated with feetwashing. In the Brethren Church, which was quite influenced by revivalism and fundamentalist theology, feetwashing came to be seen primarily as a token of our need for individual, ongoing cleansing from sin; the corporate message of humble service was relegated to the distant background.

Especially significant has been the Brethren approach to the issue of the presence of Christ in the eucharist. As I was doing my research for this presentation, two things struck me about this issue. First, there is little explicit discussion of the nature of Christ's presence in the eucharist. For example, Alexander Mack Sr. does not even address it. The foremost interpreter of Brethren theology in the nineteenth century, Peter Nead, has only this discussion:

> I do not believe that the bread and wine, in the Communion, undergoes any change, so as to become the real body and blood of our Lord Jesus Christ. It is the same as it was before it was selected for that purpose. . . . For my part, I understand the Saviour in these verses [John 6:53-56], in a spiritual, and not in a literal sense. . . .
>
> I believe the bread and wine are not the real [body and blood], but representatives of the body and blood of Jesus Christ. The object of this institution is, to set forth the death of our Lord until he come.[3]

During the twentieth century, consideration of the issue of the real presence of Christ is lacking in the eucharistic discussions of C. F. Yoder (1908) and J. Allen Miller (the first third of the century). Only more recent Brethren writers on the eucharist, Joseph Shultz (1966) and Vernard Eller (1972), enter into a more technical consideration of the issue.

Second, I was intrigued by the words of institution used by the Brethren. Today in the Brethren Church, and also in some of the earliest accounts of a Brethren love feast from the nineteenth century, the words of institution for the eucharist do not come from the synoptic Gospels or from Paul's recounting of the Lord's Supper in 1 Corinthians 11:23-26. Instead, the Brethren have typically recited Paul's statement in 1 Corinthians 10:16, rephrasing it as an affirmation: "The bread which we break is the communion of the body of Christ; the cup which we bless is the communion of the blood of Christ."[4]

Some significant conclusions can be drawn from these two observations. In developing these points, I will also be relying on discussions found in Anabaptist literature because the foundation for Brethren perspectives on the eucharist was laid in Anabaptist thought. First, when Brethren and Anabaptists read "This is my body" in both

Matthew 26:26 and Mark 14:22, they interpreted it by the lengthier statements in Luke 22:19 and 1 Corinthians 11:24, "This is my body given for you [or: which is for you]; do this in remembrance of me."

The Anabaptist leader Balthasar Hubmaier explicitly observes that Matthew and Mark recorded Jesus' words in the briefest manner, while Luke and Paul presented his words "much more richly."[5] For the Brethren and Anabaptists, the significance of Jesus' words "This is my body" was not to be found in a discussion of the manner of Christ's presence. Rather, they understood these words in light of their fuller context in the Lukan and Pauline accounts as pointing to or signifying his sacrificial death.[6] Partaking of the bread as well as the cup was to serve as a reminder of Christ's death on the cross on our behalf.

The second point that arises in Brethren and Anabaptist discussions about the presence of Christ in the eucharist relates to Jesus' "hard saying" in John 6:51-59 about eating his flesh and drinking his blood. Some Brethren prefer not to deal with the stark realism or literalism of this passage. Vernard Eller, for example, admits the difficulty posed by the sacramental overtones of this "recalcitrant passage," as he calls it. He pronounces the matter an enigma and simply moves on in his discussion without trying to reconcile the passage with his own nonsacramental position.[7] Other Brethren and Anabaptists, however, have been more than willing to enter in where Eller fears to tread.

Typically, Brethren and Anabaptists deal with the seeming sacramentalism of this passage by emphasizing Jesus' statement in John 6:63, "The words I have spoken to you are spirit and they are life."[8] Jesus' true intention was a spiritual eating and drinking, in the sense that we find our spiritual nourishment in Jesus. Brethren and Anabaptists also are insistent that any spiritual benefit of such communion with Christ is possible only through faith. (Observe that John 6:64 follows immediately: "Yet there are some of you who do not believe.")

Menno Simons makes these points quite forthrightly:

> But where the Lord's church, the dear disciples of Christ, have met in Christ's name to partake of the Holy Supper in true faith, love, and obedience, there the outward perishable man eats and drinks perishable bread and wine, and the inner imperishable man of the heart eats in a spiritual sense the imperishable body and blood of Christ which cannot be eaten nor digested. . . . Like is benefited by like. This is incontrovertible. The visible man is nourished with visible food, and the invisible man is fed with in-

visible "bread," as we learn plainly from the word of the Lord in John 6.[9]

From the foregoing, we should be able to discern that the Brethren and Anabaptist position regarding the bread and cup is that they are not "naked symbols." When faith is united with the reception of the communion elements, the believer does receive the spiritual blessings of Christ's life and spiritual presence. Thus, John Kline, a prominent Brethren leader of the mid-nineteenth century, could say that in participating in communion, the believer "is spiritualy [sic] in communion with the Lord's body, and consequently becomes partaker of his promises."[10] C. F. Yoder could speak of the "spiritual health resulting from feeding on Christ" and says that we who have "Christ in reality . . . partake of Him and live."[11] Note that there are some definite affinities with a Reformed perspective here.

A third point regarding Christ's presence relates to the issue of sacramentalism. Eller is correct in affirming that the Brethren view of the eucharist is nonsacramental. The Brethren, at least until this century, would have rejected the use of the term sacrament to refer to baptism and Lord's Supper, preferring the word ordinance.[12] Likewise, they would have rejected the idea that these acts confer grace *ex opere operato* (effective through the mere action). The *ex opere operato* view of the sacraments was originally formulated in response to the issue of the spiritual worthiness of the officiating minister; the validity of the act was not dependent on the worthiness of the minister. The Brethren, however, like the sixteenth-century Anabaptists and the seventeenth-century Pietists, shifted the focus to the spiritual state of the recipient with regard to both baptism and communion.

It is true that the Brethren during much of the nineteenth century referred to these rites as means of grace. James Quinter, a leading elder in the church during the second half of the nineteenth century, explains the meaning attached to the phrase by the Brethren: "By the phrase, 'means of grace,' we understand those means which if properly used, or those conditions which if properly complied with, will put us in possession of the grace of God."[13] However, I believe the term, means of grace, and its accompanying implications are foreign to the original view held by the Brethren. Whereas the concept of means of grace tended to create a direct link between baptism and communion on one hand, and the reception of God's gracious gifts on the other, the early Brethren would have always inserted faith as the mediating factor between the act and the grace. As Alexander Mack affirms,

"Salvation is not dependent upon the water, but only upon the faith, which must be proved by love and obedience."[14]

The early Brethren would have agreed with Menno Simons that physical acts do not serve as means or conveyors of grace, because, as Menno states, Christ is "the only means of divine grace."[15] Though these acts serve as necessary evidences of our faith and obedience, the divine blessings are given to the faith brought to and exhibited in the ordinances. Grace is not conveyed through the ordinances themselves. Again, the grace received is none other than the life of Christ and the blessings he bestows through the Spirit.[16] Note that this view shifts the emphasis away from the elements to Christ; he is both the conveyor of grace and the one whose life and blessings are received by faith. A christological focus rather than a sacramental one is therefore achieved in the Brethren-Anabaptist approach.

A final point related to the issue of the presence of Christ in communion is perhaps the most important one for the Brethren. It derives from the observation that the Brethren historically have adapted 1 Corinthians 10:16 for the words of institution: "The bread which we break is the communion of the body of Christ; the cup which we bless is the communion of the blood of Christ." Why select this passage to be read when the bread and cup are received? I believe the Brethren practice of feetwashing and love feast as well as the Anabaptist commitment to community predisposed them to using this verse.

In my introductory remarks (see chapter 8), I observed the relational dynamic in each of the three parts of Brethren communion. They have both a vertical dimension between God and the believer, and a horizontal dimension of the believer's relationship with the community of faith. The context of 1 Corinthians 10:16 incorporates both these dimensions. Verse 17 presents the community theme so prevalent in Anabaptist discourses on communion: "Because there is one loaf, we, who are many, are one body, for we all partake of the one loaf." In the ensuing verses, 18-22, Paul warns against eating sacrificial meals at pagan temples, not because the sacrifice offered to the idol or the idol itself is anything, but because there is a real sense that one participates in or fellowships with the demons to whom the sacrifices are offered. In fact, Paul reinforces his argument by citing his view of communion: there is real fellowship with Jesus Christ through the Spirit when we partake of the bread and cup.

Because this passage sets forth so powerfully the themes betokened in feetwashing and love feast, it is understandable that the Brethren drew their eucharistic language from it. Keep in mind also that the Brethren have historically used the terms *Lord's Supper*, understood as a shared meal, and *love feast* to refer to all three parts of the service. The corporate nature of the love feast inevitably led the Brethren to see the eucharist not merely as an individual act but, even more, as an act of the community of faith.

The fact that the Brethren conception of eucharist is drawn from 1 Corinthians 10:16 has some significant implications. First, it means that the eucharist is never just a personal or individual encounter with Christ but involves a community encounter with him as well. This communal aspect reminds the church of two things: Christ is the source of its life as his body; and the body, in all its members, needs to live in unity with Christ and one another.

Second, this concern for unity in the body is the rationale behind the call by Paul in 1 Corinthians 11:17-34 for self-examination prior to sharing in communion. Likewise, the Brethren and Anabaptists historically have insisted that self-examination, reconciliation of interpersonal conflicts, and corporate discipline, if necessary, must occur before the body can come together in communion. Brethren congregations would at times postpone the observance of the Lord's Supper if there were unreconciled issues in the body.

Third, when Brethren consider the idea of Christ's presence in the eucharist, their view is clearly governed by these perspectives. For the Brethren, the issue is not the presence of Christ in the elements but the presence of Christ in his body, the church. How fully do the gathered people of God reflect their Lord in holiness, purity, integrity, love? Communion is the time when the community of faith unites with their living Lord both to remember and thank him for his sacrificial love, and to receive anew his gracious blessings and love. As the Mennonite leader, Dirk Philips, stated, "By it [the Lord's Supper] we become renewed in and reminded of the spiritual fellowship which we have with Christ Jesus, namely, that he is in us with his Spirit through faith and we in him."[17]

Vernard Eller rightly notes that the Brethren perspective does affirm that Christ is "really" present. But he cautions that "there is no reason to locate that presence in the elements (in fact, to do so inevitably detracts from the *communal* aspect of the celebration)." The effect of the service is to make believers "*aware* of the presence of the one who has always been with them and always will be."[18]

Sometimes the charge is made that such a view diminishes the significance of Christ's presence in communion. There is at the heart of this charge, however, a theological assumption that can be traced back to the radically different concepts of the church held by the six-teenth-century territorial churches and by the Anabaptists. The Ana-baptist model of the church was built upon the sharp distinction be-tween the kingdom of Christ and the kingdom of this world. Unlike the territorial church model, which held that one is a citizen of both kingdoms, the Anabaptist model held that the believer must give un-divided allegiance to Christ's kingdom alone. The believer cannot be a citizen of both the kingdom of Christ and of the world; otherwise the influence of the world's values and morals will begin to corrupt one's allegiance to Christ. All of life is to be lived under the lordship of Christ, with the realization that we are constantly in his presence.[19]

With this view, the Anabaptists chastened the territorial church-es for their low view of the presence of Christ in the daily life of the church and its people. In a real sense, the debate over the real pres-ence of Christ was a battle within the *corpus Christianum* church. That church had to such a degree communed with the surrounding culture that it needed a special sense of Christ's presence. In the Brethren and Anabaptist model, believers had the vivid sense that all of life was to be lived in Christ's presence. Thus communion served not to make Christ any more real in his presence but to remind the community of his living presence and of his call to be his body by visi-bly representing him in the world.

The Brethren understanding of Christ's presence is drawn from these concepts. There is a real participation in the body of Christ both in the sense of sharing with Christ personally by the Spirit but also in the sense of sharing intimately with every other member of Christ's body. To share in the bread and cup therefore reminds the individual and community of their intimate communion with Christ, responsibil-ity to portray visibly Christ's life both individually and corporately, need to maintain the unity of the body of Christ, and responsibility to examine themselves and to reconcile differences within the body.

Thus the uniqueness of Brethren communion rests not just in the fact that we practice feetwashing and the love feast. Our understand-ing of the bread and cup likewise has unique features. Though it has many similarities with the Anabaptist view, its themes are more strongly reinforced because these themes are linked intimately with feetwashing and love feast. The vertical and horizontal dimensions of all three acts issue a reminder that our whole existence as God's peo-ple depends upon Christ's sacrificial death, upon our ongoing faith union with him, and upon a call that we are to live in unity as God's people, loving and serving one another and our neighbor.

≪§ 12 §≫

The Lord's Supper as Viewed and Practiced by the Christian Churches, Churches of Christ, and the Disciples of Christ

John Mills

The point from which one begins a journey can often determine the outcome of that journey. It has been said of our movement that we are distinctively different from other movements and denominations: our people began, not with a text from the apostle Paul to justify separation from Rome, but with the book of Acts. Our forefathers were for the most part Old Light, Anti-burger, Seceder Presbyterians. Thomas Campbell was a minister of that sect of the church, but he abhorred the disunity of the church as a whole and worked for the unity of the church in his native Ireland. Upon coming to the New World, Campbell was again pained by the divisive denominationalization of the Lord's church.

Thomas Campbell and later his son, Alexander, sought the unity of all Christians through the restoring of the church to its faith and order as seen in the New Testament. Only what was necessary to become a Christian was necessary and essential to Christian faith. Rather than beginning in a negative reaction to a state church, or in reaction to the Roman Catholic Church, they turned to the book of Acts. This was not to diminish or to neglect the rest of Scripture. They were convinced that the place to look at the basic church, its origins, faith, and practice, was in the book of Acts. They saw the actions of the apostles as obedience to the mind of the Christ, the Lord of the church. The writings of the apostles did not contradict the practices ordained in those formative years.

Second, these reformers were convinced that their beliefs and practices must be consistent with the faith and belief of the early church as found in Scripture. Sprinkled as infants, they came to reject

193

infant baptism, and they were immersed into Christ on the basis of faith in Christ. They denounced the clergy system of their heritage. The priesthood of all believers as found in Scripture was the Lord's way. They rejected institutional examination before partaking of the Supper and quarterly communion in favor of personal examination and weekly sharing in the "Breaking of Bread."

By beginning with the book of Acts, these reformers saw preaching, baptism, and the Lord's Supper all having a balanced role in the life of the worshiping church. The ordinances were thus restored to their biblical place and power. Avery Dulles, in his *Models of the Church*, discusses the five basic models or ways in which different groups view the church. When he comes to the typical Protestant model of proclamation, he says,

> Sacraments in this type of ecclesiology, as contrasted with the institutional and sacramental models, are seen as definitely secondary to the Word. For many Protestants in the Reformation tradition, the Sacrament is understood as a "visible word"—a sign or dramatization of the faith of the community in which they are administered.[1]

But does not the New Testament show the ordinances as an inherent part of the worship services as much as the proclamation of the gospel?

Dulles quotes Karl Barth on the Protestant form of ministry:

> It is very clear that the Reformation wished to see something better substituted for the mass it abolished, and that it expected that better thing would be—our preaching of the Word. The *verbum visible*, the objectively clarified preaching of the Word, is the only sacrament left to us. The Reformers sternly took from us everything but the Bible.[2]

Our heritage is not one of being "strangely warmed" at Aldersgate, as was Wesley; or "called" when told to "take up and read" in one's back yard, as was Augustine. Our forefathers sought to give themselves in obedience to the Christ as they saw that way practiced in the early church. Faith came "by hearing the word of God" (Rom. 10:17). They rejected Calvinism and subjective concepts of faith. Philosophically, our early leaders were influenced by the empiricism of John Locke and Thomas Reid. They found objectivity and balance in the book of Acts, and this was confirmed in the rest of the New Testament.

It could be said of us that we were American pragmatists. We asked, "How did the early church do this?" At times we pushed this too far and became too legalistic. But I hope this explains our uniqueness, or at least how we got to where we are.

Ordinances or Sacraments

Our history shows that we prefer the term *ordinances*. In part this can be attributed to a rejection of the term *sacrament* being seen as an automatic channel of grace, regardless of the spiritual condition of the recipient. The term *ordinance* spoke to a culture in which the ordinances were not generally practiced as the Lord had commanded. Christ was the authority behind our practice. One of our notable historians stated our dilemma well when he said, "We don't call them sacraments because the New Testament doesn't call them sacraments, so we call them ordinances which the New Testament doesn't call them either!"[3]

Alexander Campbell described an ordinance as "the mode in which the grace of God acts on human nature."[4] This definition is valid for sacrament, but Campbell preferred the word *ordinance*. A vital part of reformation to him was to restore the ordinances to their place and power as seen in the New Testament. Others feared to use his definition of ordinance.

The Campbells used two tests to determine the number of the ordinances. First, they were to be commanded by the Lord and then practiced by the early church. Second, they were to show the death, burial, and resurrection of the Lord in their action. Baptism and the Lord's Supper met these qualifications. Footwashing, which some considered to be an ordinance, failed to meet the second of these qualifications.

In following our heritage, our people see baptism in sacramental terms. Acts 2:38 is but one text that shows the immersion into Christ of penitent believers "for the forgiveness of sins" and "the gift of the Holy Spirit." But we had trouble with a sacramental understanding of the Lord's Supper. Zwingli's view was far safer than getting too close to sacramental concepts. The memorial view of the Supper is most common among our people. Engraved on almost all of our communion tables is the command "This Do in Remembrance of Me."

Frequency of Observance

A distinctive feature of our worship services is the universal practice of observing the Lord's Supper on a weekly basis. When our Presbyterian forefathers read the practice of the early church in the book of Acts, they had to give up their quarterly participation in the Supper in favor of weekly participation. Acts 20:7 tells us the practice of one early congregation: "On the first day of the week, when we were gathered together to break bread. . . ." Acts 2:42 and 46 tell us that the "breaking of bread" was a regular part of the gathering of the early church. The Lord's Supper, or breaking of bread, was at least weekly or more frequent. First Corinthians 16:2 and chapter 11 would certainly lead us to understand that the congregation at Corinth had at least a weekly observance of the Lord's Supper.[5] Jeremias is emphatic that the early church continued to celebrate the Supper weekly or even daily.[6] The correspondence of Pliny and Trajan verifies this practice. John Calvin was likewise of this opinion.[7]

Some of our more "conservative" brethren have at times objected to the Lord's Supper being held at other times, such as the Thursday before Easter, or on Christmas Eve. Others object to it being held twice on one Sunday for the same group of people, such as on Sunday morning of Christmas Eve, and then again that evening. But these views are not the norm.

It is a common practice for the elders of a congregation to take communion to the shut-ins or those in the hospital on a Sunday afternoon. Most often this is done once a month. But communion is a vital part of that visit.

Centrality in the Worship Service

So important is the weekly observance of the Lord's Supper that it is usually placed in the center of the worship service. It is central to the service. The communion table is usually placed in the center front of the sanctuary. Stepping into one of our typical sanctuaries, you can look to the front and see the communion table front and center. Directly behind the communion table would be the pulpit, and above the pulpit in the center of the front wall, you would see the baptistery. Some of the newer architectural designs vary this theme with split chancel, and so on, but the table, pulpit and baptistery speak to our understanding of the centrality of all three. Other new church buildings are built "in the round," with the table in the very center of the congregation. Many of our congregations have dared to place the

Supper after the sermon as the "climax" of the service; thus it is still central in importance. If for some reason there is no one to deliver the sermon on a given Sunday, the elders preside at the table, and the people have still worshiped.

Open Communion

It would have been easy for our people to have become legalistic and to practice closed communion, only for those immersed into Christ for the right reason. Some of our people still have trouble with the "pious unimmersed." But there was a painful incident in the history of our people that paved the way for open communion. Thomas Campbell came to Pennsylvania from Ireland as an Anti-burger, Old Light, Seceder Presbyterian clergyman. In one of his first worship services, he offered the Lord's Supper to those who were members of other branches of the Presbyterian Church. This resulted in his dismissal from his synod and much soul-searching. This incident has checked our legalistic impulses. To this day, our communion services are open "to all who wear the name of Christ, whether a member of this congregation or not." Some congregations may whisper that invitation or ignore it, but that is our heritage. Restoration for the purpose of Christian unity is our heritage, so we practice "closed membership" and "open communion."

Theology in Practice at the Table

In restoring the faith and practice of the early church, our people rejected the theology of transubstantiation and consubstantiation. These doctrines call for a clerical priest, a sacrifice, and an altar. Their reading of Scripture showed them the priesthood of all believers, a Christ sacrificed once for all, and therefore a supper at a table. Our elders preside at the communion table for the Lord's Supper. The bread and fruit of the vine (Welch's unfermented grape juice) is usually passed through the pews by the deacons (some congregations include deaconesses). Individual cups and small wafers are used. Tuberculosis put an end to the use of the single cup back in the nineteenth century, except for a few congregations on the far right, known as "one cuppers." Unleavened bread is the rule, but at times regular bread is used.

We placed importance on the Supper, its frequency, and our understanding that there is a table but no altar; therefore, we rejected the practice of altar calls. Our buildings have no altar rails. The Supper is for self-examination, repentance, covenant renewal, and assurance. Much of what others practice in their altar calls we see provided by the Lord in the Supper. Only in those congregations where little real emphasis is placed on the Supper have we seen calls for "rededications." In most of our congregations, the Supper offers abundant opportunity for rededication to Christ every week.

Our Understanding of the Supper Itself

As stated earlier, the memorial view is probably the most common understanding of the Supper in our circles. Regrettably, the use of the word *observe* is all too common. Many of us prefer the word *participation*, as found in 1 Corinthians 10:16-17. Whether we would admit it or not, our communion meditations and hymns center almost exclusively on the cross and our sins, much like the Roman Catholic mass. Some of us prefer a balance of this centering on the cross with a "celebration" of the resurrection. In such instances, the hymn prior to the Supper usually centers on the cross, and the hymn following the Supper is a hymn of victory or of resurrection.

Alexander Campbell referred to the Supper with the biblical term "Breaking of Bread." This rich picture speaks to table fellowship and participation in one body and one blood (1 Cor. 10:16-17). Such an understanding of the Supper takes us beyond just "me and my Jesus." It speaks to the unity of the church and the wholeness of the body.

The most common term used among us in reference to the Supper is *communion.* It is the "communion table" and we go to take "communion." We ask, Did you receive "communion"? We speak of the plates or trays used in the service as the "communion ware." The KJV translation of 1 Corinthians 10:16-17 using the word "communion," and Campbell's emphasis on the breaking of bread—both bring this all together. Almost unspoken, for fear of being Calvinists, the Lord is understood to be present at the table, and through the loaf and cup we commune with him. We are to ask for forgiveness and be assured of his grace. But we don't use the word *sacrament!*

I am deeply indebted to the Lord for the rich heritage I have received in the Supper. I have been blessed with grace upon grace as I have participated in the Supper and have prepared others to partake. Just this past Maundy Thursday, I had the privilege of holding the cup while an elder held the bread. People came forward, broke off a piece of bread, dipped it into the cup, and then partook of the Supper. I was deeply moved to have that close encounter with my brothers and sisters in the presence of the Lord. But I continue to challenge fellow members to look for even greater blessings in the Supper.

I believe that we are wrong when we take "Do this in remembrance of me" to mean "Take of the Supper," or "Observe communion." The Greek structure of 1 Corinthians 11:23-24 does not mean that the doing is our taking and eating. It means taking bread, giving thanks, and breaking it. We would not only be more biblical but also be more blessed by breaking a common loaf, showing the oneness of the body, and then partaking of that oneness. Hopefully, we could "discern the body" as the body of Christ, the church, and have our personal holiness include our relationship to all others who are partaking. The small individual pieces of bread point to individual communion with "me and my Jesus." Further understanding of table fellowship and of the Supper as the Breaking of Bread should lead to greater unity within the congregation and fellowship between congregations. We need to place a greater emphasis on 1 Corinthians 10:16-17 and 11:29.

I encourage my brothers and sisters to probe the richness of the term *eucharist*. We need to emphasize thanksgiving for our salvation and for our hope of eternity, as well as for the love of God and Christ's death at Calvary. We need to walk in faith and not in fear of being like the "orthodox." We need to drop the word *observe* and move on to "participate" and "celebrate" without fear of being Roman Catholic.

~§ 13 §~

A Quaker Interpretation of the Lord's Supper

T. Canby Jones

So you invited a Quaker to interpret the meaning of the Lord's Supper or eucharist! Are you sure you know what you are doing? Some Southern Baptists and others call the Religious Society of Friends a "cult." I presume they do so because we are baptized only by "the living water which wells up into eternal life," or that we feed solely on "the Bread of Life which comes down from heaven to give life to the world."

Eschewing the outward elements of water, bread, and wine, Quakers stress the sacramentality of all meals and of all life's experiences. This sense of "cosmic sacramentality," if I may call it that, is marvelously expressed in one of Kenneth Boulding's *Nayler Sonnets:*

> Lord, thou art in every breath I take,
> And every bite and sup taste firm of Thee.
> With buoyant mercy Thou enfoldest me,
> And holdest up my foot each step I make.
> Thy touch is all around me when I wake,
> Thy sound I hear, and by Thy light I see.
> The world is fresh with thy divinity,
> And all thy creatures flourish for thy sake.[1]

In Thomas R. Kelly's terms, we Quakers seek by inward attitudes of prayer and adoration so to practice the presence of God at all times and places that we come to look out on all events "through the sheen of the Inward Light."[2] In another place, Thomas Kelly says, "The possibility of this experience of Divine Presence, as a repeatedly realized and present fact, and its transforming and transfiguring effect upon all life—this is the central message of Friends."[3]

As far as I know, the only other Christian group that experiences baptism and celebrates the Lord's Supper by inward and spiritual means only is the Salvation Army. I have never learned why Salvationists spiritualize the sacraments. The movement was founded in a Quaker settlement house in East London. The Salvation Army is also notable for the parity of position and dignity given to women in the movement. These two facts give a hint of Quaker influence, but it is only a hint.

Unfortunately, many Quakers (including this writer for a number of years) feel that the Quaker testimony on baptism and the Lord's Supper amounts to a taboo. Water baptism, or as I like to term it "H_2O-type baptism," and "bread-and-wine-type eucharist" are Christian practices Quakers just *don't* do. We feel this taboo so strongly that whenever some members on the fringe of our Society of Friends encourage the use of those outward ordinances, the main body of us feel that they "have lost it" and are no longer Friends.

On the other hand, in this age of "individual choice" and "following your inward leading," a Friend may, as a sign of unity and fellowship, feel led to partake of the eucharist or Lord's Supper. Rarely if ever would that Friend be "eldered" (questioned by the elders).

So how do Friends reconcile the call to the "cosmic sacramentality" of the inward Christ experienced in all of life, with the actual taboo we feel against our engaging in the eucharistic practice of our brothers and sisters in Christ? Briefly, I think most of us don't reconcile the two. But in what follows, I will share my struggles with the "Lord's Supper" and my eventual peace found in the Supper. I hope my pilgrimage of pain and reconciliation may suggest an answer to the Quaker dilemma on this issue.

However, first we need to ask what stimulated the Quaker testimony against the use of water in baptism and bread and wine in the eucharist. I believe the basic reason that stance arose was as a protest against the superficial, banal, and even corrupt state into which sacramental rites had fallen in Roman Catholic, Anglican, and Nonconformist practice in seventeenth-century Britain and Europe. A deeper level of protest centers on tendencies in the Roman Catholic Church following the Fourth Lateran Council. That 1215 council established the sacraments as seven in number (affirming Peter Lombard, *Sentences* 4.i.2) and also taught that they were almost exclusively *the* means of grace.

As early Friends saw it and stated the problem, here was confusion between the sacramental rite and the *real* and *direct* nature of divine grace *symbolized* by the sacrament. Friends maintain that Jesus Christ has come in Spirit and in power to bring people into dire and immediate communion with himself, by whatever means he chooses and without dependence on ordinances, rites, ceremonies, or human beings ordained to celebrate them. Christ is our unseen and ever-present bishop, guide, teacher, prophet, priest, and only minister. He is seeking to raise us to newness of life through inward modes of baptism and multiple modes of communing with him.

In all worship, Friends seek direct communion with Christ the *substance*, not indirect or symbolic communion through outward means, which are *shadows* of the substance. My friend, John Punshon, professor of Quaker Studies at Earlham School of Religion, has written a concise and beautiful leaflet called, *The Shadow and the Substance*. Some words from this leaflet clearly explain the Quaker view of sacraments.

The disuse of ceremonies is a pointer to the way Quakers understand God's grace.

The most important reason for Friends' testimony is to make it impossible for Christians to mistake a real experience for an unreal one. Ceremonies in themselves have no divine power to change us one way or another, as Paul warned in the Colossians. In the second chapter of that letter, he says that they are "a mere shadow of what is to come, but the substance belongs to Christ."

The distinction drawn in Scripture between the shadow and the substance is clear. Grace is invisible and unmistakable. We are called into communion in the Spirit, inwardly. Our baptism is an appeal to God for a clear conscience (1 Peter 3:21). The communion "bread" we eat cannot be purchased at the grocery store, because it is Christ, the Bread of Life (John 6:35). So it is also with the wine, water, flame, and fire of the Spirit. To be immersed in the Spirit of Jesus Christ and filled with that Spirit is the real substance to which sacramentals point. The receiving of God's saving and empowering grace is always mediated through inward faith alone, not through outward forms of expression.

The fruit of the Spirit offers a far surer indication of spirituality than tongues, ecstasy, or rites. It is not clear how participation in ceremonies necessarily promotes these attributes, but *they* are the true outward measures of the Christian life, and it is to their

Author that one should look *directly* for transforming grace. The second consideration here is that special ceremonies can narrow our focus and make us overlook the multifarious channels God actually uses.

This is the source of the well-known Quaker phrase that all of life is sacramental. . . . Hence, the Quaker testimony leads to a particular way of life and a characteristic kind of discipleship—a continuing opening to grace . . . And this is the simple point. We live in the new order, the covenant of grace. What more do we need in our heart of hearts than to know the fountain of grace, Jesus Christ—and Him crucified?[4]

I turn now to my own struggles with the Lord's Supper. My own experience of the eucharist began with my feeling strongly the taboo described above, that "Quakers don't do sacraments." I grew up on the campus of Fisk University at Nashville, where my father, Thomas E. Jones, served as president. Fisk's African-American student body was required to attend Sunday worship in the university chapel. Our family also attended frequently. About three times during the year, they served communion, consisting of diced bread and tiny cups of grape juice passed around on trays. Horribly, my older brother, age 11, and I, age 9, would eat the bread and drink the juice. We wondered why they were so stingy with such small amounts and looked at each other and laughed, ridiculing the ceremony.

Five years later as a student at Westtown Friends Boarding School in Pennsylvania, I was led to speak out of the silence in "vocal ministry" in a Sunday unprogrammed worship at the school. Feeling this call to ministry, I became a serious student of the Bible. Imagine my consternation when I read Paul's words in Corinthians, "Whosoever shall eat this bread, and drink this cup of the Lord, unworthily, . . . eateth and drinketh damnation to himself" (1 Cor. 11:27, 29, KJV). I still cringe from that condemnation!

From this you can understand why all through my early adulthood, I felt quite uncomfortable during communion services, especially those low-church ones where they passed around the elements on trays. I rejoiced in the silence during that period, but the rest of the ceremony made me uneasy.

My discomfort with participating in the ceremony of the Lord's Supper reached a peak when some of my dearest friends in the Lord at Yale Divinity School asked me to join them in an early-morning worship group which met in the chapel for prayer and communion administered by my beloved teacher and academic adviser. As a Quaker, I felt I couldn't partake of the elements. However, I felt that my abstention was such a breach of that precious fellowship that I couldn't stand the tension and never went back.

Much later in life I was a Quaker delegate to an Ohio Council of Churches Faith and Order Conference on the Lord's Supper. The two main speakers were Robert Nelson, Methodist, and a Lutheran New Testament professor. By the time they got done presenting the evidence, there was no way, in their view, for a person to be fully Christian without partaking of the elements of bread and wine in communion. I sank into my chair feeling, as a Quaker, relegated to second-class citizenship in the body of Christ! *But*, after lunch, Father William Sherry, pastor of St. William's Catholic Church in Cincinnati, addressed us saying, "The only place to start when seeking the meaning of the eucharist is with the sixth chapter of the Gospel of John." When I heard that, my heart leapt for joy, and I began to breathe again. When Fr. Sherry finished expounding on the cosmic dimensions of "the Bread of Life which comes down from heaven to give life to the world," I was back in the body of Christ! A Quaker rescued by a Catholic! Yea!

However, my full rescue from my Quaker problems with "outward communion" came at the hands of dear and humble members of the Church of the Brethren. For years I had defended the Quaker position of "no need for outward elements in communion" by citing John 13:14-15 (KJV): "If I then, your Lord and Master, have washed your feet; ye also ought to wash one another's feet. For I have given you an example, that ye should do as I have done to you." To those who justified their failure to wash feet by saying that Jesus meant that "spiritually," signifying that we should wash feet by serving human needs, the Quaker reply came, "That's what we think Jesus meant by 'Do this in remembrance of me'; he meant it spiritually."

Later in this gathering, you will have the same experience of love feast and footwashing. The Church of the Brethren actually wash feet! Their practice did a complete "end run" around my Quaker hang-ups. In 1961 at a Friends, Brethren, and Mennonite gathering at Earlham School of Religion, my roommate was a young pastor from Pleasant Valley Church of the Brethren in rural Darke County, Ohio. He told me he had been won to the Lord by the ceremony of love feast and footwashing. The next spring I asked permission to bring my Contemporary Christianity class from Wilmington College to "observe" the ceremony. When we arrived, the dear elders of the church begged us, strangers though we were, not simply to observe but to participate. After washing one another's feet, eating a common meal, and ending with home-baked unleavened bread and fruit of the vine, how could I refuse to partake of the last part of the ceremony when I had been so deeply moved by the first two parts? I couldn't. There, and in the few later times I have shared in love feasts, my sin of eating unworthily and my spiritual block against partaking has been washed away, literally.

Since then, on special occasions of celebration of the eucharist, when I feel that more is being witnessed to than denominational tradition, I have felt at liberty to partake of the elements in a eucharist or communion service.

Beginning about 1920, many Quakers have come to think of our traditional silent-expectant-waiting form of worship, in which the Holy Spirit may prompt anyone present to speak, pray, or sing, as an experience of communion. There are many different levels and qualities in the silent worship. Sometimes we bask in the silence with joy and delight. At other times, the silence is thunderous, even deafening. Most times in the silence we feel ourselves being gathered into a living, loving community of children of the Light. On rare occasions when someone through vocal ministry shares deep anguish or seeks forgiveness, you can, through the silence, feel the surge of compassion reaching out to the petitioner from the whole group.

Many of you are aware that following the Second Great Awakening in America and its consequent revivalism, the majority of Friends Meetings in this country became evangelical, revivalistic, and missionary, complete with pastors, organized hymn singing, and a low-church Protestant order of service. Nevertheless, a period of silent-expectant-open worship is still found in the vast majority of these Friends churches. Several of them explicitly call this period "Our time of Communion after the manner of Friends."

Thomas R. Kelly, author of *A Testament of Devotion*, and my beloved philosophy teacher at Haverford College, expresses the Quaker experience of beloved community and the cosmic sacramentality of a life of daily and hourly commitment to God. In his essay, "The Blessed Community," found in *A Testament of Devotion*, he says,

> The final grounds of holy Fellowship are in God. Lives immersed and drowned in God are drowned in love, and know one another in Him, and know one another in love. God is the medium, the matrix, the focus, the solvent. . . .

Two people, three people, ten people may be in living touch with one another through Him who underlies their separate lives. This is an astounding experience. . . . We know that these souls are with us, lifting their lives and ours continuously to God and opening themselves, with us, in steady and humble obedience to Him. It is as if the boundaries of our self were enlarged, as if we were within them and as if they were within us. Their strength given to them by God, becomes our strength; and our joy, given to us by God, becomes their joy. In confidence and love we live together in Him. . . .

For daily and hourly the cosmic Sacrament is enacted, the Bread and the Wine are divided amongst us by a heavenly Ministrant, and the substance of His body becomes our life and the substance of His blood flows in our veins. Holy is the Fellowship, wondrous is the Ministrant, marvelous is the Grail.[5]

Isn't that an amazing passage? How could a Quaker describe worship and fellowship in such superbly sacramental language? Or even better, how could a true Quaker *not do so?*

I confess before all of you: In all the arguments about transubstantiation, consubstantiation, or remembrance of the Last Supper as the essential event of the eucharist—I feel strongly as a Quaker that if you don't experience *the real presence of Christ* in your celebration of the Lord's Supper, you might as well forget it. It's no use. The Zwinglian interpretation of the eucharist as only a remembrance just can't cut it. Again, if you are going to have outward celebrations of the eucharist with bread and wine, they'd better be *real!*

⋰ 14 ⋱

Seventh-Day Adventists and the Lord's Supper

Peter M. van Bemmelen

Introduction

Seventh-Day Adventists trace their historical roots to the Advent awakening of the first half of the nineteenth century. On the basis of biblical prophecies, Christians from many denominations expected that Jesus would come soon. Among these Adventists were Baptists, Methodists, Presbyterians, and others. They shared a common hope in the imminent second coming of Christ, even while they disagreed on certain points of doctrine. But to them, Christ was all in all.

That is still true for Seventh-Day Adventists today. Christ is our only hope, the center of all our faith and practice. That faith rests on the Scriptures, the Old and New Testaments, which testify of Christ. Adventists believe we are saved by grace through faith in Christ, not by works, for it is the gift of God (Eph. 2:8). We also believe that this faith will manifest itself in a response of love and a desire to obey God's will. All of this is crucial to our theology and practice of the Lord's Supper.

Theology of the Lord's Supper

To Adventists, the Lord's Supper is a sacred ordinance instituted by the Lord Jesus Christ. There is not much debate among us about terminology. We frequently refer to the Lord's Supper as the communion service, but we also speak about the service of ordinances, or the sacraments. What is important to us is that a theology of the Lord's Supper be based on Scripture in its totality. That means that we must listen carefully to everything the Gospels have to say, everything Paul has to say, everything we can learn from the book of Acts and any other part of Scripture which throws light on this Christian ceremony.

Taking a cue from Jesus' own words, "Do this in remembrance of me" (Luke 22:19; 1 Cor. 11:24, 25), Adventists understand the Lord's Supper as a memorial service with a deep spiritual significance. Worshipers, in partaking of the bread and the wine, remember and confess that Christ's body was broken and his blood was poured out for the forgiveness of our sins (Matt. 26:28), for "without the shedding of blood there is no forgiveness" (Heb. 9:22; Bible quotes from NIV).

However, the service is not only a remembrance of Christ's suffering and death. It is a participation in the life of Christ. As Jesus told the Jews and his disciples, "Whoever eats my flesh and drinks my blood has eternal life, and I will raise him up at the last day. For my flesh is real food and my blood is real drink" (John 6:54-55; cf. 1 Cor. 10:16-17). Adventists do believe that in the Lord's Supper, Christ is present in a special sense to bless his people. They do not think of Christ's presence in terms of transubstantiation or consubstantiation. Instead, Christ is present through the Holy Spirit to uplift and transform the lives of those who come together to wash each other's feet and to partake in faith of the emblems of bread and wine.

The bread and wine are understood as symbols with a deep spiritual meaning. They symbolize the sacrifice of the eternal Son of God, who in his human flesh "humbled himself and became obedient to death—even death on a cross!" (Phil. 2:8). Without a living faith in Christ and his death for forgiveness of our sins, participation in the sacramental service becomes a mere form and therefore useless, or worse; "anyone who eats and drinks without recognizing the body of the Lord eats and drinks judgment on himself." In view of this, Paul admonishes that it is important for believers to examine themselves before they eat the consecrated bread and drink the consecrated wine (1 Cor. 11:28-29).

In a brief presentation such as this, it is impossible to deal adequately with the vast spectrum of meaning associated with the Lord's Supper as understood by Seventh-Day Adventists. However, here I stress a couple of theological aspects which are of special significance to us, though not unique to Adventists alone.

The first is Jesus' example and command to his disciples to wash each other's feet, as recorded in John 13:1-17. Adventists understand this passage in the same way as the other Gospel accounts, that Jesus by precept and example was giving his disciples and the church of all ages an ordinance to be participated in by all believers. His words were emphatic, "I have set you an example that you should do as I have done for you" (John 13:15).

In washing the feet of the disciples, Christ revealed the true spirit of his kingdom: humility and service. The disciples were not ready for communion with Christ. As they had done earlier, they were arguing once more among themselves about which of them was considered to be greatest (Mark 9:33-37; 10:35-45; Luke 22:24). Jesus' earlier admonition and invitation, "Take my yoke upon you and learn from me, for I am gentle and humble in heart, and you will find rest for your souls" (Matt. 11:29), had apparently fallen upon deaf ears and hearts. They could not receive that rest as long as they were filled with pride and envy and were striving for the highest place.

So Christ—who is the Lord of the universe, God over all, one with the Father from eternity, who took upon himself our flesh and became a human being—stooped down and performed the menial task of the lowest servant. That broke the disciples' hearts. How much do I need, how much do we need to have our hearts broken so that he can minister to us anew, and so we can receive forgiveness, peace, and everlasting joy! Yes, Christ set an example for us, but in the words of one Adventist author, "It was more than an example. It was a revelation of the very inmost heart of God."[1]

Second, Jesus clearly connects the eschatological expectation with the communion service. At the Last Supper in the upper room, he told his disciples that he would not drink of the fruit of the vine until he would drink it with them again in the kingdom of his Father (Matt. 26:29; Mark 14:25; Luke 22:18). Paul alludes to this expectation when he writes to the Christians in Corinth concerning the Lord's Supper, "Whenever you eat this bread and drink this cup, you proclaim the Lord's death until he comes" (1 Cor. 11:26). Not only are we to rejoice in our present communion with Christ and with one another in the Lord's Supper. Jesus adds to that joy the anticipation, the blessed hope and expectation, that soon he will come back to gather his saints so that they may share with him the everlasting joys of the kingdom of God in the very presence of Christ and the Father (John 14:1-3; 17:24; 1 Thess. 4:16-17).

To Adventists, this hope illuminates brightly our passage through a world that is often very dark. Amidst its gloom and suffering, we hear already by faith the song of the great multitude who sing the song of the wedding of the Lamb. We cherish that wonderful promise, "Blessed are those who are invited to the wedding supper of the Lamb" (Rev. 19:9).

Practice of the Lord's Supper

According to the *Seventh-Day Adventist Church Manual*,

the Communion Service customarily is celebrated once per quarter. The service includes the ordinance of foot washing and the Lord's Supper. It should be a most sacred and joyous occasion to the congregation, as well as to the minister or elder.[2]

These words reflect the practice of Seventh-Day Adventists throughout the history of our denomination. The communion service always included the footwashing or service of humility and the Lord's Supper or sacramental service. Presently nearly eight million Adventists around the globe celebrate the Lord's Supper on a quarterly basis. Participation is for baptized believers. However, Adventists practice open communion, and all who believe in Jesus Christ as Savior and Lord are welcome to participate in all aspects of the service.

On principle, Adventists use unleavened bread and unfermented wine because we believe that was what Christ and the disciples used in the Last Supper. Only such bread and wine are fitting symbols of the purity and sinlessness of our Savior, who gave his body and blood for the sins of the world. For we were redeemed "with the precious blood of Christ, a lamb without blemish or defect" (1 Pet. 1:19).

Usually the celebration of the Lord's Supper takes place during the divine worship on Sabbath morning. The Seventh-Day Sabbath already in Old Testament times was intended as a day of sacred assembly, according to Leviticus 23:3. Seventh-Day Adventists hold that this is still true for God's people in the Christian era. So, although exceptionally the communion service is celebrated at other times, the normal practice is to do so on the Sabbath; to celebrate the Lord's Supper on the Lord's Day.

Uplifting Christ

Central to the task of the church of Christ is the proclamation of the gospel. Jesus charged his disciples to preach it to all creatures to the ends of the earth. Seventh-Day Adventists believe that Jesus Christ, crucified, risen, interceding, and coming again, should be proclaimed as the Way, the Truth, and the Life. Hence, the communion service should be closely tied to the proclamation of the Word of God. Word and sacrament belong together and should not be separated.

Ellen White, whose writings have exercised a significant influence in shaping Adventist thought and practice, wrote about eighty years ago: "Of all professing Christians, Seventh-Day Adventists should be foremost in uplifting Christ before the world."[3] These are sobering words to me as a Seventh-Day Adventist. I confess that I have often failed to uplift Christ in my life and in my words; Adventists as a people have many times failed to do so. It is my prayer that the love of Christ may dwell in our hearts through the Holy Spirit, and that all of us who are baptized into Christ may uplift him in our lives, in our proclamation of God's Word, and in our celebration of the Lord's Supper.

Adventists believe that faith in Christ leads to obedience to God's commandments. Yet their only hope of salvation from sin centers in Christ's sacrifice on the cross, in his mediatorial intercession before the Father, and in his second coming to redeem all who have believed in him, to rescue them from death and to give them life eternal. With Paul, they want to cry out, "May I never boast except in the cross of our Lord Jesus Christ, through which the world has been crucified to me, and I to the world" (Gal. 6:14).

ᴥ§ 15 §ᴥ

The Lord's Supper in the
Free Methodist Tradition

Howard A. Snyder

About a dozen years ago, I was serving on the pastoral team of a Free Methodist Church in Chicago. A young man raised in our denomination moved to Chicago and started attending our congregation. One day he said to me, "When I was growing up, I could never understand why we were supposed to feel bad at the Lord's Supper."

I was surprised, but the remark immediately struck a minor chord with me. I knew what he meant. The Lord's Supper was a somber, serious occasion when we were to "bewail our manifold sins." Too often, for my friend at least, the sense of grace and celebration was overshadowed by the accent on our sin and unworthiness and on Jesus' suffering.

My own experience was much more positive than this. The Lord's Supper was, and is, full of deep meaning. But it was something quite distant from the joyful *agape* meals that seem to have occurred in the early church.

Historical Overview

The understanding of the Lord's Supper in the Free Methodist Church has a variety of direct and indirect historical connections with the believers church tradition. The Free Methodist Church was founded in 1860 in western New York State in reaction to and protest against the growing material prosperity and accompanying spiritual decline of Methodism. The catalytic issue, and the historical basis of the term *Free*, was Methodism's growing reliance on the pew rental system to finance the building and maintenance of prominent new city church edifices. Free Methodist Churches were "free" because they offered "free seats" to all, including the poor.

The Free Methodist Church thus stands squarely in the Methodist tradition. It saw itself as maintaining the standards of primitive Methodism, with its concern for holiness, simplicity, and preaching the gospel to the poor. Free Methodism's understanding of the Lord's Supper largely accords with the Methodist tradition, as derived from the Church of England. The roots of this tradition are both Catholic, reaching back into early and medieval Christianity; and Reformed, tracing to the reforms and modifications introduced by Thomas Cranmer and other sixteenth-century English Reformers. This lineage is most obvious when one examines the Free Methodist communion ritual, particularly the prayers. Radical Protestant influences in John Wesley's life, mediated mainly through the Moravian Brethren, were also a part of early Methodism; but those features had relatively little impact on its sacramental life.[1]

This Methodist lineage means that the Free Methodist Church, like many North American denominations, inherited a "Lord's Supper" that had already been long divorced from an actual meal. The inheritance also included a generally assumed distinction between laypeople and clergy, which affected the way the Lord's Supper was practiced.

Traditional practice in the Free Methodist Church has been a quarterly celebration of the Lord's Supper with an ordained elder (a denominationally ordained pastor or superintendent) officiating. Even though (or perhaps because) communion was relatively infrequent, officiating at the Lord's Supper was and is one of the primary rights and responsibilities of an ordained pastor in the Free Methodist Church.[2]

With this background, I would like to make five observations about the understanding and practice of the Lord's Supper in the Free Methodist denomination. This illuminates several key themes.

1. *The Lord's Supper has not in itself been a prominent issue of concern* in the Free Methodist denomination, either theologically or in practice. This is clear when one examines various denominational manuals and histories. A good example is *The Story of Our Church*, by Carl L. Howland,[3] which was a basic membership-training tool in the 1940s and 1950s. The chapter entitled "Character of Worship and Evangelism" makes no reference to the Lord's Supper. The chapter's opening paragraph provides a clue to this absence:

It is universally acknowledged that worship in the early Christian Church was very simple, consisting of prayer, testimony, the singing of hymns, Scripture reading (either from the Old Testament or the inspired Letters or Gospels, as they came into being), and an exhortation or sermon. There must have been a total absence of ritualism and effort to display personal talents. In Roman Catholicism the ritual became more conspicuous and the sermon of less importance.[4]

One might have expected here a reference to the early Christian love feast. Instead, the stress on simplicity and "absence of ritualism" becomes an implicit reason for silence concerning the Lord's Supper. Interestingly, however, the denomination did occasionally practice a form of love feast, with the breaking of bread, as a service of testimony and reconciliation. This was not understood to be the Lord's Supper. By the 1950s, the love feast was becoming rare in Free Methodism.[5]

The communion ritual itself has never undergone major revision. In the 1970s, the language was modernized slightly, but the essential form was retained. An oddity of this revision is that the prayer used following the Lord's Prayer, which in the liturgical tradition is one of the prayers of confession, is designated "The Affirmation of Faith."[6]

2. To some degree, *the Free Methodist understanding of the Lord's Supper exhibits a tension between Catholic sacramentalism*, on the one hand, *and free-church themes arising from the believers church and revivalist traditions*, on the other. Sociologically, this is the familiar institutional-charismatic tension often found when new religious movements arise. In Free Methodism, it was often expressed as the tension (or conflict) between the freedom of the Spirit and dead form or ritualism. The still-unresolved tension in Free Methodism between infant baptism and infant dedication (followed by adult believers baptism) is another key example of this tension.

The discussion of ritual and sacraments in Bishop L. R. Marston's *From Age to Age a Living Witness* (the standard denominational history) shows how Free Methodists have understood and held together this tension between sacramentalism and Radical Protestantism. Marston writes, "As is true of groups generally that hold to the tradition of free worship, [in the Free Methodist Church] ritual has occupied but a minor place in its worship. However, the special occasions when ritual is in order have made a contribution of value to the stability and the spiritual depth of the congregation."[7] Clearly, in this understanding, the Lord's Supper falls under the rubric of "ritual," and as such has "a minor place," confined to "special occasions," but nevertheless serving a useful function. Importantly, the Lord's Supper is *not* understood here in its New Testament or early church simplicity.

Marston was particularly concerned about the tendency in some Free Methodist Churches to serve communion in the pews, rather than having worshipers gather at the communion rail, as implied in the ritual. He writes,

> The mangling of a beautiful service by borrowing from other traditions or attempting innovations on one's own, has been unfortunate. Members of an earlier generation who sturdily stood for their freedom in the Spirit in an ordinary service, would be deeply disturbed today by what to them would appear violence to a hallowed rite in which their turbulence of spirit was quieted by His presence as they partook of the emblems of His broken body and shed blood. Freedom of the Spirit? Yes!—in the regular services. In the Lord's Supper, let it be the solemnity of His passion and the deep unutterable joy of His salvation into which His free Spirit leads the communicants.[8]

Marston's statements suggest a kind of bipolar understanding that strongly affirms, on one hand, the freedom of the Spirit in normal or "regular" worship; and on the other hand, a more formal, sacramental worship specifically and self-consciously tied to the historic liturgical tradition. The important point for Marston is that the Holy Spirit works through both.

This tension continues in the Free Methodist (as well as many other similar) traditions. Depending on one's point of view, it can be viewed as either schizoid or profound. It could be analyzed at several levels. At an existential spiritual level, it suggests an almost instinctive sense that worship needs, from time to time, an element of sacramental mystery as a counterpoint to the more open and emotionally expressive form that was the normative pattern in Free Methodism. Obviously, this sense of sacramental mystery, expressed in a formal liturgy, traces back to medieval Christian sacramental understanding and practice more than to the early church's practice of the Lord's Supper. Yet it is an important element in the Free Methodist ethos.

3. *A major issue that arose in Free Methodist practice of the Lord's Supper concerned the appropriateness of prayers of confession* in the communion ritual. Is it suitable for Christians who testify to the experience of "entire sanctification" or heart cleansing to routinely con-

fess their sins to God? The traditional prayers of confession had been carried over from the church's Anglican and Methodist forebears. But the Holiness Movement had strongly stressed heart purity and constant victory over sin. If it is possible now to experience a deeper work of the Holy Spirit so that one lives free from conscious, intentional sin, then is it appropriate in a communion service to "bewail our sins" and pray for forgiveness?

This question surfaced in the quadrennial general conferences of the denomination, especially in the 1880s. By 1900 the debate was resolved by compromise. The solution: the "sins" mentioned in the ritual were understood to be sins of the past, not the present. The prayer of general confession was retained, but was changed. Before the revision, worshipers said, "We acknowledge and bewail our manifold sins and wickedness. . . . We do earnestly repent, and are heartily sorry for these our misdoings." After the change, they said, "We acknowledge and bewail *the* manifold sins and wickedness of *our past lives.* . . . We do earnestly repent, and are heartily sorry for these our *past* misdoings" (italics added).[9]

Officially, this settled the issue, though it has resurfaced informally from time to time.

4. *There was a gradual shift in practice* from the congregation always coming forward and kneeling, and using a common chalice and probably one loaf; to receiving either in the pews or at the altar, using broken morsels of bread and individual cups. (In Free Methodist practice, grape juice has always been used, never wine.) In this respect, Free Methodist practice paralleled that of many other American Protestant denominations in the first half of the twentieth century, as concern for hygiene spread.

A somewhat related change has been a gradual shift from a more "closed" to a more "open" communion. In some ways, both sides of this shift or tension trace back to John Wesley. Wesley saw the Lord's Supper as both a "converting" and a "sanctifying ordinance." It was both a place to repent and meet Christ and a place for committed Christians to grow in grace. In Free Methodist practice, the accent has gradually shifted to include the "converting" as well as the "sanctifying" emphasis—in this sense, at least, moving closer to Wesley.

5. Finally, and perhaps most significant, has been *a shift with regard to the early Free Methodist emphasis on the gospel to the poor.* "To preach the gospel to the poor" (Luke 4:18, KJV) was a central theme of B. T. Roberts, principal founder of the Free Methodist denomination.[10] In the beginning, this emphasis was incorporated into the com-

munion ritual in the form of a series of fourteen Scripture sentences. The elder leading the service was to begin the Lord's Supper by reading one or more of these sentences. All the listed Scriptures concerned godly living in this world, and over half spoke of the Christian obligation to care for the poor and the danger of riches.[11]

As the influence of B. T. Roberts waned (he died in 1893), and as the denomination turned inward and lost much of its Radical Reforming thrust, these Scripture sentences were removed from the communion ritual.

Current Practice

Over the past thirty to forty years, the Free Methodist Church has become increasingly diverse in practice and ethnic identity. By 1975, membership in the "overseas" church had surpassed the North American membership. Today, nearly 80 percent of Free Methodists live outside North America, and the North American membership is becoming increasingly diverse ethnically. With this has come some increased diversity in the celebration of the Lord's Supper.

A current trend seems to be toward more frequent and at times more informal celebration of the Lord's Supper. While quarterly celebration has been the norm, having the Lord's Supper on the first Sunday of each month is becoming increasingly common. An attempt to make monthly observance the norm failed in the 1979 General Conference, but the wording was modified to call for celebrating it "quarterly and more often when possible."[12]

Official policy is to discourage innovation,[13] but innovations do occur—probably both at the free-church and high-church ends of the spectrum. During the 1980s, our Free Methodist congregation in Chicago developed a modified service of holy communion which preserved most of the historic liturgical elements while adding greater stress on community and on celebrating Christ's victory. A whole loaf of bread and a common chalice were generally used. The service concluded with the praise song, "This is the feast of victory for our God."

Conclusion

The most basic and obvious lesson to be learned from the Free Methodist experience concerns the blending and the holding in tension of early-church simplicity and high-church liturgical mystery in the celebration of the Lord's Supper. This is both a strength and a weakness. The weakness is that from the beginning, for historical reasons, the Free Methodist Church never really understood or experienced the meaning of the Lord's Supper as practiced in the early church's *agape* meal: The love feast partly made up for this loss, and to some degree, so did the class meeting. Yet the particular historical inheritance shielded the church from a more genuinely biblical practice and understanding of the Lord's Supper.

The partially compensating strength is that the Free Methodist Church has been able to hold together in creative tension the sense of informal community and liturgical mystery, immediacy and history, the new and the old. David L. McKenna, in his new denominationally commissioned history of the Free Methodist Church, alludes to this trait. McKenna argues that a balance of order and freedom is a key distinctive of the tradition. In worship, he suggests, "Historically we have balanced both freedom and order." "Our distinction is in the balance."[14]

⤳ 16 ⤶

The Lord's Supper: The Perspective of the African Methodist Episcopal Church

Thomas L. McCray

The celebration of the sacrament of the holy communion for the people of God in the African Methodist Episcopal Church is the most sacred form of worship. This is true not only in "our" branch of Methodism, but in all of Methodism. The invitation to share our understanding of the Lord's Supper is a challenge and a quest to reflect more deeply on the meaning of this high act of worship. It may also help us to wedge forward to a broader view through an ecumenical interchange. A sincere thanks to the conference leaders for providing this opportunity to share and learn.

In the course of preparation and research for this presentation, I spoke to my friend, the president of Payne Theological Seminary, Dr. Louis-Charles Harvey, known by many of you. I told him of my invitation to address the conference on this important topic, and asked, "What should I say?" "Well," he said, "Tom, you can simply state the practice of our traditional Methodism, enunciated from our Wesleyan background."

The African Methodist Episcopal Church is perhaps the first branch of "Mother Methodism" in America to break off to become one of several independent denominations. Like others, it retained connection to Methodist polity. While admitting different cultural styles in the exercise of our formal worship in Methodism, we are nonetheless one in the recognition of only two sacraments: the Lord's Supper and baptism.

The African Methodist Episcopal Church, a member of the body of Christ, celebrates that membership with joy and enthusiasm. The "means of grace" is the medium by which members are able to con-

219

nect with the roots of the faith, joining in a continuum of vitality to the life of Jesus Christ, our Lord. The sacrament of the Lord's Supper constitutes the most sacred of the "means of grace" or acts of worship; it is central in the theology of our Methodism.

The Book of Discipline of the African Methodist Episcopal Church contains the "Twenty-five Articles of Religion," the basic doctrine of Methodism, and among those, articles 18 and 19 relate to the Lord's Supper. The 1992 copy of the Discipline states,

> The Supper of the Lord is not only a sign of the love that Christians ought to have among themselves one to another, but rather is a Sacrament of our redemption by Christ's death; insomuch, that to such as rightly, worthily, and with faith receive the same, the bread which we break is a partaking of the body of Christ; and likewise the cup of blessing is a partaking of the blood of Christ.
>
> The body of Christ is given, taken, and eaten in the Supper, only after a heavenly and spiritual manner. And the means whereby the body of Christ is received and eaten in the Supper, is faith.
>
> The Sacrament of the Lord's Supper is by Christ's ordinance reserved, carried about, lifted up, or worshiped. The cup of the Lord is not to be denied to the lay people: for both the parts of the Lord's Supper, by Christ's ordinance and commandment, ought to be administered to all Christians alike.[1]

In an earlier day, a minister in the Methodist Episcopal Church, (now the United Methodist Church) wrote an exposition on the "Twenty-five Articles" of Methodism. Henry Wheeler, the author, entitled his text, *History and Exposition of the Twenty-five Articles of Religion of the Methodist Episcopal Church.* In the section on the Lord's Supper, the author writes,

> The Sacrament of The Lord's Supper has always occupied a most important place in the Christian Church, and is the most sacred and divine of all God's ordinances. To be sure, this most sacred of the worship experience for the Christian is a common fellowship, although called by different names, "The Breaking of Bread," "The Eucharist," "The Communion," "The Mass," and "The Lord's Supper." It is common among Methodists of our day to refer to it as "The Sacrament of the Lord's Supper."

It is the Lord's Supper, initiated by the Lord, our Lord and Saviour Jesus Christ. "While they were eating, Jesus took a piece of bread, gave a prayer of thanks, broke it, gave it to his disciples. . . . Then he took a cup, gave thanks to God, and gave it to them. 'Drink it, all of you,' he said; 'this my blood which seals God's covenant, my blood poured out for many for the forgiveness of sins' " (Matt. 26:28).[2]

This is the form for the Lord's Supper, the fellowship for the gatherings of God's people!

The Article admits that the Sacrament is a sign of love; it does not characterize the sacramentarian view, in this respect, as false, but inadequate. The lesson of humility and love was taught by the Saviour in the washing of his disciples' feet at the time of the institution of the sacramental Supper. Their contention for precedency was a painful indication of ambition and pride; elements of character that unfitted them for the solemn events of the coming night. "Jesus, knowing that the Father had given all things into his hands, and that he was come from God, and went to God," girded himself with a towel, and washed his disciples' feet. In full consciousness of his dignity and divine origin, he performed this menial function, as a reproof of their strife, and a lesson of humility and peace. He made the application, "I have given you an example, that ye should do as I have done to you" (John 13:3, 15).[3]

In the spirit of Christ, and in the confidence of his love, members of the AME Church have endeavored to follow the humility, the command of our Lord. Aware of our history in the family of the Christian community, and the burden of conflicts our people have endured in the past and even now, it is the strength of the Presence of Christ in the Supper that enables faith and stability.

Again Wheeler states:

The Holy Communion is incompatible with pride and strife. It is in remembrance of the supreme act of the Son of God, inspired by a love which in depth and intensity can have no parallel. It had its inception in love: "For God so loved the world, that he gave his only begotten Son" (John 3:16); and equally so was its execution: "I lay down my life for the sheep. . . . No man taketh it from me, but I lay it down of myself" (John 10:15-18). So also must be its fruit in us: "Beloved, if God so loved us, we ought also to love one another" (1 John 4:11). In accordance with this is the invitation, "Ye that . . . draw near with faith, and take this Holy Sacrament to your comfort."

It is easy to imagine the scene in the room in Jerusalem where Jesus and his disciples were assembled to keep the Passover. Jesus was the head, the disciples were the subordinate members of his family. "Whosoever shall do the will of my Father which is in heaven, the same is my brother, and sister, and mother" (Matt. 12:50). As soon as Jesus had finished the ceremonial feast, he proceeded to inaugurate another, new and distinct, that was to be perpetuated in the place of the Passover. "He took bread, and gave thanks, and brake it, and gave unto them, saying, 'This is my body which is given for you; do this in remembrance of me.' Likewise also the cup after supper, saying, 'This cup is the new testament in my blood, which is shed for you' " (Luke 22:19, 20). It is expressed by Matthew thus: "And he took the cup, and gave thanks, and gave it to them, saying, 'Drink ye all of it; for this is my blood of the new testament, which is shed for many for the remission of sins' " (Matt. 26:27, 28).

Jesus kept the feast of the Passover; he knew the paschal lamb slain prefigured his own death, and that the Passover feast then being observed was the last that could ever be validly celebrated; that he himself, as the Lamb of God, would be slain, a sacrifice for the sins of the world. The analogy between the paschal lamb and Christ can be easily traced. The pure paschal lamb without spot signified Christ, the effusion of the lamb's blood signified the effusion of Christ's blood, the salvation of the children of Israel from temporal death by the lamb's blood signified our salvation from eternal death by Christ's blood.[4]

So the people of God in the African Methodist Episcopal Church come to the table of the Lord out of diverse experiences of everyday living, responding to the invitation:

> You that do truly and earnestly repent of your sins and are in love and charity with your neighbors, and intend to lead a new life, following the commandments of God, and walking hereafter in His holy ways; Draw near with faith to receive the Holy Sacrament, and make your humble confession to Almighty God, in the presence of His Church, devoutly kneeling.[5]

The *AMEC Bicentennial Hymnal* declares the following in the section entitled, "The Service of Holy Communion."

The traditional monthly experience, a custom in the AME Church, usually the first Sunday in the month, brings together hundreds of people over the world, where we are joined with sisters and brothers of Christ everywhere in the Fellowship. It is a Fellowship of love and sharing, celebrating and giving. Our people come to be renewed, after having given their strength in work and service. People regain a sense of wholeness after having been pulled asunder by torrents of daily living. At the altar of the Lord, people are renewed to go forth as strong ambassadors, with a commitment to live out their faith, hopefully in obedient service and in response to the call of God. They come to the Table of the Lord through difficult times of contradictions, disappointments, rejections, prejudices, brutality, exploitations, missing the mark, and failures. And yes, we come too out of times of great joy! It is a wonderful time on Sunday morning or evening, the African Methodist Episcopal Church, when the people gather in the fellowship of the Holy Communion.

There is a hymn almost universally sung in AME Churches over the nation that seems to captivate the spirit of the Service:

> There is a fountain filled with blood
> Drawn from Emmanuel's veins;
> And sinners, plunged beneath that flood,
> Lose all their guilty stains.
>
> The dying thief rejoiced to see
> That fountain in his day;
> And there may I, though vile as he,
> Wash all my sins away.
>
> Dear dying Lamb, Thy precious blood
> Shall never lose its power,
> Till all the ransomed Church of God
> Be saved, to sin no more.

E'er since, by faith, I saw the stream
Thy flowing wounds supply,
Redeeming love has been my theme,
And shall be till I die.

Then in a nobler, sweeter song,
I'll sing thy power to save,
When this poor lisping, stammering tongue
Lies silent in the grave.[6]

In falling on our knees to receive the broken bread and poured-out wine, and with our faces toward the rising sun, we recommit ourselves, our souls and bodies to be a reasonable, holy, and living sacrifice, calling on the Lord to fill us with his grace and heavenly benediction.

ᵛᵉ§ 17 §ᵉᵛ

A Moravian Perspective on Holy Communion

Kevin C. Frack

From their earliest days, Moravians (Unity of the Brethren) have been concerned with encouraging believers to full participation in Jesus Christ. Our highest privilege and aim is that an individual might find complete access to the benefits of Jesus' redeeming work of grace, and might make a total gift of the self to Christ's service. Only through being near to God can we know in our hearts the truth that sets us free (John 8:32ff.): "God so loved the world that he gave his only Son" (John 3:16). We experience the presence of God in the sacraments of communion and baptism, and in the Scriptures. When speaking of our call as a denomination, the *Book of Order* says: "The Unitas Fratrum (Unity of the Brethren) lives by the gifts which the Lord has given His Church on earth, His word and the sacraments of Baptism and Holy Communion. Its vocation is to proclaim His Word to its congregations and to the world and to administer the Sacraments aright."[1]

The Moravian Church owes its beginning to a growing dissatisfaction with restricted participation in faith for believers. In order to enhance the sense of ownership in the life of Jesus for common people, fifteenth-century reformer John Hus began introducing congregational hymns and developed worship in the vernacular. So non-clergy might have a deeper experience of the love and salvation of Jesus, he reversed the church's communion practice of offering the bread while withholding the cup of Christ from the masses. By lifting the authority of Scripture above the practice of church tradition, Hus and his followers found a simpler, more inclusive picture of church life. Hus held that it was essential to offer believers communion in

225

both kinds, because Paul and Christ commanded it. The image of the common cup became a symbol of the popular following his reforms created. The resultant changes shifted responsibility for salvation and life in Jesus from the church and clergy, to the individual believer.[2]

In reaction, the Council of Constance labeled Hus a heretic and reinforced its prohibition of sharing the chalice with the laity. Hus was burned at the stake, July 6, 1415. His followers, mingled with the spirit of Czech nationalism, promptly took up the banner of the common cup as their symbol of reform.[3] A tragic era of fighting and confusion ensued. Discouraged by the Council's refusal to reform, and unwilling to continue in warfare, a small band of Hus's followers decided to start a new church. In 1457, the "Unity of the Brethren" were formed, not as a separate body from the Roman Catholic Church, but as a community of faith to bring about the reforms Hus had begun.[4]

Otto Dreydoppel Jr., in his paper *The Intentions of Our Founders*, concludes that their worship life reflected the desire to reform.

> Worship in the Ancient Unity, then, was characterized by a desire to purge the liturgy of medieval corruptions and accretions and to recover the reading and the preaching of the Word, by a growing codification of liturgical forms, and by the intention to allow all of the people of God to participate in the sacramental life of the church.[5]

The new church body simplified liturgy. Anyone could receive both the bread and the cup if they believed that the elements were the body and blood, according to Christ's word and mind. They rejected any human explanation of what happens in communion, preferring a "spiritual presence" understanding. Initially, the Unity chose to hold to the Roman idea of seven sacraments (today only baptism and communion). By the time of the Luther's Reformation, a relatively defined understanding of communion had developed. According to DeSchweinitz,

> in the Lord's Supper the Body of Christ is present in the bread, and the blood of Christ in the wine. Such presence is sacramental or mysterious. The words with which Christ instituted this sacrament must be accepted in simplicity and faith, and all explanation of them avoided, except with regard to the doctrine of transubstantiation and the belief that bread and wine constitute mere symbols. The Scriptures teach neither the one nor the other

view; and, furthermore, give no authority whatever for the adoration of the host. The sacrament is to be enjoyed, not adored.[6]

Moravian worship is set within a simple, usually unadorned setting, with Christ as the center of attention. Even the places of worship for the early Unity of the Brethren, first in fields, later in plain buildings, reflected an outward simplicity more in keeping with the condition of the common folk. This simplicity freed worshipers from a legalistic symbolism they couldn't understand and let them experience Christ more directly. In a description of early Moravian communion, Edwin W. Kortz writes,

> The Lord's Supper was celebrated at least four times a year and occasionally additional celebrations were held on festival days. The service began with a sermon. Then followed a public confession, absolution, and an invitation to the Table. The Table was covered with a white cloth, and the minister wore a plain white surplice. The minister repeated the words of Institution and added a short address. The communicants came to the Table in groups and received the bread as they knelt. . . . When all had received both the bread and wine, the whole congregation knelt in prayer. During the entire service hymns dealing with the passion of Christ were sung. The service closed with the Old Testament benediction.[7]

The lack of rigid structure in early Moravian worship does not imply that it was without order. It was recognized that some form or rubric to communion would be helpful. Careful not to be encumbered with external symbolism reminiscent of Roman Catholic ritual, Unity of the Brethren communion listens to the commandments of Jesus and Paul. The Lord's Supper is usually celebrated in the context of a regular service of worship, although it can be administered at any time and place deemed needful. There is no set frequency for celebrating communion in the world Unity. "As to the time and frequency of the celebration of Holy Communion or the Lord's Supper, no fixed rule can be made that is binding on all congregations."[8]

Christ's presence in worship is normally represented by the place of the pulpit (word) and sacramental table (baptism and communion). The congregation is seen gathering as children around the Lord in God's "living room." The simplicity of Jesus-centered living is enacted in each worship service. We believe that it is the outer simplicity that allows the believer to focus without distraction or constraint on an inner experience of God. In this simple experience of God, the Body finds unity.[9]

> The main features of the communion service are prayer, the right hand of fellowship (a visible symbol of fellowship with one's brother and sister), the words of institution (quotations of Scripture without interpretation, allowing the communicant freedom of interpretation), and hymns. The hymns are chosen to reflect the theme of each particular communion (Epiphany, Lent, etc.). There is no sermon in the communion service itself, but preaching is a part of the preparation for communion.[10]

Early Moravians experienced a deep affinity for the suffering Savior. So powerful was their appreciation of his sacrifice on our behalf, that the Lord's Supper itself became a tangible opportunity for the believer to meet Jesus, doing in his death what we ourselves could not in our living. The centrality of the work of Jesus to and for us shifts our attention from an altar to which believers go, offering sacrifice. Instead, we have an inner and continual meeting with the one whose death was "once for all" (Heb. 10:10). Therefore, the communion table is set on the level of the congregation, the center of worship attention. With the focus upon the present act of Christ bringing salvation to us, rather than upon any action on our part, communion allows us to physically experience "Emmanuel, . . . God is with us" (Matt. 1:23). "In this is love, not that we loved God but that he loved us and sent his Son to be the atoning sacrifice for our sins" (1 John 4:10). The focus of worship is no longer the "holy of holies" as a place in the room, but a place in our hearts. Christ at the center of our bodies and Christ the center of corporate worship—this communion allows us to gather in a circle of fellowship with him and one another.

Before the consecration of the elements of communion and then again at the conclusion of the service, participants share the right hand of fellowship (the peace of Jesus). The first occurrence is a tangible act of unity as an indication of our common need for God's forgiveness and the merits of Jesus' death. The second, as conclusion to communion, is a physical expression of the oneness we share as we go forth in proclamation of what Jesus does for, in, and through us to the world.[11]

Moravians practice open communion. We see ourselves as but one part of the larger body of Christ; thus all Christians who confess

Jesus as Lord and Savior are welcome to partake. Baptized children who have given indication of a love of Jesus to parents, pastor, and elders—such children are also welcomed to commune with the congregation. The inclusion of children is seen as a means of encouraging whatever work of the heart the Savior is undertaking. In a paper on his own belief, Arthur Freeman writes concerning the scriptural mystery of Jesus at work in communion: "The Moravian position, following Zinzendorf, is that persons may bring differing understandings of the Lord's Supper to the Lord's Table and still take communion together. If we had to define it before we joined together around the Lord's Table, we would never be able to take Communion together."[12]

The imagery of Christ coming to us is further enhanced as the elements are brought to believers. Serving communicants thus is a personal reminder that the very present Savior has come to us, that we might have life in him (John 3:17). Participants stand as the server approaches, indicating personal readiness of heart to meet with Jesus. Standing protests any elevation and veneration of the "host" in favor of the person of Jesus. Participants wait to partake at the same time, thus to symbolize our unity in Christ.[13]

The followers of Hus saw the "function" of priest or clergy changed significantly. Instead of effective worship performed *for* the congregation by those "set apart," Brethren clergy were seen as those "set apart" to stimulate others into full participation in Christ. By 1467, the Brethren began a fully autonomous clergy, desiring priests chosen for holiness of life and spiritual giftedness. Greater importance was ascribed to the purity of leadership than to the intellectualism of later Protestant reforms. The desire for holiness was further expressed by the expectation that the clergy would lead the whole flock into purity of life before God. Clergy were to set a good example, willingly to acknowledge guilt, to live humbly and non-argumentatively, and objectively to discern the hearts of believers, not swayed by tears. Authority was given to clergy to refuse communion to the unrepentant, to avoid the appearance of giving false grace.[14]

Reaction to the abuses of total authority in the position of clergy in medieval Roman Catholicism gave a different image to the "position" of clergy in the Unity of the Brethren. While expectation was high for clergy to exemplify Christlike living, they were not viewed as "different" from the laity. Ordination in the Unity of the Brethren is only an ordination to sacramental function, not to a position. Pastors are "set apart," not because of their special knowledge or ability to administer the sacraments, but to function on behalf of Christ.

In certain traditions robes are conferred upon the clergy as marks of distinction. Moravian clergy wear a plain white robe called a surplice. This covering is an "erasure" of the pastor's personality. As one who is completely submissive to Christ, the servant becomes invisible so that the believer might experience Jesus himself, heart to heart. Count Zinzendorf introduced the idea of the surplice as a celebrative symbol of the eternal image of Revelation 7:9-17. The robe's whiteness would underscore the Christians' need for purity. The Synod of 1769 officially recognized the valuable function of the surplice, but it discarded the use of Zinzendorf's added red belt.[15]

According to the *Book of Order* of the Northern Province of the Moravian Church in North America, ministers are expected to wear the surplice in functions where they act in a specific sense as a representative of the Lord: when administering the sacraments and the rites of confirmation, marriage, ordination, and consecration.[16]

Moravian communion practice provides an open invitation to meet Jesus. Regardless of a believer's heritage, age, geography, experience, and understanding—the invitation comes from the Lord to participate: "This is my body that is for you. . . . This cup is the new covenant in my blood. Do this, as often as you drink it, in remembrance of me" (1 Cor. 11:24-25). It is our hope that all people will come to know Jesus in the full intimacy of his death and resurrection for our salvation.

❧ 18 ❧

Sacrament, Ordinance, or Both? Baptist Understandings of the Lord's Supper

William H. Brackney

This essay is not intended to present an exhaustive discussion of the Lord's Supper. Instead, it is a synopsis of the historical development of Baptist beliefs, practices, and key questions about the Supper. In addition, I give some contemporary observations about the Supper's celebration in the denominational tradition, primarily in North America and its extended influence, with reference to the British experience.

Preliminary Questions

First, it is important to distinguish between the terms *sacrament* and *ordinance* in Baptist usage. Baptists, among many of the English dissenters of the sixteenth and seventeenth centuries, looked to the Bible for clear teaching on matters of faith, life, and church order. Early General and Particular Baptists worked hard at ridding their vocabulary and practice of "popish" influences and the trappings of the English Establishment.[1] The reader of John Smyth's work, for instance, is confronted repeatedly with his use of the term *ordinance,* by which he meant those acts which Christ "ordained" to be observed in the true church. He identified two essential ordinances, baptism and the Lord's Supper. Later others added the laying on of hands, footwashing, anointing with oil, preaching, and the magistracy.[2]

General and Particular Baptists used these key terms in different contexts. Some writers are convinced that John Smyth (fl. 1605) and later General Baptists derived their understandings and practices of the Lord's Supper primarily from the Mennonites.[3] This conclusion is based on the silence of contrary evidence from early accounts, plus Smyth's *Propositions and Conclusions* (1612) and correspondence describing Smyth's worship about 1608 in Amsterdam. Further, it can be noted that in 1626 the General Baptists corresponded with Hans de Ries (fl. 1610), leader of the Waterlander Mennonites, about the infrequency of the Lord's Supper in the English General Baptist community, among other matters. Finally, in this vein, at least one General Baptist congregation at Warboys practiced the love feast before the Supper in 1655, a feature possibly derived from the Mennonites.[4]

But Smyth and other General Baptists also used the term "sacrament," apparently as others had in the Puritan-Reformed tradition of which he was a part.[5] Some English Separatists like Smyth had modified Puritan theology to emphasize the method and drama of Jesus at the Last Supper. The key word was "signify": the Supper symbolized something deeper, experiential in nature. Both Puritans and Independents stressed the christological role of the minister at the Supper, which enabled "a supernatural and special blessing" or presence of the Lord in communion. Additionally, the frequency of celebration, urged by Calvin to be weekly, was transformed to monthly observance among the Independents and General Baptists in the first half of the seventeenth century in England.[6] John Smyth was educated under the celebrated Francis Johnson (1562-1618) at Cambridge and had early experience in ministry. Hence, he would have been conversant with these trends in the Puritan-Separatist tradition long before his emigration to live with the Dutch Mennonite community.[7] One is resigned, therefore, to an inconclusive position as to the precise origins of General Baptist understandings of the Lord's Supper.

Among the English Particular Baptist churches before 1675, any detailed explanation of the Lord's Supper is lacking. One may assume again that doctrine and practice evolved from the Separatist-Independent models out of which the Particular Baptists also emerged.[8] In the Particular Baptist "Second London Confession" (1677), a definitive article explained the Supper as a "memorial" in which "worthy receivers . . . spiritually receive and feed upon Christ crucified,"[9] which blends both the Zwinglian[10] and Calvinistic traditions. The terms *sacrament* and *ordinance* were used broadly (and sometimes interchangeably) of the Supper in the early Baptist communities—General and Particular—until late in the eighteenth century, when *ordinance* became the more acceptable term.[11]

What emerged from the wide variety of practices by the mid-eighteenth century was a fellowship meal referred to as "the breaking of bread" or the Lord's Supper. Commonly, the Supper was also seen as a celebration of Christ's work for believers. Some seventeenth-century Baptists took great liberties with scriptural bases for the Supper, such as the Leg-of-Mutton Baptists mentioned in D'Assigney's *Mystery of Anabaptism Unmasked* (1709). This group braised and served a rack of lamb in recognition of the Christian Passover.

It is fair to say that neither early Baptists in England nor North America had much affinity for understanding the Supper as a means of grace. Most believed that the "thing signified" took priority over the symbol, and this allowed Baptists to deny miscreant church members admission to the table, in the interests of church order. This "mere memorialism" of the sacrament reached a peak in the writings of John Clifford (1836-1923), president of the Baptist Union of Great Britain, whose position was widely influential on both sides of the Atlantic. In response, with a stroke of creative sacramental theology, Charles H. Spurgeon (1834-1892) recovered from the Puritan tradition the idea of the real presence of Christ:

> As surely as the Lord Jesus came really as to His flesh to Bethlehem and Calvary, so surely does He come by His Spirit to His people in the hours of their communion with Him. . . . No power upon earth can henceforth take from me the piece of bread which I have just eaten; it has gone where it will be made up into blood, and nerve, and muscle and bone. That drop of wine has coursed through my veins and is part and parcel of my being.[12]

Great variety thus characterized Baptist thinking and practice with respect to the theological meaning of the Lord's Supper. Baptists never followed a pattern suggested by any single writer or source, such as John Smyth, considered to be a type of "founder." Few in the local churches of Britain (not to speak of North Americans!) would have been widely read in the Reformation literature of the sixteenth century. Rather, Baptists have been more concerned with the reenactment of the Last Supper. The confessions show attention to the terms of admission to the Lord's table, as suggested in the New Testament. The preferred scriptural basis for early Baptists was the Pauline tradition (itself a dramatic recollection of the Last Supper), rather than the Gospel narratives.[13] Debates over the meanings of the relevant biblical passages often overrode classical ecclesiological disputation on the matter.

Terms of Communion

The matter of admission to the Table was particularly important to Baptists from the eighteenth century, and it was bound to the issue of membership qualifications. Strict "close communion"[14] standards were applied among most English and Welsh Baptists, with a few notable exceptions.[15] John Bunyan (1628-1688) of Bedford practiced a form of open communion and was chastised bitterly for so doing.[16] Typical of the classic position was that of John Gill (1697-1771) at Horseley Down, Southwark:

> After the ordinance of baptism, follows the ordinance of the Lord's Supper; the one is preparatory to the other; and he that has a right to the one has a right to the other; and none but such who have submitted to the former should be admitted to the latter.[17]

Robert Hall (1764-1831) of Arnsby, a major controversialist on the subject, noted the principal reasons for closed communion were (1) the priority of baptism before communion, (2) the implications of the apostolic commission, (3) the apostolic practice of believers baptism before the Lord's Supper, and (4) the united practice of all the Christian churches to his time. Hall's response to his adversaries was to assert that no "rules" existed at the time of Jesus' ministry, and that only logic favored such conclusions. Contrariwise, he argued in favor of open communion because of Christian love and recognition of pedobaptists as part of the Christian church. Also, he believed the issue of priority was a secondary matter, and that correct views on baptism had never been prerequisite to salvation.

Joining Hall among the more progressive English thinkers were Benjamin Beddome (1717-1795) of Bourton on Water, Robert Robinson (1735-1790) of Cambridge, John Ryland (1753-1825) of Northampton, and Daniel Turner (1710-1798) of Abingdon. There were also strong adherents to the traditional position, such as Andrew Fuller (1754-1815) at Kettering, Abraham Booth (1731-1806) at Prescott Street in London, Joseph Kinghorn at St. Mary's in Norwich (1766-1832), and Joseph Ivimey (1773-1832). These latter declared in 1850 that Particular Baptists had three weaknesses: open communion, ignorant ministers, tyrannical deacons.[18]

In the nineteenth century as the open communionists came to outnumber the closed communionists in the newly formed British Baptist Union, a new sect, the Strict Baptists, emerged behind the high Calvinism of William Gadsby (1773-1844) and Joseph C. Philpot (1802-1869). Some historical theologians believe this return to strict communionism was a Baptist response to the Tractarian movement, a theory validated by the crosscurrents of Victorian renewal and the Evangelical revival. But this conservative reaction was largely mollified in the Union when Charles H. Spurgeon declared himself an open communionist, while advocating closed membership, a more palatable and conciliatory position.

The American Baptist Calvinistic associations in the seventeenth and early-eighteenth centuries confessed a uniformly closed communion stance: no one was to be admitted but baptized believers. Pastors like Samuel Jones (1735-1814) of Lower Dublin, Pennsylvania, and Isaac Backus (1724-1806) of Middleborough, Massachusetts, taught from Scripture that believers baptism was the outward, visible sign that the people of God had been reconstituted a true church. Only such persons had a right to "communicate" at the Lord's Table. To do otherwise was to "walk in a disorderly way." This included pedobaptists and other professing Christian believers who were not part of the covenanting congregation. Following believers baptism as an adult, the individual would assent to the covenant of the church and be admitted to the Lord's Supper. Church discipline for unruly persons might require prevention from participation until the person was restored.

In the eighteenth-century American Baptist communities, there were increasing instances of changing patterns and thinking. Reports from both New England and Pennsylvania indicated the practice of "mixed communion."[19] In the Revolutionary period, Benjamin Randal (1749-1808) of New Durham, New Hampshire, reacted to the Yankee determinism of his region in the 1780s by calling for "free grace, free will, and free communion."[20] Founder of the Freewill Baptists, Randal until the early twentieth century was considered a pariah among Regular, Calvinistic, Closed Communion Missionary Baptists.[21]

Three powerful forces had profound effects upon Baptists in the Jacksonian era. The first was local church protectionism, the ecclesiological equivalent of rugged individualism; the second was nativism. The nativist crusade caused Baptists to redouble their efforts to eradicate Catholicism, in part by asserting Baptistic distinctives. A third troubling influence was the debate with the Campbellite churches, who held to more frequent celebrations of the Supper in a form of sacramentarianism, which mainstream Baptists eschewed. A number of high-profile debates between Baptists and Campbellites dominate the literature of the 1830s and 1840s in the Ohio Valley region.

Most importantly, beginning in the 1830s in the northern United States, a form of local church protectionism articulated in the "New Hampshire Baptist Confession of Faith" (1832) called for immersion as a "pre-requisite to the privileges of a church relation . . . and to the Lord's Supper."[22] With equal vehemence in the southern states, the phenomenon called "Landmarkism" strictly forbade communion except among immersed believers.[23] J. R. Graves (1820-1893), the fiery advocate of Landmarkism, wrote, "The Lord's Supper is a church ordinance and as such can only be observed by a church as such and by a person in the church of which he is a member."[24] Likewise, J. M. Pendleton (1811-1891), in *Three Reasons Why I Am a Baptist* (1853), declared himself on the matter: "Faith precedes baptism and baptism precedes communion."

Here was the ultimate theological exclusivism within the Baptist position: neither Graves nor Pendleton would consider compromise for the sake of fellowship or love of the brethren. It was a matter of self-denial and loyalty to Jesus. Moreover, loyalty to the Landmark principles would lead inevitably to a triumph of the Baptist form of Christianity. Doctrinal positions like closed communion would hold solid prominence until the urban congregations came under the influence of cooperative mission and sociopolitical egalitarianism in the late nineteenth and early twentieth centuries.

The communion question in Canadian Baptist history has provided its share of deep division. In the eighteenth century, New Light stir led to congregations being established in the Maritime provinces. The first churches there observed open communion, later switching to a closed position. Maritime historians believe this led to a long-term sense of denominational loyalty not found elsewhere among Baptists in Canada. In the central provinces, however, there were differences of opinion depending on mission affiliation. Those churches started by American Baptists along the lakeshores practiced closed communion, those in the Ottawa Valley of English origin favored open communion, and those of Scottish Haldane vintage north of Lake Ontario held to closed communion.

Early mission societies were formed around a respective theological position; much organizational competition and discord ensued.[25] Not a small amount of confusion occurred in both the Maritimes and central provinces as the Freewill Baptists from New England started congregations on an open principle.[26] In the twentieth century, Canadian Baptists tended to follow the trends of their coreligionists in the

United States rather than in Great Britain.

Partly in response to the ecumenical movement and partly as a victim of the breakdown of Christian consensus in the period 1955-1970, few Baptists in North America retained a stance close to restricted communion. While closed membership still prevails among most Baptists, open communion to all professing believers is uniformly recognized among the groups associated with the Baptist World Alliance and others like the General Association of Regular Baptists and the Canadian Fellowship of Evangelical Baptists.[27] In Britain, Baptist participation in the national Free Church movement and the Council of Churches has led to uniformly open communionism, except among the remaining Strict Baptists.[28]

Secondary Issues

In addition to disagreement over the terms of communion, Baptists have also debated the appropriate beverage to symbolize the Lord's shed blood. All of the seventeenth- and eighteenth-century confessions assume that alcoholic wine was used in various vintages and types.[29] The First Baptist Church in Providence, Rhode Island, (oldest in the U. S.) even used beer when wine was unavailable! However, partly with the advent of the temperance crusade, and also due to the discovery of a chemically feasible means to preserve unfermented grape juice, many Baptists rushed to substitute juice for wine.

Theologians and biblical scholars on both sides contended for the exact scriptural meaning of the Greek word *oinos*.[30] In the end, largely for ethical reasons, Baptists in Britain and North America switched to the use of wine with water or commercial grape juice by the 1880s. Ironically and somewhat awkwardly, Baptist officiants today still use the terminology "fruit of the vine" or "wine," meaning "grape juice," a term which seems to carry with it an overly household tone for true disciples.

Related to choice of beverage was the question of whether to use a single cup or individual communion glasses. Until the mid nineteenth century, Baptists used a common cup or chalice from which all communicants would drink.[31] Again, technology and the advance of medical science called forth modifications to "orthopraxy." The "germ theory" of medical science reached the pew in the 1880s through schools like Johns Hopkins University and the University of Rochester. Advocates suggested that serious illnesses could be spread by unsanitary habits. Drinking from a common cup could lead to cancer, tuberculosis, diphtheria, scarlatina, influenza, tonsillitis, whooping cough and others; the greatest of these is tuberculosis, the "Great White Plague" which, like the poor, we have always with us.[32]

To counteract these possible maladies (especially as the grape beverage was no longer alcoholic!), Central Presbyterian Church and a neighboring Baptist congregation in Rochester, New York, pioneered the use of individual, sterilized glass cups in 1894. The glasses were soon patented in North America along with a convenient squeeze bottle to fill them![33] Theology had literally been shaped by social concern!

Where Baptists Are Today

Baptist theology of the Lord's Supper has been substantially modified by social and political trends. The vast majority of mainstream Baptists in North America and Great Britain offer an open Lord's table to other Christians. Many congregations enthusiastically seek fellowship with non-Baptists on special occasions like World Communion Day or during Lent. Many pastors in the American Baptist tradition and the mainstream churches of the Canadian Baptist family follow prescribed liturgies derived from service books.[34]

What one finds in the typical North American Baptist celebration of the Lord's Supper does not vary greatly. At the close of a regular worship service, the celebration of the Lord's Supper takes place, with the pastor and deacons assembled in the front of the congregation. In most local churches, Baptists use individual glasses filled with grape juice, euphemistically referred to as "the cup" or "the blood" in order to avoid the problem of "the wine."

"The cup" is served in tandem with either a symbolic loaf (which the ladies of the church prepare for the occasion), or matzoth crackers, or precut dry pellets of meal to symbolize the body of Christ. Deacons generally distribute the elements, and selections from the Pauline or Gospel accounts are read to shape the progression of the service. The Lord's Supper is celebrated typically once per month (summers possibly excepted). This reflects the ongoing pattern established in the Puritan-Reformed traditions. It is uncommon for anyone but the pastor of a congregation to officiate, designated deacons being an exception.[35]

In general, twentieth-century Baptists, strongly influenced by

North American nineteenth-century thought, seem to have adopted a "memorialist" position as their theological understanding of the Supper. The elements are only symbols of the Lord's completed sacrifice. The real thrust of the event is obedience to Christ's command, "Do this in remembrance of me," which is frequently carved in the front of Baptist communion tables. The widespread reproduction of Leonardo da Vinci's "Last Supper" painting in many sanctuaries or educational facilities leaves with Baptists the popular image of Jesus and his followers gathered about a wooden table at supper. Thus to the observer, the pastor visually assumes the position of Christ in the middle of the table, with the inner semicircle of deacons gathered around.

Many pastors will emphasize prayer and confession at the beginning of the service as vehicles of preparation; some borrow statements of invitation from other traditions and even request persons to come and take communion at the front of the sanctuary. The concept of "communion" with God is mixed with celebration. Canadian Baptists, for instance, widely employ a form of service which blends phraseology from a variety of Baptist and non-Baptist literature.[36] Care is still taken to avoid the terminology "means of grace" and any priestly role for the pastor.[37]

There are signals in the worldwide Baptist family that indicate reconsideration of both theory and practice. Through the Baptist World Alliance, theological faculties, and regional bodies, Baptists have interacted with important ecumenical statements like the World Council of Churches statement, *Baptism, Eucharist, and Ministry* (*BEM*, 1982), and other cross-confessional studies.[38] Such efforts have already enhanced Baptist approaches to the Lord's Table.[39] Canadian Baptists, as in Ontario and Quebec, have modified a Canadian Presbyterian view of the Supper with material from the Mennonite tradition, referring to it successively as an ordinance, sacrament, holy communion, eucharist, memorial, and a "joyful mystery."[40] In a recent scholarly work published by the Study and Research Committee of the Baptist World Alliance, one writer responded to the *BEM* document by affirming much that Baptists have in common with other Christians. But he took strong exception to the use of the term *sacrament* and the need to mention a "common table for all Christians."[41] Written from a U.S. Southern Baptist perspective, the official statement would not reflect the more ecumenically inclined American Baptists or the Baptist Union of Great Britain and Ireland. American Baptists, across their constituency, promote intercommunion at both the local and regional levels. British Baptists continue to advocate a Free

Church contribution in full ecumenical dialogue with national and international councils of churches.[42]

It is always safe to assert that each local Baptist church has the authority to define its understanding of the ordinances/sacraments, thus allowing much diversity. Yet it is also helpful to trace patterns which have emerged in the overall historic Baptist understandings of the Lord's Supper. In that approach, there is a remarkable similarity of confessional traditions and practices within specific cultural contexts of Baptist life and thought. From those presently existing contexts, it is refreshing to witness winds of openness and transformation, such as the theological conversations among Baptists and Roman Catholics, Lutherans, Reformed churches, Mennonites, and soon perhaps the Orthodox communion and the Church of England. Slowly, the Baptist community is coming to realize that Christ's invitation is open to many.

❧ PART 5 ❧

SPECIAL PRESENTATIONS ON THE LORD'S SUPPER

✎§ 19 §❧

Toward an Anabaptist Theology of the Lord's Supper

John D. Rempel

The Lord's Supper entered my life as a reality I knew I would long contend with the day I was baptized. When we got to the breaking of bread, I realized that more was happening than met the eye. In our catechism class, we had been given a "Zwinglian" formulation of the Supper as a memorial, but when a hush overtook the congregation —and me—the formulation fell short of what we experienced. We did not have a theology to express a reality we believed in, that of entering the mystery of the broken body and shed blood, of entering the very presence of Christ. It took me years of worship and reflection simply to put words to the dissonance between our theology and our practice of the Lord's Supper.

Early in my seminary career came my first chance to help lead a chapel service in which I tried to bring together personal faith in Christ with liturgical form. Afterward, John Howard Yoder remarked to me, "You are the first person I've met, other than myself, who wants to bring together evangelical piety and liturgy." He went on to say that what evangelical theology and church life lack is liturgical and sacramental expression. It seemed bizarre to me that people for whom personal faith was so important did not know how to incarnate it. They were too often sloppy in worship and superficial in their celebration of the eucharist.

With the beginning of my doctoral studies, I was able to examine this phenomenon with scholarly tools. I was knocked over by the fact that I could not find more than a half dozen substantive articles on the Lord's Supper in Baptist or Mennonite writings. Neither of those traditions had produced a single book-length treatment of the subject!

My doctoral advisers pressed me in vain for a list of books out of my tradition on the Lord's Supper. My consolation was that I had hit upon a dissertation topic not previously dissected by fifty other people.

Once I immersed myself in Anabaptist writings on communion, I realized how diverse they were. Many authors, including Menno Simons, confine themselves to brief pastoral or apologetic comments. I found one outstanding, sustained treatment of the subject in each of the streams of Anabaptism. None of the figures I chose was at the center of the community to which he belonged; but I judged each of them to be the most profound and most systematic of their type.

Balthasar Hubmaier carried forward the theology of the Swiss German Reformation in general and of the Swiss Brethren in particular. Hubmaier, a liturgical scholar, was the only Anabaptist who sought to recreate the mass in evangelical form. His "Form of Christ's Supper" masterfully expresses Anabaptist beliefs about the Supper as a covenantal meal and a pledge of obedience, with participation modeled on 1 Corinthians 14.

Pilgram Marpeck represents the mature form of Anabaptism in the South German realm. His defense of "ceremonies" against the attacks of Spiritualists, most formidably, Caspar Schwenckfeld, led him on a theological journey that still awaits most believers churches. Protestantism as a whole gave the spiritualist impulse, the quest for the inner reality behind the outward form, greater rein than had been permitted in Catholicism. Anabaptism went far in this direction because of its emphasis on faith as the wellspring of the Christian life. It feared sacraments as realities which automatically brought into being what they signified without a necessary response of obedient faith.

Marpeck was convinced that, unless the spiritual impulse were balanced by the sacramental one, the gospel would be reduced to biblical, ahistorical, nonchurchly, individualized piety. He judged Spiritualism to be a movement that cut off the limb it was sitting on. He turned to a theology of the incarnation as the source of the outwardness of the Christian life in general, and of the church and its ceremonies in particular.

Dirk Philips systematized what Menno Simons had set forth in occasional pastoral discourses. He went beyond Menno in a significant and fascinating way. Dirk was steeped in late medieval Sacramentarianism, a eucharistically inspired mysticism focused on union with Christ. He thus preserved a strand of medieval piety within an Anabaptist theological framework.

The Reformation as a whole, particularly Anabaptism, presupposed God's initiative in salvation but became preoccupied with the human response to it. Anabaptism contended that even other forms of Protestantism did not sufficiently stress the indispensability of faith to the work of grace. By means of its baptismal theology, Anabaptism was more consistent than other forms of Christian tradition in insisting that a sacrament is the point of intersection between grace and faith. Churches which continued to baptize infants (with the possible exception of Zwinglianism) continued to hold to an objective presence of grace, whether or not it is received by the faith of the individual to whom it is offered.

At its best, Anabaptism conceived of a sacrament not as an object infused with grace but as a relationship in which grace is given and received. In my view, Anabaptism subverted the consistency of its insight by focusing so much on the human response to grace. What began as a corrective became a new, fixed position. Marpeck represents a balance between the divine initiative and the human response that continues to leave its mark on the tradition, in the High German Confession of 1660 (Dutch-North German), the Shorter Catechism of 1690 (Swiss-South German), and the Mennonite Brethren Confession of Faith of 1902. But for much Anabaptist thought, ordinances almost ended up exclusively as signs of faith but not of grace. The eucharistic piety I mentioned at the beginning, not the theology, kept a balance between the offer of grace and the response of faith.

Let me conclude this probing into issues affecting our theology of the Lord's Supper with a summary of the views of the three theologians I scrutinize in *The Lord's Supper in Anabaptism*. Balthasar Hubmaier's focus was on the Holy Spirit. The Spirit always works inwardly and even prior to the response of faith; God works in spiritual ways while the church works in material ways. This conviction led Hubmaier to undertake the most drastic and fundamental reinterpretation of sacraments of anyone I have worked with in the Anabaptist tradition.

In Hubmaier's mature theology, the breaking of bread was no longer an encounter with grace but exclusively a response to grace. This motif has dominated Free Church thought through the centuries. But Hubmaier's view was not a mere memorialism. His focus lay on the Supper as the moment of recovenanting, when believers pledge themselves to give up their body and blood for their neighbor, just as Christ gave his body and blood for them. It is a rigorous view of communion, one which opens the door to the separation of grace and obedience. But it is not graceless; grace precedes the breaking of bread. Hubmaier's Supper is sacramental in that it is a visible act of covenanting in a particular congregation. It was precisely this emphasis on the visible and communal that the Spiritualists spoke against.

Marpeck's theology of the eucharist could be aptly summarized by Augustine's dictum that we both are the body of Christ and receive the body of Christ. Marpeck's greatness is that he placed the doctrine of the incarnation within a believers church perspective. For him, the church is made up of people who have received Christ by an existential act of faith. The church as an outward, historical community is the point of intersection between grace and faith. In the incarnation and in its prolongation in the church, God befriends the created order and comes to us through it. Marpeck is not embarrassed by God's use of matter to reveal himself. He reads these thoughts out of the Gospel of John and through the lens of that Gospel, assuming them as the foundation for his understanding. The church prolongs the incarnation, and ceremonies prolong the church; ceremonies are the hands or at least the fingers of the body of Christ.

For Marpeck, a sacrament is not an isolated, static object but the self-expression of the church and of Christ, a dynamic event, an organic outflowing of life in Christ. Though he may be credited with sacramental realism, he is not at all preoccupied with bread and wine as objects and what happens to them in and of themselves. We are given union with Christ in the event of believers gathering in faith and love to share bread and wine with one another.

The sub-Zwinglian view that entrenched itself in the age of rationalism, that the Lord's Supper is merely a human act of remembrance, emerged from a long tradition that had set out to refute two Catholic teachings. One is *ex opere operato* sacramentalism, the view that a sacrament automatically effects what it signifies. The other is that the body and blood of Christ are corporeally present in communion. Marpeck holds to neither of these views and yet avoids the barren reductionism of later Free Church eucharistic thought. His appeal to the Trinity, even if present in embryonic form, introduces a dynamism; Christ's presence in the Supper flows from the life of the Trinity and shows how God moves in himself and toward the world.

Whereas Hubmaier emphasizes being the body of Christ, and Marpeck places weight on receiving as well as being that body, Dirk's emphasis is on receiving it. According to him, we are given union with Christ at the time of our conversion. The paradigm, the outward expression of this union, is the breaking of bread. We reappropriate our relationship with Christ every time we commune. Dirk makes clear that the Supper is only a sign of a reality which precedes it. But it is a sign pointing to a participation in Christ which may be most fully described as eating his flesh and drinking his blood. Dirk emphasizes the community that gathers and the importance of the presiding minister and the message he preaches. Yet in Dirk, the focus remains on the individual believer who encounters Christ.

Late in life, when erstwhile friends like Sebastian Franck denounced not only sacraments but the visible church, Dirk realized that Spiritualism left no room for the visible working of God in history—in the Bible, the church, or the ordinances. For the Spiritualist, the age of the Spirit was the age of inwardness, when true believers needed no outward signs of God's work in the world. Dirk came to see that sacraments were particular evidences for belief in the outwardness of the church. So then, on the basis of his theology of sanctification—that the believer and the church are being divinized, made to participate in the very nature of Christ—he tentatively acknowledged sacraments as expressions of our participation in the life of Christ.

Most believers churches seem to me to be where Dirk was at the end of his life: aware of the fact that Spiritualism is a denial of God's work in history, a denial of the church as the extension of Christ's incarnation. But anti-Catholic prejudice and rationalism have us stumped as to what it might mean to believe that "the bread that we break, is it not a sharing in the body of Christ?" (1 Cor. 10:16).

What did Hubmaier, Marpeck, and Dirk think they were doing? They thought of themselves as biblicists doing exegesis. They did that, but fundamentally, they were systematic theologians, thinkers who tried to arrive at a teaching adequate to guide their community and refute their detractors. From their Christology flowed their ecclesiology; from these two sources flowed their belief about ordinances. Their great inspiration is the Gospel of John. They turn to the Synoptic and Pauline institutional narratives when they have to argue with their opponents. But their home territory is the Gospel of John.

For Hubmaier, the key to understanding communion is the Son's ascension so the Spirit can come. For Marpeck, the key is the inward working of the Father through the Spirit and the outward working of the Son. For Dirk, the key is the Son's ascension but also his ongoing offering of himself to the believer in his body and blood. The words of institution, including an exegesis of "this is my body, . . . this is my blood," are secondary to the primary interest in Christology. Who Christ is, in his divine and human natures, is ultimately what matters for their ecclesiology and, in incomplete and inconsistent fashion, for their sacramentology.

How did Anabaptist communities celebrate communion? The scattered and fragmentary nature of the references makes it hard to answer this question. We have Hubmaier's "Form for Christ's Supper." It emphasizes a confession of sin, preaching on the sacrifice of Christ, the pledge of love as the basis of worthy participation in the breaking of bread. Peter Riedemann talks about a simple administration of bread and cup. Michael Sattler counsels his congregations to break bread whenever they assemble. Early in the seventeenth century, we have Leonard Clock's three communion prayers (a general prayer plus one over the bread and one over the cup) and Hans de Ries's fully worked-out service, embodying motifs from all three of my subjects.

As to frequency of observance, we know that the late medieval norm was communion once or twice a year. The priest carried out the consecration weekly, but worshipers rarely communed because of their exclusion from the liturgy and their dread of unworthy communion. Protestants tried to restore frequent communion in the sixteenth century! My interpretation of the fragmentary evidence is that Anabaptism, like other forms of Protestantism, was unable to overcome the ingrained dread of unworthy communion. Anabaptists, in addition, were so scattered by persecution that most congregations could not meet weekly. Besides, their emphasis on being at peace not only with God but with their neighbor added a moral dimension to the medieval dread.

In Catholicism, it had come to the point where a priest communed without a congregation; in Anabaptism, the congregation communed without a priest. Since the congregation was the actor in communion, if it was not reconciled in itself, it could not break bread together. We know that at the time of the Swiss division in the 1690s, the congregations in Switzerland broke bread once a year. Jacob Ammann pleaded for twice-yearly communion, appealing to the Dutch-North German congregations as his model.

Twice-yearly communion remained the norm among Mennonites until the Mennonite Brethren turned, under Baptist influence, to a monthly observance. Their reasoning was that the Supper was not only celebration of the church's unity but equally of God's grace. This pattern and theology have gradually taken root in other Mennonite and Brethren circles. We are still near the beginning of a theology and practice of the Lord's Supper which holds to the oneness of the church not only as our offering of obedience but also as Christ's offering of grace. To put it into the form of a prayer,

> Eternal God, you have graciously accepted us
> as living members of your Son, our Savior, Jesus Christ,
> and you have fed us with spiritual food
> in the sacrament of his body and blood.
> Now send us into the world in peace,
> and grant us strength and courage to love and serve you
> with gladness and singleness of heart,
> through Christ our Lord.
>
> Amen.

❧ 20 ❧

"Mary, Please Pass the Bread": Social Implications of the Lord's Supper in the Early Church

Reta Halteman Finger

Acts 2:42-47

They devoted themselves to the apostles' teaching and fellowship, to the breaking of bread and the prayers. Awe came upon everyone, because many wonders and signs were being done by the apostles. All who believed were together and had all things in common; they would sell their possessions and goods and distribute the proceeds to all, as any had need. Day by day, as they spent much time together in the temple, **they broke bread at home and ate their food with glad and generous hearts, praising God** and having the goodwill of all the people. And day by day the Lord added to their number those who were being saved. [emphasis added]

Acts 6:1-4

In those days, when the disciples were increasing in number, there was a grumbling of the Hellenists against the Hebrews because **their widows were being neglected in the daily (table) service.** And calling to themselves the whole community of disciples, the twelve said, "It is not pleasing to us to leave behind the word of God to serve tables. Examine therefore, brothers and sisters, men from among you who are well-spoken of and full of the Spirit and of wisdom, whom we will appoint for this need. And we will devote ourselves to prayers and to the service of the word." [emphasis added; author's translation]

These texts, about which I write in my doctoral dissertation, have a direct bearing on our discussion on the Lord's Supper.

In the first text in Acts 2, daily communal bread-breaking is included with other aspects of the early believers' common life and worship, such as hearing the apostles' teaching and worshiping in the temple. With this intimate relationship between ordinary and sacramental life, it seems logical to assume that these daily communal meals also included the ritual of wine and bread.

The second text in Acts 6 notes that when the number of disciples was increasing, the logistics involved in dealing with all these people became more complex. They were dealing with more than minor or temporary problems. The text says the Hellenistic widows were being overlooked in the daily table service. Some people were regularly missing out on lunch.

These texts have not figured prominently in theological reflections upon the Lord's Supper. However, they may give us an important window into early-church practices of the Lord's Supper—especially its social implications.

Through the history of scholarship, there has been resistance to using these texts to provide normative understandings for the Lord's Supper. Why? Mainly because they are embedded in a description of the believers church as a community of goods. The idea of Christians sharing material possessions has not been well-received in the church at large. Generally, church history shows a bias by both theologians and church leaders against a Christian community of goods.

Let me mention a few brief examples.

1. Communal life has been taken seriously within Roman Catholicism, but only for a minority of Christians who remain celibate. The laity have not generally been encouraged in this direction, assuming it would be destructive of family life.[1]

2. The Reformers Martin Luther and John Calvin formed their theologies about communal life against the background of, on one hand, the sixteenth-century corruption within the Roman Catholic Church and its monasteries and convents; and on the other hand, the communal emphases of the Anabaptists and the agitation of the peasants for more social justice. After some waffling, Luther concluded that such community of goods as described in Acts 2, 4, and 6 must be entirely voluntary. He did not advocate it for the majority of lay Christians.[2]

John Calvin is even more negative about a concrete sharing of possessions. He prefers to think that Luke is describing, not a literal community of goods, but a more spiritualized unity. The believers' liberality was the result of this harmony; the rich sold their goods to help the poor. Calvin is concerned about this text "on account of fanatical spirits who devise a *koinōnia* of goods whereby all civil order is overturned."³ Here he has the Anabaptists in mind because "they thought there was no Church unless all men's goods were heaped up together and everyone took therefrom as they chose."⁴

3. Much later, other commentators so feared a breakdown of Western capitalism that they saw the early communalism of believers as either a short-lived experiment that didn't work out, or as an actual evil. Commenting in *The Expositor's Bible* in 1903, G. T. Stokes saw the community of goods as a mistake that should never have happened. The event is recorded in Acts as "a significant warning for the mission field," to encourage missionary churches "to strive after a healthy independence amongst their members."⁵ Indeed, the conflict between the Hellenists and Hebrews concerning the widows can be compared to the same evil spirit that bursts forth in almshouses, asylums, and workhouses, where charity cases are suspicious and quarrelsome in spite of receiving assistance.⁶

4. The presence of Soviet communism in the twentieth century contributed to Western reaction against taking seriously any kind of actual community of goods and regular table fellowship in the Acts account. One German scholar, Werner Elert, voicing the concerns of many, emphasized that a community of goods did not work then and would not now because it suspends the natural order of economics.⁷

5. A more recent method of dismissing these texts is one which is generally held by scholars today: Luke was idealizing the early church by making it sound like a utopian dream or a primeval "Golden Age." Hans Conzelmann perhaps said it most bluntly: "We cannot speak of a failure of the experiment because it never happened in the first place."⁸

One of the reasons modern Western middle-class Christians have difficulty accepting the communal sharing of these early Jerusalem believers is that we don't understand their socioeconomic situation. What was it like to live in a world that had no concept of market capitalism, no democracy, and no social welfare system? What was it like to live in a society composed of a small minority of rich and powerful people, almost no middle class, and a great mass of lower-class people who lived from year to year on a subsistence level? In such a culture, then, what was it like to follow the practices of their Master and model Jesus, who had sent his Spirit upon them to give them power to create a new community? Sketching out that picture will be one of my dissertation tasks.

In the meantime, however, if we can dare to think that daily communal meals could have plausibly been the experience of those Jerusalem believers, what implications can we draw from this? What social implications would this practice have had for the early church, and what might it say to our church life and practice of the Lord's Supper today? I will briefly suggest three.

Communal Table Fellowship Nothing New for the Jesus Movement

Rather than a new practice created rashly during the aftermath of the Holy Spirit's wind and fire, the believers were simply continuing on a larger scale the meal practices of Jesus and his disciples. When we speak of the Lord's Supper, let's not forget that the Lord had many suppers where he ate with all the wrong people and continually challenged the hierarchical, exclusive, Greco-Roman-style meals explained by Ben Witherington. According to the Gospels, Jesus' meal practices stood out as distinctive; they were a continual irritant to the religious leaders in his culture. The innovation of daily communal meals began much earlier than the account in Acts 2.

Communal Meals a Form of Social Welfare

What happens when the whole community meets in various homes for a daily meal together? The bottom line is that the most basic needs of the poor are being met. The petition in the Lord's Prayer, "Give us this day our daily bread," is being literally fulfilled.

I don't think this means the rich were providing all the food. Barnabas is likely mentioned because he's one of the few wealthy people in the group. Rather, the subsistence believers were taking care of each other, along with the destitute. As we know, the cheapest way to do that is to buy or produce food in bulk and eat together. If so, you don't have a eucharistic, agape meal only once a month, or even once a week. You'd starve. You have it every day. As a result, it says in Acts 4:34, "there was not a needy person among them."

There is evidence in other New Testament writings of this practice of Christian groups eating together and sharing the Lord's Supper as part of their common meals. Paul criticizes the rich Corinthians (1 Cor. 11) for abusing this practice by eating their own food before the poor have a chance to get there, which means they literally go hungry (11:21). Robert Jewett has done research on tenement churches among the lower classes, in contrast to house-church groups, who evidently had a patron wealthy enough to own a large house for group meetings. Jewett's work leads one to the conjecture that many small Christian cell groups were meeting in tenements for a daily common meal, for which they each contributed something.[9] The command in 2 Thessalonians 3:10 about "those who do not work shall not eat" can make sense only in a situation where there is a common table and where food intake can be controlled.[10]

Bo Reicke's 1951 study[11] shows how the New Testament ceremony of the Lord's Supper celebrated in the context of a common meal continued the Old Testament festival traditions and was maintained by a broad stream of Christianity through the fourth century. There are references to the *agape* meal in John 13:1, Jude 12, and Ignatius' letter to Smyrna 6:2; 7:1; and 8:2, as well as discussions of common meals in Acts 2 and 1 Corinthians 11. These show that the Lord's Supper was combined with diaconal service—serving and eating meals as a community.

Seen in this light, perhaps the closest models we have today of communal eucharistic meals are soup kitchens and people eating together in the Catholic Worker Movement.

The Essential Role of Women in the Agape Meals

When the Lord's Supper is embedded in a daily common meal, what happens to "women's work"? In all cultures I know of, past and present, women are mainly responsible for food preparation and serving, as well as home management. This was certainly true of the Mediterranean culture of the first century, where gender roles were more sharply divided than in our contemporary American culture. Men were expected to operate in the public, political sphere; women lived their lives in the private sphere of home life.

So what happens if the Lord's Supper is continually reenacted in the private sphere of the home, in the context of a common meal? Luke already recorded in his Gospel that Jesus had said, in the context of the Last Supper, that he was among them, not as one who reclined at the table, but as one who serves (Luke 22:27)—essentially as one who does women's work. What kind of role reversals were going on during these revolutionary communal meals in Jerusalem? What kind of honor was given to the women's work of serving food? Who *really* served the eucharistic bread and wine?

Ironically, during the history of the church, one of the last places women have been allowed to serve is at the Lord's table. But when communion is served in the context of a communal meal, it becomes that much easier to see how the reenactment of Jesus' serving bread and wine as his body and blood is really "women's work" which has been elevated to a sacred ceremony.

Daily communal meals among the early Jerusalem believers must have involved a lot of planning and organization, not unlike church potlucks of our present experience. Did a church potluck ever take place without women's planning and preparing of food? Some things never change in two thousand years!

The problems in Acts 6:1-6 have something to do with inequality regarding women. Most commentators have seen the widows in Acts 6:1 as the community's most vulnerable members. This could be, but the text says nothing about the widows being poor. Is it not possible that an order of widows—single women or older women less tied to domestic duties—handled the communal meals and food distribution? They perceived the inequality that was happening and complained to the apostles so that action was taken to correct it.

Of course, in an overall patriarchal society, male deacons are chosen. However, we do not see that any of these men took an active part in the actual organization of the meals; two of them were preachers and evangelists just like the apostles. Who was actually doing the basic, day-to-day organization of food production, buying, cooking, and serving to make sure everyone was fed? I'd be surprised if women were not the backbone of the whole operation.

Perhaps at this conference the people who have been doing the most eucharistic, sacramental service within our group are the two women who have planned and prepared and served our lunches.

Conclusion

A theology of the Lord's Supper should include the social implications reflected in Acts 2:42-47 and 6:1-6, texts which themselves hark back to Jesus' communal table practice. Communion as part of a communal meal both symbolizes and provides the context for equality of social status and equally full stomachs. No one should go hungry at the Lord's table.

Communion as part of a communal meal focuses on the essential role of women, who traditionally have prepared and served food. It reminds believers that Jesus came in the female role of food server, not in the role of the one sitting at the table. So enacted, the Lord's Supper calls us to consider issues of social equality, community, and gender role reversal in our lives and church communities today.

ᴥᵹ 21 ᵹᴥ

Proposed Theses for a
Believers Church Theology
of the Lord's Supper

Thomas Finger

Given the variety among believers churches, unanimous agreement on a complete theology is unlikely. The following theses, then, are not attempts at prescribing a uniform perspective, and I certainly make no claims to comprehensiveness. They are simply brief discussion proposals to help discern what degrees and kinds of similarities and differences exist among believers churches.

I hope that this presentation will elicit suggestions for additions to or subtractions from the list of theses below, as well as for different wordings, nuancings, combinations, and arrangements. Many of these themes are handled in my *Christian Theology: An Eschatological Approach.*[1]

Theses Describing a General Believers Church Orientation

1. **Believers churches can affirm the general principle of "sacramentality."** "Sacramentality," broadly considered, means that the material world is God's good creation, and that God always wills to impart revelation and salvation through it and by means of it. Believers churches, by emphasizing visible holiness in concrete relationships and tasks, have affirmed this principle, largely in an ethical-social sense.

Recognition of the compatibility of this emphasis with the broad "sacramental" principle can encourage believers churches to consider ways of expressing it more fully in worship. Such recognition can open avenues for dialogue and understanding with churches who have been more sacramental in the liturgical sense.[2]

2. The Lord's Supper, by sharing many features with ordinary common meals, expresses God's desire to be present at such meals and at similar corporate, daily events. While the Lord's Supper has many unique features and a distinct focus, its use of common foods and its frequent connection with aspects of ordinary meals, especially in Scripture, make it not so much a specialized religious rite as an event illuminating and directing attention to God's desire to be more fully present in more ordinary corporate events.

Celebrations of the Supper should involve features associated with ordinary meals. The communal character of the Supper can be well expressed by sharing among participants in partaking of the elements.

3. The meaning of the Lord's Supper is found more in the acts performed than in the elements involved. Most theological discussion has located the Supper's meaning in the physical elements, the words pronounced, the participant's attitude, or in some relation among these. The believers church emphasis on common sharing suggests that this meaning might be connected at least as much with the overall pattern of activities involved.

This corresponds with the original Supper's character as a dramatic foreshadowing of events about to occur and of subsequent celebrations as symbolic re-enactments of these events. Moreover, the "this (*touto*)" that we are commanded to do (1 Cor. 11:24-25), which "proclaims" Jesus' death (11:26), may well refer to the acts of sharing.[3]

Theses Describing the Celebration of Lord's Supper Itself

4. The Lord's Supper involves remembrance of Jesus' life, teaching, passion, and crucifixion. Believers churches have emphasized Jesus' concrete life and death and have resisted treating him simply as a general spiritual principle. Accordingly, while celebrations of the Supper may include many features, they should always recall his historical suffering and crucifixion. The words of institution, often connected with the Supper in Scripture and regularly used by almost all churches, form an appropriate part of every celebration.

5. Since Jesus is risen, he is not only remembered at every authentic Supper, but also present, offering communion with himself. The bread and wine represent not only the life Jesus once offered up for us, but also his risen life, in which he now invites us to participate. Accordingly, the Supper should include features which focus on

Jesus' presence and celebrate his presence. In this way, Christ is "really present" in authentic celebration of the Supper. This presence, however, is not restricted to the physical elements. Christ is personally present throughout the activities of the Supper through the Holy Spirit.

6. The Lord's Supper is a foretaste and anticipation of the eschatological banquet. The Supper not only remembers Jesus' death and celebrates his presence. It also points forward to the culmination of his saving work, when people from all nations will gather together in harmony, material want will be abolished (cf. Isa. 25:6-9), and Jesus Christ will be fully present among them all. The Supper arouses joyful hope for this event.[4]

7. Authentic remembrance of Jesus' passion, participation in his risen life, and hope for his future involves thankfully acknowledging him as the Source and Lord of the individual's and the community's life. Since Jesus' death was his total self-giving for us, genuine response to this gift includes reciprocal giving of ourselves to him. Through offering us the elements, Jesus offers us his very life through the Holy Spirit, which becomes operative in us only as we likewise offer our lives to him.

8. Authentic remembrance of, participation in, and anticipation of Jesus' self-giving involves the participants' willingness to give themselves for each other. Since Jesus' death, life, and future coming are activities of self-giving, participation in them involves giving oneself for others. Authentic celebration of the Lord's Supper, therefore, always involves mutual pledging of the participants to each other. Since this extends, in principle, to giving one's life, it cannot be limited to "spiritual" matters; it must involve willingness to share material goods. Where economic differences impede fellowship, the Lord's Supper cannot be rightly celebrated (1 Cor. 11:17-22).

9. Authentic remembrance of, participation in, and anticipation of Jesus' self-giving involves willingness to share life, goods, and gospel with the world. Since Jesus lived, died, and lives again for the whole world, the participants' self-pledging cannot be limited to each other. It must include willingness to give themselves for anyone, friend or enemy, for whom Christ came. In light of the universality of the Supper's eschatological orientation, this involves willingness to share the gospel with all peoples, to work toward harmony among them, and to improve their material situations.

Theses Touching on Historic Issues
Concerning the Lord's Supper

10. While Jesus desires to be present in all celebrations of the Lord's Supper, his presence, since it is his self-giving through the Holy Spirit, can become actual only where it is being received, as described in theses 4-9. Christ, then, will not be actually present in the elements, words, or any other feature of the Supper simply by themselves. His presence, however, does not depend on human action as a meritorious work, since he alone can bestow himself. Human receptivity is not an initiating cause of his presence, but simply the way that our self-giving intention, in conjunction with the Holy Spirit, becomes actual as a mutual reality.

11. The Lord's Supper may be called a "sacrifice" with respect to the activities of Jesus and the participants involved. The risen Christ's self-offering to the participants and their responding self-offering, both of which are taken up into Jesus' continual self-offering to the Father, can be characterized in sacrificial terminology. Yet such "sacrifice" does not repeat Jesus' once-for-all sacrifice on Calvary.

12. Jesus is present chiefly among the participants, though he may be absent or present to individuals in unusual situations. Where features 4-9 characterize a celebration, participants can normally assume that Jesus' life-bestowing presence is active among them through the Holy Spirit, even if this is not experienced in any definitive way. Yet while Jesus' presence is primarily a communal reality, individuals authentically open to it may expect to receive something of it even in a celebration closed to it (which is not characterized by all the above features); individuals closed to Jesus' presence cannot expect to receive it even in a celebration which is open to it.

13. The elements symbolize, among other things, communion among participants, and "the body" refers to this reality, though it cannot be exclusively identified with this reality. Believers churches have often emphasized the similarity between bread and wine, formed from many grains and grapes crushed together; and the Christian community, composed of many individuals similarly united. Since Christ is present chiefly throughout this "body" (though through the Holy Spirit and not in a directly material way), the congregation can be called a eucharistic "body." Yet bread also symbolizes Jesus' historical body, and his risen presence, bestowed through the Spirit, cannot be wholly divorced from that of his glorified body; hence, the eucharistic meanings of "body" can neither be wholly identified with the community nor reduced to the community.

14. **The bread and wine of the Lord's Supper can be called Christ's "body" and "blood" in terms of their functions**. Physical realities are sometimes spoken of as functionally equivalent to broader personal ones. Giving one's "hand" in marriage, for instance, means dedicating one's life. When bread and wine function to communicate Christ's risen life, a function quite different from their ordinary use, they may be appropriately called his "body" and "blood" even though no change occurs in their substance. The modern Roman Catholic theory of *transignification* can help believers churches articulate such conceptions.[5]

PART 6

REFLECTIONS, ECUMENICAL DIALOGUE, AND FINDINGS

✦ 22 ✦

The Lord's Supper
in the
Mennonite Brethren Church

David Ewert

The Lord's Supper played an important role in the birth of the Mennonite Brethren Church in 1860. In the eighteenth century, thousands of Mennonites came from Prussia (now Poland) and established colonies in the Ukraine, by invitation of the Russian czarina. Although the colonies eventually became prosperous economically, spiritual life among Russian Mennonites in general left much to be desired. They never forgot their sixteenth-century Anabaptist roots, but they had lost their spiritual fervor; church life had become formal and rigid. This had also led to a breakdown in ethical practices.

Through a variety of influences, among them the preaching of Eduard Wuest, a Lutheran evangelist from Germany, new life began to stir. Small groups began to meet for Bible study and prayer. These spiritually awakened members began to feel uncomfortable when they found themselves partaking of the Lord's Supper with people who had been drunk on Saturday night. In one of their communities, the leading elder was asked whether he could lead those who had truly committed their lives to Christ in celebrating the Lord's Supper separately from the larger body of Mennonites. This seemed like a dangerous precedent, and the request was denied.

In the end, a group of believers met together for communion. They signed a document of secession from the larger Mennonite body on January 6, 1860. I need not review the events that followed; suffice it to say that a new church emerged and chose as its name the Mennonite Brethren.

Let me tell you, briefly, how I, as a member of this church, experienced the Lord's Supper when I was baptized and became part of this body of believers. I was born in the Ukraine and emigrated to Canada with my parents in the latter 1920s, after the Revolution, the famine, and the beginning of Stalin's reign of terror. We spoke German in the home and in the church, so I was unaware of disputes about appropriate vocabulary to designate the Lord's Supper. We called it simply *"das Abendmahl."*

As a child I did not know how the Lord's Supper was practiced, for in our church, children were not present at communion. Only baptized members (and in the first hundred years of our history, only immersed members) were allowed to be present at the Lord's table. When I was baptized at age 17, I thought of the Lord's Supper as a rather awesome event; I watched others to see what one did at this solemn occasion.

Under the influence of Russian Baptists, the Mennonite Brethren from their beginning celebrated communion once a month, and they still do. In my younger years, we literally broke bread. Regular loaves lay on the communion table, and deacons and ministers broke them into smaller pieces in the presence of the congregation. The deacons passed the bread along the pews, and each of us ate one piece. Following that, wine was poured into glasses (since we came from Europe, the question of wine versus grape juice had not yet been raised); then the glasses were passed around. We drank from a common cup.

It was stressed by our ministers that self-examination should precede participation in communion, and most of us took that quite seriously. Communion was normally attached to a regular worship service. Sometimes people would get up and leave because they did not feel worthy to partake. Church discipline was connected with communion. The life of our members was rather carefully monitored. When members failed in their Christian life, they were often asked to refrain from participating in communion. Of course, if they repented and confession was made before communion, they were restored.

Always, before the words of institution were spoken, one of our ministers would give a brief meditation on the death of our Lord. I do not recall that any great effort was made to interpret the meaning of the Lord's Supper for us. Since it was understood as a celebration at which we "remembered" Christ's death, I tended to think that the blessing of communion depended on how well I could concentrate and reflect on Christ's passion. Since then I have discovered that "remembrance" in the Hebraic sense of the word has more to do with re-enacting or reliving the Christ-event. However, I found comfort in a saying of C. S. Lewis on the Lord's Supper: Jesus said, "Take, eat." He did not say, "Take, understand."

The aspect of fellowship was strongly underscored at communion. We still practiced the holy kiss, and the Lord's Supper was an occasion to assure our neighbors in the pew of forgiveness and love. Men and woman were always separate in our churches. After we had partaken of the elements, we turned to our neighbors and gave them the kiss of peace.

The concern for the needy was also part of the communion service; to this day, as a rule, we always have a collection for the needy at the Lord's Supper.

Since the days of my youth, a number of changes have occurred in our churches with respect to the Lord's Supper. Some of the changes are of an external nature. We now use individual cups instead of common cups—not for theological but for sanitary reasons. Also, we have changed to grape juice (or something that resembles it), although there was some resistance to that change. Moreover, there has been considerable experimentation with different ways of celebrating communion. Sometimes the members sit around small tables, and sometimes the setting is a regular supper, with communion attached to it.

In earlier years our church practiced feetwashing (often attached to the communion service). However, that has been dropped and is generally held to be a Palestinian custom which need not be perpetuated in a different culture. That has also led to the abandonment of the "brotherly kiss," as it was often called.

The celebration, rightly or wrongly, is no longer as solemn an occasion as it used to be. Also, the Lord's Supper is no longer closely tied together with discipline. Perhaps the greatest change was introduced only a year ago, when our conference decided to allow believers who are not yet baptized to participate. This has raised the question of the place of believing children at communion—a question that is far from answered. Generally, one gets the impression that members in all of our churches are looking for ways and means of making the Lord's Supper more meaningful.

⌘ 23 ⌘

Reflections on the Conference

Timothy George

We have talked a lot about symbols. I am not sure what symbolic significance there is in the fact that two Baptists are holding down the right and left wings of this table, one from north of the border and the other from south of the Mason-Dixon line! I do resonate with almost everything my colleague Bill Brackney has said about the Baptist tradition, because I feel that deeply and personally myself.

This is the third Believers Church Conference I have attended. I first learned about these conferences from my teacher and great mentor, George Hunston Williams, who read a paper at the first one of these meetings on the history of the believers church from A.D. 30 to 1967, the date of that inaugural conference. Professor Williams used to tell us as doctoral students in his seminar, "The purpose of studying history is to enlarge one's coordinates, and the purpose of studying church history is to catholicize one's heresies." This is the kind of conference where that latter process of catholicizing our own heresies takes place, as we listen and engage one another.

I want to say a special word of appreciation to both Jeffrey Gros and Vladimir Berzonsky for what they've brought already to this discussion. In our open dialogue, I am sure they will contribute further. Both of them, Jeffrey quite gently and Vladimir a little more sternly, have pointed us toward the need for looking more broadly at the Christian tradition.

I'd like to talk about three elements that are indigenous to the traditions of believers churches. They also connect us to this wider Christian reality: *confession, covenant,* and *catechism.*

Confession

I begin with *confession*. One of the New Testament texts that we have talked about is Paul's declaration that we are "proclaiming the Lord's death until he comes," as we gather around his table. The element of proclamation, the kerygmatic dimension of the Lord's Supper, implies that there is a confessional reality to which we bear witness when we come to the table of the Lord. Jaroslav Pelikan has a wonderful aphorism: tradition is the living faith of the dead, whereas traditionalism is the dead faith of the living.

Many of our churches and traditions began as a conscious protest against what we perceived to be traditionalism, in an effort to re-affirm—to reenact—the New Testament church, as it was often called. Often we preferred to talk about that in terms of restitution or restoration, rather than reformation. But in any event, as I read our history, we were not intending to do something novel and new and strange and totally different from the Christian faith. We were seeking to reaffirm what we understood, under God, through our reading of holy Scripture, to be a true, articulate expression of the one, holy, catholic, and apostolic church. That's an important fact for us to remember as we think about the deep roots of our own history theologically.

To what do we bear witness at the table of the Lord? We have spoken a lot about the experience of fellowship we share together as the people of God in the believers church. But what is the objective reality to which we all bear witness as we come to the table of the Lord? Is it not the reality of the holy Trinity, the one God who is Father, Son, and Holy Spirit? Is it not the person and work of Jesus Christ, the eternal Son of God, who in the fullness of time was conceived by the Holy Spirit, born of the Virgin Mary, suffered under Pontius Pilate, was buried, raised again from the dead, ascended into heaven, and one day is coming again in power and glory?

This is a common Christian faith, to which we too bear witness. Often we've done it in formal confessions, some of us; others have been more reluctant to express those commitments and beliefs in formal confessional documents, claiming the Bible only as our creed. But whether we do that in formal confessional documents or in other ways, that is a part of the common faith that we share. The Lord's Supper is a place where that is given visible expression.

The Reformation talked about the coinherence of Word and sacrament. We have seen that demonstrated in the beautiful service of the Lord's Supper at the Brethren Church. President Finks gave us a homily and read Scripture, and that was integrated into the sharing of the elements of that special meal. Thus the confession of faith to which we bear witness is very important. That leads me to talk about the diversity of understanding we have as to what goes on at the table of the Lord: real presence versus memorialism, and all those issues related to eucharistic theology proper.

I would simply add a side note here that I think believers churches might find it helpful to reengage some of the debates of the Reformation on this issue. The differences between Luther and Zwingli have led us to be more polarized in the way we think about that issue. The differences between those two great Reformers reflect philosophical and exegetical differences they themselves were well aware of, both advocating a kind of selective literalism. Luther: "This is my body" must be taken literally. Zwingli: "Christ is at the right hand of the Father." "X" marks the spot, literally. But it was a different literalism.

When we move on to the second generation, with Calvin and the Reformed tradition, we have something of a mediating way of understanding that things separated in space can be united in time through the presence and the power of the Holy Spirit. Luther talked about the ubiquity of Christ's body; Calvin talked about the ubiquity of the Holy Spirit, and particularly the idea of our being lifted up, not bringing Christ down, but the *sursum corda*, the elevation of our hearts into the presence of the heavenly court. That's a good motif for believers churches to think about theologically.

One final point on confession. The word *confessores* in the early church had to do with bearing witness to the faith at the point of danger and death, martyrdom. We cannot gather as a believers church conference without being reminded of the tremendous role of suffering and martyrdom among those who gave shape and gave birth to so many of our traditions in the sixteenth century and beyond. When we read the *Martyrs Mirror* or *Foxe's Book of Martyrs*, very often the point of engagement, before the martyrs were sent to the stake or the gallows or drowned in a river, wasn't simply believers baptism; it was also the Lord's Supper, and a distinctive understanding of the Lord's Supper that was at variance with the received tradition. This was something for which men—many women also, and children, even—willingly gave their lives. So we cannot take that witness lightly as we seek to be faithful to what we have been given.

Covenant

My second word is *covenant.* Again, this is a word that is deeply embedded in who we have been as the people of God. The Baptist tradition often would print a covenant and even post it on the side of our church, and we would read it from our hymnals from time to time. By now, that's almost completely dropped out of many of our Baptist traditions. It's there on the books, but we seldom, if ever, have anything to do with it.

Confession speaks of what we believe; covenant speaks of how we live, our ethical obligations—we've heard much about that in this conference. But it also deals with other issues that are still controverted: the whole question of open and closed communion. I hear differing ideas of that expressed in this conference. There's a sense in which we're drawn to those who can talk about the Lord's Supper being open for anybody and everybody. It's a converting ordinance, as Wesley himself talked about it. It's an evangelistic opportunity.

But as we think about that, what really are we saying in terms of our historic tradition and our scriptural understanding of that? We have insisted that baptism be reserved for those who are consciously committed to Christ, expressed in believers baptism. We won't even extend that to the infants of believing parents. What does it mean, then, when we can feed them but not wash them? What does that say about the covenantal character of the community of faith and our relationship with the world, out of which, Vladimir has reminded us, we have been called?

Deeply connected to that, and almost not mentioned at this conference, is the role of church discipline in relation to the Lord's Supper. I only remember one brief comment here on that. We did have a Believers Church Conference at Goshen centered around this theme. Many of us have reacted against church discipline; it's dropped out of our tradition, and presumably for a good reason: the legalism, all the negative things that go with the way discipline has been abused. As one of my students put it not long ago, rather crassly, "What does one have to do to be kicked out of the Baptist church these days?" Well, the answer is, hardly anything would qualify unless it's capital murder in front of fifty witnesses!

However, isn't there such a thing, as "redemptive excommunication"? That's a part of our history. That gave distinctive shape to who we were as believers churches. Even in the time of slavery, there are cases, several instances, where slaves were a part of the congregation, a believers church congregation. Though they had no legal standing to protest against anything their master might do to them, in that church they could bring charges, so to speak. They could register a complaint in the context of a community of faithful people against masters who abused them. Now that didn't eliminate the institution of slavery, but that gets at what discipline ought to be as a part of the reality of the church. I think the relation of discipline to the Lord's Supper needs more discussion.

Catechism

My final word is *catechism.* Again I have to say, lamentably, in many of our traditions, my own included, that's a word we almost never use anymore. We say Baptist catechism is about as much of an oxymoron as a Protestant pope. Yet catechisms have been a part of our tradition. The first catechism of the Reformation was not by Luther in 1527 but by Hubmaier in 1525. Later, Charles Haddon Spurgeon, in the English Baptist tradition, also published a Baptist catechism.

This is a way of intentionally passing on the faith to the rising generation. We greatly need to give attention to that in relation to the Lord's Supper. We should not view the Lord's Supper simply as a tool of teaching, but as an experience of the presence of the community which shapes a character, a life, and a commitment to Christ. So the way we understand and the way we do the Lord's Supper in terms of our worship, the Supper's centrality, its frequency—these are important questions as we think about the catechetical dimension of the Lord's Supper.

⁖ 24 ⁖

The Lord's Supper in Ecumenical Dialogue

Jeffrey Gros

A word of appreciation for the invitation to sit in on your work, as an outsider. Indeed, I come from a Brethren community within the sacramental church, officially known as The Brothers of the Christian Schools! We have successfully kept the clergy out for over three hundred years, in service of our calling to educate the poor. We receive communion every day. But to insure our thoroughly lay Brotherhood, our discipline forbade the learning or teaching of Latin, serving the priest at mass, or wearing the surplice.

I also must confess that this has been my first experience of the Brethren love feast, though I worked with Church of the Brethren folks to see that the general board of the National Council of Churches could experience the footwashing. After this conference, I must revise my evaluation of it when teaching sacramental theology in an ecumenical context.

However, I do have on my desk a 1964 picture of my freshman high school class gathered around the table with food piled high next to the chalice and the breadbasket of matzo. In the background, trophies of the homeroom are arrayed around the Dali Last Supper. We were celebrating together one of our "meal masses." I can assure you that the Christ-centered, biblically based, objective faith in the Lord's presence in the Supper only enhances the significance of the experience of this meal, as can be noted in the Base Christian Community movement of Latin America. There we find William's Second Edition[1] finding much success. The same faith appears in the enculturation of the Lord's Supper among our people in Africa in a myriad of diverse style and customs.

Introduction

Given the time constraints, this will not be a theological, ecumenical reflection. Instead, it will be a brief word of gratitude, appropriate for a conference on the eucharist—even if we don't often use that word! I will make a few words of thanksgiving for: (1) the contribution of the Believers Church Conference and movement; (2) specific contributions to the World Council of Churches' *Baptism, Eucharist, and Ministry (BEM)* process; and, time permitting, a few challenges for the future, arising from these contributions.

However, in this community I must start with a spiritual note, taking my cue from the Salvation Army response to *BEM*.[2] We would all live our lives in the spirit of General Orsborn's hymn:

> My life must be Christ's broken bread,
> My love his outpoured wine,
> A cup o'er filled, a table spread
> Beneath his name and sign,
> That other souls, refreshed and fed,
> May share his life through mine.

To this diaconal eucharistic spirituality, I would also challenge us to a Quaker attitude. We need this if we are to become capable of any competent Christian approach to confession and ritual. We should realize that, because of Christ's presence in the community, acting and speaking must first be grounded in the Holy Spirit. Second, we should approach the acts and proclamations of the community with a profound silence before the Mystery.[3] Indeed, in theological method, this is the classical Orthodox apophatic way (separate from speech), or way of the negative.

Gratitude to the Believers Churches and Conference

The witness and contribution of persons representing your traditions, including some here, to national and international texts and scholarship is immense. I merely recall the names of Marlin Miller, James Leo Garrett, Dean Freiday, David Shannon, Dale Brown, Melanie May, Raoul Diedra, Cheryl Bridges Johns, Fred Norris, Cecil Robeck, Mark Heim, Michael Kinnamon, the late John W. V. Smith, and many more. I can assure you that my Roman Catholic students doing an ecumenical sacramental theology paper dare not neglect these if he or she expects an *A*, and I suspect that is true for your students as well. Your churches' witness shows up in the texts in ways that have influenced the lives and thinking of the Protestant, Anglican, Orthodox, and Roman Catholic traditions with which you are in dialogue. I trust a similar richness has come to your people, in Christ, through these encounters.

This meeting itself must be counted as historic. I cannot imagine that in 1967 anyone would have thought that the Lord's Supper would have emerged as an item of discussion among these churches within the ensuing thirty years or as the theme for the eleventh conference! This would have been as true inside as among those of us outside of your traditions, I suspect. Who would have thought that by 1983, the World Council's *BEM* would reflect so much of the believers church input and faith? Who would have thought that by 1990, some of the over 180 churches from all over the world to respond to *BEM* with official church testimonies would be such believers church groups as Seventh-Day Adventists, Quakers, Salvation Army, the World Evangelical Fellowship,[4] Church of the Brethren, and varieties of Mennonites, Baptists, and Wesleyans?

It is amazing to see, in these ecumenical witnesses from your churches, some major agreement. The conference has joined in affirming (1) Christ's will for the unity of the church; (2) the richness and diversity of Christian witness to the centrality of word and sacrament or ordinance within the biblical mandate to celebrate the Lord's Supper; (3) the importance of Christians seeking unity in the Lord's Supper—for Christian witness, for ethical integrity, and for theological faithfulness to the free grace of Christ by which we are alone justified; and (4) an openness to be together in a journey, empowered by the Holy Spirit, to overcome those differences which still divide us in our commemoration and understanding of the Lord's Supper.

We are grateful for the ecumenical fortitude of some of the senior speakers we have heard here. Indeed, it is pioneering work to serve the reclamation of the common patristic and medieval heritage for the believers churches, within a restorationist-Campbellite ethos.

It is risky business to take up scientific religious history and hint of Baptist origins in the Landmark ethos of early-twentieth-century Southern Baptist culture.

Wesleyanism is the most American, culturally adapted, and experienced-based Christian movement. As it explores worship reform through scientific biblical research or proposes a countercultural community of character, it stands at the ecumenical margins of Methodist and Holiness communities.

We do hope that others will follow in the footsteps of pioneering scholars and their ecumenical concerns. They can bring the best of modern ecumenical resources to bear in the next generation of believers church scholarship in service to the church worldwide. Thus they can correct deficiencies of the past and explore prospects of deeper reconciliation for the future.

Yes, I am grateful for the historic character of this gathering. It promotes and signifies ecumenical reconciliation among your churches. In addition, it provides a basis for witness to those within the wider Christian family to which your churches have a unique and compelling witness in the ecumenical encounter.

Specific Contribution to *Baptism, Eucharist, and Ministry*

In expressing particular gratitude for the contribution of believers churches to the *BEM* process, I can only (1) outline the stages of the process, (2) note some of believers church concerns that may be found in the *Eucharist* text, and (3) suggest some challenges remaining. I will leave it to others to fill in the theological content of this outline.

It would have been most useful in this conference if all of the papers had taken account of the *BEM* literature and the Believers Church Conference literature that relates to it. I look forward to reading a synthesis of the believers churches' responses to *BEM*, analyses of your common faith, questions still outstanding among you, and the common witness you wish to bring in conversation with other churches. I suspect the quality of the papers in this conference would have been enhanced if they had been informed by what your scholars are doing, by what has been done in previous conferences, and by the contribution of your traditions in the ecumenical context.

The Faith and Order movement began before the founding of the World Council of Churches (WCC). Its first World Conference was held in Lausanne, in 1927,[6] with almost all of your traditions being represented. The Lord's Supper was one of the points of discussion. This theme, together with various other issues that divide the churches, continued to be discussed. In the Accra meeting of 1974, a text "Baptism, Eucharist, and a Mutually Recognized Ministry" was produced and sent to the churches for their reaction and suggestions for revision.[7]

During this same period, a wide range of bilateral dialogues added to the reconciling research. These were national and international exchanges, and conversations between two churches or two families of churches, like the Baptist World Alliance or the Lutheran World Federation.[8] There were hundreds of meetings on issues of disagreement around the Lord's Supper, baptism, and ordination. One was a conference at Southern Baptist Seminary in Louisville in 1978.[9] This wide international consultation, biblical and historical research, and dialogue provided the basis for the convergence text, released from the Lima meeting of Faith and Order, in January 1982: *Baptism, Eucharist, and Ministry (BEM)*.

The text has become the most widely discussed text in the history of the World Council of Churches. As noted above, the formal responses are rich and diverse. The Believers Church Conference took up the text in its seventh conference, providing a response to the baptism section of the text, allowing for the witness of those theologians whose churches did not formally respond to the ongoing conversation.[10] The eighth conference took up the theme of the "Ministry of All Believers," with the ministry section of *BEM* in mind.[11] In all of the churches, the Lord's Supper is linked with questions of ministry and initiation, and therefore a conference like ours is built on its earlier work.

In the United States, two conferences were sponsored to assist the churches in the process of responding, one before official responses were produced,[12] the second after many of the U.S. church responses were available. The proceedings were published in *American Baptist Quarterly*.[13] Finally, the World Council published a *Report* in 1990 synthesizing the responses available by that time, elucidating issues that the churches did not understand or were not sufficiently clear in the text, and outlining the needs for further research, particularly in the areas of (1) Scripture and tradition, (2) ecclesiology, and (3) sacramentality.[14]

Today we know more about our common faith, common research, and continuing differences on the Lord's Supper than at any time since the Reformation. At the Fifth World Conference on Faith and Order, in 1993 at Santiago de Compostela, Spain, further work was done on these issues, including their relationship to the Lord's Supper.[15] At this meeting, there was a rich representation of believers church theologians, both from WCC member and nonmember churches.

The *Eucharist* segment of the *BEM* text itself will continue to be analyzed from a believers church perspective for a long time to come. Indeed, without allusion to this text, any future course in worship, history, or church will fall short of academic or seminary standards. This text includes sections on the institution of the Lord's Supper; its meaning, including thanksgiving, memorial (with subsections on what can be said together about sacrifice and presence), invocation of the Holy Spirit, communion of the faithful, and kingdom meal; and the structure and nature of the celebration of the Supper.[16] Marlin Jeschke's paper, especially, indicates the significant congruence of the communion and kingdom sections in particular with believers church concerns.

Future Challenges

As I have noted above, I am particularly looking forward to a synthesis and analysis of the believers churches' responses to the Lord's Supper section of this text. There are rich fields of research here for believers church scholars and students. Indeed, the historical judgments of the sixteenth century and later, even some of which we have heard in this conference, will have to be tested and possibly revised in the light of this text and the fifty years of research that stands behind it. Scholarship cannot stand that continues the judgments of the past, unless it faces the modern ecumenical agreements and takes account of their research and results, even if it comes to disagree with them after careful study. Our religious education material will have to take account of these texts and of their evaluation by the churches that have responded to it.

It will be most interesting to see what this text will contribute to the mutual understanding and relationship among the churches whose traditions are represented in the Believers Church Conferences, and between this gathering of churches and other Christian bodies. It will also be interesting to study the relationship *among* the believers churches as their diverse relationships with *other* Christian bodies develops as a result of different evaluations of this agreement.

For example, Roman Catholics and Lutherans are contemplating reevaluating the condemnations of the sixteenth century[17] on the basis of the work in this country on justification by grace through faith.[18] This will have profound implications on the evaluation of the Catholic Lord's Supper as "works righteousness." Lutherans, Anglicans, and Roman Catholic scholars, officially commissioned by their churches, already claim substantial agreement on the Lord's Supper.[19]

What will be the evaluation of the Reformation, if these proposals are successful? What will be the implications for other Reformation and post-Reformation churches? Certainly all Christians in the West will have to evaluate these texts and the research behind them in light of their own judgments in the past and their present relationship to the churches from whom they have been divided for centuries.

A second specific challenge for us is to develop an ecumenical hermeneutic, a method of interpretation that contributes to the reconciliation of Christians. We search the Scripture for common biblical warrants, for common bases for renewal, rather than legitimations for our divisions and support for historic polemics. We allow Christ's call for unity and Paul's admonitions toward reconciliation to guide our scholarship together. We search Christian history for continuities and complimentarities, not for polemics and polarization.

We seek to get inside the piety,[20] rituals, confessions, and lived faith of the other Christian body, looking first at its fidelity to the gospel before bringing the critical eye of judgment, condemnation, and alienation. We try to see and represent the other Christian group as they understand their own faith and piety. We work to criticize together those elements of our history and our lived Christianity that have been divisive and polarizing. We seek the common ground that can be found, submitting areas of division to the Holy Spirit's healing graces and to the keenest reconciling conceptualization with which God has gifted our intellects.

These are challenges that serve the reconciliation among the believers churches and encourage the believers churches in service to the wider unity of Christ's church. They provide a rich opportunity for renewal of all of our scholarship, for enriching the devotional and relational lives of our churches and all their members. Above all, they serve our fidelity to Christ's eschatological call, which is uniting all Christians for his mission to the whole world. Part of our gratitude for God's gift in communion is work to make communion among all Christians a deeper reality.

ᴥ§ 25 §ᴥ

A Baptist Response

William H. Brackney

It has been a wonderful experience for me to be part of this conference for the first time, and to recognize the values that Baptists share in common with a number of other Christian groups.

I want to focus on three issues: (1) What I think we bring to these kinds of discussions, (2) what we may lack in the believers church tradition, and (3) an overall observation.

As we listen to each other, we hear a distinct emphasis upon Christian experience. When we talk about the Lord's Supper, we yearn for a vital Christian experience. I don't wish to denigrate or deny the importance of symbol or ritual, but I hear coming from the heart and soul of the believers churches an affirmation of experience with Christ, experience with each other, experience in the great moments of our faith, one of which—the Lord's Supper—we have emphasized here. The principle of a regenerate membership, the related ideals common to us, point ultimately back to a deep sense of Christian experience.

Another asset we bring to the larger church is a sense of unity that is new among us in the last three or four decades. An important defining factor of the believers church is the unity we have achieved in these periodic conferences. There is, thankfully, a unified body of believers churches which can now participate in the larger ecumenical church. We surely have come a long way since the early sixteenth century when we were "nonconformists" or "outcasts."

Second, mention must also be made of some of our vulnerabilities. Speaking as a Baptist, I think we in the Baptist tradition need to recover a sense of the larger body of Christ. We are local church enthusiasts. We use congregational terminology, sometimes to a fault. There is a localism and a decentralizing tendency, not only evident in American but Canadian culture as well. This local church protectionism diminishes the associational principle and deemphasizes our national and regional expressions of the church.

We can also become victims of our own exclusivity. When Baptists and other believers talk about "paedo-Baptists," it is reminiscent of the "Jew/Gentile" categories of the early church. Some of the language that we use in the believers churches needs to be modified to help us recognize that beyond deeply held differences in polity, behavior, and process—surely biblically and traditionally based—we share other ideals which unify us. A broader sense of what the body of Christ encompasses is a timely need among us.

Some years ago, I heard about a wonderful moment in which the World Communion of Reformed Churches actually retracted their defamation of Baptists and Anabaptists for the first time in almost four hundred years. This should be an invitation for us to reconnect with the larger Reformation traditions for the sake of dialogue and growth. We need experience as believers churches in talking about the matters of the faith with other people in a post-Christian North America and in a not-so-Christian world that is little interested in religious fragmentation.

Third, there is a sense in which we need "respect." We first need respect among our brothers and sisters within the believers churches and then beyond. Conferences like these are beginning to earn that respect for each other; the subsequent publications and personal relationships also move us beyond being perceived as "troublesome dissenters."

Respect needs to be earned and reearned. We experience a great deal of distrust and anxiety and exclusivism toward each other. I remember in the first two sessions with the Mennonite World Conference, as I chaired the Baptist World Alliance theological discussion team, one of our members, not well-acquainted with Mennonites, continued to refer to Mennonites as "Midianites." Mennonites listened for an entire day. Their patience was astounding. Finally one Mennonite gently said, "Now can I just explain the difference between what I think the *Midianites* were and what *Mennonites* are?" The person listened patiently and replied, "Well, thank you for that. I guess it's a matter of spelling!"

We also need to grow beyond our traditional boundaries of recognition. I find it fascinating and uplifting to hear the presentation of our Seventh-Day Adventist colleague, because for so many years Baptists often categorized Seventh-Day Adventists as "not yet arriving in the mainstream of evangelical and believers church traditions." What other groups, one wonders, also might belong in our fellowship?

Finally, particularly as Baptist, we need to tone down our rhetoric. There is a 26-volume series printed by the American Baptist Historical Society called "The Baptist Bibliography," the subtitle of which reads, "Works By, For, About, and Against the Baptists." The largest amount of literature in that set is material of an antagonistic and polemic nature. It would be appropriate to spend the second half of our history talking about what we have in common with other Christians.

I conclude with one general observation. Our presence around the table of the Lord these past few days reminds us that, as believers churches, we serve and share the same Lord of the church. Perhaps that is the point of commonality into which the Believers Church Conference can now lead us.

ᴈ§ 26 §ᴂ

Observations
from the
Orthodox Perspective

Vladimir Berzonsky

I have been invited as an observer to represent the Orthodox Church and, evidently in some sense, official clergy as well; other observers, even from the Roman Catholic Church, are from the laity. We have a saying in Russian, a *biely voron*, which means "white crow." But it may be for the best that I come from a background different from the majority of you.

It appears to me that in general the Orthodox perspective is overlooked in the framework of this symposium. I have been invited precisely as an Orthodox Christian, so my observations will not always harmonize with the tenor of the presentations. However, this doesn't imply that our differences are irreconcilable, and they certainly are not to be taken as intentionally divisive or mean-spirited. I shall just reflect on what I have witnessed these last four days and offer observations from my own tradition and background.

Only one paper, as I recall, touched on the idea of Orthodox Christianity in passing, a brief reference at that. However, I feel it to be a serious fault if evangelical theology were to forego the opportunity to enhance their vision of the gospel by reaching out toward the Orthodox experience. If we may set aside the stereotypes built up against Orthodoxy, you may discover we have much to contribute to the *plērōma* (fullness) of Christian witness and faith.

I grant that we are polarities apart. The Orthodox have a fixed place for liturgy, for beauty in worship, and for the enhancement of the Lord's table—which is questionable in the eyes of those from the Reformed tradition. From listening to all the papers presented during the course of this program, it appears to me there is as much reflection on what is to be omitted from worship as what should be included.

I hope this does not appear to be overly simplistic, but our different perspectives on the Lord's Supper can be presented in the following way: The Orthodox Christian would seek to make the meal as beautiful as humanly possible. If the thought is that Jesus Christ is the invisible host and special guest, or as we state liturgically, "The offeror and the offered, the receiver and the received," how can we make this meal different from the conventional manner in which we gather for supper? We adorn the table with candles, with flowers at certain seasons, with specially sewn and rather ornate tablecloths. We prepare ourselves by fasting in order to enjoy the food all the more, preparing ourselves in cleanliness of soul through confession of sins and repentance. Then we try to imagine what we may have left out.

How strange it would be for an Orthodox Christian to ask if all this is necessary—whether we could do without the adornments, stripping to the essentials of what we absolutely require for a meal with the Lord. I recognize the background from which this reduction came about: the excesses, indulging of clergy, indulgences in another sense, and the reaction of austerity which followed. Nevertheless, I wonder if the reaction may not be overreaction. Is there not time now for a new look at liturgy?

Also, in the presentations on the Lord's Supper, it seemed painfully apparent to me there is a concerted avoidance of the very meal in the Gospels which is a sublime moment of sharing between the disciples and the Lord, the Last Supper. Many scholars have pointed to the varieties of references in the Johannine Gospel to the eucharist; for instance, at the post-resurrection appearances of Christ, he makes a point of sharing a meal, not only as proof that he is risen in the flesh, but to affirm the bond of union he anticipated at the Last Supper.

I was interested in the sterling use of tradition by St. Paul in his first letter to the Corinthians, for a reference to the words of institution. Yet it seemed to me rather odd not to lift up the actual Last Supper scenarios from the Gospels themselves. I felt something is escaping me in regard to the preference of epistle over Gospels. Nevertheless, let us proceed to Corinthians. Here we have the admonition of Paul: "When you assemble as a church" (11:18). Fortunately or unfortunately, *ekklēsia* has never been defined in the literal sense, if definition means circumscribing. By its very nature, the church remains a mystery transcending definition. Here then is a term which we might profitably reexamine. How is this assembly special? May we introduce other terms and come to some agreement as to what we mean when we say, for instance, *sacrament? eucharist?*

Some presenters have lifted up other terms for the Lord's Supper, such as *eucharist*. However, I felt one term was omitted, a term that might be quite helpful for our mutual edification: *liturgy.*

Liturgia simply means "work," just ordinary work, a rather mundane term, which makes it possible to begin anew without a great deal of theological luggage. Certainly we would have an overload of ideas describing what we meant by the term; but at least we could return to the definition of the word itself.

We might do the same with *ekklēsia*. It means "to be called out." We all know enough Greek to understand that we are called out for a specific purpose, to become the people of God, the new Israel. This is the meaning of "holy" as well. To be in the church is thus to be among the holy ones.

Now the goal of the assembly is eucharist, which means "to give thanks." This is something developmental. We don't just thank or not thank; we learn how to give thanks. We do this by expanding our personalities, realizing all the reasons why we should be glorifying the Lord and Source of all blessings. To take this a step further, we soon realize how limited we are by our feeble reason and vision. We simply don't see far enough nor broadly enough to grasp all that the Lord has been, is, and intends to be doing on our behalf.

I feel we have to continually return to what we have in common, for we shall soon realize that these far outweigh what keeps us apart. I believe also that the Orthodox can be quite helpful. We affirm the place of the Scriptures, and I feel that on this basis, with people who speak of *sola Scriptura*, we can discuss, analyze, and even take apart the Scriptures.

Yet I ask myself, Why are these people able to evaluate in a very touching and sensitive way the various phases of your Reformation, discussing an early Luther and a later Luther, a Luther who was arguing with Zwingli, a Luther who was too involved in the world to develop an elaborate systematic theology? And how is it possible they can be so sensitive to the nuances of a Zwingli who at times was courageous and even foolhardy, at other times cautious, a man who evolved from his early stages of being a priest into a paragon of reform against the Catholic Church?

On the other hand, what is wrong with treating St. Augustine with the same sensitivity to his nuances of understanding, seeing in him vestiges of his Manichaean philosophical beginnings? Can we not speak of an early and a later scholar? If we could come to that evaluation of the theologian who so influenced Western Christian thought, Catholic and Reformed, we might recognize his role in setting Western Christianity apart from its Eastern base.

Many scholars recognize today that if Augustine had been capable of reading Greek, he might have mitigated some of his speculations by the insights of the Greek fathers of the church.

Taking this thought a step further, we Orthodox Christians look from outside at the traditional arguments that have never been resolved among Western Christians. Yet there are other viewpoints which have never been explored, such as the ancient Syriac tradition lying outside of both Latin and Greek fields of learning.

In other terms, we have revisited the ancient divisions that have set apart Reformists from Catholics. By using the agape meal, we have created somewhat of a Lord's Supper setting. I feel this gathering will be most helpful in serving as a catalyst for subsequent explorations of the place of the Lord's Supper among the varieties of evangelical communities assembled for this occasion.

⤳ 27 ⤶

Report of the Findings Committee

The delegates to the Eleventh Believers Church Conference gratefully acknowledge the fine work of the program committee in planning the conference around the theme of "The Lord's Supper." The well-prepared papers and the sharing of insights and concerns by those in attendance made this conference a significant learning experience.

Also, the delegates wish to express their thanks to Ashland Theological Seminary for hosting the conference, planning meaningful worship services, and leading the guests in an agape and feetwashing celebration.

The Findings Committee presented a number of tentative observations to the conference at the Saturday morning session. After receiving additional responses and suggestions from the delegates, the committee shares the following items.

Although the Lord's Supper has played such an important role in the history of believers churches, it is rather surprising that so little has been written on this topic by those who stand in this tradition. Therefore, a conference on this topic was probably long overdue.

As we read and listened to the various papers on the biblical, historical, and theological aspects of the Lord's Supper, we became aware of the great diversity both in the practice and the understanding of the Lord's Supper in churches standing in the believers church tradition. Some of this diversity is due, no doubt, to the different historical occasions that gave rise to the various branches of believers churches. These bodies often represent reactions to the church traditions with which they broke.

Items on Which Believers Churches Generally Agree

1. That the Lord's Supper was instituted by Jesus.
2. That believers churches recognize the great significance of the Lord's Supper for the life of the church.
3. That the Lord's Supper is to be practiced by believers only—people who are in fellowship one with another and who have committed their lives to Christ in faith and obedience.
4. That there are important personal, ethical, and social dimensions in the celebration of the Lord's Supper.
5. That the Lord's Supper is not only a memorial of the past Christ-event, but also witnesses to Christ's promised presence with his people. Moreover, when the church gathers at the Lord's table, it does so in the hope that Christ will return at the end of the age.

Areas in Which Different Practices Are Readily Observed

1. On frequency of communion, our churches range all the way from weekly to annual celebration of the Supper.
2. There are different settings for the Supper. Some celebrate it in the context of a meal (the agape); others limit themselves to the bread and cup. Some have participants come forward to receive the elements; others have them served by deacons.
3. There are differences in the elements. Some use ordinary bread; others use unleavened bread or wafers. Some use grape juice; others, particularly Europeans, use wine; churches differ on whether the elements should be "consecrated" or not.
4. Not all believers churches practice feetwashing as part of the communion service.
5. Some churches leave the examination of the life of the participant to the individual's own conscience; others try to monitor the life of the members of the congregation.
6. Some still connect the Lord's Supper with some form of church discipline (when necessary); others do not. Churches disagree on whether communion should be open or closed.
7. Some restrict the Lord's table to baptized believers; others encourage nonchurch members, even children, to participate.
8. Some always combine the proclamation of the Word of God with the Supper; for others, the celebration of the Lord's Supper itself is the proclamation.
9. Some make the Lord's Supper a special event; for others, it is part of the regular worship on a Sunday morning.
10. Some frown upon the practice of small groups celebrating

communion in homes or other places; others encourage koinonia groups to do just that.

11. In the Quaker tradition, every meal is sacred and thought of as a Lord's Supper.

Cases in Which Different Meanings Are Discerned

We gather that there is not only diversity in practice but also in understanding the meaning of the Lord's Supper in our churches.

1. There is still some confusion on how we understand Christ's "presence" at the Lord's Supper. Some, in fact, are concerned that we have lost the consciousness of the living Christ at the Lord's table.

2. Because of our antisacramentalist heritage, we are not quite sure whether we can legitimately use the word *sacrament*.

3. Not all members of our churches understand "in remembrance of me" in the same way. Is it mental, or is it a dramatic re-living of the great historical event of Christ's death?

4. There are also different views of the concept of *koinōnia* as this relates to the Lord's Supper. Some stress the vertical relationship of the participants with Christ; others put the emphasis on the horizontal.

5. Then, too, there are still different understandings on the question of what it means to participate in the Supper "worthily."

6. There is also a lack of understanding of the concept of "covenant" as it relates to communion. How does the participant renew one's covenant at the Lord's table?

7. The eschatological dimension is, sadly, often lacking in our celebration of communion.

8. We have some difficulty in keeping the solemnity of the occasion in balance with the joy that characterized the early church when it broke bread.

Challenges to All Believers Churches

1. To be more creative in our efforts to make the communion service meaningful. Although constant experimentation would be unsettling, we should not be too set in the way we have always done things.

2. We need to learn better the significance of symbolism, not only in worship generally, but in communion in particular.

3. We need to make sure that we do not practice any discrimination at the Lord's table—economic, social, ethnic, or gender. One of the concerns that surfaced was how to make communion more

gender inclusive. Evidently in some churches, women are not allowed to serve the eucharistic elements.

4. We should also clarify our position on how to relate to those Christian bodies that do not stand in the believers church tradition.

5. We need to clarify our position on the place of children and guests from other church traditions at the table of the Lord in our congregations.

"The grace of the Lord Jesus Christ, the love of God, and the communion of the Holy Spirit be with all of you" (2 Cor. 13:13).

Prepared by
    David Ewert, Chairman
    Christina Bucher
    Timothy George
    Luke Keefer

Appendix

Believers Church Conferences and Associated Publications

First Conference
Convened: June 26-30, 1967, at Southern Baptist Theological
Seminary, Louisville, Kentucky
Theme: "The Concept of the Believers' Church"
Publication: James Leo Garrett Jr., ed., *The Concept of the
Believers' Church: Addresses from the 1967
Louisville Conference* (Scottdale, Pa.: Herald Press,
1969).

Second Conference
Convened: June 29–July 2, 1970, at Chicago Theological
Seminary, Chicago, Illinois
Theme: "Is There a Christian Style of Life in Our Age?"
Publication: *Chicago Theological Seminary Register* 60 (Sept.
1970), includes the report of Findings Committee
and the major presentations.

Third Conference
Convened: May 26-29, 1972, at Laurelville Mennonite Church
Center, Mount Pleasant, Pennsylvania
Theme: "A Conference for Laity"
Publication: No publication of papers

Fourth Conference
Convened: June 5-8, 1975, at Pepperdine University, Malibu,
California
Theme: "Restitution, Dissent, and Renewal"
Publication: *Journal of the American Academy of Religion* 44
(Mar. 1976): 3-113, includes many of the papers.

Fifth Conference
    Convened: May 15-18, 1978, at Winnipeg, Manitoba
       Theme: "The Believers' Church in Canada"
  Publications: Jarold K. Zeman and Walter Klaassen, with John D.
          Rempel, eds., *The Believers' Church in Canada:
          Adresses and Papers from the Study Conference in
          Winnipeg, May 15-18, 1978* (Waterloo, Ontario:
          Baptist Federation of Canada, and Mennonite
          Central Committee [Canada], 1979).
          Philip Collins, *The Church of Tomorrow: The
          Believers' Church* (Toronto, Ontario: Baptist
          Federation of Canada, 1982), provides a study
          guide for the above work.

Sixth Conference
    Convened: October 23-25, 1980, at Bluffton College, Bluffton,
          Ohio
       Theme: "Is There a Believers' Church Christology?"
    Publication: J. Denny Weaver, "A Believers' Church
          Christology," *Mennonite Quarterly Review* 57 (Apr.
          1983): 112-131, presents Weaver's address as well
          as a summary of the proceedings and information
          where other papers were separately published.

Seventh Conference
    Convened: June 5-8, 1984, at Anderson School of Theology,
          Anderson, Indiana
       Theme: "Believers' Baptism and the Meaning of Church
          Membership: Concepts and Practices in an
          Ecumenical Context"
    Publication: Merle D. Strege, ed., *Baptism and Church: A
          Believers' Church Vision* (Grand Rapids, Mich.:
          Sagamore Books, 1986).

Eighth Conference
    Convened: September 2-5, 1987, at Bethany Theological
          Seminary, Oak Brook, Illinois
       Theme: "The Ministry of All Believers"
    Publication: David B. Eller, ed., *Servants of the Word: Ministry
          in the Believers' Church* (Elgin, Ill.: Brethren Press,
          1990).

Ninth Conference
   Convened: March 30–April 1, 1989, at Southwestern Baptist
          Theological Seminary, Fort Worth, Texas
     Theme: "Balthasar Hubmaier and His Thought"
  Publication: No complete compilation of conference papers was
          published. *The Mennonite Quarterly Review* 65
          (Jan. 1991): 5-68, includes the papers by John H.
          Yoder, James W. McClendon Jr., H. Wayne Pipkin,
          and George H. Williams.

Tenth Conference
   Convened: May 20-23, 1992, at Goshen College, Goshen,
          Indiana
     Theme: "The Rule of Christ (Matthew 18:15-20): A
          Conference on Church Discipline and the
          Authority of the Church"
  Publication: No complete compilation of conference papers was
          published. *Brethren Life and Thought* 38 (Spring
          1993): 69-107, includes the papers by Estella B.
          Horning, Melanie A. May, and Lauree Hersch
          Meyer. An abridged version of Everett Ferguson's
          paper appears in *Restoration Quarterly* 36 (1994):
          81-100.

Eleventh Conference
   Convened: June 1-4, 1994, at Ashland Theological Seminary,
          Ashland, Ohio
     Theme: "The Lord's Supper"
  Publication: Dale R. Stoffer, ed., *The Lord's Supper: Believers
          Church Perspectives* (Scottdale, Pa.: Herald Press,
          1997).

Twelfth Conference
   Convened: October 17-18, 1996, at McMaster Divinity
          College, Hamilton, Ontario
     Theme: The Believers' Church: A Voluntary Church

Continuation Committee: Richard E. Allison, Luke L. Keefer Jr., and
          Dale R. Stoffer, all of Ashland (Ohio) Theological
          Seminary; Marlin Jeschke, Berlin, Ohio; and
          J. Denny Weaver, Bluffton (Ohio) College

Sources for the History of the Believers Church Conferences

Materials from the Believers Church Conferences are preserved in the Archives of the Mennonite Church, at Goshen (Ind.) College.

Donald F. Durnbaugh, *The Believers' Church: The History and Character of Radical Protestantism* (Macmillan, 1968; Scottdale, Pa.: Herald Press, 1985), ix-x, calling attention to the earlier "Study Conference on the Believers' Church" held by the General Conference Mennonite Church, August 23-25, 1955, and reported in *Proceedings of the Study Conference on the Believers' Church* (Newton, Kan.: Mennonite Press, 1955).

_____, "Believers' Church." In *The Brethren Encyclopedia*, vol. 1 (Philadelphia: The Brethren Encyclopedia, 1983), 113-114.

John Howard Yoder, "Introduction," and "The Conferences on the Concept of the Believers' Church: Themes and Reports." In *Baptism and Church: A Believers' Church Vision*, ed. Merle D. Strege (Grand Rapids, Mich.: Sagamore Books, 1986), 3-7, 207-208.

Donald F. Durnbaugh, "Origin and Development of the Believers' Church Conferences." In *Servants of the Word: Ministry in the Believers' Churches*, ed. David B. Eller (Elgin, Ill.: Brethren Press, 1990), xvii-xxx.

_____, "Believers Church." In *The Mennonite Encyclopedia*, vol. 5 (Scottdale, Pa.: Herald Press, 1990), 63-64.

John H. Yoder, "The Believers' Church Conferences in Historical Perspective." *Mennonite Quarterly Review* 65 (Jan. 1991): 5-19.

Notes

Editor's Preface

1. Howard John Loewen, "Editor's Preface," in John D Rempel, *The Lord's Supper in Anabaptism: A Study in the Christology of Balthasar Hubmaier, Pilgram Marpeck, and Dirk Philips* (Scottdale, Pa.: Herald Press, 1993), 17.

1. The Lord's Supper in Church History: Early Church Through Medieval Period

1. A fine older survey from a non-Roman Catholic perspective is J. H. Srawley, "Eucharist (to end of Middle Ages)," *Encyclopedia of Religion and Ethics*, ed. Jas. Hastings (New York: Scribner's, 1922), 5:540-563. For more extensive surveys, see Y. Briolioth, *Eucharistic Faith and Practice Evangelical and Catholic* (London: SPCK, 1930); A. J. MacDonald, ed., *The Evangelical Doctrine of Holy Communion* (Cambridge: W. Heffer & Sons, 1930); R. E. Clemens et al., *Eucharistic Theology Then and Now* (London: SPCK, 1968); William R. Crockett, *Eucharist: Symbol of Transformation* (New York: Pueblo, 1989); more popularly, Gary Macy, *The Banquet's Wisdom: A Short History of the Theologies of the Lord's Supper* (New York: Paulist, 1992). For a Roman Catholic interpretation of the ancient period, see P. Battifol, *L'Eucharistie: La présence réelle et la transsubstantiation*, 9th ed. (Paris: J. Gabalda, 1930). For a good collection of texts from the patristic period, see Daniel J. Sheerin, *The Eucharist* (Wilmington: Glazier, 1986); for texts from the whole period topically arranged, P. F. Palmer, *Sacraments and Worship* (Westminster, Md.: Newman, 1963), 38-215; for the ancient period and arranged by literary categories, André Hamman, *The Mass: Ancient Liturgies and Patristic Texts* (Staten Island: Alba House, 1967); a more extensive collection of texts in the original languages with Spanish translation is Jesus Solano, *Textos eucaristicos primitivos*, 2 vols. (Madrid: La Editorial Catolica, 1952-54).

2. Exod. 12:14 uses *mnemosunon* for "remembrance," the same word as Matt. 26:13. Cf. *anamnēsis* in 1 Cor. 11:24-25.

3. Scott McCormick Jr., *The Lord's Supper: A Biblical Interpretation* (Philadelphia: Westminster, 1966), 73-84; Xavier Leon-Daffier, *Sharing the Eucharistic Bread* (New York: Paulist, 1987), 102-116. On the theme of "remembering" in the Old Testament, Brevard S. Childs, *Memory and Tradition in Israel* (Naperville, Ill.: Alec R. Allenson, 1962); in the New Testament, Nils A. Dahl, "Anamnēsis: Mémoire et Commémoration dans le christianisme primitif," *Studia Theologica* 1 (1947): 69-95, esp. 71-72 on this point; reprinted in English without complete annotation, "Anamnēsis: Memory and Commemoration in Early Christianity," in *Jesus in the Memory of the Early Church* (Minneapolis: Augsburg, 1976), 11-29.

4. E. G. C. F. Atchley, *On the Epiclesis of the Eucharistic Liturgy and in the Consecration of the Font* (Oxford: Oxford Univ. Press, 1935), surveys the history of an

epiclesis or invocation in consecrating the eucharistic elements and the water of the baptismal font.

5. For the second century, see H. B. Swete, "Eucharistic Belief in the Second and Third Centuries," *Journal of Theological Studies* 3 (1902): 161-177, repr. in E. Ferguson, *Studies in Early Christianity*, vol. 15: *Worship in Early Christianity* (New York: Garland, 1993), 109-125; E. Ferguson, *Early Christians Speak*, rev. ed. (Abilene: ACU Press, 1987), 93-127.

6. Crockett, *Eucharist: Symbol of Transformation*, 62, describes the shift as from Jewish and biblical models to naturalistic and philosophical models. He notes that there were biblical models for a language of transformation, but these were eschatological, having to do with resurrection and new creation.

7. L. W. Barnard, *Justin Martyr: His Life and Thought* (Cambridge: Cambridge Univ. Press, 1967); E. F. Osborne, *Justin Martyr* (Tübingen: Mohr, 1973); T. Stylianopoulos, "Justin Martyr," *Encyclopedia of Early Christianity*, ed. E. Ferguson (New York: Garland, 1990), 514-516.

8. M. Jourjon, "Justin," in W. Rordorf et al., *The Eucharist of the Early Christians* (New York: Pueblo, 1978), 71-85.

9. J. Nilson, "To Whom Is Justin's Dialogue with Trypho Addressed?" *Theological Studies* 38 (1977): 538-546.

10. E. C. Ratcliff, "The Eucharistic Institution Narrative of Justin Martyr's First Apology," *Journal of Ecclesiastical History* 22 (1971): 97-102.

11. Atchley, *On the Epiclesis*, section 3, understands Justin's phrase as "through the word [logos] of prayer" and as meaning a form of words, that is a prayer which he thought came from Christ; G. J. Cuming, "*DIA EUCHES LOGOU*," *Journal of Theological Studies*, n.s. 31 (1980): 80-82, translates, "a prayer of the form of words which is from Jesus," with reference to Justin, Apol. 1.13.1. A. Gelston, "*DI' EUCHES LOGOU* (Justin, *Apology* 1.66.2)," *Journal of Theological Studies* 33 (1982): 172-175 translates, "through the word of prayer from him," according to the example of Jesus' thanksgiving. See my discussion of other options in *Early Christians Speak*, 112-114.

12. Ferguson, *Early Christians Speak*, 113.

13. J. Lawson, *The Biblical Theology of St. Irenaeus* (London: Epworth, 1948); M. T. Clark, "Irenaeus," *Encyclopedia of Early Christianity*, 471-473.

14. A. Hamman, "Irenaeus of Lyons," in Rordorf, *The Eucharist of the Early Christians*, 86-98; Ferguson, *Early Christians Speak*, 114.

15. *Adv. haer.* 4.17.5; 4.18.4-5; 4.33.2; 5.2.2-3.

16. *Adv. haer.* 5.2.3, the cup and bread "receive the word of God and the Eucharist becomes the body of Christ." The parallel with 4.18.5, "receive the invocation of God," might indicate a reference to the prayer (so Atchley, *On the Epiclesis*, section 4); but "word of God" for Irenaeus normally means Christ, the Eternal Word, and if that is the meaning here, we have a possible explanation of what the heavenly reality in the quotation below is. Other possibilities besides the heavenly Logos for this heavenly reality would be the body and blood of the risen Christ, or the Holy Spirit, but these seem to me less likely.

17. Hence, there could be no change in the substance of the elements, or else his argument that our real physical bodies are raised would be compromised; everything depends on the physical elements being what they appear to be, nourishing food and drink. Fragment 13 (Harvey, 2.482-483) affirms that the "divine communion" is the blood and body of Christ but not "true blood and flesh." This extract that Oecumenius attributes to Irenaeus appears to be based on the Letter of the Churches of Vienne and

Lyons (Eusebius, *Ecclesiastical History* 5.1.14-17).

18. He does report with scorn the quite literal changes in the elements effected as if through magic by the Gnostic Marcus, in *Adv. haer.* 1.13.2.

19. E. F. Osborn, *The Philosophy of Clement of Alexandria* (Cambridge: Cambridge Univ. Press, 1957); Walter Wagner, "Clement of Alexandria," *Encyclopedia of Early Christianity*, 214-216.

20. Charles Bigg, *The Christian Platonists of Alexandria* (Oxford: Clarendon, 1913), 103-107; André Méhat, "Clement of Alexandria," in Rordorf, *The Eucharist of the Early Christians*, 99-131.

21. John 6 was a major source of both a realistic identification of the elements with the flesh and blood of Jesus (as witnessed by the frequent substitution of "flesh" for "body" in comments on the Eucharist) and of a symbolic interpretation of the benefits derived from participation.

22. In Clement's collection of Excerpts from Theodotus 82, we read, "And the bread and oil are sanctified by the power of the Name, and they are not the same as they appeared to be when they were received, but they have been transformed by power into spiritual power. Thus, the water, also, both in exorcism and baptism, not only keeps off evil, but gives sanctification as well" (R. P. Casey, *The Excerpta ex Theodoto of Clement of Alexandria*, Studies and Documents 1 [London: Christophers, 1934], 88-91). This statement could have been subscribed to by Justin and Irenaeus; it contrasts with the kind of change expressed in the fourth century by Cyril, Gregory of Nyssa, and Ambrose.

23. T. D. Barnes, *Tertullian: A Historical and Literary Study* (Oxford: Oxford Univ. Press, 1971); R. D. Sider, *Ancient Rhetoric and the Art of Tertullian* (Oxford: Oxford Univ. Press, 1971); idem, "Tertullian," *Encyclopedia of Early Christianity*, 883-885.

24. F. R. M. Hitchcock, "Tertullian's Views on the Sacrament of the Lord's Supper," *Church Quarterly Review* 134 (1942): 21-36; V. Saxer, "Tertullian," *The Eucharist of the Early Christians*, 132-155; Ferguson, *Early Christians Speak*, 115.

25. In a similar way Crockett, *Eucharist: Symbol of Transformation*, 80-81, says the distinction between a "realist" and "symbolic" understanding would have had no meaning in the early church, for whom the symbol is participating in the reality rather than just representing it. Because the symbol is the reality, yet distinguished from it, both kinds of language could be used interchangeably (p. 87).

26. Fred W. Norris, "Cyril of Jerusalem," *Encyclopedia of Early Christianity*, 250-251.

27. The translations from Cyril and Gregory of Nyssa below are taken from Ferguson, *Early Christians Speak*, 108-109; briefly discussed on 116.

28. David Balas, "Gregory of Nyssa," *Encyclopedia of Early Christianity*, 400-402.

29. John of Damascus in his presentation of the orthodox position on the Eucharist, in *Fide orth.* 4.13, borrows extensively from Gregory of Nyssa.

30. The same situation obtained in the arguments from the Eucharist in the fifth-century christological controversies. Both Cyril of Alexandria and Nestorius believed in a conversion of the elements without defining the manner of the change. But they drew opposite conclusions as to the relation of the divine and human in Christ. See Henry Chadwick, "Eucharist and Christology in the Nestorian Controversy," *Journal of Theological Studies* n.s. 2 (1951): 145-164. Crockett, *Eucharist: Symbol of Transformation*, 61-62, notes the shift to the language of transformation in the liturgies of the fourth to sixth centuries. The Liturgy of St. John Chrysostom uses the language of "make" and "change" (*metaballō*) with reference to the elements, instead of the

language of "consecration" or "epiphany" as in the earlier liturgies.

31. Louis J. Swift, "Ambrose," *Encyclopedia of Early Christianity*, 30-32.

32. Margaret Miles, "Augustine," *Encyclopedia of Early Christianity*, 121-126. The literature on Augustine is enormous; for an introduction to him, see Roy Battenhouse, ed., *A Companion to the Study of St. Augustine* (Oxford: Oxford Univ. Press, 1955).

33. For the interpretation of Ambrose and Augustine, I follow C. W. Dugmore, "Sacrament and Sacrifice in the Early Fathers," *Journal of Ecclesiastical History* 2 (1951): 24-37, repr. in E. Ferguson, *Studies in Early Christianity*, vol. 15: *Worship in Early Christianity* (New York: Garland, 1993), 178-191; see also Crockett, *Eucharist: Symbol of Transformation*, 88-98. The characterization of the two positions as realist and symbolic follows A. J. MacDonald, ed., *The Evangelical Doctrine of Holy Communion* (Cambridge: W. Heffer & Sons, 1930); Ambrose and Augustine are discussed in chap. 2.

34. Doubts about the authorship of this work appear to "have been laid to rest" (J. Quasten and A. Di Berardino, *Patrology*, vol. 4 [Westminster, Md.: Christian Classics, 1986], 172).

35. Theodoret, *Eccl. Hist.* 5.17, quotes Ambrose as speaking in terms of literal realism when he denies the sacrament to the emperor Theodosius for the massacre at Thessalonica. These words reflect Ambrose's thought, since Theodoret himself often speaks in symbolical terms.

36. The passage begins at Ambrose, *Sacram.* 4.4.13.

37. Similarly, the eucharistic sacrifice is called an "image of truth," an image of future reality (Ambrose, *Enarrationes in Is.* 38.25).

38. The following sentences summarize some thoughts from *De mys.* 9.50-58, where the language is more precise than in *De sacram.*

39. Cf. *Enarrationes in Psalmos* 118, *Serm.* 18.26: "Christ is food to me; Christ is drink to me; the flesh of God is food to me, and the blood of God is drink to me. . . . Christ is ministered to me daily."

40. Cf. *Serm.* 234.2, "Not all bread, but only that which receives the blessing of Christ becomes the body of Christ"; *Sermo Denys* 6, "Add the word [prayer] and it becomes something very different"; *Trin.* 3.4.10 refers to consecration by "mystic prayer" and the Spirit of God working invisibly.

41. *In Psalm.* 98.8 (Engl. 99.8); cf. *In Psalm.* 33:1, 3, and 11 (Engl. 34), where Augustine speaks of Christ carrying his own body.

42. *Sermo Mai* 129 refers to eating Christ not just sacramentally but by abiding in him. Cf. *Doct. Chr.* 3.16.24, where John 6:53 is interpreted as a "figure" that we should have a share in the Lord's suffering.

43. Cf. *Serm.* 272, "These things, my brothers, are called sacraments because in them one thing is seen but another is understood. What is seen has a physical appearance, but what is understood has spiritual fruit."

44. Augustine's fullest definition of a sacrament occurs in reference to the salt given to catechumens: "The signs of divine things are, it is true, things visible, but the invisible things themselves are also honored in them, and that species which is then sanctified by the blessing is therefore not to be regarded merely in the way in which it is regarded in common use" (*Catech. rud.* 26.50).

45. *Serm.* 57.7 [7.7]; 272; *Sermo Denys* 3; *Sermo Morin* 7 ("sacrament of unity"); *In euang. Ioh.* 26.13.

46. "Sacrament and Sacrifice," 24-37, esp. 33-34.

47. Brief but helpful summaries are in A. Harnack, *History of Dogma*, vol. 5 (New York: Dover, 1961 reprint), 312-322; and J. Pelikan, *The Christian Tradition*, vol. 3: *The Growth of Medieval Theology (600-1300)* (Chicago: Univ. of Chicago Press, 1978), 74-80.

48. My quotations are taken from the selections translated by George E. McCracken for the *Library of Christian Classics*, vol. 9: *Early Medieval Theology* (Philadelphia: Westminster, 1957), 94-108.

49. J. F. Fahey, *The Eucharistic Teaching of Ratramn of Corbie* (Mundelein, Ill.: St. Mary of the Lake Seminary, 1951).

50. I quote the English translation of George E. McCracken, *Early Medieval Theology*, 118-147.

51. "Whether it contains some hidden element which becomes patent only to the eyes of faith, or whether without concealment of any mystery the appearance of the body is seen outwardly in what the mind's eyes see inwardly" (*Corp.* 5). If meant to reflect Radbertus's view, this is not a fair representation, but it may be an accurate statement of how the king interpreted him.

52. "Whether it is that body which was born of Mary, suffered, died, and was buried, and which, rising again and ascending into heaven, sits on the right hand of the Father" (*Corp.* 5).

53. Cf. *Corp.* 69 for the body of Christ that suffered as different from the "body which daily in the mystery of Christ's Passion is celebrated by the faithful."

54. *Corp.* 7-10; on "figure," cf. 91.

55. *Corp.* 37-38.

56. "This [change] was done figuratively, since under cover of the corporeal bread and of the corporeal wine, Christ's spiritual body and spiritual blood do exist" (*Corp.* 16). Cf. the reference to "the spiritual body" in the Lord's Supper (*Corp.* 62).

57. Ratramnus would say more so, for he sees the realist interpretation as removing the need for faith (*Corp.* 11).

58. A Protestant perspective by A. J. MacDonald, *Berengar and the Reform of Sacramental Doctrine* (London: Longmans, Green & Co., 1930); Roman Catholic by C. E. Sheedy, *The Eucharistic Controversy of the Eleventh Century Against the Background of Pre-Scholastic Theology* (Washington: Catholic Univ. of America, 1947); balanced surveys by R. W. Southern, "Lanfranc of Bec and Berengar of Tours," in *Studies in Medieval History Presented to F. M. Powicke* (Oxford: Clarendon, 1948), 27-48; and J. Pelikan, *The Growth of Medieval Theology*, 184-204; Gary Macy, *The Theologies of the Eucharist in the Early Scholastic Period: A Study of the Salvific Function of the Sacrament according to the Theologians c. 1080-1220* (Oxford: Clarendon, 1984), 1-72.

59. "In the course of the Middle Ages, the Platonic dialectic between symbol and reality was obscured and the salvation-historical perspective gave way to a greater preoccupation with metaphysical questions" (Crockett, *Eucharist: Symbol of Transformation*, 87). The rediscovered philosophy of Aristotle provided a new way of looking at the problem and of explaining a change in the elements themselves.

60. Teresa Whalen, *The Authentic Doctrine of the Eucharist* (Kansas City: Sheed & Ward, 1993), 5-6, summarizes some of these.

61. These two arguments are explained by R. W. Southern, "Lanfranc of Bec and Berengar of Tours," 43-45.

62. Macy, *The Theologies of the Eucharist*, 39.

63. Margaret Gibson, *Lanfranc of Bec* (Oxford: Clarendon, 1978), 92.

64. Gibson, *Lanfranc*, 89.

65. Macy, *The Theologies of the Eucharist*, 73ff.

66. Macy, *The Theologies of the Eucharist*, 40.

67. A. J. MacDonald, *Lanfranc: A Study of His Life, Work, and Writing*, 2d ed. (Oxford: Oxford Univ. Press, 1944); Gibson, *Lanfranc* (Oxford: Clarendon, 1978), 63-97, on the controversy with Berengar.

68. R. W. Southern, "Lanfranc of Bec and Berengar of Tours," 34, 40.

69. Macy, *The Theologies of the Eucharist*, 36.

70. This represents a fourth kind of change in addition to the three stated by Berengar: a change from being to nonbeing, from nonbeing to being, and being into being.

71. Macy, *Theologies of the Eucharist*, 37.

72. J. Pelikan, *The Growth of Medieval Theology*, 203; James F. McCue, "The Doctrine of Transubstantiation from Berengar Through Trent: The Point at Issue," *Harvard Theological Review* 61 (1968): 385-430, esp. 387; dependent on Hans Jorissen, *Die Entfaltung der Transsubstantiationslehre bis zum Beginn der Hochscholastik* (Münster, 1965). McCue notes that Bandinelli favored a doctrine of succession rather than transubstantiation (394).

73. During this same period of time, the late-twelfth and early-thirteenth centuries, the words of consecration were fixed. See Pierre-Marie Gy, "Les paroles de la consécration et l'unité de la prière eucharistique selon les théologiens de Pierre Lombard à S. Thomas d'Aquin," in *Lex Orandi Lex Credendi: Miscellanea in onore di P. Cipriano Vagaggini*, ed. G. J. Békés & G. Farnedi (Studia Anselmiana 79; Rome: Anselmiana, 1980), 221-233.

74. H. J. Schroeder, *Disciplinary Decrees of the General Councils* (St. Louis: Herder, 1937), 238-239.

75. Macy, *The Banquet's Wisdom*, 84, 104, following McCue, "The Doctrine of Transubstantiation," 385-412, esp. 389-403.

76. For a brief introduction, Ralph McInerny, "Aquinas, St. Thomas," in *Dictionary of the Middle Ages*, ed. J. R. Strayer, vol. 1 (New York: Charles Scribner's Sons, 1982), 353-366, but not discussing his views on the sacraments.

77. I use the translation in *St. Thomas Aquinas Summa Theologiae*, ed. Thomas Gilby, vol. 58 (New York: McGraw-Hill, 1965), 53-91.

78. J. J. Megivern, *Concomitance and Communion: A Study in Eucharistic Doctrine and Practice* (New York: Herder, 1963), 237, points out that concomitance is an aspect of the doctrine of the real presence and a consequence of transubstantiation.

79. B. Augier, "La transsubstantiation d'après S. Thomas d'Aquin," *Revue des sciences philosophiques et théologiques* 17 (1928): 427-459.

80. Macy, *The Banquet's Wisdom*, 109-112.

81. McCue, "The Doctrine of Transubstantiation," 403-407.

2. Contrasting Views of the Lord's Supper in the Reformation

1. Quoted in Roland H. Bainton, *Here I Stand: A Life of Martin Luther* (New York: Abingdon Press, 1950), 207.

2. Eric W. Gritsch, *Thomas Müntzer: A Tragedy of Errors* (Minneapolis: Fortress Press, 1989), 48-49.

3. George Huntston Williams, *The Radical Reformation* (Kirksville, Mo.: Sixteenth Century Journal Publishers, Inc.), 118.

4. Edward Waite Miller and Jared Waterbury Scudder, *Wessel Gansfort: Life*

and Writings, 2 vols. (New York: G. P. Putnam's Sons, 1917), 1:191.

5. Herbert B. Workman, *John Wycliffe: A Study of the English Medieval Church,* 2 vols. (Oxford: Clarendon Press, 1926), 2:15. See also William R. Estep, *Renaissance and Reformation* (Grand Rapids: Eerdmans, 1986), 66-67.

6. Matthew Spinka, *John Huss and the Czech Reform* (Chicago: The Univ. of Chicago Press, 1941), 56-57.

7. Estep, *Renaissance and Reformation,* 73.

8. Miller and Scudder, *Wessel Gansfort,* title page.

9. Miller and Scudder, *Wessel Gansfort,* 1:4.

10. Miller and Scudder, *Wessel Gansfort,* 2:5-6.

11. Miller and Scudder, *Wessel Gansfort,* 23.

12. Cited in Williams, *The Radical Reformation,* 108.

13. Martin Luther, *The Babylonian Captivity of the Church,* 1520, trans. A. T. W. Steinhauser et al., in *Luther's Works,* 55 vols. (Philadelphia: Muhlenberg Press, 1959), 36:31. All of the known works of Luther are included in *Werke,* the Weimarer Ausgabe ed. (1883ff.), from which the English translation is made.

14. Luther, *Babylonian Captivity,* 40.

15. Zwingli's mature position on the eucharist is set forth in many separate tracts in both Latin and German. In addition to titles that have survived from the sixteenth-century editions, all are found in a 1829-1832 edition of his works in eight volumes. A more recent edition is titled *Huldreich Zwinglis samtliche Werke,* edited by E. Egli et al. (Berlin/Leipzig/Zurich: 1905-in progress). Unfortunately, the complete corpus of Zwingli's writings has never been translated into English. A newer edition of a part of Zwingli's more important works was edited by Fritz Blanke, et al. (1940-1963), titled *Zwingli Hauptschriften.* In this work, the Latin writings are translated into German. The abbreviations of the editions I refer to are as follows: ZW for the edition of 1829-1832; Z for the 1905- edition, and ZH for the *Hauptschriften* of 1940-1963.

Zwingli had written three tracts in which he took issue with Luther's concept of the "real presence" in 1527 and 1528. They are: *Fründlich verglimpfung und ableinung über der predig treffenlichen Martini Luther's wider die schwarmer; uiber Luther's buch das sacrament betreffende, Huldreich Zwingli's christenlich antwurt; uiber doctor Martin Luther's buch, bekenntnuss genannt, antwort Huldreich Zwingli's.* ZW, vol. 2.

16. ZH, 1:143

17. Peter Stephens, "Zwingli's Sacramental Views," in *Prophet, Pastor, Protestant: The Work of Huldrych Zwingli After Five Hundred Years,* edited by E. J. Furcha and H. Wayne Pipkin (Allison Park, Pennsylvania: Pickwick Publications, 1984), 159.

18. Stephens, "Zwingli's Sacramental Views," 160.

19. The modern student can follow the development of Zwingli's eucharistic theology to 1525 through his five Latin works on the subject. They are: *De Canone Missae epichiresis, De Canone Missae libelli apologia, Adversus Hieronymum Emserum Canonis Missae adsertorem apologia, De vera et falsa religion, Subsidium sive Coronis de Eucharistia. Huldrici Zuinglii Opera,* ZW (Latin works), vol. 3.

20. *The Mennonite Quarterly Review* 30 (Apr. 1956): 113-114.

21. Fast, "First Anabaptists," 115.

22. Fast, "First Anabaptists," 115.

23. John D. Rempel, *The Lord's Supper in Anabaptism* (Scottdale, Pa.: Herald Press, 1993), 47ff.

24. H. Wayne Pipkin and John H. Yoder, trans. and eds., *Balthasar Hubmaier, Theologian of Anabaptism* (Scottdale, Pa.: Herald Press, 1989), 27. I have worked

through the text of the Second Zurich Disputation as recorded in Z, 2:768-788, but at times I prefer to use Pipkin and Yoder's translation instead of my own.

25. J. C. Wenger, trans., *Conrad Grebel's Programmatic Letters of 1524* (Scottdale, Pa.: Herald Press, 1970), 21-23.

26. Leonhard von Muralt and Walter Schmid, eds., *Quellen zur Geschichte der Täufer in der Schweiz*, vol. 1 (Zurich: S. Hirzel Verlag, 1952), 41.

27. Muralt and Schmid, *Quellen*, 1:41.

28. Fritz Blanke, *Brothers in Christ*, trans. Joseph Nordenhaug (Scottdale, Pa.: Herald Press, 1961), 24.

29. Gunnar Westin and Torsten Bergsten, eds., *Balthasar Hubmaier Schriften* (Heidelberg, Germany: Verein für Reformationsgeschichte, 1962), 317.

30. Westin and Bergsten, *Balthasar Hubmaier*, 318. See also Pipkin and Yoder, *Balthasar Hubmaier*, 355.

31. I am indebted to Pipkin and Yoder, *Balthasar Hubmaier*, 393-408, for most of the quotations from "A Form of the Supper of Christ." I have taken the liberty to revise them in light of *Balthasar Hubmaier Schriften*, 355-364.

3. Believers Church Perspectives on the Lord's Supper

1. Hans-Jürgen Goertz, "Foreword," and Howard John Loewen, "Editor's Preface," in John D. Rempel, *The Lord's Supper in Anabaptism: A Study in the Christology of Balthasar Hubmaier, Pilgram Marpeck, and Dirk Philips* (Scottdale, Pa.: Herald Press, 1993), 13, 17.

2. Information on the background of the "Baptism, Eucharist, and Ministry" consensus is provided in Merle D. Strege, ed., *Baptism and Church: A Believers' Church Vision* (Grand Rapids: Sagamore Books, 1986), 125-155, 173-192, in chapters written by Lewis S. Mudge, Michael Kinnamon, and Jeffrey Gros. The document itself was issued as *Faith and Order Paper No. 111* (Geneva: World Council of Churches, 1982). For summaries of the current status of intercommunion and similar issues in the ecumenical movement, see the special issue on "Eucharistic Hospitality," *The Ecumenical Review* 44 (Jan. 1992): 1-90.

A sketch of the beginnings and course of the present series of conferences, with bibliographical citations, is found in Donald F. Durnbaugh, "Origin and Development of the Believers' Church Conferences," in *Servants of the Word: Ministry in the Believers' Church*, ed. David B. Eller (Elgin, Ill.: Brethren Press, 1990), xvii-xxx; the text was unfortunately printed in an incomplete form. See also the introduction by John Howard Yoder in Strege, *Baptism and Church* (1986), 3-7, and his article, "The Believers' Church Conferences in Historical Perspective," *Mennonite Quarterly Review* 65 (1991): 5-19. The initial conference is well documented in James Leo Garrett, Jr., ed., *The Concept of the Believers' Church: Addresses from the 1967 Louisville Conference* (Scottdale, Pa.: Herald Press, 1969).

3. Based on personal observation and articles in the Church of the Brethren periodical: "Russian Orthodox Delegation to Be Guests of Brethren in November," *Messenger*, Oct. 26, 1967, 18-19; "The Russians: Reflections on the Exchange," *Messenger*, Jan. 18, 1968, 15-19; "A Bridge Built by Dialogue," *Messenger*, Apr. 25, 1968, 10-11, 20-21.

4. Rempel, *Lord's Supper*, passim.

5. John D. Rempel, "Communion," in *The Mennonite Encyclopedia* (Scottdale, Pa.: Herald Press, 1955-59 [vols. 1-4], 1990 [vol. 5]), 5:170-172, esp. 171.

6. Ernest A. Payne, *The Fellowship of Believers: Baptist Thought and Practice*

Yesterday and Today, enlarged ed. (London: Carey Kingsgate Press, 1952), 57-70. The recent article by the Baptist theologian Millard J. Erickson is remarkably unhelpful, joining a cursory review of doctrinal and practical issues with attention to the risk of contracting AIDS through sharing a common cup. See "The Lord's Supper," in Paul Basden and David S. Dockery, eds., *The People of God: Essays on the Believers' Church* (Nashville: Broadman Press, 1991), 51-62. He asserts that a "merely symbolic view of the elements" is "held by many Baptists" (52).

7. *Christian Faith and Practice in the Experience of the Society of Friends* (London: London Yearly Meeting of the Religious Society of Friends, 1960), 61, 208 (refers to paragraphs rather than pages).

8. Robert Barclay, *A Catechism and Confession of Faith* ([n.p.: 1673]), taken from Hugh S. Barbour and Arthur O. Roberts, eds., *Early Quaker Writings, 1650-1700* (Grand Rapids: Eerdmans, 1973), 314-349, esp. 339-340.

9. Dean Freiday, ed., *Barclay's Apology in Modern English* (Lebanon, Pa.: Sowers Printing Company, 1967), 327-361, esp. 361.

10. Trueblood considers Barclay's concession about the limited utility of the ordinance a remarkable evidence of "tenderness to those who had not moved into what he thought was the new day" (233). Hugh Barbour comments on Barclay's motivation: "When in his later chapters he gave clear, compact summaries of Quaker views on the Bible and sacraments, society and the state, he gave credit to people who conscientiously still used sacraments or bore arms on their way (he said) to the fuller Light of Quakerism." Hugh S. Barbour and J. William Frost, *The Quakers* (New York: Greenwood Press, 1988), 65. For a recent Quaker view on sacraments, see the pamphlet by John Punshon, *Shadow and the Substance* (Philadelphia: Wider Quaker Fellowship, 1993), originally published in *The Evangelical Friend* (Nov./Dec., 1992). See also Howard Brinton, *Friends for 300 Years* (New York: Harper & Brothers, 1952), 69-71.

11. On the Polish Brethren, see George H. Williams, *The Radical Reformation,* 3d ed. (Kirksville, Mo.: Sixteenth Century Journal Publishers, 1992), 1146. The letter was written by Christoph Ostorodt; it is published in English translation in Donald F. Durnbaugh, ed., *Every Need Supplied: Mutual Aid and Christian Community in the Free Churches, 1525-1625* (Philadelphia: Temple Univ. Press, 1974), 126-130.

For the letter from Grebel to Müntzer, see George H. Williams, ed., "Documents Illustrative of the Radical Reformation," in *Spiritual and Anabaptist Writers,* eds. G. H. Williams and Angel M. Mergal (Philadelphia: Westminster Press, 1957), 71-85, esp. 77. Other recent translations are found in Leland Harder, ed., *The Sources of Swiss Anabaptism: The Grebel Letters and Related Documents* (Scottdale, Pa.: Herald Press, 1985), 284-292; and Michael G. Baylor, *The Radical Reformation* (Cambridge: Cambridge Univ. Press, 1991), 36-48.

12. John A. Hostetler, *Amish Society,* 4th ed. (Baltimore: Johns Hopkins Press, 1993), 33; Steven M. Nolt, *A History of the Amish* (Intercourse, Pa.: Good Books, 1992), 26-27. The documents of the schism are given in John D. Roth, with Joe Springer, eds., *Letters of the Amish Division: A Sourcebook* (Goshen, Ind.: Mennonite Historical Society, 1993), replacing John B. Mast, ed., *The Letters of the Amish Division* (Scottdale, Pa.: Christian J. Schlabach, 1950).

Weekly observance of the Lord's Supper was a key plank in the platform of the Restorationist movement of Thomas and Alexander Campbell: W. E. Garrison and A. T. DeGroot, *The Disciples of Christ: A History* (St. Louis, Mo.: Bethany Press, 1948), 163. Brief information on the practice of the Lord's Supper in many churches is contained in Frank S. Mead, *Handbook of Denominations in the United States,* 6th ed. (Nashville:

Abingdon, 1975), and comparable references.

13. John H. Yoder, trans. and ed., *The Legacy of Michael Sattler* (Scottdale, Pa.: Herald Press, 1973), 37. The same view is expressed in the second of the "Five Articles" (ca.1547); Franklin H. Littell, *The Anabaptist View of the Church*, 2d rev. and enlarged ed. (Boston: Starr King Press, 1958), 98.

14. Williams, *Anabaptist Writers* (1957), 77. For a discussion of the "Rule of Christ," see Marlin Jeschke, *Discipling in the Church: Recovering a Ministry of the Gospel*, 3d rev. and enlarged ed. (Scottdale, Pa.: Herald Press, 1988).

15. Walter Klaassen and others, eds., *Anabaptism in Outline: Select Primary Sources* (Scottdale, Pa.: Herald Press, 1981), 190.

16. Williams, *Anabaptist Writers* (1957), 76; published also in Klaassen, *Outline* (1981), 191.

17. Quoted in Williams, *Radical Reformation* (1992), 281; the quotation is taken from Robert Friedmann, ed., *Glaubenszeugnisse oberdeutscher Taufgesinnter*, Quellen zur Geschichte der Täufer, 12 (Gütersloh: Verlagshaus Gerd Mohn, 1967), 33. Rideman repeated the imagery in his *Account of Our Religion, Doctrine and Faith*, 2d English ed. (Rifton, N.Y.: Plough Publishing House, 1970), 86. The passage is also published in Durnbaugh, *Every Need Supplied*, 107.

Luther used it in his *Sermon on the Sacrament of the Body of Christ* (1519), *Werke*, Weimarer Ausgabe ed., 2:748; see Robert Friedmann, "Lord's Supper," *The Mennonite Encyclopedia*, 3:394, where Hutterite use is also detailed. Calvin's reference is: "The bread shown in the Sacrament represents this unity. As it is made of many grains so mixed together that one cannot be distinguished from another, so it is fitting that in the same way we should be joined and bound together by such great agreement of minds that no sort of disagreement or division may intrude." John T. McNeill, ed., *Calvin: Institutes of the Christian Religion*, trans. F. L. Battles (Philadelphia: Westminster Press, 1960), 1415; see also Willem Balke, *Calvin and the Anabaptist Radicals*, trans. W. Heynen (Grand Rapids: Eerdmans, 1981), 56-58.

18. On the history and spirit of the Society of Brothers, see Emmy Arnold, *Torches Together: The Beginning and Early Years of the Bruderhof Communities*, 2d ed. (Rifton, N.Y.: Plough Publishing House, 1971); and Merrill Mow, *Torches Rekindled: The Bruderhof's Struggle for Renewal* (Ulster Park, N.Y.: Plough Publishing House, 1989). For a highly critical personal account by the daughter of an exiled community leader, see Elizabeth Bohlken-Zumpe, *Torches Extinguished: Memories of a Communal Bruderhof in Paraguay, Europe, and the USA* (San Francisco: Peregrine Foundation, 1993).

19. For information on Mennonite divisions, see Cornelius J. Dyck, *An Introduction to Mennonite History*, 3d ed. (Scottdale, Pa.: Herald Press, 1993), and Adolf Ens's, "Schisms," *Mennonite Encyclopedia*, 5: 796-797. Harold S. Bender's landmark article, "The Anabaptist Vision," originally published in *Church History* 13 (1944): 3-24, was republished in slightly revised form in *The Mennonite Quarterly Review* 18 (1944): 67-88; and in Guy F. Hershberger, ed., *The Recovery of the Anabaptist Vision: A Sixtieth Anniversary Tribute to Harold S. Bender* (Scottdale, Pa.: Herald Press, 1957), 29-54. Two conferences marking the fiftieth anniversary of Bender's article were held at Elizabethtown College and at Goshen College in 1994.

20. John C. Wenger, ed., *The Complete Writings of Menno Simons (c.1496-1561)*, trans. Leonard Verduin (Scottdale, Pa.: Herald Press, 1956), 740; also published in Durnbaugh, *Every Need Supplied*, 86-87.

21. See the discussion on religious liberty in Donald F. Durnbaugh, *The Believers'*

Church: The History and Character of Radical Protestantism (New York: Macmillan, 1968), 249-254.

22. Rempel, *Lord's Supper*, 27.

23. Williams, *Radical Reformation* (1992), 1286-1287. On the tenet of free will among Anabaptists, see Jan Kiewit, *Pilgram Marbeck: Ein Führer in der Täuferbewegung der Reformationszeit* (Kassel: J. G. Oncken Verlag, 1957); and Robert Friedmann, *The Theology of Anabaptism: An Interpretation* (Scottdale, Pa.: Herald Press, 1973), esp. 58-77. On mission outreach, see Durnbaugh, *Believers' Church* (1968), 226-241.

24. Cornelius J. Dyck et al., eds., *The Writings of Dirk Philips, 1504-1568* (Scottdale, Pa.: Herald Press, 1992), 101.

25. Hostetler, *Amish Society* (1993), 224-225.

26. For a vivid description of the traditional practice, see Reuel B. Pritchett with Dale Aukerman, *On the Ground Floor of Heaven* (Elgin, Ill.: Brethren Press, 1980), 16-17.

27. The queries, thirteen in all, are quoted in Howard Brinton, *Meetinghouse and Farmhouse*, Pendle Hill Pamphlet, 185 (Lebanon, Pa.: Sowers Printing Company, 1972), 15-16.

28. *Church Government* (London: London Yearly Meeting of the Religious Society of Friends, 1968), par. 1701-1702.

29. Quoted in Durnbaugh, *Every Need Supplied*, 36.

30. Among English Baptists, however, there was a long tradition of open communion—"opening the Lord's Table to all Christians"—which clashed with the American practice of close communion in Canada, causing controversy; see G. Gerald Harrop, "The Baptist Convention of Ontario and Quebec," in *Baptist Advance: The Achievements of Baptists in North America for a Century and a Half* (Nashville: Broadman Press, 1964), 159-177.

31. James Leo Garrett Jr., *Baptist Church Discipline* (Nashville: Broadman Press, 1962), 19.

32. Rolland Perry Smith, in "Bethany Memories and Visions," ed. Debra L. Eisenbise, *Brethren Life and Thought* 39 (Winter 1994): 34-35.

33. William Woys Weaver, ed., *The Marlborough Footwashing: A Remarkable Anecdote of Peace and Harmony* (Chester Springs, Pa.: Firbank Press, 1981), originally published in John and Isaac Comly, *The Friends' Miscellany* 5 (1834): 369-373. According to Weaver's research, the building actually constructed was a schoolhouse rather than the Quaker meetinghouse.

34. See the discussion in Durnbaugh, *Believers' Church*, 264-282.

35. H. Wayne Pipkin and John H. Yoder, trans. and eds., *Balthasar Hubmaier: Theologian of Anabaptism* (Scottdale, Pa.: Herald Press, 1989), 403-404.

36. Freiday, *Barclay's Apology* (1967), 346-348. For thorough study of its biblical basis, see John Christopher Thomas, *Footwashing in John 13 and the Johannine Community* (Sheffield, England: Journal for the Study of the New Testament, 1991).

37. Donald F. Durnbaugh, *Pragmatic Prophet: The Life of Michael Robert Zigler* (Elgin, Ill.: Brethren Press, 1989), 189. The Mennonite service contribution is summarized in Robert S. Kreider and Rachel Waltner Goossen, *Hungry, Thirsty, a Stranger: The MCC Experience* (Scottdale, Pa.: Herald Press, 1988). See also the discussion in Durnbaugh, *Believers' Church*, 264-282.

38. In *The Mennonite Encyclopedia*, see J. Winfield Fretz, "Insurance," 3:42-43; Harold S. Bender, "Life Insurance," 3:343-344; J. Winfield Fretz and Harold S. Bender,

"Mutual Aid," 3:796-801; Calvin W. Redekop, "Cooperatives," 5:206; Laban Peachey, "Mennonite Mutual Aid," 5:572-573; "Mutual Aid," 3:613-615. In *The Brethren Encyclopedia*, 3 vols. (Oak Brook, Ill.: The Brethren Ency., 1983-84), see James C. Gibbel, "Insurance," 1:657; and Arthur G. Gish, "Mutual Aid," 2:901-903.

39. See the discussions on mutual aid and disaster relief in the volumes in the Mennonite Experience in America Series (Scottdale, Pa.: Herald Press): Richard K. MacMaster, *Land, Piety, Peoplehood* (1985); Theron F. Schlabach, *Peace, Faith, Nation* (1988); James C. Juhnke, *Vision, Doctrine, War* (1989).

40. "Appendix. By the younger Alexander Mack," in *A Short and Plain View of the Outward, Yet Sacred Rights and Ordinances of the House of God; . . . Also Ground Searching Questions Answered by the Author Alexander Mack*, eds. Henry Kurtz and James Quinter (Columbiana, Ohio: 1860), 141-148, slightly altered; see also Donald F. Durnbaugh, "The Brethren and Schism," *Brethren Life and Thought* 12 (Summer 1967): 24-33.

4. "Making a Meal of It": The Lord's Supper in Its First-Century Social Setting

1. See my discussion in *The Christology of Jesus* (Minneapolis: Fortress, 1990), 33ff.

2. See J. T. Squires, *The Plan of God in Luke-Acts* (Cambridge: Cambridge Univ. Press, 1993), 59ff.

3. See the discussion in B. Malina, *The New Testament World; Insights from Cultural Anthropology* (Louisville: Westminster/John Knox, 1993), 117ff.; M. McVann, "Rituals of Status Transformation in Luke-Acts: The Case of Jesus the Prophet," in *The Social World of Luke-Acts*, ed. J. Neyrey (Peabody: Hendrikson, 1991), 333-360; and in the same work, Neyrey, "Ceremonies in Luke-Acts: The Case of Meals and Table Fellowship," 361-387.

4. It may be taken as a sign of our confused times that we have mistaken the ritual of marriage for a ceremony. To judge from the NT evidence, early Christians would surely have seen marriage as a boundary-crossing rite that was basically unrepeatable, since it was meant to be "until death do you part," involving a one-flesh union that was irrevocable. By contrast, most modern Christians treat marriage as though it involved a repeatable ceremony.

5. See Neyrey, "Ceremonies in Luke-Acts," 363ff.

6. Cf. J. Jeremias, *The Eucharistic Words of Jesus*, 3d ed. (Philadelphia: Fortress, 1968); and I. Howard Marshall, *Last Supper and Lord's Supper* (Grand Rapids: Eerdmans, 1980).

7. M. Douglas, "Deciphering a Meal," in *Implicit Meanings* (London: Routledge and Kegan Paul, 1975), 249-275, esp. 249.

8. Most conveniently found in the Loeb ed. of Martial, 1:201 (cf. *Epigrams* 1.20; 4.85; 6.11; 10.49).

9. See my commentary *Conflict and Community in Corinth* (Grand Rapids: Eerdmans, 1994).

10. Cf. section on John 13-17, below.

11. Cf. W. Burkett, "Oriental Symposia: Contrasts and Parallels," in *Dining in a Classical Context*, ed. W. J. Slater (Ann Arbor: Univ. of Michigan, 1991), 7-24, esp. 18.

12. The Romans called such a feast *cēna* and drinking parties *convivia*.

13. Cf. G. Paul, "Symposia and Deipna in Plutarch's *Lives* and other Historical Writings," in *Dining in a Classical Context*, 157-169.

14. Cf. Juvenal, *Sat.* 125-127.

15. A. Booth, "The Age for Reclining and Its Attendant Perils," in *Dining in a Classical Context*, 105-120, esp. 106.

16. Emperors such as Claudius had a practice of bringing their children to such *convivia* to show them off, allowing them to sit at the end of the table quietly. This should not be taken as characteristic of all such occasions. Cf. Suetonius, *Claudius* 32. It did happen on occasion at a different sort of meal in private homes, when an employed rhetor would share a meal with his charges; thus Quintilian laments, "I do not approve of boys sitting with young men. For even if the teacher be such a one as we would desire to see in charge of the morals and studies of the young, . . . it is nonetheless desirable to keep the weaker members separate from the more mature." (*Inst. Or.* 2.2.14-15). He is concerned about homosexual advances, because he knows the kinds of activities that often went on at banquets and drinking parties.

17. A. O. Wire, *The Corinthian Women Prophets* (Minneapolis: Fortress, 1990), 103, suggests that women, other than those who provided the entertainment, prostitutes, or *hetairai*, regularly attended such dinner parties in temples; that is both unlikely and without basis in the sources. Her argument is strange since she also wishes to argue that the Corinthian women prophets were *ascetics*! It is true that a family might well attend at least the meal portion of a public cultic feast, or family sacrifice, but it is doubtful that Paul has the former in view, and probably not the latter either. He is discussing dinner parties, perhaps in particular those put on by *collegia* in temple precincts. In 1 Cor. 10, he turns briefly to a meal in a private home.

18. K. E. Corley, "Were the Women Around Jesus Really Prostitutes? Women in the Context of Greco-Roman Meals," *SBL 1989 Seminar Papers*, ed. D. J. Lull (Atlanta: Scholars Press, 1989), 487-521, esp. 513.

19. Cf. K. M. D. Dunbabin, "*Triclinium* and *Stibadium*," in *Dining in a Classical Context*, 121-148; here 122-123.

20. Cf. P. Gardner, "The Gifts of God" (Ph.D. diss., Cambridge, 1981), 120.

21. Gardner, "Gifts of God," 126, rightly says that what is uppermost in Paul's mind is not the sacraments and their abuse, but the community to which all belonged. The point is, these Israelites were truly part of that community, "baptized" into Moses, no less, and yet they were judged in the desert. The focus of the passage is on immoral behavior. As a secondary implication, it is possible that the Corinthians had a magical view of the sacraments, thinking participation in them secured them from any future judgments.

22. Gardner, "Gifts of God," 137, helpfully surveys the development of all the wilderness-wandering traditions in the Hebrew Scriptures and beyond. He concludes that the *function* of these traditions is markedly similar. They show the people sinned in forgetting God's gifts to them, in always craving more, *and* in turning to other gods, which inevitably led to divine judgment. The function of the tradition was to recall God's ongoing faithfulness and to make sure a later generation didn't make the same mistake of sinning.

23. R. MacMullen, *Paganism in the Roman Empire* (New Haven: Yale Univ. Press, 1981), 52ff. points out quite rightly that most pagans were not searching for eternal life, but rather present benefits from religion. There is evidence that they believed that certain rites of passage conveyed some spiritual benefits here and now. For example, cleansing in the blood of a bull was thought to convey an extension of one's earthly life in a state of ritual purity; cf. *CIL* (*Corpus inscriptionum Latinarum*, 1863ff.), 6.510, 13.511, 13.520. Theon of Smyrna, during the reign of Hadrian, speaks of initiation rites (which ones are uncertain) that bestow "a blessed state of divine grace and com-

panionship with the gods"; cf. MacMullen, *Paganism*, 172, n. 20. Perhaps most telling is Plutarch, *Mor.* 1105B, asserting that many people feel no fear of death, believing that initiation rites will assure them a happy afterlife.

24. This may also explain the "*gnōsis* (knowledge)" cry in Corinth (cf. 1 Cor. 1:5; 8:1, 7, 10-11; 13:2, 8; etc.), since esoteric knowledge is what some of these pagan cults offered to the initiated; knowledge was considered to be the key to "salvation" in some circles. E. Ferguson, *Backgrounds of Early Christianity* (Grand Rapids: Eerdmans, 1987), 205-220, stresses that the deliverance the mysteries offered was from fate and the terrors of the afterlife. The initiate was brought into favor with the deity, promised protection now, and sometimes promised a blessed afterlife.

25. Gardner, "Gifts of God," 153ff.

26. The force of Paul's argument is vitiated if one follows J. D. G. Dunn, *Christology in the Making* (Philadelphia: Westminster, 1980), 183-184, who maintains that Paul is saying that Christ is now the equivalent of what the rock was then. This defeats the power of the analogy, which depends on arguing that God's activity in Christ was the same then as now. Paul does not say that the "rock *is* Christ" or "the rock represents Christ" but rather that the rock *was* Christ. The tense of the verb is crucial.

27. Rightly interpreted by Gordon Fee, *First Corinthians* (Grand Rapids: Eerdmans, 1987), 449ff.

28. One may point, for instance, to the example in Josephus, *Ant.* 18.65-80, where the lady Paulina after dinner in the temple precincts had night-long sex with Mundus, assuming he was the god Annubis.

29. In 1 Cor. 10:8b, we have a notable problem. Paul says 23,000 fell in the desert; Num. 25:9 clearly says 24,000. In fact, all known Jewish sources have 24,000, and there is really no textual evidence to suggest that 1 Cor. 10:8 ever read anything other than it does—23,000. One may say Paul deals in round numbers, just as the OT does, which is true, but it isn't the correct round number.

30. MacMullen, *Paganism*, 40.

31. On Christians refusing to participate in or partake of a sacrifice in a temple, cf. R. Gordon, "Religion in the Roman Empire," in *Pagan Priests: Religion and Power in the Ancient World*, eds. M. Beard and J. North (Ithaca: Cornell Univ. Press, 1988), 235-255. Gordon rightly notes that this refusal separated Christianity from all other religions, including Judaism, which at least offered sacrifices *for* the Emperor. The ideological implications of this were considerable, especially since, as Gordon shows, during the empire the Emperor tied himself closely to such; all over the empire, he placed numerous statues of himself sacrificing, including in Roman Corinth. This was part of the larger propaganda agenda of portraying the emperor as the great benefactor of the empire (cf. Gordon, "The Veil of Power," 201-231, in the same volume). The rejection of idol meat, especially at a festival in honor of Caesar, would carry the larger message of the rejection of imperial patronage.

32. This is another allusion to Christ's preexistence.

33. Cf. H. Seesemann, *Der Begriff Koinōnia im Neuen Testament* (Giessen: Töpelmann, 1933), 99-100, who argues for the sense "participation" in most Pauline contexts, and that it is a religious concept for Paul. The exception to both these dictums, Seesemann says, is 2 Cor. 6:14, which may point to its non-Pauline origins. Cf. below, the next two pages. Seesemann follows J. Y. Campbell, "*Koinōnia* and Its Cognates in the NT," *Journal of Biblical Literature* 51 (1932): 375-377. *Koinonia* is now also a loanword in English.

34. C. K. Barrett, *First Corinthians* (New York: Harper & Row, 1968), 232.

35. Fee, *First Corinthians*, 469ff.

36. This however was not unknown in the Greek sources. In a paper given at the annual SBL meeting in San Francisco in Nov. 1992, entitled "The Warmth and Breath of Life," L. J. Ciraolo has shown that in the Greek magical papyri from Egypt, animals (e.g., birds) would be strangled and then held up to the deity's statue to provide breath and animate the statue. This is especially clear in *PGM* (*Papyri Graecae magicae*, 1928-31), 7. The point is to endow the statue with magical potency, not make the animal sacred to the god. These references are interesting because they may provide a further clue to understanding the reference to "things strangled" in the decree of Acts 15:20, 29. Strangling was not a Roman practice. In Roman sacrifices, the throat was slit. Nevertheless, these papyri show that such practices were known in the pagan Greco-Roman world.

37. As Fee says in *First Corinthians*, 489, causing "offense" doesn't mean to hurt someone's feelings; instead, it means either to cause a believer to stumble or to put a stumbling block in front of a potential convert.

38. *Aresko* (1 Cor. 10:33) can mean "give pleasure to."

39. Notice how E. A. Judge, "The Social Identity of the First Christians," *Journal of Religious History* 11 (1980): 212, describes the early Christian meetings as "the talkative, passionate, and sometimes quarrelsome circles that met to read Paul's letters over their evening meal in private houses."

40. Cf. S. M. Pogoloff, *Logos and Sophia* (Atlanta: Scholars Press, 1992), 239.

41. Lucian is not exaggerating the differences between the Saturnalia and ordinary meals. Cf. Martial, *Epigram* 3.60, quoted in text above, just before note number 8.

42. It may be significant that at Roman banquets the religious ceremonies were regularly reserved to the end of the dinner proper (or even after the *sumposia*, if it was to follow). If the Christian meal was analogous, the Lord's Supper may have transpired at the end of the meal. Cf. D. E. Smith, "Meals and Morality in Paul and His World," *SBL 1981 Seminar Papers* (Scholars Press, 1981), 319-339.

43. S. C. Barton, "Paul's Sense of Place: An Anthropological Approach to Community Formation in Corinth," *New Testament Studies* 32 (1986): 225-246. Here is another telltale piece of evidence that it is a mistake to assume that Paul simply applied the structure of the household and its conventions to the community of faith. When the community meets in a house, Paul insists they meet in a way that comports with the equality that exists in the body of Christ, and thus without regard to social status and social distinctions.

44. On homes as a place where a *collegium* would meet for dinner, cf. *CIL*, 9.148: "collegium quod est domo Sergiae Paullinae." Normally they met in a temple or in their own clubhouse. J. D. G. Dunn, "The Responsible Congregation," in *Charisma und Agape*, ed. L. De Lorenzi (Rome: St. Paul, 1983), 201-238, esp. 204, n. 12, points out that the meeting of clients with the patron in his house in the morning is not a parallel to what we find in 1 Cor. 11.

45. With due respect to Barton, "Paul's Sense of Place," 242. For Paul, if there is a rite of passage or incorporation, it is baptism.

46. Cf. R. MacMullen, *Roman Social Relations* (New Haven: Yale Univ. Press, 1974), 73.

47. Smith, "Meals and Morality in Paul," 323. Very striking are the rules of the guild of Zeus Hypsistos, a religious association in Egypt in the first century B.C. which prohibited factions (*schismata*), "chattering" (cf. 1 Cor. 14:33ff.), and indicting one

another, which might lead to going to court (cf. 1 Cor. 6).

48. If this is correct, it would explain some of the chaos described in 1 Cor. 14; some participants were inebriated.

49. Nero's regular practice was to call in the teachers of *sophia* after dinner to amuse the guests; the teachers could include philosophers and rhetors. Cf. MacMullen, *Enemies of the Roman Order* (Cambridge: Harvard, 1966), 59.

50. The association meals, though somewhat more democratic, still involved a pecking order in terms of seating and likely food also.

51. W. A. Meeks, *The First Urban Christians* (New Haven: Yale Univ. Press, 1983), 78-79. Meeks, however, also points out great similarities. Both groups were small and involved intense face-to-face interactions, with membership decided by free decision rather than birth, although trade associations had the prerequisite of being involved in a particular trade.

52. Cf. E. A. Judge, *Social Pattern* (London: Tyndale, 1960), 44-45: "There need be no doubt that . . . they were not distinguished in the public's mind from the general run of official associations. Like many others, they could be labelled conveniently from the god whose patronage they claimed. 'Christ-ites' is certainly not the sort of name they would have chosen for themselves. . . . The term *ecclēsia* (sc. meeting) itself and the names for the various officials may have developed special connotations within the Christian community, but to non-Christians, and to Christians themselves in the early stages, they need have suggested nothing out of the ordinary." Cf. Pogoloff, *Logos and Sophia*, 248ff.

53. Cf. Gerd Theissen, *The Social Setting of Pauline Christianity: Essays on Corinth*, ed. and trans. John H. Schütz (Philadelphia: Fortress, 1982), 145-174.

54. It also depends on stressing *prolambanei* ("he takes before") in 1 Cor. 11:21. Cf. S. Scott Bartchy, "Table Fellowship with Jesus and the 'Lord's Meal' at Corinth," in *Increase in Learning: Essays in Honor of J. G. Van Buren*, eds. R. J. Owens and B. E. Hamm (Manhattan: Manhattan Christian College, 1979), 45-61.

55. Cf. J. Jeremias, *Unknown Sayings of Jesus* (London: SCM, 1957), 59-61.

56. Cf. the remarks of Murphy-O'Connor, *St. Paul's Corinth* (Wilmington, Del.: M. Glazier, 1983), 158-159.

The mere fact that all could not be accommodated in the *triclinium* meant that there had to be an overflow into the atrium. It became imperative for the host to divide his guests into two categories: the first-class believers were invited into the triclinium; the rest stayed outside. Even a slight knowledge of human nature indicates the criterion used. The host must have been a wealthy member of the community, and so he invited into the triclinium his closest friends among the believers, who would have been of the same social class. The rest could take their places in the atrium, where conditions were greatly inferior.

Only if the meal was not held indoors would such a division of the group be unnecessary. Paul's reference to houses suggests that it was indoors.

57. *Apo* in 1 Cor. 11:23 indicates source.

58. Cf. C. Senft's attempt to compare Paul's version to that found in Mark, in *La première épître de Saint-Paul aux Corinthiens* (Neuchâtel: Delachaux, 1979), 151.

59. Perhaps they both got it from the congregation at Antioch.

60. Fee, *First Corinthians*, 549.

61. The breaking of bread would not do this anyway, since no bone of his was broken.

62. Cf. the chart in Fee, *First Corinthians*, 546.

63. Cf. J. Jeremias, *The Eucharistic Words of Jesus* (London: SCM, 1966), 15ff.

64. This is found in the Markan version of the Lord's Supper.

65. The present aspect is the present proclamation and perhaps also the presence of the risen Christ with the community.

66. See 1 Cor 16:22. The fact that this letter concludes with such a phrase may suggest it was to be orally transmitted during the all-congregation Lord's Supper meal. Cf. Rev. 22:20.

67. That would include every believer. One doesn't share in the Lord's meal because one is personally worthy of doing so; it is a gift of God's grace.

68. Yet this is a deliberative use of forensic language, which simply shows once again that when one is evaluating the rhetorical thrust of a discourse, one must ask about the function of the language used, not simply the usual provenance.

69. The least probable option is that it means forgetting the sacramental presence in the elements and thus committing a sacrilege against the sacrament.

70. For the word *paideuometha* (1 Cor. 11:32) meaning "discipline," cf. 2 Cor. 6:9 and 1 Tim. 1:20.

71. D. A. Carson, *John* (Grand Rapids: Eerdmans, 1991), 475, speculates that the Feast of Unleavened Bread is in view, but the only festival mentioned in this passage (13:1) is the Passover Feast. In view of how intrusive the Evangelist is into the text of this Gospel, it is difficult to believe he would not explain if he was referring to another Feast. On the other hand, the reference to giving something to the poor has been taken to allude to the custom of giving alms to the poor on Passover night; cf. Jeremias, *Eucharistic Words*, 54. But, in view of the sources cited by Jeremias, it is not certain that this was a known practice as early as Jesus' day.

72. Cf. G. K. Beasley-Murray, *John* (Waco, Tex.: Word, 1987), 240ff.; and J. W. Pryor, *John Evangelist* (Downers Grove: IVP, 1992), 58ff.

73. F. Craddock, *John* (Atlanta: John Knox, 1980), 100.

74. A clear hint that the Evangelist would move in this direction is found in the exclamation of the Baptist in John 1:36.

75. What follows can be found in much fuller form in my *Conflict and Community in Corinth*, 241ff.

76. Nero's regular practice was to call in the teachers of *sophia* (wisdom) after dinner to amuse the guests, which could include philosophers and rhetors. Cf. R. Mac-Mullen, *Enemies of the Roman Order* (Cambridge: Harvard Univ. Press, 1966), 59.

77. It is understandable why this custom would be assumed to be a necessary and regular part of hospitality in the Middle East. Dust and dirt covered one from traveling during nonrainy seasons. Roads for the most part had not been laid or "repaved" by the Romans.

78. These sorts of remarks are not found in the Synoptic portrayal of the Last Supper in Mark 14 and parallels. Only Luke's brief remark about the cup of wine being shared *"after supper"* (Luke 22:20) points in the direction of a Greco-Roman meal.

79. It is intriguing that Luke portrays the Last Supper as including a discussion by the disciples of who is the greatest. Jesus calls attention to his own servant leadership as a pattern for the disciples to follow in Luke 22:24-27, in a similar fashion to what we find in John 13. This suggests that they are both drawing on common tradition about this sort of closing meeting and teaching session.

80. On the guilds and trade associations, including burial associations, see my discussion in *Conflict and Community in Corinth*, 243ff. Here again is a striking Johannine similarity to material in Luke 22, this time in 22:35-38, where the issue of money and purse is raised.

81. Notice how the Last Supper is depicted as ending with a religious act, a hymn (Mark 14:26 and par.).

82. In other words, Jesus is portrayed as Wisdom, while the disciples are portrayed as the simple and spiritually immature, as in Prov. 9.

83. The definitive study on the footwashing aspect of the material found in John 13 is J. C. Thomas's *Footwashing in John 13 and the Johannine Community* (Sheffield: JSOT Press, 1991). The interpretation which follows differs from Thomas's in several regards:

(1) I do not think this material should be interpreted as if it is addressed to the Christian community. On the contrary, it is portrayed as a more common Greco-Roman meal which anyone could recognize and identify, as is appropriate in a missionary document.

(2) In my view, it is a mistake to assume an overlap between washing rituals and anointing rituals. For one thing, anointing rituals have royal overtones that washing rituals do not. What may be true about the meaning of John 12, probably has little bearing on the meaning of John 13.

(3) Nothing in our text suggests that the subject is postbaptismal sin of Christian believers. The disciples are not portrayed in this discourse as fully Christian. Indeed, they are portrayed as lacking essential Christian understanding and basic spiritual perceptivity (cf. 14:5, 8).

(4) If the rite has theological overtones, the issue here is the cleansing work of Christ, as symbolized by footwashing, not repentance or the seeking and obtaining of forgiveness by a Christian. Peter is threatened with having no part in Christ (13:8). In other words, the focus is on the Godward side and divine activity, not on the human response or preparation. This ritual is portrayed as basically a passive one, something one receives from another. In this regard, it is unlike the Lord's Supper.

(5) Washing feet is seen as an example of serving others, a lifestyle that believers are to follow. In view of the highly symbolic nature of the Johannine treatment of a variety of signs and actions, it may be doubted that this text is meant to institute a new ritual. This text inculcates self-sacrificial service for others, following the example of Christ's self-sacrificial and cleansing service.

84. But see the discussion in Carson, *John*, 455-458; Brown, *John XIII-XXI*, Anchor Bible (Garden City: Doubleday,1970), 555ff.

85. See Beasley-Murray, *John*, 238.

86. Notice how once we get to the Passion narrative, Jesus controls the action. He no longer suggests that he must wait on the Father's go-ahead, or for his hour to arrive; Jesus will lay down his life at a time and under the circumstances of his own choosing.

87. Mekilta no. 1 on Exod. 21:2 says that Jewish slaves should not even be required to perform this menial task. Instead, it should be reserved for Gentile slaves, or for women, children, and pupils of a great teacher.

88. For the language, cf. Luke 15:12; Matt. 24:51; Rev. 20:6; and Beasley-Murray, *John*, 234.

89. Carson, *John*, 462ff.

90. Cf. R. Schnackenburg, *John III* (London: Burns & Oates, 1982), 19-20.

91. Schnackenburg, *John III*, 19-20.

92. This makes especially problematic the practice of those who wish to perform footwashing at the end of celebrating the Lord's Supper. If the rite is going to be performed, it should surely come *before* partaking of the bread and wine. Cleansing must

precede receiving the other benefits of Christ's death.

93. For those who think another ritual is here mandated, it has always been awkward that nothing whatsoever is said in the Synoptics about this rite, in connection with the Lord's Supper or otherwise. If the Johannine community practiced such a rite, it was something distinctive to that community and apparently unknown or unendorsed by the communities of Matthew, Mark, and Luke.

94. Beasley-Murray, *John*, 238.

5. Ecclesiology and the Lord's Supper

1. Richard Slotkin, *Gunfighter Nation: The Myth of the Frontier in Twentieth Century America* (New York: HarperCollins reprint ed., 1993). This book is the third volume in a trilogy wherein Slotkin explores the myth of redemptive violence woven through American culture. The earlier volumes are entitled *Regeneration Through Violence* (1973) and *The Fatal Environment* (1985).

2. Slotkin, *Gunfighter Nation*, 351.

3. This film, released in 1950 and one of three Ford "cavalry Westerns," starred John Wayne and Maureen O'Hara. Wayne played starring roles in the other two as well—*Fort Apache* (1948) and *She Wore a Yellow Ribbon* (1950).

4. Walter Brueggemann, *Old Testament Theology: Essays on Structure, Theme, and Text*, ed. Patrick D. Miller (Minneapolis: Fortress Press, 1992).

5. Walter Brueggemann, *Israel's Praise: Doxology Against Idolatry and Ideology* (Philadelphia: Fortress Press, 1988).

6. Brueggemann, *Israel's Praise*, 108.

7. Brueggemann, *Israel's Praise*, 105.

8. Brueggemann, *Israel's Praise*, 113.

9. Brueggemann, *Israel's Praise*, 117.

10. "The Constantinian Sources of Western Social Ethics" in *The Priestly Kingdom* (Notre Dame: Univ. of Notre Dame Press, 1984), 136. Yoder's sentence calls to mind Kierkegaard's dictum: "When everyone is a Christian, no one is a Christian."

11. Yoder, "Constantinian Sources," 139. On this point, see also Stanley Hauerwas, "A Sermon on the Sermon on the Mount" in *Unleashing the Scripture. Freeing the Bible from Captivity to America* (Nashville: Abingdon Press, 1993), 63-72.

12. Yoder, "Constantinian Sources," 136.

13. Gary Macy, *The Banquet's Wisdom: A Short History of the Theologies of the Lord's Supper* (Mahwah: Paulist Press, 1992), 30.

14. Macy, *Banquet's Wisdom*, 30.

15. Macy, *Banquet's Wisdom*, 58-59. Macy offers a wry comment in conclusion: "Of course, such dignity could, and sometimes did, go to the head of the person who was bishop."

16. Quoted in Macy, *Banquet's Wisdom*, 60-61.

17. In those days "relevance" also often dictated the substitution of Pepsi and potato chips for bread and (in my tradition) grape juice as the elements of communion. We reasoned that the former were the common fare of our culture even as the latter were of Jesus' culture. Such conclusions may be some of the less harmful consequences of our iconoclasm, but still in need of forgiveness.

18. Two recent works by L. Gregory Jones address this connection, explicitly in the first case, and implicitly in the second. See *Transformed Judgment: Toward a Trinitarian Account of the Moral Lies* (Notre Dame: Univ. of Notre Dame Press, 1990); and Jones and Stephen E. Fowl, *Reading in Communion: Scripture and Ethics in Chris-*

tian Life (Grand Rapids: Eerdmans, 1991). Earlier than either of these is William H. Willimon, *The Service of God: How Worship and Ethics Are Related* (Nashville: Abingdon, 1983).

19. Richard Bondi, "The Elements of Character," *Journal of Religious Ethics* 12:2 (Fall 1984): 201-218.

20. Bondi, "Elements of Character," 214-215.

21. Bondi, "Elements of Character," 215.

22. Peter Lampe, "The Eucharist: Identifying with Christ on the Cross," *Interpretation* 48:1 (Jan. 1994): 36-49.

23. Lampe, "Eucharist," 36. Lampe cites the following texts as examples: 1 Cor. 6:8-11; 12:13, 20-26; 10:1-22; Rom. 6:1-6, 11-13.

24. Lampe, "Eucharist," 44-45.

25. Lampe, "Eucharist," 45.

26. Willimon, *The Service of God*, 125.

27. James McClendon, *Systematic Theology: Ethics* (Nashville: Abingdon, 1986), 31.

28. Commenting on Barnabas's mission from Jerusalem to Antioch in Acts 11:19-30, William Willimon writes in *Acts,* Interpretation series (Atlanta: John Knox Press, 1988), 106-107:

> We do know that time and again the church has attempted to keep itself on track by looking back and letting itself be judged by tradition. Today's church may not be so convinced of the necessity for contemporary practice conforming to traditional norms. Why should we submit to the judgment of the Creed, the scrutiny of Scripture, the opinions of dead people? Many are suspicious of the past, seeing it as a repository of misunderstanding, injustice, and benighted ideas. The Bible is an ancient book, full of old, culturally determined values. Therefore, we must make our own way, using our own experience as our only guide. We thus ignore our own culturally determined biases (for the bias of the past is usually easier to see than our own) and cut the church loose from its moorings. Jerusalem and the Twelve who reside there stand as a warning to the church that we ignore our past, we jettison the apostolic "facts" of our faith, at the greatest of peril.

29. On this point, see Hauerwas' essays in part one of *A Community of Character: Toward a Constructive Social Ethic* (Notre Dame: Univ. of Notre Dame Press, 1981); and John Howard Yoder, "The Hermeneutics of Peoplehood," in *Priestly Kingdom.*

30. I have explored some of the ethical and political issues entailed in historical remembering in my essay, "History as a Moral and Political Art," in my *Tell Me the Tale: Historical Reflections on the Church of God* (Anderson: Warner Press, 1991), 137-159.

31. I have explored these themes in an essay entitled, "The Malling of the Church," in my *Tell Me Another Tale: Further Reflections on the Church of God* (Anderson: Warner Press, 1993), 147-161.

32. Second Kings 6:8-23. See Brueggemann's insightful commentary on this text in his essay, "The Embarrassing Footnote," in *Interpretation and Obedience: From Faithful Reading to Faithful Living* (Minneapolis: Fortress Press, 1991), 28-40.

6. Eschatology and the Lord's Supper

1. Robert G. Clouse, Robert D. Linder, and Richard V. Pierard, eds., *Protest and Politics: Christianity and Contemporary Affairs* (Greenwood, S.C.: The Attic Press, 1968).

2. Robert G. Clouse, Robert D. Linder, and Richard V. Pierard, eds., *The Cross*

and the Flag (Carol Stream, Ill.: Creation House, 1972).

3. Among publications which illustrate this point are Robert G. Clouse, "Johann Heinrich Alsted and English Millennialism," *The Harvard Theological Review* 62 (1969): 189ff.; Peter Toon, Robert G. Clouse, et al., *Puritans, The Millennium and the Future of Israel: Puritan Eschatology* (Cambridge, England: James Clarke, 1970); Robert G. Clouse, "The Apocalyptic Interpretations of Thomas Brightman and Joseph Mede," *Journal of the Evangelical Theological Society* 11 (1968): 181ff.; Robert G. Clouse, ed., *The Meaning of the Millennium: Four Views* (Downers Grove, Ill.: Inter-Varsity Press, 1977); Robert G. Clouse, *Millennialism and America* (Portland: Western Baptist Press, 1977).

4. David Allan Hubbard, *The Second Coming: What Will Happen When Jesus Returns?* (Downers Grove, Ill.: InterVarsity Press, 1984), 9f.

5. For the Grace Brethren service, see *The Brethren Minister's Handbook* (Winona Lake, Ind.: n.p., 1945), 37ff. Also David R. Plaster, *Ordinances: What Are They?* (Winona Lake, Ind.: BMH Books, 1985). For a Church of the Brethren view of the Lord's Supper, see Vernard Eller, *In Place of Sacraments: A Study of Baptism and the Lord's Supper* (Grand Rapids: Eerdmans, 1972). For other Brethren groups, notice relevant articles in *The Brethren Encyclopedia*, 3 vols. (Oak Brook, Ill.: The Brethren Ency., 1983-84).

6. Geoffrey Wainwright, *Eucharist and Eschatology* (New York: Oxford Univ. Press, 1981), 92.

7. For various types of hunger, see the thoughtful meditation by Monika K. Hellwig, *The Eucharist and the Hunger of the World* (New York: Paulist Press, 1976). An excellent study of human need and the Eucharist is Tissa Balasuriya, *The Eucharist and Human Liberation* (Maryknoll, N.Y.: Orbis Books, 1979).

8. Quoted in Robert McAfee Brown, *Unexpected News: Reading the Bible with Third World Eyes* (Philadelphia: Westminster Press, 1984), 19.

9. For more discussion of this issue, see Robert G. Clouse, ed., *Wealth and Poverty: Four Christian Views of Economics* (Downers Grove, Ill.: InterVarsity Press, 1984), 221ff.

10. For more on Christian attitudes toward violence, see Robert G. Clouse, ed., *War: Four Christian Views*, rev. ed. (Downers Grove, Ill.: InterVarsity Press, 1991).

11. Quoted in Horton Davies, *Bread of Life and Cup of Joy: Newer Ecumenical Perspectives on the Eucharist* (Grand Rapids: Eerdmans, 1993), 208.

12. Robert G. Clouse, Richard V. Pierard, and Edwin Yamauchi, *Two Kingdoms: The Church and Culture Through the Ages* (Chicago: Moody Press, 1993), 595ff., deals with categories of social action that I suggest in this paper plus several others. Also, an excellent presentation of the global problems faced by believers is Robin Keeley, ed., *Christianity: A World Faith* (Oxford: Lion Publishing, 1986). On the definition of justice, note Karen Lebacqz, *Justice in an Unjust World: Foundations for a Christian Approach to Justice* (Minneapolis: Augsburg Publishers, 1987).

13. John Stott, *Decisive Issues Facing Christians Today* (Old Tappen, N.J.: Fleming H. Revell Co., 1990), 225f.

14. Quoted in Bonnidell Clouse and Robert G. Clouse, eds., *Women and Ministry: Four Views* (Downers Grove, Ill.: InterVarsity Press, 1989), 21.

15. Stephen Travis, *The Jesus Hope* (London: Word Books, 1974), 125f.

16. Travis, *Jesus Hope*, 125f. See also his *I Believe in the Second Coming* (Grand Rapids: Eerdmans, 1982).

7. Making the Lord's Supper Meaningful

1. See R. Lee Cole, *Love Feasts: A History of the Christian Agape*, 1916.

2. According to Peter Lampe, "The Eucharist: Identifying with Christ on the Cross," *Interpretation* 48:1 (Jan. 1994): 36-49, one could mention also Hellenistic influence; cf. *Meaning and Practice of the Lord's Supper*, ed. by Helmut T. Lehmann (Philadelphia: Muhlenberg Press, 1961), 59-60.

3. Joseph R. Shultz claims the emperor Constantine "built nine new churches in Rome . . . [and] magnificent church buildings at Ostia, Naples, Albano, Carthage, Jerusalem, Bethlehem, Mamre, Antioch, Thessalonica, and scores of other places in the provinces, besides a number in the new capital at Constantinople"; *The Soul of the Symbols: A Theological Study of Holy Communion* (Grand Rapids: Eerdmans, 1966), 97.

4. "Under Emperor Constantine it became Christianity on parade, with vast congregations meeting in large churches not only recognized but approved by the society surrounding it. Now it was hierarchically celebrated, with the leaders entering in solemn procession in distinctive garb"; Horton Davies, *Bread of Life and Cup of Joy: Newer Ecumenical Perspectives on the Eucharist* (Grand Rapids: Eerdmans, 1993), 264-265.

5. "Plastic 'fish food,' " says James F. White, in *Introduction to Christian Worship*, rev. ed. (Nashville: Abingdon, 1990), 252.

6. Unfortunately, high-church voices seem to be heard by default. Look into even your believers church seminary libraries to notice how little has been written in recent years by believers church theologians on the Lord's Supper.

7. E.g., Harold E. Fey, *The Lord's Supper: Seven Meanings* New York: (Harper & Row, 1948).

8. "There are differences in the administration of the Lord's Supper among Protestant churches [such as Anglicans, Methodists, Baptists, Congregationalists, and Presbyterians], but its meaning is the same." Horton Davies, *Christian Worship: Its History and Meaning* (New York: Abingdon, 1957), 100. Similarly, White says, "Whatever the name, the content throughout Christianity is the same"; *Introduction*, 219.

9. Alister McGrath, *Christian Theology: An Introduction* (Cambridge, Mass.: Blackwell Pubs., 1993), 428.

10. Alan M. Stibbs says we should call it the Lord's Supper rather than the Eucharist because it is not what we are doing in giving thanks but what our Lord is giving us, seeing it is the Lord's Supper; *Sacrament, Sacrifice and Eucharist* (London: Tyndale, 1961), 58-59.

11. Arthur Cochrane says, "By sacrament is meant a religious and cultic act whereby Jesus Christ is made present and his body and blood are eaten and drunk. . . . This time-honored doctrine had to go . . . because it violates the plain teaching of Scripture"; *Eating and Drinking with Jesus* (Philadelphia: Westminster, 1974), 9-10.

12. "Baptists have agreed on the symbolic interpretation of the Lord's Supper," says one Southern Baptist writer, citing the 1963 "Baptist Faith and Message": "The Lord's Supper is a symbolic act of obedience whereby members of the church, through partaking of the bread and the fruit of the vine, memorialize the death of the Redeemer and anticipate his second coming"; James E. Carter, "The Lord's Supper: A Baptist Perspective," *Southwestern Journal of Theology* 31 (Spring 1989), 36.

13. Horton Davies, *Bread of Life*, 79. Cochrane says, "Anamnēsis means . . . a recollection in the consciousness or mind, . . . a recollection by word, and . . . a recollection by act. In this threefold sense, anamnēsis is a human ethical activity"; *Eating*

and Drinking, 60.

14. Happily, many Catholic churches now have excellent preaching. At least my last two visits to Notre Dame exposed me to superb preaching.

15. "Only by actively loving and caring for others does the participant in the Eucharist 'proclaim' Christ's death as something that happened for others"; Lampe, "The Eucharist," 45.

16. This tradition has been revived symbolically in recent Catholicism in the practice of lay people—perhaps a family—bringing the bread and wine up the aisle to the altar.

17. "It will be clear from what Paul has said that he does not think of the Lord's Supper as itself a sacrifice in any sense of the term, despite a long history of Christian interpretation to the contrary. The supper is likened not to a sacrifice at an altar but to the meal which follows the sacrifice and which is celebrated with a table and a cup"; I. Howard Marshall, *Last Supper and Lord's Supper* (Grand Rapids: Eerdmans, 1980), 122-123.

18. John Howard Yoder in *The Politics of Jesus* (Grand Rapids: Eerdmans, 1972), 134, says, "There is but one realm in which the concept of imitation holds: . . . at the point of the concrete social meaning of the Cross in its relation to enmity and power. . . . Thus—and only thus—are we bound by the New Testament thought to 'be like Jesus.' "

19. Paul in Col. 1:24, "In my flesh I am completing what is lacking in Christ's afflictions for the sake of his body, that is, the church."

20. For this reason the custom in many churches nowadays of a monetary offering at the end of the Lord's Supper is fitting. The Catholic scholar Arthur A. Vogel raises a question that should disturb us all: How difficult it is to get people to "move out of their church buildings into the world. . . . People do not seem to understand better how the action of the liturgy leads to action in the world"; *Is the Last Supper Finished?* (New York: Sheed and Ward, 1968), 176-177. Says Jon L. Berquist, "At the table the community begins its transformation. . . . In our world this means a concern for economics"; *Ancient Wine, New Wineskins: The Lord's Supper in Old Testament Perspective* (St. Louis, Mo.: Chalice Press, 1991), 7.

21. The real presence of Christ is not in the bread and cup in the Lord's Supper any more than it is in the water in baptism, says Stibbs, *Sacrament,* 74.

22. Even Edward Schillebeeckx states that the real presence of Christ is "ultimately situated in the believing community itself"; *The Eucharist,* trans. N. D. Smith (New York: Sheed and Ward, 1967), 103, 110. Stibbs says Christ comes to us, not to the bread and cup (*Sacrament,* 75).

23. "For Paul, the [original] ethical implications of the Eucharist were far more vital than the later intricate theological discussions of how Christ might be present in the Lord's Supper. The fact that Christ is present matters for Paul; and the function in which Christ is present (saving and judging) is of importance"; Lampe, "The Eucharist," 43. Likewise, Geoffrey Wainwright, "Eucharist and/as Ethics," *Worship* 62 (Mar. 1988):137, "What we receive in the Eucharist, we are to do and to recognize in the world: we are to initiate and join in the works that bespeak the kingdom of God."

24. Horton Davies, *Bread of Life,* 229.

25. Robert L. Brawley, "Anamnēsis and Absence in the Lord's Supper," *Biblical Theology Bulletin* 20 (Winter 1990): 142.

26. Or is it like with the Southern Baptist who said God does not hear the prayers of Jews?

27. Schillebeeckx, *Eucharist*, 107-151.

28. Recently some leaders in the Mennonite Brethren Church have proposed the access of unbaptized Christians, both children of church members and Christians of goodwill who attend a given congregation regularly but for some reason have not yet been baptized *(Direction,* Fall 1989). Marshall, *Last Supper*, 156, says, "The Lord's Supper today should be open to all who wish to . . . profess faith in him. This implies that unbaptized believers may take part."

29. This is usually based upon the words of Jesus in Matthew 5:23-24, about being reconciled to one's brother or sister before bringing one's gift to the altar.

30. Wouldn't there be something wrong if at every checkup the patient confessed to continuing smoking and drinking and overeating and lack of exercise and sleep, and the doctor assured the patient of forgiveness? Wouldn't there be something wrong with an annual Thanksgiving Day family reunion at which family members would always be making up and never getting over old grudges?

31. Ronald S. James, "Communion and the Coming Kingdom," *Weavings* 2 (Jan.-Feb., 1987): 28-31. Scott McCormick Jr. devotes an entire chapter to this theme in his *The Lord's Supper: A Biblical Interpretation* (Philadelphia: Westminster, 1966).

32. Vernard Eller speaks of the "form . . . of a commemorative funeral for Jesus" as the mood of too many communions. According to Davies, *Christian Worship*, 93, the Lord's Supper surely stands in line with the Hebrew understanding of feasting and joy: "Joy was unembarrassingly associated with . . . the pleasure of a good meal. . . . Many reasons were given for the expression of joy: . . . the birth of children, long life, love of a spouse, and prosperity and abundance at the harvest of grain and vintage. . . . Joy was seen as a gift of God and was often associated with religious feasts and liturgical worship."

33. "Luke's contribution is to stress that the Lord's Supper is the joyous celebration of the experience of salvation in the presence of the risen Lord"; Marshall, *Last Supper*, 133.

34. According to Berquist in *Ancient Wine*, 82, Old Testament visions of the kingdom include "good food and plenty of it." For example, Isa. 25:6 says, "On this mountain, Yahweh of hosts will make for all peoples a feast of rich food [low cholesterol, I presume], a feast of aged wines, of delicacies filled with richness, of aged wines strained clear."

35. According to White, the Swedish Lutheran theologian Brilioth claims, "The rediscovery of the idea of communion [fellowship] is the greatest positive contribution of the Reformation in regard to the Eucharist"; White, *Christian Worship*, 246. If this is so, it was only some forms of pietism that appropriated the "rediscovery."

36. Berquist, *Ancient Wine*, 133, makes the point that the Lord's Supper means covenant. Of course it does. The word covenant is in Jesus' words of institution and in Paul's; see essay by Ben Witherington III, above, on 1 Cor. 11. The concept of covenant is so basic that one could equate it with "Christian." To come to the Lord's table is to confess oneself to be Christian, which equals confessing oneself to be bound up in the new covenant. Christians are New Testament people. That basic meaning of covenant is what I am talking about in this whole section. The question is merely one of meaningfulness of language. Does the word *covenant* communicate to people in our churches today? Yet I do not doubt the necessity for members of the church to be conscious that coming to the Lord's table is to confess that we are bound together in the body of Christ.

37. Markus Barth, "This means nothing less than that there is no, not even

sacramental, communion with Christ when the social community is considered irrelevant or of secondary import and is in fact broken up"; *Rediscovering the Lord's Supper: Communion with Israel, with Christ, and Among the Guests* (Ann Arbor: Books on Demand, 1988), 60.

38. Cochrane draws attention to the fact that churches in the U.S. and Canada actually do "celebrate" or "administer" the Lord's Supper in an austere religious atmosphere in the church sanctuary (a holy place) and then have a coffee hour or a potluck supper in the church parlors for fellowship and a social get-together"; *Eating and Drinking*, 74.

39. I remember the first times I participated in communion in my home church. I almost choked. I had no problem with Sunday dinner at home. We were Mennonites, and we were at home with food! But even though—or maybe because—I had attended church regularly since childhood and observed many a communion, the Lord's Supper never conveyed the overtones of fellowship. That is why it seemed so awkward to be eating—receiving the abbreviated tokens—in the church sanctuary.

40. "The Lord's Supper, as practiced in our congregations, is not only loveless but inhuman! Each partakes alone. It is all so impersonal. No one greets his neighbor with a handshake or a 'holy kiss.' One does not speak to or listen to those around him. . . . Is it any wonder that in many congregations a coffee hour or a church supper will be served where the members and visitors can get to know one another, speak to one another, and to help one another?" Cochrane, *Eating and Drinking*, 87.

41. "Symbolism and tokenism have been the destruction of genuine Christian fellowship"; Cochrane, *Eating and Drinking*, 83.

42. Martin Marty, *Baptism* (Philadelphia: Westminster, 1962), 18.

43. I once attended a Catholic church where the priest complimented his congregation for their friendliness. Visitors at a previous Sunday had stayed over after a weekend sports event, had attended the local service, and had commented upon how friendly the congregation was. As I left the church, no one so much as spoke to me coming or going. I said to myself, "If this is a friendly church, save me from an unfriendly one."

44. Some theological writings properly suggest that the benediction of the Lord's table should carry over into and grace all eating we do. In the words of Paul, "So, whether you eat or drink, or whatever you do, do everything for the glory of God" (1 Cor. 10:31), "giving thanks to God the Father at all times and for everything in the name of our Lord Jesus Christ" (Eph. 5:20). Says Cochrane, "The Lord's Supper is the model and criterion of all meals"; Cochrane, *Eating and Drinking*, 77.

45. Elder D. B. Gibson, *The Lord's Supper* (Elgin, Ill.: Brethren Publishing House, 1902), 22, says, "If [baptism] requires enough water to cover a [person], [*deipnon*] with greater certainty requires enough food to fill the person and as many as are to partake of it." Gibson, 24, argues cogently also for the importance of time—*deipnon* was an evening meal. He also shows that the Supper was at a table with dishes on it.

46. Says Arthur Cochrane, a Presbyterian, "The simplest yet most necessary reform of the Lord's Supper in our congregations is that it must become again a meal for the nourishment of the physical body. In these pages we will give many reasons why it should be a meal"; *Eating and Drinking*, 40. Even Australian Anglican John Wilkerson says, "In order to carry out Christ's command that we should 'Do this,' it will usually be necessary to reproduce in some physical form the arrangement of the upper room in the place where the Eucharist is to be celebrated"; *The Supper and the Eucharist: A*

Layman's Guide to Anglican Revision (New York: St. Martin's Press, 1965), 145. Canadian United Church minister Paul Miller says, "The time has come for the United Church to rediscover the love feast or agape"; "Let Us Break Bread Together," *Touchstone*, Sept. 1990.

47. "There is nothing to suggest that the love feast was a separate kind of meal from the Lord's Supper, and it seems more probable that these were two different names for the same occasion." "By the second century the Breaking of Bread or Lord's Supper had been completely separated from the church meal, but they belonged together in New Testament times"; Marshall, *Last Supper*, 110, 145.

48. Some years ago I was amused to read an Anglican theologian's disparagement of the pattern of receiving communion while seated in pews. He called it irreverent "lounging." He either didn't know his Bible or else had forgotten who it was who really had "lounged": Jesus and his disciples, who reclined at the Last Supper! Let us permit ourselves to note, though, that when participants are seated, communion need not lose the spirit of reverence. Yet "cafeteria" communion does lose the opportunity—and responsibility—of fellowship.

49. Some readers may wonder why I have not discussed frequency of communion, especially since I have appealed to the restorationist impulse in our tradition. Numerous writers note the New Testament and early church references to observance of the Supper every Lord's day. I may be charged with inconsistency, but I personally do not find any direct and immediate connection between frequency of celebration and the meaning of the Lord's Supper. In other words, I do not see the supper necessarily becoming more meaningful the oftener it is celebrated. Instead, I see it the other way around: let us restore the New Testament agape form of the supper, and then congregations will find a practical rhythm. For starters, I am inclined to suggest a quarterly carry-in meal.

50. Although even they seem to have succumbed to the temptation to abbreviate some of their celebrations.

8. Brethren Heritage of the Lord's Supper

1. See, for example, Alexander Mack, *Rights and Ordinances*, in *The Complete Writings of Alexander Mack*, ed. William R. Eberly (Winona Lake, Ind.: BMH Books, 1991), 45, 60-63.

2. See Donald F. Durnbaugh, comp. and trans., *European Origins of the Brethren* (Elgin, Ill.: Brethren Press, 1958), 287; and Donald F. Durnbaugh, ed., *The Brethren in Colonial America* (Elgin, Ill.: Brethren Press, 1967), 76-77, 217, 449.

3. See Peter Nead, *Theological Writings on Various Subjects* (Dayton, Ohio: B. F. Fells, 1850), 139, 147. Note also John Kline's similar emphasis in Nead, *Theological Writings*, 387-388.

4. See, for example, C. F. Yoder, *God's Means of Grace* (Elgin, Ill.: Brethren Publishing House, 1908), 285; J. Allen Miller, *Christian Doctrine: Lectures and Sermons* (Ashland, Ohio: Brethren Publishing Company, 1946), 255; Joseph R. Shultz, *The Soul of the Symbols: A Theological Study of Holy Communion* (Grand Rapids: Eerdmans, 1966); Vernard Eller, *In Place of Sacraments* (Grand Rapids: Eerdmans, 1972); The Vindicator Committee, *Doctrinal Treatise*, 3d ed. (Covington, Ohio: The Vindicator, 1970); *Dunkard Brethren Church Polity* (n.p., 1980); William M. Beahm, *The Brethren Love Feast* (Elgin, Ill.: Brethren Press, n.d.).

5. The Brethren followed the Pietists and Radical Pietists in seeking balance on controversial issues. The Pietists typically sought a "blessed middle-way" on dialectical

issues such as the Word and Spirit, the inner and the outer, the individual and the community, individual freedom and corporate accountability. For further discussion of this concept, see Dale R. Stoffer, *Background and Development of Brethren Doctrines, 1650-1987* (Philadelphia: Brethren Encyclopedia, Inc., 1989), 24, 31, 36, 83-84, 97.

6. Durnbaugh, *Colonial America,* 235. Peter Nead, *Theological Writings,* 148, makes a similar point about the accounts of the Lord's Supper: "So, by taking the four Evangelists together, in conjunction with what the apostles have written, we have the Gospel in full."

7. For a more detailed discussion of this point, see Stoffer, *Brethren Doctrines,* 23-24, 26-28, 52, 61, 73-74.

9. The Agape in the Brethren Tradition

1. See Dale R. Stoffer, "The Background and Development of Thought and Practice in the German Baptist Brethren (Dunker) and the Brethren (Progressive) Churches (ca. 1650-1979)" (Ph.D. diss., Fuller Theological Seminary, 1980), 15-277. The dissertation has been published as *Background and Development of Brethren Doctrines, 1650-1987* (Philadelphia: Brethren Encyclopedia, 1989). See also Donald F. Durnbaugh, *Brethren Beginnings: The Origin of the Church of the Brethren in Early Eighteenth-Century Europe* (Philadelphia: Brethren Encyclopedia, 1992), 1-31.

2. Alexander Mack, "A Brief and Simple Exposition of the Outward but Yet Sacred Rights and Ordinances of the House of God as the True Householder Commanded and Bequeathed in Writing in His Testament; Presented in a Conversation Between Father and Son in Question and Answer by Alexander Mack, One also called to the Great Supper" ([Berleburg?], 1715), in William R. Eberly, ed., *The Complete Writings of Alexander Mack* (Winona Lake, Ind.: BMH Books, 1991), 62. The translation is that of Donald F. Durnbaugh, in his *European Origins of the Brethren* (Elgin, Ill.: Brethren Publishing House, 1958).

3. Some texts of 2 Peter 2:13 read "*agapais* (love feasts)" instead of the better-attested "*apatais* (dissipations)"; or "deceptions," Reike), showing assimilation to the Jude text. However, some texts of Jude 12 read "*apatais* (blemishes)" in place of the better-attested "*agapais* (love feasts)." See Bo Reicke, *The Epistles of James, Peter, and Jude* (Garden City, N.Y.: Doubleday, 1964, 1982), 166-168, 205-208. The singular form, *agapē,* has become a loanword in English, meaning "love feast" or "love."

4. Hans Lietzmann, *Mass and Lord's Supper* (1926, 1979).

5. Michael J. Townsend, "Exit the Agape?" *The Expository Times* 90 (Sept. 1979): 360.

6. Graydon F. Snyder, *First Corinthians. A Faith Community Commentary* (Macon, Ga.: Mercer Univ. Press, 1992), 156-158, 239-241. See also his article, "Love Feast," in *The Brethren Encyclopedia,* ed. Donald F. Durnbaugh, 3 vols. (Oak Brook, Ill.: The Brethren Encyclopedia, Inc., 1983-84), 2:762. He distinguishes the two strands as memorial (*anamnēsis*) and fellowship (*koinōnia*) meals.

7. Cave's *Primitive Christianity: or, the religion of the ancient Christians in the first age of the Gospel,* first appeared in 1673 in London; the first German translation, *Erstes Christentum, oder Gottesdienst der alten Christen in der ersten Zeiten,* appeared in Leipzig in 1694, with 2d ed. in 1696.

8. Peter C. Erb, *Pietists, Protestants, and Mysticism: The Use of Late Medieval Spiritual Texts in the Work of Gottfried Arnold (1666-1714)* (Metuchen, N.J.: Scarecrow Press, 1989), 31-32, 226, n. 55.

9. Ernst Christoph Hochmann von Hochenau, "Letter to Alexander Mack and

Georg Grebe," in Donald F. Durnbaugh, ed., *European Origins of the Brethren* (Elgin, Ill.: Brethren Publishing House, 1958), 113.

10. Mack, "Rights and Ordinances," 61.

11. Erb, *Pietists, Protestants and Mysticism*, 27-41. See also Hans Schneider, "Der radikale Pietismus im 17. Jahrhundert," in Martin Brecht, ed., *Der Pietismus vom siebzehnten bis zum frühen achtzehnten Jahrhundert*, vol. 1 in *Geschichte des Pietismus* (Göttingen: Vandenhoeck & Ruprecht, 1993), 394-415.

12. A[lexander] M[ack], "Eberhard Louis Gruber's Basic Questions which were especially submitted to be answered by the New Baptists of the Wittgenstein Area along with the accompanying Brief and Simple Answers to the Same, previously published in manuscript by an Artless Member of the church at Wittgenstein" (Berleburg?, 1713), translated by Donald F. Durnbaugh in William R. Eberly, ed., *The Complete Writings of Alexander Mack* (Winona Lake, Ind.: BMH Books, 1991), 39. Thus the early Brethren, like many radical Pietists, believed they were living in the "Philadelphian church age," a period in the grand scheme of biblical time when the persecuted yet faithful remnant church (as described in the letter to Philadelphia in Revelation 3) would be strengthened to endure before the dawn of the new kingdom.

13. Mack, "Rights and Ordinances," 43.

14. Mack, "Rights and Ordinances," 61. This appears in the discussion of the Lord's Supper. See also 62.

15. Peter Nead, *Theological Writings*, new ed. (Dayton, Ohio, 1866), reprinted by Dunker Reprints, 1985), 144. A letter by John Kline, appended to the volume, argues the same point, that the eucharist is a memorial of the death of Jesus, and the agape is an eschatological meal anticipating the wedding banquet of the Lamb. See 387.

16. Nead, *Theological Writings*, 139, 387.

17. Martin Grove Brumbaugh, *A History of the German Baptist Brethren in Europe and America* (Elgin, Ill.: Brethren Publishing House, 1906), 156-159.

18. Johann Adam Gruber, "Extract from J. A. Gr[uber's] Letter from Germantown, Oct. 28, 1730," in *Geistliche Fama*, no. 3 (1731), 51, quoted in Felix Reichmann and Eugene E. Doll, trans. and eds., *Ephrata as Seen by Contemporaries* (Allentown, Pa.: Pennsylvania German Folklore Society, 1953), 3. Among radical Pietists, "Breaking of bread (*Brotbrechen*)" became a technical term for the Lord's Sup-per. Among Brethren-related groups, it referred to the full love feast.

19. Conrad Beissel [?] [with Peter Miller?], "Vorrede" to *Das Gesang der Einsamen Turtel-Taube* (Ephrata, Pa.: Press of the Brotherhood, 1747), folios 6-19, especially folios 18-19.

20. Lamech and Agrippa, *Chronicon Ephratense* (Ephrata, Pa., 1786), translated by J. Max Hark (Lancaster, Pa.: S. H. Zahm & Co., 1889), reprint (New York: Burt Franklin, 1972), 62.

21. Note the controversy over Beissel's visit to the daughter congregation on the Antietam (today's Snow Hill), when the local group was still observing the love feast in the manner of the Schwarzenau Brethren, in which all participants passed the elements to each other; Lamech and Agrippa, *Chronicon Ephratense*, 260-261.

22. Lamech and Agrippa, *Chronicon Ephratense*, 91.

23. Vernard Eller, *In Place of Sacraments* (Grand Rapids: Eerdmans, 1972), 98, 101-105.

24. Eller does advance a layer of eschatological interpretation for the cup shared during the eucharist; *In Place of Sacraments*, 124-127.

25. Donald F. Durnbaugh, ed., *Meet the Brethren* (Elgin, Ill.: Brethren Press, 1984), 31, 46, 51, 77, 97, 107.

10. Footwashing Within the Context of the Lord's Supper

1. J. C. Thomas, *Footwashing in John 13 and the Johannine Community*, JSNTS, 61 (Sheffield: JSOT Press, 1991).

2. F. Hauck, "*Opheilō*," in *Theological Dictionary of the New Testament (TDNT)*, ed. G. Kittel, trans. G. W. Bromiley, 10 vols. (Grand Rapids: Eerdmans, 1964-74), 5:562-564, esp. 563.

3. D. A. Carson, *The Gospel According to John* (Grand Rapids: Eerdmans, 1990), 467-468.

4. J. Shultz, *The Soul of the Symbols* (Grand Rapids: Eerdmans, 1966), 62.

5. L. Morris, *The Gospel According to John* (Grand Rapids: Eerdmans, 1971), 621, n. 36.

6. H. Schlier, "*Hypodeigma*," in *TDNT*, 2:33. Apollonius of Citium uses *hypodeigma* on a number of occasions with the sense of "illustration, (or) picture showing how something is to be done" (Liddell-Scott, 1878). Cf. especially Apollonii Citiensis, *In Hippocratio de articulus commentarius*, ed. F. Kudlien (Berlin: Akademie-Verlag, 1965), 38, 60-64, and 112.

7. H. Schlier, "*Amēn*," *TDNT*, 1:338.

8. Raymond E. Brown, *The Gospel According to John*, Anchor Bible (Garden City, N.Y.: Doubleday, 1970), 2:563.

9. P. G. Ahr, "He Loved Them to Completion? The Theology of John 13-14," in *Standing Before God: Studies on Prayer in Scripture and in Tradition with Essays in Honor of John M. Oestereicher*, ed. A. Finkel and L. Frizzell (New York: KTAV Publishing House, 1981), 77. M. Hengel, *Crucifixion*, trans. J. Bowden (Philadelphia: Fortress, 1977), 29, notes 21, 87: often crucifixion victims died naked.

10. Brown, *Gospel According to John*, 2:551.

11. Despite some strong support for *deipnou genomenou* ("when supper had ended"), *deipnou ginoumenou* is to be preferred as the original reading. This judgment is based upon (1) slightly better external evidence (Aleph° B W it^d syr^pal arm) and (2) internal coherence, for it is obvious from the context (John 13:26) that the meal continued after the footwashing episode is complete. Cf. B. M. Metzger, *A Textual Commentary on the Greek New Testament* (London: United Bible Societies, 1971), 239. However, either reading demonstrates the point that Jesus washes the disciples' feet at an unusual time.

12. Translation of K. Lake, *The Apostolic Fathers* (Cambridge: Harvard Univ. Press, 1912), 1:273-275.

13. Translation of K. Lake, *The Apostolic Fathers*, 2:330-331.

14. Cf. F. F. Segovia, "John 13:1-20, The Footwashing in the Johannine Tradition," *Zeitschrift für die neutestamentliche Wissenschaft und die Kunde der älteren Kirche* (ZNW) 73 (1982): 43, "An acceptance of that which the washing symbolizes grants the disciples continued union with Jesus." The context of belief, the Book of Glory, demonstrates that the footwashing does not initiate fellowship, but continues it.

15. J. Owanga-Welo, "The Function and Meaning of the Johannine Passion Narrative: A Structural Approach" (Ph.D. diss., Emory Univ., 1980), 241.

16. Translation of Gummerie, *Seneca: Epistulae morales* (London: Heinemann, 1920), 2:317.

17. One or both of the suggested meanings for *leloumenos* are the only viable options for the disciples in the narrative or the implied readers. However, the author knows of another possibility which the reader will encounter in John 15:3. In this verse, Jesus tells the disciples, "Already you are clean (*katharoi*) because of the word which I

have spoken to you." If it were legitimate to take *leloumenos* in 13:10 as the referent of *ton logon* in 15:3, then perhaps the difficulty would be solved. On one occasion in the LXX (Greek Old Testament: Judges 3:19), *logos* does refer to a "prophetic" action, when Ehud told King Eglon that he had a *logos* for him in private and then killed the king. However, such a parallel (if it be a parallel) is too far removed to explain John 15:3. In addition, it appears that the *logos* of 15:3 has reference to Jesus' collective teaching, not one specific event. Approaching 13:10 in the light of 15:3, Bultmann argues that cleansing comes on the basis of the Revealer's word and on that basis alone. Therefore, *leloumenos* is used to describe the bath in the word; this makes cleansing with water secondary at best.

However, one of the difficulties in explaining John 13:10 on the basis of 15:3 is the difference in context. While 13:10 speaks of cleansing from some uncleanness or defilement, 15:3 uses cleansing in the sense of pruning the branches in order to produce good fruit. There does not seem to be sufficient evidence to demand that 13:10 must be interpreted by means of 15:3. Yet there may be a deeper connection between cleansing by means of pruning and cleansing through washing. Rather than playing 13:10 and 15:3 off against one another, the two statements about cleansing should be allowed to speak independently, perhaps at different levels of meaning. C. H. Dodd offers a most helpful analysis through comparison with a similar dilemma found elsewhere in the Fourth Gospel: "The disciples are *katharoi* through washing with water [13:10]: they are *katharoi*, also, *dia ton logon* [15:3]. Similarly, eternal life comes by eating the flesh and blood of the Son of Man (6:54) and also, *ta rhēmata ha lelalēka humin* are *zōē* [6:63]. The treatment of the two sacraments are analogous." So, for the evangelist, cleansing takes place through water and the word, and both are dependent on the cleansing effects of Jesus' death.

18. As P. Grelot concludes, "When one gives thought to this background, it is difficult not to see a baptismal allusion in the declaration by Jesus." P. Grelot, "L'interprétation pénitentielle du lavement des pieds," in *L'homme devant Dieu, I: Mélanges offerts au père Henri Lubac* (Paris: Aubier, 1963), 86. Obviously, there are other passages which do not equate *louō* with baptism. For example, cf. Acts 9:37 and 16:33.

19. C. H. Dodd, *Interpretation of the Fourth Gospel* (Cambridge: Cambridge Univ. Press, 1953), 401, n. 3.

20. B. F. Westcott, *The Gospel According to St. John* (Grand Rapids: Eerdmans, 1975), 191; B. W. Bacon, "The Sacrament of Footwashing," *Expository Times* 43 (1931-32): 221; O. Cullmann, *Early Christian Worship*, ed. A. S. Todd and J. B. Torrance (London: SCM Press, 1953), 108-110; Dodd, *Interpretation of the Fourth Gospel*, 401, n. 3; F. Hauck, "*Katharos,*" *TDNT*, 3:426; A. J. B. Higgins, *The Lord's Supper in the New Testament* (London: SCM Press, 1952), 84; W. L. Knox, "John 13:1-30," *Harvard Theological Review* 43 (1950): 163; G. H. C. MacGregor, *The Gospel of John* (London: Harper, 1959), 76; A. Maynard, "The Role of Peter in the Fourth Gospel," *New Testament Studies* 30 (1984): 534-535; A. Maynard, "The Function of Apparent Synonyms and Ambiguous Words in the Fourth Gospel" (Ph.D. diss., Univ. of Southern California, 1950), 329-330; A. Oepke, "*Louō,*" *TDNT*, 4:306.

21. Carson, *Gospel According to John*, 465-466, remarks, "In his first epistle, addressed to Christians, to people who have already believed (1 John 5:13) and received eternal life (2:25), John insists that continuing confession of sin is necessary (1:9), as is continued dependence upon Jesus Christ, who is the atoning sacrifice for our sins (2:1-2). The thought of John 13:10 is not dissimilar."

22. J. R. Michaels, *John* (New York: Harper & Row, 1984), 227. Cf. also G. R. Beasley-Murray, *John* (Waco: Word, 1987), 235; and "Baptism," in *New International Dictionary of New Testament Theology*, ed. Colin Brown, 4 vols.(Grand Rapids: Zondervan, 1986, 1:154; Raymond E. Brown, *Gospel According to John*, 2:586; F. F. Bruce, *The Gospel of John* (Grand Rapids: Eerdmans, 1984), 283; W. K. Grossouw, "A Note on John XIII 1-3," *Novum Testamentum* 8 (1966): 129-130.

23. Such an interpretation dovetails neatly with the preoccupation with post-conversion sin in 1 John and the interpretation of footwashing in the early church. Cf. Thomas, *Footwashing in John 13 and the Johannine Community*, 149-172.

24. Translation of Lake, *The Apostolic Fathers*, 1:331.

25. Cf. esp. the remarks of Origen, *Genesis Homily* 4.2; Ambrose, *Mysteries* 6.31; and Augustine, *Homilies on John* 58.5.

26. Ben Witherington graciously sent a copy of his paper to me before the conference, which contained a critique of my work on footwashing. I appreciate both his courtesy and the honor of his attention. In this closing footnote, I would like to respond to several issues he raises in note 83 of his paper.

(1) While there is room for disagreement on the issue of intended audience, I must confess that I am genuinely puzzled by the argument that the Fourth Gospel was not written primarily for the Christian community but was a missionary document. (2) To argue that there is no, or little, connection between Mary's action in John 12 and the footwashing in John 13 seems to ignore both the flow of John's narrative and the way that footwashings could be quite elaborate in antiquity. (3) To argue that the disciples are not fully Christian appears to ignore John's intention of contrasting the faith of the disciples with those who have inadequate faith. (4) To say that footwashing signifies cleansing and forgiveness from Jesus is not to say that believers have no role to play in signs which convey such cleansing. While it might be fair to say that one aspect of footwashing is passive, in that one believer receives from another, I fail to see the significance of this dimension in that eucharist and baptism are also rites that are received. (5) To interpret the meaning of the practice of footwashing solely as an example of serving others is to ignore the interpretation of the rite which is provided in John 13 itself. Based on the relevant data, it is still more likely that the first readers of the Fourth Gospel took John 13 as the institution of a rite of cleansing.

11. Brethren Heritage of the Lord's Supper

1. Alexander Mack, *Rights and Ordinances*, in *The Complete Writings of Alexander Mack*, ed William R. Eberly (Winona Lake, Ind.: BMH Books, 1991), 60-61.

2. C. F. Yoder, *God's Means of Grace* (Elgin, Ill.: Brethren Publishing House, 1908), 390-394.

3. See Peter Nead, *Theological Writings on Various Subjects* (Dayton, Ohio: B. F. Fells, 1850), 153.

4. Nead, *Theological Writings*, 151-152; and Henry R. Holsinger, *History of the Tunkers and The Brethren Church* (Oakland, Calif.: Pacific Press Publishing Co., 1901), 249-255. The original declaration over the cup was "the cup of the New Testament is the communion of the blood of Christ."

5. H. Wayne Pipkin and John H. Yoder, trans. and ed. *Balthasar Hubmaier: Theologian of Anabaptism*, Classics of the Radical Reformation, 5 (Scottdale, Pa.: Herald Press, 1989), 322.

6. Nead, *Theological Writings*, 153. For the same point among Anabaptist writers, see Menno Simons, *Foundation of Christian Doctrine*, in *The Complete Writings*

of Menno Simons, c.1496-1561, trans. Leonard Verduin and ed. John C. Wenger (Scottdale, Pa.: Herald Press, 1956), 143-144; and the statements by Balthasar Hubmaier and Dirk Philips in Walter Klaassen, ed., *Anabaptism in Outline*, Classics of the Radical Reformation, 3 (Scottdale, Pa.: Herald Press, 1981), 193, 206-207.

7. Vernard Eller, *In Place of Sacraments: A Study of Baptism and the Lord's Supper* (Grand Rapids: Eerdmans, 1972), 81-84.

8. Nead, *Theological Writings*, 153.

9. Menno, *Christian Doctrine*, 153-154.

10. Nead, *Theological Writings*, 388. In his work, Nead includes an essay by John Kline on the Lord's Supper.

11. Yoder, *God's Means of Grace*, 392.

12. Dale R. Stoffer, *Background and Development of Brethren Doctrines, 1650-1987* (Philadelphia: Brethren Encyclopedia, Inc., 1989), 107.

13. James Quinter, "Means of Grace," *The Christian Family Companion and Gospel Visitor* n.s. 2 (Jan. 26, 1875): 58. For a detailed discussion of this point, see Stoffer, *Brethren Doctrines*, 109-110.

14. Alexander Mack, *Basic Questions*, in *Complete Writings of Alexander Mack*, 32.

15. Menno, *Christian Foundation*, 131.

16. Menno, *Christian Foundation*, 123-125, 130-131; and *Christian Baptism*, in *Complete Writings of Menno Simons*, 244-245; Mack, *Basic Questions*, 28-29, 32-33. By calling the ordinances "means of grace," the Brethren of the nineteenth century were moving in the direction of a more sacramental model.

17. Klaassen, *Anabaptism in Outline*, 207.

18. Eller, *Sacraments*, 34.

19. This perspective is reinforced in the early Anabaptist confession of faith, the Schleitheim Confession (1527). Note the following statements drawn from the article on "Breaking of Bread."

> As Paul points out, we cannot at the same time drink the cup of the Lord and the cup of the devil. That is, all those who have fellowship with the dead works of darkness have no part in the light. Therefore all who follow the devil and the world have no part with those who are called unto God out of the world. All who lie in evil have no part in the good.

John H. Leith, ed., *Creeds of the Churches* (Garden City, N.Y.: Anchor Books, 1963), 285.

12. The Lord's Supper as Viewed and Practiced by the Christian Churches, Churches of Christ, and the Disciples of Christ

1. Avery Dulles, *Models of the Church* (Garden City: Image Books, 1978), 88.

2. Dulles, *Models*, 176.

3. Joe Dampier, former professor, Emmanuel School of Religion.

4. William Robinson, *What Churches of Christ Stand For* (Birmingham: The Churches of Christ Publishing Committee, 1926), 85.

5. See Joachim Jeremias, *The Eucharistic Words of Jesus* (London: SCM Press LTD, 1973), 118-122; F. F. Bruce, *Commentary on the Book of the Acts* (Grand Rapids: Eerdmans, 1955), 79; Richard Longenecker, *The Acts of the Apostles*, The Expositor's Bible Commentary (Grand Rapids: Regency, 1981), 289-290.

6. Jeremias, *Eucharistic Words*, 62, 137.

7. John Calvin, *Institutes of the Christian Religion* (Philadelphia: Presbyterian

Board of Publication and Sabbath School Work, 1911), 2:580.

13. A Quaker Interpretation of the Lord's Supper
1. Kenneth Boulding, *The Nayler Sonnets* (Nyack, N.Y.: F.O.R., 1945), 13, #13.
2. Thomas R. Kelly, *A Testament of Devotion* (New York: Harper's, 1941), 32.
3. Kelly, *Testament of Devotion*, 91.
4. John Punshon, *The Shadow and the Substance* (Philadelphia: Wider Quaker Fellowship, 1992).
5. Kelly, *Testament of Devotion*, 82, 86-87.

14. Seventh-Day Adventists and the Lord's Supper
1. M. L. Andreasen, "The Ordinance of the Lord's House," *Ministry* (Jan. 1947): 44.
2. *Seventh-Day Adventist Church Manual*, rev. (General Conference of Seventh-Day Adventists, 1990), 78.
3. Ellen G. White, *Gospel Workers*, rev. and enl. ed. (Washington, D.C.: Review and Herald Publishing Association, 1915), 156.

15. The Lord's Supper in the Free Methodist Tradition
1. See Howard A. Snyder, *The Radical Wesley and Patterns for Church Renewal* (Downers Grove, Ill.: InterVarsity Press, 1980).
2. Some Free Methodists have occasionally commented on the irony that the denomination puts more restrictions on who may officiate at the Lord's Supper than on who may preach or teach in the church. Clearly this is a carryover from medieval Catholic sacramentalism.
3. Carl LeRoy Howland, *The Story of Our Church: Free Methodism: Some Facts and Some Reasons*, rev. (Winona Lake, Ind.: Free Methodist Publishing House, n.d. [ca. 1940]; rev. ed., 1951).
4. Howland, *Story* (1951 ed.), 94.
5. See L. R. Marston's comment in his *From Age to Age a Living Witness: A Historical Interpretation of Free Methodism's First Century* (Winona Lake, Ind.: Light and Life Press, 1960), 354-355.
6. *The Book of Discipline 1979* (Winona Lake, Ind.: Free Methodist Publishing House, 1980), 286. Cf. *The Book of Common Prayer* (New York: Seabury Press, 1979), 332.
7. Marston, *From Age to Age*, 339.
8. Marston, *From Age to Age*, 340.
9. Compare *The Doctrines and Discipline of the Free Methodist Church* (Rochester, N.Y.: B. T. Roberts, 1879), 124; and *Doctrines and Discipline of the Free Methodist Church* (Chicago: Free Methodist Publishing House, 1931), 209. The newer version also provided that the officiant might substitute the Lord's Prayer for the general confession, in contrast to the earlier form, which provided a way to excise the confession of sin—though the Lord's Prayer included, "Forgive us our debts" (Matt. 6:12, KJV).
10. See Howard A. Snyder, " 'To Preach the Gospel to the Poor': Missional Self-Understanding in Early Free Methodism (1860-90)," unpublished manuscript, 1992 (prepared for the Oxford Institute of Methodist Theological Studies), 23 pages.
11. The Scriptures listed were Matt. 5:16; 6:19-20; 7:12; 6:21; Luke 19:19; 2 Cor. 9:6-7; Gal. 6:10; 1 Tim. 6:6-7; 1 Tim. 6:17, 19; Heb. 6:10; 13:16; 1 John 3:17; Prov. 19:17;

and Ps. 41:1 (in that order). Following the reading of one or more of these passages, an offering was to be received. See *The Doctrines and Discipline of the Free Methodist Church* (Rochester, N.Y.: The General Conference, 1870), 116-118.

12. *The Book of Discipline 1979*, 218.

13. See "Instructions for Elders and Deacons Who Serve Communion," *Pastor's Handbook of the Free Methodist Church*, 2d ed., ed. Clyde E. Van Valin (Winona Lake, Ind.: Light and Life Press, 1986), 135.

14. David L. McKenna, "A Future with a History," *Light and Life* 128:3 (Mar. 1995): 13.

16. The Lord's Supper of the African Methodist Episcopal Church

1. *The Doctrine and Discipline of the African Methodist Episcopal Church* (Nashville, Tenn.: The African Methodist Episcopal Church Sunday School, 1992), 17.

2. Henry Wheeler, *History and Exposition of the Twenty-five Articles of Religion of the Methodist Church* (New York: The Methodist Book Concern, 1908), 317ff.

3. Wheeler, *Twenty-five Articles*, 319.

4. Wheeler, *Twenty-five Articles*, 321.

5. *Discipline of AME Church*, 436.

6. *AMEC Bicentennial Hymnal* (Nashville, Tenn.: The African Methodist Episcopal Church, 1994), no. 256.

17. A Moravian Perspective on Holy Communion

1. *The Book of Order of the Moravian Church (Unitas Fratrum) Northern Province* (Bethlehem, Pa.: Provincial Elders' Conference, 1991 ed.), art. 19 (a).1-7.

2. Matthew Spinka, *John Hus, A Biography* (Westport, Conn.: Greenwood Press, 1968), 240.

3. Spinka, *John Hus*, 256.

4. Albert H. Frank, "History of the Moravian Church—Ancient Unitas Fratrum," class lectures, Sept. 9, 1981, Moravian Theological Seminary, Bethlehem, Pa.

5. Otto Dreydoppel Jr., "The Intentions of Our Founders: A Historical Review of Moravian Worship," in *A Symposium on Moravian Theology, November 18, 1988*, rev. (Bethlehem, Pa.: Moravian Theological Seminary, May 1989), 4.

6. Edmund DeSchweinitz, *The History of the Church Known as the Unitas Fratrum* (Bethlehem, Pa.: Moravian Publication Concern, 1901), 204.

7. Edwin W. Kortz, "The Liturgical Development of the American Moravian Church," *Transactions of the Moravian Historical Society* 18 (1962): 287.

8. *Book of Order*, art. 1084, XI-28.

9. Edwin W. Kortz, "Moravian Seminar," class lectures, Nov. 3, 1982, Moravian Theological Seminary, Bethlehem, Pa.

10. Kortz, "The Liturgical Development of the American Moravian Church," 27.

11. *Hymnal and Liturgies of the Moravian Church* (The Moravian Church in America, Northern and Southern Provinces, 1969), 149-201.

12. Arthur J. Freeman, Personal Statement of Faith, "I Believe," 6.

13. Kortz, "Moravian Seminar."

14. Marianka S. Fousek, "The Pastoral Office in the Early Unitas Fratrum," *The Slavonic and East European Review*, 40.95 (1962).

15. Edwin W. Kortz, "Moravian Seminar" paper on "The Moravian Surplice," material dated December 1978, Moravian Theological Seminary, Bethlehem, Pa.

16. *Book of Order*, XI-29.

18. Sacrament, Ordinance or Both? Baptist Understandings of the Lord's Supper

1. Horton Davies, *Worship and Theology in England, From Andrewes to Baxter and Fox, 1603-1690*, vol. 2 (Princeton: Princeton Univ. Press, 1975), 2:495, 509. See also *Confession of Faith Put Forth by the Elders and Brethren of Many Congregations of Christians (Baptized upon Profession of Their Faith) in London and the Country* (London: n.p., 1677), chap. 30.

2. John Smyth, *The Differences in the Churches of the Separation: Contayning a Description of the Leitourgie and Ministerie of the Visible Church* (Amsterdam?: n.p., 1608); Thomas Grantham, *Christianismus Primitivus, or the Ancient Christian Religion* (London: Francis Smith, 1678).

3. E. P. Winter, "Calvinist and Zwinglian Views of the Lord's Supper Among the Baptists of the Seventeenth Century," *Baptist Quarterly* 25:3 (July 1954): 325ff. Another major difficulty with Smyth's work is the lack of demonstrable continuity of ideas. No contemporary (or later) Baptist thinker credited John Smyth with laying a foundation for a Baptist theology of the Lord's Supper. Even the General Baptists themselves form a historical divergence from the main current of Anglo-North American Baptist life. On this latter point, consult Norman H. Maring, "Editorial," *Foundations* 1:3 (1958): 93-94.

4. Davies, *Worship and Theology*, 1:500-505; E. B. Underhill, ed., *Fenstanton, Warboys and Hexham Records* (London: Hanserd Knollys Soc., 1854), 212. This thesis is vulnerable at the point of assuming too large an influence of John Smyth on those who returned with Helwys to England, and the present silence of other potential factors acting on the early General Baptist churches.

5. See "Propositions and Conclusions, Concerning True Christian Religion, Conteyning a Confession of Faith of Certain English People, Living at Amsterdam," in William T. Whitley, ed., *The Works of John Smyth, Fellow of Christ's College, 1594-8*, vol. 2 (Cambridge: Cambridge Univ. Press, 1915), 2:733-750. Ernest A. Payne, *The Fellowship of Believers* (London: Kingsgate Press, 1944), 52, observes that Smyth and later General Baptists "had no scruples about using the term Sacrament" in a Calvinistic sense.

6. Davies, *Worship and Theology*, 2:317-319.

7. Whitley, *Works of John Smyth*, 1:xvii-lxxiv.

8. Davies, *Worship and Theology*, 1:507-508.

9. *Confession of Faith Put Forth by the Elders and Brethren of Many Congregations of Christians* (London: n.p., 1677), chap. 30. Winter, "Calvinist and Zwinglian Views," 325, points out that in this confession, English Particular Baptists excluded the word *sacrament* and preferred terms like *figurative*, as in the "Westminster Confession of Faith" (1646, Presbyterian).

10. Many modern Baptist writers use the term "Zwinglian" to designate the historic position of "memorialism." But this is problematic, because no Baptist writer before the present century ever credited Zwingli with that position. See, for instance, Payne, *Fellowship of Believers*, 50ff.

11. John H. Y. Briggs, *The English Baptists of the Nineteenth Century* (Didcot: Baptist Historical Society, 1994), 65, places the change in terminology among many British Baptists in the context of Robert Hall and the Evangelical Revival.

12. Charles H. Spurgeon, *Till He Come: Communion Meditations and Addresses* (London: Passamore & Alabaster, 1894), 148, 319. See also Spurgeon's *The Right Observance of the Lord's Supper* (St. Paul, Minn.: Asher Pub. Co., n.d.).

13. Note the Scripture references in the confessional documents; Davies, *Worship and Theology*, 2:504.

14. The terms "close communion" and "closed communion" are used interchangeably, with the former being preferred in the seventeenth century, and in later periods among some British Baptists and southern U.S. Baptists.

15. For an authoritative discussion of the seventeenth-century issues, compare Winter, "The Lord's Supper: Admission and Exclusion . . . ," with B. R. White, "Open and Closed Membership Among English and Welsh Baptists," *Baptist Quarterly* 24 (1972): 330-334.

16. John Bunyan, *Differences in Judgement: About Water Baptism No Bar to Communion* (London: John Wilkins, 1673), 3-4. B. R. White at Oxford is reluctant to allow Bunyan as a Baptist; he finds no direct evidence of a Baptist denominational decision.

17. John Gill, *A Body of Doctrinal Divinity* (London: The author, 1770), 519.

18. Kinghorn and Ivimey charged Hall with "reductionism," minimizing the sacraments to mere symbols. More recently, Michael Walker, *Baptists at the Table* (Didcot: Baptist Historical Society, 1992), 98ff., and John H. Y. Briggs, *The English Baptists*, 62-65, have agreed with the charge Kinghorn and Ivimey make against Hall.

19. Winthrop S. Hudson, "The Ecumenical Spirit of Early Baptists," *Review and Expositor*, 55.2 (Apr. 1958): 190, believes that Baptists in the mother congregation at Philadelphia had "communion" with Presbyterians. There may be a problem in his source, however, with the specific definition of the term *communion*. In New England the prime example of this phenomenon was John Males of Swansea, Massachusetts, who was virtually the town pastor for a wide variety of communicants in the period 1660-1675.

20. John Buzzell, *The Life of Elder Benjamin Randal* (Limerick, N.H.: Hobbs, Woodman Co., 1827), 75-76.

21. Though there are significant divergences, this was the prevailing stream in the United States and British North America. See William G. McLoughlin, *New England Dissent, 1630-1833* (Cambridge, Mass.: Harvard Univ. Press, 1971), 1:79-91.

22. "The New Hampshire Baptist Confession of Faith," in William L. Lumpkin, *Baptist Confessions of Faith* (Valley Forge: Judson Press, 1959), 366.

23. Compare J. R. Graves, *Old Landmarkism: What Is It?* (Texarkana, Ark.: 1880), 17-26, with a contemporary Southern Baptist view in H. Leon McBeth, *The Baptist Heritage: Four Centuries of Baptist Witness* (Nashville: Broadman Press, 1987), 447-461.

24. J. R. Graves, *The Supper, A Church Ordinance and Was So Observed by the Apostolic Churches* (Memphis: Baptist Book House, n.d.), 1-2.

25. Harry A. Renfree, *Heritage and Horizon: The Baptist Story in Canada* (Mississauga, Ont.: Canadian Baptist Federation, 1988), 72-81; Phillip A. Griffin-Allwood, "The Canadianization of Baptists: From Denominations to Denomination, 1760-1912" (Ph.D. diss., Southern Baptist Theological Seminary, 1986), 148-179.

26. Craig A. Cameron, "The Freewill Baptist Experience in Lower and Upper Canada, 1800-1867: Crosscurrents of Canadian-American Religious Life" (Th.D. diss., Univ. of Toronto, 1994), 84-144.

27. A telephone survey conducted by the writer on 1 June 1994 revealed that the American Baptists, Southern Baptists, North American Conference, General Association of Regular Baptists, General Association of General Baptists, and Fellowship of Evangelical Baptists, plus those affiliated with the Canadian Baptist Federation— virtually all practice open communion. The lone exception is the Baptist Missionary Association of churches, formerly the Landmark Baptists in the southern United States,

who have even modified their stance to "close communion," by which many congregations allow immersed believers to enjoy communion from church to church.

28. White, "Open and Closed Membership," 334.

29. "The Orthodox Creed" (1679), in Lumpkin, *Confessions,* 321; "Second London Confession" (1677, 1688), in Lumpkin, *Confessions,* 293. William Whiston, an Anglican, suggested that eighteenth-century English Baptists would do well to mix their communion wine with water; see his *A Friendly Address to the Baptists* (Stamford: n.p., 1747).

30. Compare Abraham Coles, *Wine in the Word; An Inquiry Concerning the Wine Christ Made, the Wine of the Supper, Etc.* (New York: Nelson & Phillips, 1878) with Alvah Hovey, "What Was the 'Fruit of the Vine' Which Jesus Gave His Disciples at the Institution of the Supper?" *Baptist Quarterly Review* 9 (1887): 302-303. Coles was a prominent medical doctor, and Hovey was a seminary president.

31. These were often crafted in pure silver and displayed prominently in the church sanctuaries; scores of them were presented to the American Baptist Historical Society and other repositories when the change was made.

32. "Report of the Committee on Individual Communion Cups," Fifth Baptist Church, Philadelphia, Pa., 10 December 1897. Archives, American Baptist Historical Society.

33. Quoted in William H. Brackney, ed., *Baptist Life and Thought, 1600-1980: A Sourcebook* (Valley Forge: Judson Press, 1983), 279.

34. See, for instance, John Skoglund, *A Manual of Worship* (Valley Forge, Pa.: Judson Press, 1968), 43-60; Larry Matthews, ed., *A Manual for Worship and Service* (Mississauga, Ont.: Canadian Baptist Federation, 1976), 71-75.

35. Controversy on the domestic mission field flared in 1905 when Woman's American Baptist Home Mission Society missionary in Oklahoma, Isabel Crawford, with a layman presided over a service for the Lord's Supper in the absence of an ordained clergyman. Crawford was forced to resign; years later the Board reconsidered its position. See Matthews, *A Manual for Worship and Service,* 303-310.

36. Matthews, *A Manual for Worship and Service,* rev. (1981), 71-76. The Canadian Baptist Federation also commissioned a resource guide: Ronald F. Watts, *The Ordinances: A Baptist Perspective* (Mississauga, Ont.: Canadian Baptist Federation, 1988).

37. Some pastors complain that because Baptists believe the Supper is a community event, they may not take the elements to shut-in persons, as ministers of other sacramental traditions would.

38. American Baptists, for instance, have an official response: Genna Rae MacNeil and George D. Younger, *A Study Guide for the BEM Document* (Valley Forge: Office of the General Secretary, 1986); plus others like David M. Scholer, "The *Baptism, Eucharist, and Ministry* Document: An Outline of One Baptist Reflection," *Perspectives in Religious Studies* 13.4 (Winter 1986), 121-125, which summarizes the study of the faculty at Northern Baptist Theological Seminary in Illinois.

39. Writers in the believers church traditions have explored new definitions of sacrament and symbol. See, for instance, Joseph R. Shultz, *The Soul of the Symbols: A Theological Study of Holy Communion* (Grand Rapids: Eerdmans, 1966); Vernard Eller, *In Place of Sacraments: A Study of Baptism and the Lord's Supper* (Grand Rapids: Eerdmans, 1972). These books, among others, have enjoyed a wide readership among Baptists in the United States and Canada.

40. *This We Believe: Resources for Faith, A Baptist Study Guide* (Toronto: Baptist Convention of Ontario and Quebec, 1987), 30.

41. William R. Estep Jr., "A Response to Baptism, Eucharist, and Ministry: *Faith and Order Paper No. 111,*" in William H. Brackney, ed., *Faith, Life and Witness: The Papers of the Study and Research Division of the Baptist World Alliance, 1986-1990* (Birmingham, Ala.: Samford Univ. Press, 1990), 10-13.

42. Compare the American Baptist "Statement on Denominational Identity" (1987) section on the Lord's Supper with the British Baptist resource, Paul R. Beasley-Murray, *What We Do at the Lord's Supper* (London: Baptist Union, n.d.). Some modern British Baptists still have a fondness for sacramental terminology: D. S. Russell, "The Ministry and the Sacraments," *Baptist Quarterly* 27.1 (1957-58): 21, recalls the position of C. H. Spurgeon in arguing for a "real Presence of Christ at the Supper," though not in the elements.

20. Social Implications of the Lord's Supper in the Early Church

1. J. Hoffner, *Christliche Gesellschaftslehre* (1968), 173, as quoted in Hans-Joachim Kraus, "Aktualitat des 'Urchristlichen Kommunismus'?" *Freispruch und Freiheit* (Munchen: Chr. Kaiser Verlag, 1973), 312. Hoffner, Bishop of Münster, writes, "After the Fall the community of goods could be realized without destructive results only in the family and in the cenobitic communities of the cloister, which are a 'copy of the holy church' in Jerusalem and therein represent the possessions of a holy 'commune.'"

2. Martin Luther, "Ordinance of a Common Chest" (1523), and "The German Mass and Order of Service," in *Luther's Works*, American ed., vol. 53 (Philadelphia: Fortress, 1965), 161, 63-64.

3. John Calvin, *The Acts of the Apostles 1-13*, Calvin's Commentaries, trans. John W. Fraser and W. J. G. McDonald, ed. David W. Torrance and Thomas F. Torrance (London: Oliver and Boyd, 1965), 87.

4. Calvin, *Acts 1-13*, 87.

5. G. T. Stokes, *The Acts of the Apostles*, The Expositor's Bible, ed. W. Robertson Nicoll (New York: A. C. Armstrong & Son, 1903), 200.

6. Stokes, *Acts*, 203.

7. Werner Elert, *Das christliche Ethos* (1961), 173f.; referred to in Kraus, "Actualitat," 315.

8. Hans Conzelmann, *Acts of the Apostles* (Philadelphia: Fortress, 1963), 24.

9. Robert Jewett, "Tenement Churches and Pauline Love Feasts," *Quarterly Review* 14.1 (Spring 1994): 43-58.

10. Jewett, "Tenement Churches."

11. Bo Reicke, *Diakonie, Festfreude und Zelos in Verbindung mit der altchristlichen Agapenfeier*, Uppsala Universitets Årsskrift 5 (Uppsala: A.-B. Lundequistska Bokhandeln, 1951).

21. Proposed Theses for a Believers Church Theology of the Lord's Supper

1. See *Christian Theology: An Eschatological Approach*, vol. 2 (Scottdale, Pa.: Herald Press, 1989), 331-342.

2. For a modern Roman Catholic discussion of this theme, see Bernard Cooke, *Sacraments and Sacramentality* (Mystic, Conn.: Twenty-third Publications, 1983).

3. For this exegesis, see Graydon Snyder, "The Text and Syntax of Ignatius' *Pros Ephesious* 20.2c," *Vigilae Christianae* 22 (1968): 11. For a modern Catholic critique of overemphasis on the elements and a positive emphasis on activity in the eucharist, see Tad Guzie, *Jesus and the Eucharist* (Ramsey, N.J.: Paulist, 1974), and *The Book of*

Sacramental Basics (Ramsey, N.J.: Paulist, 1981).

4. See Geoffrey Wainwright, *Eucharist and Eschatology* (New York: Oxford Univ. Press, 1981).

5. See Joseph Powers, *Eucharistic Theology* (New York: Herder & Herder, 1967).

24. The Lord's Supper in Ecumenical Dialogue

1. George H. Williams, *La Reform Radical* (Mexico City and Madrid: Fondo de Cultura Economica, 1983).

2. See *Churches Respond to BEM: Official Responses to the "Baptism, Eucharist, and Ministry" Text*, vol. 4, ed. Max Thurian (Geneva: World Council of Churches, 1987), 242.

3. Cf. "Religious Society of Friends (Quakers) in Great Britain," in *Churches Respond to BEM*, 4:214-229. Given that the Quakers have been involved in the discussion of the Lord's Supper, it was a disappointment to me when the 1982 *BEM* text omitted even a commentary note on their faith and witness. The Canberra Assembly of the World Council (1991) and the World Conference on Faith and Order (1993) did not make the same mistake. They declared, "We gladly acknowledge that some who do not observe these rites share in the spiritual experience of life in Christ." Cf. Michael Kinnamon, ed., *Signs of the Spirit: Official Report, Seventh Assembly* (Grand Rapids: Eerdmans, 1991), 174. Thomas Best, ed., *On the Way to Fuller Koinonia* (Geneva: World Council of Churches, 1994).

4. World Evangelical Fellowship, "An Evangelical Response to *Baptism, Eucharist, and Ministry*," Wheaton, Ill., June 1989.

5. *Churches Respond to BEM: Official Responses to the "Baptism, Eucharist, and Ministry" Text*, vols. 1-6, ed. Max Thurian (Geneva: World Council of Churches, 1986-88).

6. Ruth Rouse and Stephen Neill, eds., *A History of the Ecumenical Movement 1517-1948* (London: SPCK, 1954). Lukas Vischer, ed., *A Documentary History of the Faith & Order Movement: 1927-1963* (St. Louis: The Bethany Press, 1963).

7. Gunther Gassmann, ed., *Documentary History of Faith and Order: 1963-1993* (Geneva: World Council of Churches, 1993).

8. Lukas Vischer and Harding Meyer, eds., *Growth in Agreement: Reports and Agreed Statements of Ecumenical Conversations on a World Level* (New York: Paulist Press, 1984); Jeffrey Gros and Joseph Burgess, eds., *Growing Consensus* (New York: Paulist Press, 1994); Jeffrey Gros and Joseph Burgess, eds., *Building Unity* (New York: Paulist Press, 1989); Ross T. Bender and Alan Sell, eds., *Baptism, Peace, and State in the Reformed and Mennonite Traditions* (Waterloo, Ont.: Wilfrid Laurier Univ. Press, 1991); Hans Georg von Berg, et al., eds., *Mennonites and Reformed in Dialogue* (Geneva: World Alliance of Reformed Churches, 1986); Marc Lienhard and Pierre Widmer, eds., *Les Entretiens Luthero-Mennonites (1981-1984)* (Montbeliard: Les Cahiers de Christ Seul, 1984); "Issues in Southern Baptist–Roman Catholic Dialogue," *Review and Expositor* 79.2 (Spring 1982); "Grace, Roman Catholic–Southern Baptist Dialogue (1982-1984)," *Southwestern Journal of Theology* 28.2 (Spring 1986); "Reports of the International Roman Catholic–Pentecostal Dialogue (1985-1989)," *Pneuma* 12.2 (Fall 1990): 117-142.

9. "Louisville Consultation on Baptism," *Review and Expositor* 77.1 (Winter 1980).

10. Merle D. Strege, ed., *Baptism and Church: A Believers' Church Vision* (Grand Rapids: Sagamore Books, 1986).

11. David B. Eller, *Servants of the Word: Ministry in the Believers' Church* (Elgin, Ill.: Brethren Press, 1990).

12. Jeffrey Gros, ed., *The Search for Visible Unity* (New York: Pilgrim Press, 1984); "Baptism, Eucharist, and Ministry Conference," *Midstream* 25.3 (July 1986): 322-329.

13. *American Baptist Quarterly* 7.1 (Mar. 1988): 38-49.

14. *Baptism, Eucharist, and Ministry: Report 1982-1990* (Geneva: World Council of Churches, 1990).

15. Best, *Fuller Koinonia.*

16. It was a disappointment to me that the Anabaptist martyrs' witness did not merit a commentary in *BEM*. Surely many of our churches will need to confess repentance for the behavior of our forebears before a credible fellowship in the Lord's Supper will be possible. For all of us, the Lord's Supper is a witness, a pledge of our own willingness to proclaim Christ in the face of martyrdom. Archbishop Romero was gunned down because of his witness, during the course of celebrating the Lord's Supper; this is a searing testimony to the demands of Christian proclamation in our time.

17. Karl Lehmann and Wolfhart Pannenberg, eds., *The Condemnations of the Reformation Era: Do They Still Divide?* trans. Margaret Kohl (Minneapolis: Fortress Press, 1989).

18. H. George Anderson, T. Austin Murphy, and Joseph A. Burgess, eds., *Justification by Faith* (Minneapolis: Augsburg, 1985).

19. Cf. Vischer and Meyer, *Growth in Agreement;* Gros and Burgess, *Growing Consensus*; and Gros and Burgess, *Building Unity.*

20. June 7 is Corpus Christi, in my tradition. I am sure that it is challenging for you to communicate to your people and students the Christian import of this celebration for us. It is just as challenging for us to witness the Christian content of your infrequent and apparently casual commemoration of the Lord's Supper. Ways of worship are often bracing when not one's own. For many of you, it is difficult to understand why a George Washington or Abraham Lincoln, a Sts. Constantine and Helen, or a St. James the Moorslayer would be imaged in some churches. Likewise, it is difficult for others to understand why the arts are banned by some in service of the gospel. To reflect the other's history, piety, and culture requires a major conversion and a serious discipline; cf. Jeffrey Gros, "Towards a Hermeneutics of Piety for the Ecumenical Movement," *Ecumenical Trends* 22.1 (Jan. 1993): 1-12.

The Editor

Dale R. Stoffer was born in Cleveland and raised in Hamden, Connecticut, and in Canton, Ohio, where his family was involved with the Trinity Brethren Church from 1962. His father was raised in the Brethren Church.

Stoffer received a B.A. degree from Ashland (Ohio) College in 1972, an M.Div. from Ashland Theological Seminary in 1975, and a Ph.D. from Fuller Theological Seminary in 1980. During his doctoral studies, his area of concentration was historical theology, and his mentor was Geoffrey Bromiley. His dissertation focused on the background and development of Brethren doctrine and practice.

Dale married Marcia L. McPherson in 1973, and they have two children, Anne and Paul. In 1980 the Stoffers moved to Columbus, Ohio, where Dale served as the mission pastor of the new Smoky Row Brethren Church. He pastored the congregation for twelve years, saw it grow from four to nearly fifty families, and guided it through two building projects.

Stoffer was an adjunct professor at Ashland Theological Seminary from 1984 until he began full-time service in 1992. He is an associate professor of historical theology at the seminary, teaching in the areas of history; theology; Anabaptist, Pietist, and Brethren studies; and church planting.

Active in the Brethren Church, Stoffer served as Ohio District moderator in 1986-87 and as moderator of the General Conference of

The Brethren Church in 1987-88. He has served on numerous committees and boards at district and national levels and as co-chair of the Task Force for the Centennial Statement of Faith of The Brethren Church.

Stoffer has published one book, two church manuals (one on church planting and one as co-author on discipleship), and numerous articles in books, journals, and church periodicals.

The Stoffer family resides in Ashland, Ohio, where they participate in the Park Street Brethren Church.